The Tree That Bends

The Tree That Bends

Discourse, Power, and
the Survival of the Maskókî People

Patricia Riles Wickman

THE UNIVERSITY OF ALABAMA PRESS

Tuscaloosa and London

Copyright © 1999
The University of Alabama Press
Tuscaloosa, Alabama 35487-0380
All rights reserved
Manufactured in the United States of America

1 2 3 4 5 6 7 8 9 • 07 06 05 04 03 02 01 00 99

∞
The paper on which this book is printed meets the minimum requirements of American National
Standard for Information Science–Permanence of Paper for Printed Library Materials, ANSI
Z39.48-1984.

Library of Congress Cataloging-in-Publication Data
Wickman, Patricia Riles, 1944–
    The tree that bends : discourse, power, and the survival of the
Maskókî people / Patricia Riles Wickman.
        p.   cm.
    Includes bibliographical references and index.
    ISBN 0-8173-0966-7 (pbk. : alk. paper)
    1. Creek Indians—History—Sources. 2. Creek philosophy. 3. Creek
Indians—Social life and customs. 4. Florida—History—Spanish colony,
1784–1821. 5. Spain—Colonies—America—Administration. 6.
Spain—Foreign relations. I. Title.
    E99.C9 W58   1999
    975.9′004973—ddc21   98-58025

British Library Cataloguing-in-Publication Data available

Uuh . . . Pat, this is Jim Billie. How 'bout grabbin' your guitar and comin' on over. We'll sit around the fire and sing some songs about ol' Osceola.

Thank you, my dear. I'd love to.

I once heard someone quote Salvador Dalí, saying that the principal objective of all his work was "to systematize confusion and discredit reality." I never checked that quotation. I didn't need to. In that moment, Dalí made total sense to me, and I felt a closer kinship than ever to that fascinating Catalan. That's as close to "truth" as I could ever hope to come.

Contents

Illustrations

Maps

Plates

Tables

Preface

When I began my earlier book, *Osceola's Legacy* (Tuscaloosa: University of Alabama Press, 1991), over ten years ago now, I actually believed that the "legacy" about which I was writing was solely a material one and that my involvement with Native American studies was beginning and ending with that work. Osceola (ca. 1804–1838) was a Native American war leader whose passion and commitment to the survival and freedom of his "Creek" people (an eighteenth-century British generic for Maskókî tribes of south-eastern North America) caught the interest of his white adversaries, nationally and internationally. They romanticized him and his too-real cause into a stereotyped image of "savage" valor that fulfilled broad social—ergo national—expectations concerning the tragic plight of Indians whose very lives were giving way, more rapidly than ever, before the advance of "white civilization." His was a high price to pay but not, ultimately, the white man's price; therefore it was—taken with an appropriate modicum of sang-froid—acceptable.

In closing my research, it seemed as though his personal effects were all that Osceola had left for the later world and that his story somehow climaxed with them and with the echoing passions that still reverberated around them. I realized that, in order to present a clear story of the survival and evolution of ownership of his possessions, I had had to refute several myths about the man, but the information seemed so clear and incontrovertible—and final—to me that I failed to realize that those myths were not dependent elements in a closed story.

Over the first year after the book's publication, however, as letters and calls and reviews began to come in from two continents, I began to see with new eyes not only the strength with which non-Native keepers of his image held their myths but also, far more important, the larger social discourse sets of which those myths were the foundations. The primary sets centered on no less than the rights of conquest, and the true nature of the resultant "civilization," and all of the Spencerian icons of white supremacy that had quietly entrenched themselves in the face of twentieth-century social challenges and gone to live in the dark, threatened corners of the hearts of too many "law-abiding citizens." The passions that Osceola had held, and had aroused, had shaped themselves into profoundly disquieting specters of conquests past.

History, as we often must be reminded, does not teach lessons. But, if we are wise, we do learn from it nonetheless. We learn, for instance, that altering our view of the past in the service of social and political expedience is an ultimately harmful experience. It engenders a false self-image that will always be at variance with a larger, collective reality. It serves only a limited sector of any society, usually that overtly or covertly manipulative group in whose interests it was originally advanced. It creates unrealistic expectations, both positive and negative, and erroneous images. And, perhaps most important for all of us at any moment in time, it impedes the social responsiveness and interpersonal understanding that comes with seeing ourselves clearly and, consequently, others.

So I soon realized that Osceola's story did not begin with his birth in 1804. It began when the first Europeans entered the southeastern quadrant of the North American continent and when the Native Americans whom they encountered—Osceola's ancestors—began to see themselves mirrored in the expectations of a culturally antithetical, powerful, and confrontational Other. Nor did his story end with his physical death in 1838; that was merely climax. In the three short years of his public career, his life was elevated to legend by the very people who sought to end it. Consequently, in the denouement since that time, his story has become a metaphor for the idealized American experience. I realized, then, that if Osceola were to have any real and enduring legacy—and he does—that legacy must be one of understanding. We must choose to see his story, and the story of his ancestors and descendants, both for what it is and for what it represents in the cultural lexicon of a strong nation where, for far too long, there have been only "winners" and "losers." Such a scenario leaves a future peopled only with survivors.

Of course, I still had no clear idea of how, specifically, I would go about continuing Osceola's story in a useful manner, especially in the light of the excellent research that was already being conducted by anthropologists in the field of sixteenth-century contact analysis. But, then . . . I took a bus ride with James Billie.

On a muggy August afternoon in South Florida, in 1992, I was on a chartered bus, sitting next to James E. Billie, Chairman of the Tribal Council of the Seminole Tribe of Florida, enjoying a much-needed respite in the air conditioning. We had spent the day squiring a group of Venezuelan governmental dignitaries around the Big Cypress and Hollywood Reservations and out "the Trail" (the Tamiami Trail) into the Everglades. I was serving as translator for the chairman. All day we had talked about the history of the Seminoles and Miccosukees in and out of Florida, and I had found Florida's Native Americans themselves asking at least as many questions about the past as the visitors did. It was wonderful; the kind of day about which historians can usually only dream.

Suddenly, James turned to me and said: "You know what you ought to do? You ought to move out to the Reservation and teach those Indians some of their own history!" (James's personal style and his rhetoric are so congruent that it is virtually impossible to quote him without *hearing* the force of his personality.) "Do *what?*" I said, so shocked that I could not even muster a coherent answer. "I mean it," he continued. "They don't know this stuff. You could tell 'em about their past because a lot of these young ones, and some of us old ones too, don't have enough people left to teach them."

And so, just that easily—and inauspiciously—it began. Now, a short six years later, that moment seems eons away. If, at any second during the feverish next few weeks of battening down my Miami apartment and packing for life "on the Res," I actually envisioned myself as going forth to impart great stores of wisdom to the Seminoles, I was quickly disabused of that notion. Perhaps hurricane Andrew, which hit us on the very day that I had planned to move, August 24, 1992, was the messenger. (I'll take my lessons in smaller packages from now on, if I can arrange it!) As a Floridian born and raised, I have lived through a lot of hurricanes, but this one really was "The Big One." Perhaps it was because the imminent prospect of death has a way of placing all life in brilliantly clear perspective, but as road crews began to clear the trees and glass and power lines off of I-95, I headed out to the Big Cypress Indian Reservation almost overwhelmed by the enormity of the task that I had so quickly accepted and, most of all, as a non-Native and a woman heading into what I had been taught to view as a male-dominated society, by my own effrontery.

By the time I held my first "class," I was so unsure of exactly how best to proceed that I could only fall back upon my most basic instincts. I faced a room filled with about thirty hot, sweaty men in bluejeans and T-shirts, who were there because their chairman (their "chief" as some called him, although he was an elected official) had told them to be there and had provided them with a home-cooked lunch. No women came, at first, because they had not been specifically invited and their traditional norm

(I learned) is not to intrude themselves upon a group of men unless specifically invited. I was not even sure that all of the people in the room could speak English.

Nevertheless, James welcomed them to the "history talk," which, he said, was only the first of an ongoing series. He told them, "Do you remember when your uncles and your grandmother used to tell you about things that happened 'a long time ago'? Or, maybe they said, 'Well, that was something that they did back in the Old Days.' You know, I've always wondered, just when the hell *were* 'the Old Days'? Well, here's someone who can tell us. She knows when all those old times were. So I want you to listen and pay attention."

While that mandate had a certain value, I knew that it could only get me attention, not acceptance. So, once again, I resorted to my own best instincts. I began: "Before I begin to talk to you about your own past, I think that there are a few things that you should know about me, so that you can make up your minds about whether to 'hear' me or not. The first thing that you need to know is that I'm not a 'wantabe.' I'm not going to sprout turquoise tomorrow and start looking for a sweat lodge. Second, I'm not some snooty little white lady who's coming in here to tell you how to run your lives. Finally, I haven't really come here to *teach* you at all. I've come here to *share* the information that I have with you. Because, above all, I know that everything I 'know' I have learned from the things that white men have written down. So, no matter how much information I have, it still can never be more than half of the story. You have the other half. And, I hope that you will choose to share some of your story with me so that, between us, we can put back together a better picture of what really happened in your past."

It turned out to be the right thing to say. Over the coming months, I would find out that I had established my own humanity and made myself approachable with those words. Slowly, the people began to respond, in their own ways, and to share magnificent insights into a cosmogony that has profoundly altered my view of their universe—and of my own. I also began to perceive their genuine allegiance to their unique heritage, which they realize is being eroded at a more rapid rate than ever before by the onslaught of all the positive and negative elements of a white culture—by fast foods and crack cocaine, by pickup trucks and beer, and by shyster salespersons of everything from cheap sneakers to a rosy heaven run by, and for, a white god. It is the fear underlying that realization that has prompted them to share their culture with me (in spite of strong traditional injunctions to keep silent), in hopes of preserving it through writing. It is also, I realize, a profound trust that they offer, and one that I carry as one of the proudest responsibilities of my life.

As we continued the "history talks," I found myself rethinking all of the information that I had accumulated over almost three decades of my work in history. I began to test every conclusion that I had so easily formed in sterile libraries and archives against the reality of their lives today and the image of their culture that they have been required to objectify in the crucible of an oppressive and tumultuous past. Many of my conclusions came up wanting.

One, in particular, that appeared less and less defensible as I heard myself saying it was the long-accepted axiom among social scientists that the Seminoles were not "native" to Florida but, rather, were transplants with only about a two- to three-hundred-year equity in the state, and even that amount is equivocal, depending upon the author whom one consults.

Robert Remini's conclusions regarding the southeastern Native Americans are typical of many Euroamerican historians' assessments, even those of historians who trained and work in Florida. In his monumental *Andrew Jackson and the Course of American Empire, 1767–1821,* he writes of the fate of the southeastern Native Americans, indicating that, following the 1814 Treaty of Fort Jackson, Alabama, which ended the disastrous Creek War of 1813–1814, "Within twenty-five years, the entire family of red men, Creeks, Cherokees, Chickasaws, Choctaws, and Seminoles, were swept away from the south and either buried under the ground or banished to the remote western country beyond the Mississippi River."[1]

Even though the drama of that statement is undeniable, and although the profound drama of the Creek War and its consequences upon the Native American peoples of the Southeast are undeniable, the reality of the people who were sitting before me in our history talks was also undeniable. How could I accept that imagery and still face the members of the Seminole Tribe of Florida who, very obviously, were not either "banished" or "buried under the ground"? Not only are there descendants of the southeastern groups still firmly ensconced in the Southeast today but, in the case of Florida, the area's European history has been so culturally discontinuous as to make the Seminoles of Florida, ostensibly by default, the oldest remaining coherent ethnic group in the state today. The longest-running non-native Natives, apparently. The entire situation was ludicrous.

Ultimately, it was this point, this dichotomy between "Florida's indigenous peoples," whom I had been taught to consider as extinct, and the

"Seminoles of today," whom I *and* they had been told to consider as non-indigenous (although, as I was to learn, they still knew the difference), that became the fulcrum upon which balanced all the rest of the image of the past—not only that past that had impact upon those peoples inside the geopolitical area that is called Florida today, but also that collective conception of a past shared by the occupants of the Southeast and of the entire United States.

Every responsible social scientist knows that it is no longer defensible, either intellectually or ethically, to paint our collective past Cultural White. But what does that change really mean? What are its ramifications relative to all the individuals—of all ethnic and racial groups—the trajectories of whose lives have been formed, over centuries, by what we now know to have been misconceptions? Obviously, we must first identify our myths in order to find the power of those myths. That is the search that I have begun with this work.

For ultimately, giving answers to those questions is the purpose of the humanities—the only critical reason thinking humans think about themselves and the world that they have created. It is no longer sufficient, or even defensible, to propound unsubstantiated cultural fiats, the sole function of which is to buttress some particularistic social status quo. If we are truly rational, viable branches on the great evolutionary tree, and not just some cosmic trial and error, then every leaf has its value, every part contributes to the whole. Florida's Native Americans do not exist merely to draw non-Native tourists to South Florida. Nor are they merely thorny reminders of an unpleasant episode in our history. They *are* we, and we *are* they. Their disappearance will diminish us all significantly and damage us irreparably as myth-bearing animals. Our survival, therefore, is inextricably intertwined with theirs. Pogo had it right all along.

Acknowledgments

There are a number of persons who deserve public thanks for their parts in the process of bringing this work to fruition. Foremost are those colleagues whose trust and interest sustained me. Dr. Thomas Abercrombie, formerly of the University of Miami (Florida) and now of New York University, introduced me to ethnohistory and to an entirely new vocabulary that was capable of giving shape to those critical elements of human existence previously considered inconsequential or too amorphous to capture on paper. Dr. Robert Levine, former Chair of the Department of History at the University of Miami, facilitated the research with all of the resources at his disposal.

But it was James E. Billie, Chairman of the Tribal Council of the Seminole Tribe of Florida, who opened the door to the Native American universe and, quite literally, gave me carte blanche there. I have never completely returned from that trip, and I hope that I never shall. My debt of gratitude to the Seminole, Miccosukee, and Maskókî (Creek) peoples of Florida and Oklahoma is beyond measure. I have only a profound respect and admiration, plus my words, with which to repay their open-hearted trust. Perhaps these may, in some small measure, recompense.

Equally important in other ways, however, has been the unwavering belief of my sons, Chris and Tony, who have seen me through these twenty-eight years (thus far) of historical preoccupations and who have been my toughest critics and my staunchest fans. Pat Diamond, James Billie's administrative assistant, is a dear friend and a kindred spirit. Her twin admonitions, "Stick with me, kid!" and "Play the game to win!" have gotten us into (and, fortunately, out of) a lot of great adventures. Her insights into conducting successful negotiations in an intercultural environment have been critical.

I owe a special debt of gratitude to Dr. Eugene Lyon, Director of the Center for Historic Research at Flagler College, St. Augustine, Florida. Gene is the undisputed dean of historians of the sixteenth-century Southeast, and his work has been my benchmark for many years. His comments on the work presented here have strengthened it significantly. In addition,

I wish to thank Dr. George Lowis, sociologist with the Departments of Epidemiology and Public Health at Skidmore College (New York) and the University of Miami Jackson Memorial Medical Center (Florida), for his gracious and useful comments and discussions on various portions of the manuscript. Last, but hardly least, I gratefully acknowledge the confidence of the National Endowment for the Humanities, which provided a grant award in support of the writing.

The Tree That Bends

1 Introduction: A People Obscured by Their Past

> To uncover [the Southeastern Indians'] histories in anything like the detail
> available for the European components of the early American population is,
> in my view, the greatest challenge in the whole realm of research.
>
> —Bernard Bailyn[1]

Ask any moderately studious Florida fourth grader about the Seminoles, and you will hear a story that erases Native Americans from Florida through the agency of Spaniards and diseases, making it an empty frontier at the time of European expansion. The aboriginal inhabitants of Florida were destroyed over the period 1513 to 1763, the story concludes, and the people known today as the Seminoles are an indistinct amalgam of survivors from tribes and territories outside of the geographic entity known today as Florida. The documentary sources that are used to buttress this imaging have been presented, time and again, as an inescapable reality. Florida thus becomes a place for guilt-free development and the progress of civilization.

Some accounts picture twentieth-century Miami settlers encountering colorful Seminoles at tourist attractions with names such as Musa Isle or Tropical Paradise, where they are presented as having adapted to the land by learning to "wrestle" alligators for tourist dollars. These Seminoles, our fourth-graders learn, arrived in Florida from the outside, at about the same time as the "Americans" came. Indigenous peoples have no prior claim on the land in this recension and, if they now occupy the wetlands of the Everglades, this was their lot as marginal interlopers. This chauvinist vision is not only the stuff of primary school histories, it is also the condensed form of the received wisdom of historical scholarship on the Southeast.[2]

It is my contention, however, that Euroamerican scholars have, wittingly or not, colluded in the projection of an American myth, one that has undermined Seminole land claims and, what is more, has questioned the legitimacy of Seminole culture. Positing early Native American societies as well-bounded, discrete, timeless, and unchanging cultural units amounts to a form of ostensive self-identification through negative projection, making natives the imaginary antithesis of progress and civilization. "Indians" cannot master the land because they are natural beings, who are of the land. They occupy space, rather than owning and developing it. Control of the land is thus tacitly assigned to those who can best employ it—the Europeans—for whom use reaffirms rights.

When the culture of modern Euroamericans differs radically from the culture of the settlers at Charles Towne, it is a testament to the progress inherent in European society: but if modern Seminoles differ from the Abalachi, the Timuguana, and other *La Florida* peoples of the Spanish colonial period, it must be because there is no continuity between them. Timeless cultures are static and nonadaptive, not dynamic as Euroamericans imagine themselves. And these beliefs, conceived, confirmed, and institutionalized in the histories of the United States, are the character for white claims to Florida. Florida children receive them as early as the fourth grade and they become operative elements of lifelong imaging. It is to these basic myths of cultural imaging and entitlement that the present work addresses itself.

This book is an investigation into the ethnohistory of cultural transformation, based upon the interrelations of Native Americans and Iberians along the cultural frontiers of interior and lower *La Florida* in the first colonial period, 1510 to 1763. Its primary objective is to describe the cultural genesis of those Native groups known today as the "Creeks," "Miccosukees," and "Seminoles," in an effort to uncover the multicultural origins of Florida and the Southeast as fundamental components of United States history. Methodologically, this is an interdisciplinary study of cultural transformation, which uses the approaches of ethnohistory, discourse analysis, archaeology, and cultural anthropology to reexamine long-neglected facets of southeastern Native American history.

The first Europeans to enter the region we know today as the southeastern United States were the Iberians. They entered through the area that has become the state of Florida, but there was no such designator when Iberians first encountered the land, about 1510 c.e.[3] That area, which they did not for some time understand as merely one quadrant of a continent previously unknown to them, they named *La Florida,* from the Roman Catholic liturgical season of their discovery, *Pascua Florida,* or Easter.[4]

The scope of their claim was at its zenith, however, only during the initial stages of discovery and settlement, in the sixteenth century, before other European powers were able to breach successfully the immense, but amorphous, borders of territory that the Spaniards could not physically protect.

The appropriate historical characterization of this amorphous area has been the topic of some discussion. The Spaniards tended to refer to their spheres of occupation as *las provincias de la Florida,* with discrete provinces demarcated linguistically. Sometimes, they included their spheres of interest in this designator as well.[5] However, we must not confuse the provinces of *La Florida* with the modern geopolitical state of Florida, "two-thirds of which remained outside European control throughout the time of Spanish occupation."[6] This irregularity of usage serves as an important reminder that the Spanish reach always exceeded the Spanish grasp. If we are to rediscover the processes and products of Native American–Spanish interactions then we must, at the very least, accept the imaging by which they characterized themselves and their worlds. Spanish maps designated the land "La Florida," and Spanish contracts did the same.

Over the almost half-millennium since the entrance of Europeans, the names *La Florida* and *Florida* have not been merely variants of discrete linguistic usages, or even of a single diachronic concept, but rather designators of very disparate cultural, political, and geographic entities. The disparities among these entities are basic to our uncovering the Native American transformation that was taking place within the larger context. Therefore the terms *La Florida* and *Florida* will be used throughout this work as the two distinct geographic, synchronic, and politicocultural entities that they actually were, in order to maintain the philosophical and physical distances between the two disparate culture bases and political agendas.

The paradigm of power relations, within the setting of colonial discourse, also is a basic element of the conceptualization of the entire investigation. It diverges from the simplistic "domination versus resistance" models in that it approaches the cultural phenomena under investigation infused with a discussion of the dynamics of the equality, as well as the inequality, of power as couched in the discourse of all of the concerned groups. The indigenous peoples described here, confronted with the interposition of Iberian discourse, in all its forms, remade themselves. The proof of their ability to perform this feat is the cultural products that are known today by Euroamericans as the Creeks, Seminoles, and Miccosukees.

The process attendant upon the contact that took place in the Southeast was one of a continuous cultural *negotiation:* a reciprocal process predicated upon the desire of one or more parties to effect an outcome that might or might not be in the best interests of one or more of the other concerned parties and upon the reality that neither party has sufficient resources to exercise absolute control. In this case, the Europeans, irrespective of their ethnicity, wanted total control and maximum benefit in the Southeast, while the Native Americans, irrespective of their ethnicity, sought to maintain a full range of prerogatives, including the unilateral right to increase their power at will. Two tactics were the hallmarks of the megaprocessual level of this negotiation, which has proceeded for almost five hundred years, thus far.

One was the multifaceted use of *discourse,* which I define here in its broadest functionalist terms, as a continuous series of social functions that run the gamut from the rhetorical and symbolic to the textual and are identifiable as discrete but interrelated informational sets, where such sets are direct products of the structure of the initiating culture.[7] The second tactic was the systematic inclusion of the element of *power* in the negotiating process, where power is defined as any type of nonphysical or physical function, introduced by one or more parties as an overt or covert means of effecting any degree of involuntary change on the part of the other party or parties to the negotiation.

It is important not to lose sight of the fact that, from the point of view of both the Maskókî peoples and the Spaniards, exactly the same set of tactics comprised their strategies. This is a critical point because its realization marks the classic difference between defining the Native Americans solely as reactive, disempowered victims and defining them as proactive, empowered participants in the process. The defining differences in the process were matters of degree only: to what extent could each of the parties draw upon resources sufficient to swing the balance of power toward effecting its desired changes, and to what extent was each of the involved parties willing to commit its available resources toward effecting those changes? In every negotiation, however, we must remember that the ultimate power is the physical destruction of one or more parties by another. It is an old story, which repeats itself ad infinitum in all our worlds today, for politics is merely the art of negotiation, and as Carl von Clausewitz, the Prussian military theorist, phrased the concept in state-level terminology, war is merely the continuation of politics by other means.

An analysis of the discourses created in these historical processes provides a key to a reappraisal of this cultural objectification. Discourse in all of its manifestations, rhetorical and semiotic, and realized as the discourse sets that order its oral and rhetorical modes and inform its actions, is, in any age, the most viable indicator of cultural objectification. These discourse sets also mutate over time, in direct response to changing sociocultural values and the unuttered desire to maintain a cultural equilibrium, as defined at the functional level by the most powerful social group in a society. Consequently, not only the micro-recalibrations of these discourse sets but also their macro-adjustments are mirrors of shifting internal loci of power. That is to say, in a circularity that belies Aristotelian linealism, discourse is the mirror of power, which informs discourse.

To reappraise the Maskókî peoples' past, then, the analyst must engage in a triple project that involves going back to primary sources, reexamining them from a fresh vantage point while at the same time critically reexamining the histories that have been forged from them. Finally, no account of the Maskókî past would be complete without questioning the Maskókî people themselves, past and present, about their own past.

The sources of information available to us, upon which we may base our reexamination of the subjects outlined above, are of only two major types: linear and nonlinear. The linear sources are a group of documents produced by the Europeans, especially the Spaniards, over the period 1510 to 1763. This is the first continuous period of interaction between Native Americans and Europeans in the Southeast and the period that effectively encompasses the complete range of critical strategies for cultural survival in which the Maskókî peoples engaged and by which they would be characterized by the English in the late seventeenth and eighteenth centuries. It is also this partially arbitrary and misleading characterization of the Maskókî peoples that would constitute the Euroamerican legacy to twentieth-century social scientists.

Linear documentation is available to us today in three groupings: published accounts of exploration, official administrative documents of occupation, and secondary documentary products of occupants of the Southeast. Of these three categories, only the final one includes information generated by or directly solicited from the Native Americans themselves, and its volume is, admittedly, relatively small.

The nonlinear sources available for examination fall into two groups:

first, the materials recovered through the archaeological process and, second, the discourse produced and maintained by the descendants of the Native Americans themselves, whose holding environment, historically, is oral. The descriptor *preliterate* is favored by some researchers today to characterize cultures that historically have not employed written documentation. However, this term implies that the development of writing is incipient in the culture or that the culture would undoubtedly, and necessarily, evolve into a literate culture, given time. This teleological judgment is consistent with Aristotelian linealism and with Euroamerican cultural chauvinism, but not with a circular Native American cosmogony and not with the reality of the Maskókî peoples whom we are discussing here. Therefore, a value-neutral term, *orally transmitted culture,* will be used here.

The integration of these nonlinear sources into the overall documentary process is critical to the production of any viable image of the Native Americans and their past. Taken together, the opportunities for interpretation presented by the total range of these materials are great indeed, as we shall see. First, however, we must begin by examining the ideological milieu in which the Maskókî peoples objectified themselves prior to the interposition of European expectations.

In the case of the present work, 174 Seminole sources, cited in Appendix 2, are available. They are the core of the group of individuals with whom I have discussed various topics addressed in this work. Our discussions have taken the form of long, formal "talks," in the traditional manner, and casual conversations held in every available setting where, also in a manner consistent with the traditions of oral transmission of culture, my Seminole teachers have amplified and reinforced my learning. They have answered questions that I have posited but, most important, over the six and a half years that we have lived and worked together thus far, as they have come to trust my respect for the information and my ability to understand, they have initiated teaching sessions in which my single responsibility was to hear and remember. Consequently, my research files contain thirty-five audiotaped and videotaped interviews, but the majority of the data occur as written notes.

On the basis of the sources indicated here, then, the present work seeks out and examines first, the dynamic nature of the Maskókî culture as various tribes endured but transformed themselves during their contact with Europeans; second, the specific nature of Spanish cultural transfer, which most directly informed the engagement; third, the networks of power relationships that were manipulated by the various groups as their discourses; fourth, the symbolic dimension created by the colonial setting in which the discourses took place; and fifth, the synthetic product of the discourses, which Euroamerican historians would manipulate into their own cultural context as the Creek, Seminole, and Miccosukee Indians.

Three discrete diachronic units will constitute the frontiers of interaction between the Spaniards and Native Americans in *La Florida*. The first unit is the symbolic frontier created by the routes of the entradas of the European explorers, particularly in the period 1510 to 1568. Despite the fact that the locus of enunciation of the accounts is exclusively the cultural Other, these accounts construct a rhetorical universe that has a degree of its own validity beyond the primary mediated message. The interposition of a completely new set of requirements and expectations carried by the Europeans initiated a profound process of self-objectification among the southeastern Maskókî peoples that allowed them to begin to modify themselves, within the flexible parameters of their own discourse, while maintaining a maximum number of their own prerogatives within any given circumstance.

The second unit is composed of the Iberian-dominated cultural and administrative centers at Santa Elena (near Beaufort, South Carolina; the first capital of *La Florida*, abandoned in 1587), San Agustín (St. Augustine), and Pensacola (after 1698), where interactions between Iberians and indigenous peoples were the most formalized and limited but which were the core areas of Iberian cultural transfer. The third unit is the mission chain that spread northward between Santa Elena and San Agustín and westward from San Agustín through Abalachi and, sporadically, southward to the lower east and west coasts of the peninsula and that operated intermittently during the late sixteenth through the early eighteenth centuries. Taken together, the missions constitute a core area for this investigation because they were the sites of maximum interaction and cultural transformation, as well as sources of document production.

During the sixteenth and seventeenth centuries, as the English and the French *avant garde* made physical inroads into the Spaniards' claimed territory, the European powers battled each other for the right to exercise hegemony over the land and over peoples who had, for thousands of years already, exercised their own forms of hegemony there. Native peoples survived the process, and they continue to survive, as coherent and viable cultural inheritors of 12,000 years of southeastern occupation. Illuminating and confirming the vital differences between these two potential states of being—cultural subordination and cultural destruction—is the single most important objective of this work.

Because over the past 485 years both the Spaniards and Euroamericans have, through their discourse, created taxonomic parameters advantageous to Euroamericans, we must define yet another taxonomic parameter: the Native American construct. It is the one that constituted the primary reality of the earliest inhabitants and that continued to inform their world view even as Europeans pursued their own visions. It is also the one that has been most obscured by the non-Native reporters.

The Southeast in that world view neither had nor has a single name. It existed as no single geographic, political, or cultural entity. Its borders were amorphous in any documentary sense and its population was culturally diverse and socially heterogeneous. Its very conceptualization was shaped by precepts that were alien to non-Natives. Europeans there were not merely strangers; they were truly strangers in a strange land.

One of the larger sets of descriptors that has any validity when applied to the southeastern Native American peoples upon whom this research focuses is linguistic, but even this set is amorphous at best, and, at worst, it is sometimes misleading. At least five separate languages and their dialectic families are currently believed to have been in use throughout the Southeast in the sixteenth century.[8] Our inability to assign specific geocultural borders to these families, even after a century of research, is strong evidence of the dynamism of their constituent culture groups and of the great care that must be exercised whenever language is imposed as a cultural designator.

Principal Iroquoian speakers were the large culture group whom Maskókî speakers designated by the word *Tcilokit* (var., Chalaque, Xalaque), a generic indicator meaning "people of a foreign tongue," which, as we shall see, the Maskókî applied and continue to apply to various groups. The English would apply it only to one people, and only in the transliteration *Cherokee*. Catawban, a language distantly affiliated with Siouan, existed in at least two dialectic forms. Algonquian-speaking Shawanoe (Shawnee) peoples were an enigmatic, but durable, culture group across the Southeast. Yuchî, a language isolate, also proved durable.[9]

By far the largest linguistic group throughout the region was composed of Maskókî speakers, and it is principally to this geographically widespread linguistic family that the members of the Creek, Seminole, and Miccosukee speakers belong. Linguistic affiliates ranged, geographically, from the tip of *La Florida* in the south (the Teguesta and Calusa), northward and westward into present-day eastern Mississippi, Alabama, and eastern Tennessee (including the Abalachi, Chactá [Choctaw], Chicaça [Chickasaw], and the most northerly, Koasati), and eastward across modern Georgia to the Atlantic (including Yamásî, Guale, and probably Timuguana).[10]

Attempts to classify the linguistic affiliations of this latter group, known today by the single term *Timuguana* or *Timucua*, have engendered much controversy, principally among archaeologists.[11] Ultimately, however, it would be impossible to segregate this region from the Mississippian picture, as if these peoples had existed in total linguistic exclusion despite their geographic and cultural inclusion. Moreover, the larger areas of controversy make these people an excellent example of many of the cultural processes that are reexamined and redefined in the present work.

John Hann's recent study, *A History of the Timucua Indians and Missions*, makes this quite clear.[12] Their zone of occupation, extending across much of what is today north Florida and south Georgia, was controlled by at least fourteen or fifteen distinct tribes, speaking as many as eleven separate dialects of a common language. Whether these dialects ultimately had their origins in the core Maskókî language or comprised a discrete base language with numerous Maskókî borrow words remains a subject of conjecture.

The Spaniards, who actually knew very little about them, "seemed to have continued to refer to them by tribal names . . . rather than generically as Timucua," a practice entirely consistent with the imaging of the peoples, which will be discussed further in a later chapter.[13] Nevertheless, they appear to have shared many cosmogonic traits with their Mississippian neighbors. Therefore language and culture were not coterminal. However, in their very heterogeneity in the areas of those traits that archaeologists most often wish to use as cultural definitors—language, name, ceramic tradition, and military alliance—they stand as an excellent example of the entire dynamic process posited in this work.[14]

Further, Hann's conclusion that the Spaniards really knew little about these people even though theirs was the first and principal territory in which the Spaniards settled, reminds us that Spanish documentary pronouncements must not be taken as either all-inclusive or definitive, despite Spanish attempts to adopt such a tone. Indeed, the author concludes that several of our traditional views of these people may have been drawn inaccurately from "a document-based bias."

Finally, Hann's investigation concludes that despite the cultural pressures of Spanish interposition, these people exercised many of their own cultural prerogatives for at least as long as they can be tracked in the Spanish documents, that is, for well over two centuries, until the Spanish exodus from *La Florida* in 1763. The Timuguana people picked and chose those elements of Spanish culture and society that they would accept and maintained those elements of their own that were basic to their continuity, down to and including the practices of medicine, public civic functions, and distinct leadership attachments (which Hann calls "subgroup identities").[15] In all of this, their actions paralleled those of the majority of their Maskókî neighbors.

Consequently, the term *Maskókî peoples* will be used throughout this work as the primary designator for all of those southeastern tribes that were, and remain, linguistic affiliates of the Maskókî family, regardless of the manner in which their sixteenth- to eighteenth-century territories related to what are today discrete states of the United States. However, it is important to remember that the term *Maskókî peoples* is not a projection of self-representation or sociocultural objectification but, rather, an impositional construct representative of a symbolic dimension. Its application confers no legitimization other than that assumed by its enunciators.

More important than the Maskókî language per se, and intimately tied to it from the Native American viewpoint, was, and is, the cosmogony inherent in the designator "Maskokálgî." Among Maskókî peoples, this term signifies "the People of the Maskókî Way," and the Maskókî Way is a cosmogony, not a language. Use of the term infuses the discussion of linguistic context with a cosmogonic message significantly greater than its content, for, although there exists an inextricable bond between language and the culture that creates it, the two are not synonymous; they are synergistic. In addition, communication forms are not constant across cultures; they are unique. As one writer explains: "Cultural conceptions of communication are deeply intertwined with conceptions of person, cultural values, and world knowledge—such that instances of communication are never free of the cultural belief and action systems in which they occur."[16]

Certain major assumptions implicit in the traditionalist, narrative renderings of the history of Florida make it an ideal laboratory for the application of these new methodologies and the reexamination of the process of cultural transformation. These assumptions have perpetuated themselves as integral parts of the larger evolutionary reading of southeastern

Native American history. Primary among them is the belief that the Native American story is merely a subset of the general Euroamerican occupation and development. Two historical "realities" have informed this view.

First is that no representatives of Florida's pre-Contact groups are currently available, as discrete cultural entities, to challenge the theory. Second is the Eurocentric belief that the Native Americans in Florida today are all descendants of certain Maskókî peoples arbitrarily and generically labeled "Creeks" by the seventeenth-century English and that, consequently, they are not direct evolutionary descendants of the pre-Contact "Florida" Natives, where the geopolitical limits of the modern state are retroactively applied to the movements of peoples to whom they neither had, nor have, any meaning. Particularly illustrative of the generally accepted view of Florida's contemporary native groups is the belief that all "Florida" natives became extinct by 1763 as a result of the introduction of European pathogens and warfare or as a result of their few survivors' departing *La Florida* with the Spaniards, by choice.

After years of revising estimates upward, it is currently considered probable that at least 200,000 Native Americans were living within what are now the borders of Florida when the first Europeans arrived in the early sixteenth century, and probably 400,000 altogether were living throughout what is now the southeastern United States. In a hypothesis that has been repeated so many times that it has become axiomatic, however, social scientists have concluded that, in 1763, at the end of the First Spanish Period, the last eighty-six Christianized Indians left Florida with the Spaniards.[17] That is to say, as the direct result of two and a half centuries of Native-European contact, a natural disaster of such magnitude befell the Native Americans that they had no defense, no recourse, and no hope. They succumbed to overwhelming European superiority (even including biological superiority) and, as a consequence, by 1763, they "disappeared."

Social scientists then speak of a demographic void across the northern frontier of "Florida" and the migration of non-native Natives (so to speak) into that void, whose attachment to an adopted land would be strong, but whose tenure would be relatively short: within the subsequent century they too would be hunted relentlessly unto death, or pushed well beyond the line of vision of the Euroamerican settlers flooding into the newly christened "Florida." Either way, they would be gone, and Euroamerican "Floridians" could get around to the business of naming incorporated towns after extinct tribes and touting an exotic Native past as an advertising draw for tourists who might be persuaded to migrate southward—temporally and temporarily—in order to fill what had become an economic void.

As one anthropologist summarized this explicit view, "Florida did not remain *empty* of native peoples. During the first half of the eighteenth century *Creek* Indians moved southward into Florida, often occupying lands previously inhabited by the Apalachee and Timuguana peoples. These Creeks were the ancestors of the modern Seminole and Miccosukee peoples" (emphasis added).[18]

Over the period 1817 to 1858, Florida's Native Americans fought three wars against the United States, predicated solely upon their determination to resist dispersion and removal from the land that was their home. It was the United States government that unilaterally decided to declare the fighting ended and leave the Native American survivors in relative peace. Then, after another three-quarters of a century, a period of seclusion and respite from war, the Seminoles "emerged" from the Florida Everglades during the real estate Boom Period of the 1920s. In the words of one well-known Florida historian, this time they came out as "tourist attractions."[19] There, it was discovered (but not by the Native Americans), they had been not only living but prospering in the most vital and basic sense: they had been successfully exploiting the Florida Everglades, one of the most inhospitable environmental zones in the world, *and* their numbers had been slowly increasing.

Who were these Indians? the twentieth-century Euroamerican visitors to Florida asked. And the Euroamerican Floridians answered for them: they are quaint reminders of a bygone era. They are docile tourist attractions, making pinestraw baskets and patchwork skirts, little "dugout" canoes, and children's toy bows and arrows. For over five centuries, their natural resources, their sociocultural repertoires, their language, their survival skills, and the very lives of their men and women had been selectively—if not ruthlessly—subjected to pressures by numerically superior non-Native cultures. Now, in yet another profound indignity, even their ideological heritage was being coopted by a culture that saw the possibility of profiting economically by pandering to tourists, the ultimate nationalist ideologues. Very few Euroamericans ever asked the "Indians" who they were, and even those who did were not predisposed to hear discomforting answers.

However, evidence exists today in the discourses of the descendants of these groups that the symbolic universe embraced by them continues to be infused with a historical dimension encompassing both these discrete constituent groups and the mediated paths by which they have been endowed with their current recontextualized image. It is, in fact, this endurance of the historical dimension of their cultural voice, encoded in discourse, that accounts for their cultural survival, notwithstanding the disparity between their self-representation and their objectification by cultural Others. They are, in their current existence, a people obscured by their own past: both by the transformational process of survival and by the obscurantist vision of Euroamericans. At present, they are also a people saved by their own ability to internalize their past as a viable element of their sociocultural present. This flexible historical present is the matrix in which they endure.

Yet another factor bears upon the obscurantist vision of Euroamericans as regards the Native American history of Florida. Modern Florida has been legitimated as a facet of American studies primarily from the period of the American Revolution forward only as it complements the birth and growth of the Anglo-Saxon core of the political entity known as the United States. At the same time, its Latin American heritage has been downplayed or negated by scholars whose single criterion for inclusion in "Latin" America is the denominator of language (i.e., the use of Spanish versus English as the current base language).[20] Only within the most recent generation have studies begun to appear that attempt to situate the Iberian phase of southeastern occupation relative to later Anglo-European settlement interests.[21] Consequently, the application of approaches that have proven successful within the research endeavors on the core areas of Latin America can now provide a clearer view of the interactional process that culturally transformed the Southeast during the first colonial period and reintegrate Florida's Iberian and Native American past into the larger Euroamerican colonial experience.[22]

Although Latin Americanists have begun, within the past two generations, to acknowledge and delineate the forms of power that were retained and wielded by the native peoples of Mexico and Central and South America, despite continuous Spanish cultural pressure, and the extent to which the discourse generated by the groups informed the resultant society, no comparable work has yet been undertaken for the southeastern United States. Euroamerican histories have relied almost exclusively upon Euroamerican voices to provide baseline data for histories of Native American groups. That is, Native American historical images have been formed as projections of the dominant culture and objectifications of its value structures. The more than 250 years of discrete Native American–Iberian discourse during which Maskókî men and women replicated and transformed their own self-representations in the colonial Southeast, within the flexible parameters of their own cultural contexts, have been obscured or obliterated by the Euroamerican locus of enunciation.

It becomes, then, not merely practical to effect such a shift in focus in order to incorporate a significantly heightened awareness of the cultural Other but, rather, culturally and intellectually imperative. For, as Anthony Pagden reminds us, "the early modern observers . . . were more concerned with evaluation than understanding," and they consequently framed their evaluations in moralistic terms.[23] The objective and result of their rationalization was to encrypt all conceptualization of the cultural Other firmly inside an Aristotelian linealism, coopted by Roman Catholicism, that judged each group in terms of a ubiquitous *telos,* or evolution toward a universal goal of reunion with a Christian deity.

Pagden states:

> The painstaking description, and the recognition of the "otherness" of the "other," which is the declared ambition of the modern [social scientist] would have been unthinkable to most of the [early modern] writers. . . . None were attempting, consciously or unconsciously, to grope their way through an intellectual miasma raised by the "prejudices" of education, social background or ideological commitment towards a more complex, more "objective" vision of reality. Those prejudices constituted their mental worlds. . . . To have wished to abandon them would have seemed foolish, dangerous, possibly even heretical.[24]

Further, the "mental world" that they objectified for themselves did not bloom and die in the sixteenth century. Its Aristotelian discourse completely permeated western European Christianity, creating a highly durable dogma of cultural superiority that placed "civilized" Christians sufficiently far along its evolutionary route as to instill in them a moral imperative to lead erring, *un*civilized, Native American "children" back to its straight and narrow path.

Within the radical Roman Catholicism of the Spaniards, this moral mandate was contextualized as a holy war, in which conversion was but the necessary first step to salvation, and death—early or late—was its sine qua non. (Indeed, one modern writer has characterized Roman Catholicism as "the Cult of Death."[25]) With this mandate subsequently reconfigured as an evolving Protestant ideology and mediated by the dialog of an emerging Humanism, seventeenth- and eighteenth-century English Christians retained the utilitarian cultural superciliousness of Aristotelian linealism even as they reframed their drive to convert within economic parameters and politicized their discourse of dominance.

Regardless of the framework, however, the legacy left to the present generation of social scientists remains the same. Pagden posits that the ultimate conceptual failure of the Spaniards (and, we might add, of all Euroamericans) "lay simply in their unwillingness to face the true dimension of what stood self-evidently before them."[26] In all fairness, we might add that this assessment is only partial, and Pagden himself pronounces it "imperfect." Any generation has the choice to be "unwilling" but, in order to effect substantive change in the concept of its discourse relative to a cultural Other, the cultural locus of enunciation must first also contain within its own cultural repertoire an analytic of alternatives, coupled with a stronger impetus to change than to stasis. Neither the former nor the latter was within the ideology of the Spaniards, and the English, while embracing the former, also eschewed the latter, in pursuit of political and economic self-interests.

Even in the late twentieth century, a willingness to seek change in our examination of the cultural Other has not yet become generally accepted. The human mind moves from the known to the unknown; from the relational to the nonrelational. Thus, when existing paradigms begin to change, they do so only "in response to a very gradual recognition that the system can no longer be made to account for all the facts of the case. Even the new paradigm is likely to be—indeed *must*—retain enough of the old to make it recognizable as a paradigm capable of explaining the facts of that particular case."[27] Such is the situation in the present work.

There are a number of national functional myths, or principles of perception, that have informed social scientists' interpretations of the history of the Native American Other. These myths may be stated or unstated in the syntheses, but their power to color perceptions and speak in the conclusions remains equal.

The major myths that propel our continuing conceptions and misconceptions of the Native Americans are grounded in the earliest perceptions of the male Europeans who first met their antecedents and in the unique discourse sets that evolved in their negotiations. Those same myths have been preserved, some of them almost intact, for almost five hundred stormy years and have been used very effectively to disempower the Native

Americans in socially, politically, and economically significant ways. The element of power has been the key to their survival and the degrees of power available to the groups internalizing the myths have largely determined their shapes and the force of their impact upon the societies involved.

Foremost is the myth that the Maskókî speakers were in a state of social stasis at the moment when the first Europeans arrived. That is to say, whether or not we can conceptualize, rationally, that no society is static—that there is always a dynamic of action and a reciprocal dynamic of interaction—the effect of an antithetical conceptualization upon the study of southeastern history has been the same. Our attempts to conceptualize and reconstruct a theoretical past have always been flawed by an unwillingness, or an inability, to deal with the reality of a social dynamism. This is partially because this particular past was always taking place just beyond our field of historical vision. That is, it began in a time when no Europeans were available to document the process, and so it proceeded in an "undocumented" context, promulgated by societies whose own mythologies were, and continued to be, orally held and transmitted and not readily available to Euroamericans.

A particularly persistent myth is that the meeting of Native Americans and Europeans in the Southeast was a case of Conquest (literally, with a capital *C*) and that, consequently, the prerogatives of power rested solely with the Europeans throughout the ensuing centuries. Despite the fact that this also-flawed paradigm has been discarded by so many in the social science fields, especially those engaged in Latin American history where the Black Legend had to be discarded before any theoretical progress could be made, southeastern social scientists have failed to move beyond it, with few and minimal exceptions.[28]

I will demonstrate, however, that the Maskokálgî cosmogony was fluid, not brittle like that of the Europeans. Their world was capable of incorporating new concepts and exigencies, without being destroyed by the process. In the parallel (but not analogous) process, the European cosmogony was unfolding, to a far greater extent, within the parameters of its own internal benchmarks. The primary basis of this dichotomy was also the fundamental difference between the cosmogonic approaches of the two cultures. The cosmogony of the Maskókî peoples was and is a circular one that makes allies of humans and nature. Therefore, the natural propensity of all elements is movement in concert, but this movement implies no direction, linear or otherwise. In this world view, all creatures and events have an ab initio right to being, and a consequent right to acceptance.

In stark contrast to this cosmogony was and is that of the Europeans, whose Aristotelian-based, linear trajectory, rooted in exclusionism, was expropriated and institutionalized by Christianity. In this millennia-old scenario, Man and Nature are locked in a perpetual battle of wills in which one must be the victor and the other the vanquished. Nothing is allowed except that which is specifically permitted, and nothing is permitted except that which specifically advances the "good fight."

As yet another principal and interrelated myth, this militaristic, male-centered paradigm excluded acceptance, toleration, and/or incorporation of the New and assimilation of any Other that might threaten the brittle construct. In this paradigm, women were a singularly fearsome Other, whose sexuality and whose very lives were legally and institutionally proscribed. Legally, Spanish women were controlled by a body of statutory law concerning the interrelated spheres of family honor, purity of blood, kinship and inheritance, dower and real property rights, and female sexuality and procreation. Institutionally, the Roman Catholic Church used fear and intimidation to promulgate double standards for the genders and enforce them through the physical and social power of a church-state alliance. The resultant society objectified itself as the consummate projection of honor and power, where honor was invested in its women and championed by its men, and power was the ultimate reward for successful manipulation of the symbolic universe.

Sufficient has been written on this and related topics that they need not be dwelt upon at length here. That the trajectory of European occupation and growth of the *civis* and *polis* in the Southeast, as recorded in the European documents, proceeded strictly along male lines of kinship and power, however, is a given. Feminist history of this period in the Southeast is almost totally submerged in the larger image of males as unilateral decision makers and literal makers of history. In a culture in which cosmogony was defined by antagonisms, the separatist roles of women and men decreed for them an inherently antagonistic relational mode.

Conversely, among the Maskókî speakers, whose cosmogony was framed as a universal symbiosis, women occupied discrete positions as mediators and arbiters of many portions of the symbolic universe. Matrilineal kinship patterns anthropomorphized the transmission of both the symbolic and the real universe, including the orderly transfer of power spheres from generation to generation. Despite the assertion of some anthropologists that matrilineality is consistent only with an agrarian-based culture, the southeastern Native Americans developed what one researcher describes as "the richest culture of any of the native peoples north of Mexico . . . by almost any measure."[29] And, despite the best efforts of the Spaniards and Roman Catholicism to exorcise this "pagan" system, matrilineality and its concomitants of exogamy and matrilocality have persisted to the present as hallmarks of the Maskôkî peoples.[30]

The Conquest paradigm also gives rise to two other, correlative and mutually supportive, myths. One regards the exact nature of the process of Native American–European intercourse, which has been assumed to be impositional, rather than propositional. The assertion that this process was and, in fact, continues to be, one of negotiation, as opposed to rule by mandate, is presented above. Part of the basis for this myth is the indisputable fact that there are more Euroamericans in the United States today than Native Americans. Therefore, if one falls prey to the historiographic fallacy of *post hoc, ergo propter hoc*, the conclusion that Europeans were the "victors," *ergo* Europeans must have had all the power, becomes inescapable: fallacious, but inescapable.

Then, closely allied to the myths of total power and total victory is the myth of total destruction, that is to say, extinction. According to this myth, the "aboriginal Indians" of Florida are gone, and there are no descendants to speak with their true voices today because the Seminoles are only adopted children of Florida. Yet, a closer examination of the dynamic nature of Maskôkî culture, as well as the negotiative process by which many *La Florida* Natives evolved in the face of constant and mounting cultural pressures, coupled with an examination of the historiographic and physical processes by which the Creeks and Seminoles emerged in the historical literature, will reveal an alternative to this view.

The cultural repertoire of today's Seminoles and Miccosukees holds strong memories of Hitchitî, Yuchî, and Yamásî ancestors and songs from the Calusa (a southwest Florida tribe considered by Euroamericans to have been extinct for two hundred years). At least one family honors memories of tall Abalachi women (a north-central Florida tribe considered by Euroamericans to have been extinct for two hundred years) as Clan Mothers. Numerous Oklahoma Seminoles preserve a Spanish heritage as a part of their tradition. And Maskôkî peoples in both Florida and Oklahoma support an active, ongoing kinship system based partially on the relationships of core Clans and "found people" (adopted Clan remnants of various southeastern tribes). Regardless of the vitality of this living past, the non-Native world clings to the orthodoxy of the myth that the Florida Indians are extinct. The "Seminoles," by the ritual passage of being renamed, in English, in the late eighteenth century, also passed into a new incarnation in their eyes, an identity completely distinct from their antecedent amalgamants, which justifies Euroamericans in clinging to the spurious validity of their Conquest paradigm.

How are the ancestors of the Seminoles to be reevaluated? The present work is organized in two parts, each of which addresses distinct facets of the reevaluation. Part I, "The Maskokálgî," is a conceptual redrawing of those elements of Maskókî cosmogony that were critical to the survival of the people as bearers of a culture that has survived to the present. In Chapter 2, I identify those peoples who were, within the largest framework, the cultural ancestors of today's Seminoles, the Maskókî peoples of the Southeast. These are the peoples whose cosmogony, social networks, and, to certain extents, linguistic matrices placed them in a Maskókî world, within a differentiated Maskokálgî cosmogony. I examine the cosmogonic matrix of the Maskokálgî—the People of the Maskókî Way—as they functioned separately from, and prior to, the demands of the European cultural Others in order to glimpse the ways in which they objectified themselves with a degree of cultural flexibility unavailable to the European Others.

Chapter 3 includes an investigation of the bases of Maskókî cosmogony that set it apart from the teleological framework that informs Euroamerican culture. These include the circular matrix and the dynamism created by it. I also discuss the specialized nature of an orally transmitted society. In Chapter 4 I continue the discussion of the dynamic nature of Maskókî life and the specific elements of that dynamism that have been obscured by European concerns with antithetical goals. These include various types of power relationships, especially in relation to the power to name, and rename, and power as it related to the internal social structures of the Native Americans themselves. The relationships of gender and sex among the Maskókî peoples are examined in Chapter 5, along with some of the power systems by which Europeans manipulated away female power in the documents. I also examine public power, as an extension of the discussion of matriliny, and the relationships of warriors and the Maskókî system of war to the larger cultural patterns.

Part II, "Enter the Spaniards," is an essential rereading of the traditional Euroamerican sources as regards the direct relationships of would-be Spanish conquerors and the people whom they sought to conquer. Chapter 6 reviews the application of the Entrada model to the Southeast by the Spaniards, introducing to the Maskókî peoples the basic range of demands and negotiating tactics that would be pressed upon them repeatedly by the first European interpositions. In this model, I differentiate among some general elements of Spanish demands that were inherent to the Iberian Roman Catholic cosmogony, others that were inserted in response to Native American negotiations outside of *La Florida,* and those that were direct responses to the unique negotiants whom the Spaniards encountered in *La Florida.*

In Chapter 7 the discussion shifts to the Spaniards, specifically, and to the range of Spanish and Roman Catholic cultural templates and institutions that were transposed to *La Florida* and that formed the negotiating base, both physically and philosophically, for their interactions with the unique Native American cultural Others. Chapter 8 is a reexamination of the expectations of the Spaniards and the imaging that they sought to impose through their documentation. In it we apply our revised understanding of the Maskókî culture to a reappraisal of the mechanics of the direct negotiations between the Maskókî peoples and the Spaniards and the range of prerogatives maintained by the former. Were these prerogatives forfeited by those Native American peoples who appeared, from the viewpoint of the Spanish-produced documents, to succumb to what historians have labeled the system of "Conquest by Contract" or "Conquest by Gifts"?[31] To what extent did they evolve cultural voices capable of speaking effectively within the field of changing colonial circumstances? Most important, did they carry out this evolution by losing and replacing culture, or was it possible to effect the changes necessary for survival wholly within the framework of their own cosmogony?

Finally, Chapter 9 examines how, as the first Spanish colonial phase closed, another and profoundly more burdensome set of demands was introduced to the Maskókî peoples, with the opening of the English colonial phase. The entrance of the French, as well, into their own set of negotiations with the westernmost tribes of Maskókî peoples brought yet another set of demands into the larger negotiation. What may we conclude about the impact of these ostensibly disparate rhetorical sets, from the viewpoint of the Maskókî peoples who bore the brunt of them? Were they, indeed, disparate demands? The negotiations were not all "one-way" exercises, following the trajectory of successful "Conquests." How, then, were the Natives able to affect the outcomes of the negotiations, and what is the evidence of those effects?

Chapter 10 provides a summation of all the elements of the discourses between the Maskôkî peoples and the Spaniards during the first Spanish colonial period. In it I draw conclusions about the realities of the Spaniards' interposition in the light of the cultural self-imaging against which modern non-Native researchers must measure their own conclusions, rather than against the artificial and arbitrary yardstick of Euroamerican cultural expectations, as so often has been done in the past.

Then, it will only be left for us, as products and producers of the linear cosmogony, to admit the validity of what seems to be, but is not in fact, an antithetical universe. The alternative to lineality in human existence (order, in Western Christian terms) is not randomness and chaos (in scientific terms), or anarchy (in political terms), because what has been perceived as disorder, even at the cosmogonic level, is finally being unveiled as our own unique lack of perception. Researchers within the field of quantum mechanics have been among the first segments of Euroamerican society to make the transition in understanding. Their realizations have direct application to our reevaluation of the Maskôkî experience; perhaps they are the signposts to what could really be a "New World." As some of these researchers have put it,

> The magnificent successes in the fields of natural sciences and technology [have], for many, fed the illusion that the world on the whole function[s] like a huge clockwork mechanism, whose laws were only waiting to be deciphered step by step. Once the laws were known, it was believed, the evolution or development of things could—at least in principle—be ever more accurately predicted. Captivated by the breathtaking advances in the development of computer technology and its promises of a greater command of information, many have put increasing hope in these machines.
>
> But today it is exactly those at the active core of modern science who are proclaiming that this hope is unjustified; the ability to see ever more accurately into future developments is unattainable. One conclusion that can be drawn from the new theories, which are admittedly still young, is that stricter determinism and apparently accidental development are *not* mutually exclusive, but rather that their coexistence is more the rule in nature.[32]

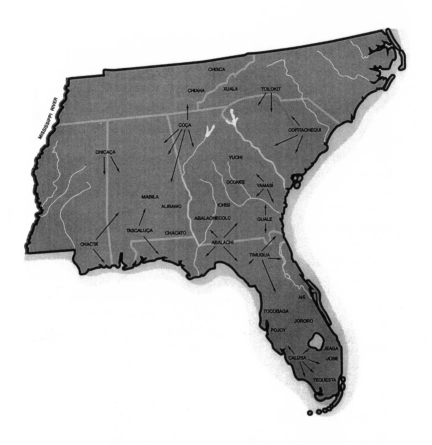

Principal Native Tribes of Lower *La Florida* at European Contact
(Map by Synergy Design Group, Tallahassee, Florida)

I would add, this is so in humans no less than stars.

As long as Maskókî peoples continue to survive, to exist as discrete cultural entities, they constitute proof positive of the errors of the Conquest myth and the inefficacy of the discourse of dominance. It is left only to non-Natives to cease generating the rhetoric of destruction and begin substituting the rhetoric of survival.

I   The Maskokálgî

2   The Four-Cornered Circle

How does the reproduction of a structure become its transformation?

—Marshall Sahlins[1]

Kósa, Kúsa 1) nom pr. of ancient town of the Upper Creeks on Coosa river, Ala. 14, I. 23. The Cheroki call all the Creek tribes Kusa-people. 2) Kósa, isti Kósa, coll. Kóasalgi: *Kusa Indian* 14.3.

—Albert Gatschet[2]

The Cultural Genesis of the Maskókî Peoples

The cultural genesis of the Maskókî peoples whom the Spaniards would encounter in the Southeast in the sixteenth century was the rise and spread of the ideological phenomenon characterized by some archaeologists as "Mississippianism," which began around 800–1000 C.E. and was a cosmogonic phenomenon of significant proportions, in every sense of the phrase. That is, its adherence was far more than a religious experience in the Western sense, in which a spiritual belief system may or may not influence significant areas of secular society. Mississippianism was a cosmogony that included a broad-ranging set of beliefs and practices that permeated every major facet of life, from rituals covering life passages, to social and political organization, to the production of a complex material culture repertoire directly supportive of, and springing from, its canons.

Arising somewhere in the area of the confluence of the Ohio and Mississippi rivers, the field of its florescence eventually encompassed parts of the northeastern, almost all of the southeastern, and parts of the western North American continent. No definitive answers have previously been put forward, by Euroamerican researchers, to the basic questions of its existence. What was the impetus for the rise of the phenomenon? Were there initiating individuals or events? How and from what source, physical or ideological, did it gain its coherence over time and space? And, finally, was the diminution of its coherence—but not, I would argue, its demise—precipitated by the interposition of Spanish Europeans, or were they merely the coincidental observers of a process already in progress?[3]

Most researchers identify the rise of Mississippianism with the introduction and spread of sedentary agriculture and, specifically, with the wide-ranging ramifications of maize cultivation. Indeed, one recent writer restricts use of the term *Mississippian* to "those societies that practiced cleared-field agriculture with maize as the dominant crop."[4] While the majority of Mississippian societies were agriculture based, *La Florida* provided a controversial exception to this theory, especially in the Native American groups along the Atlantic and Gulf shores and interior peninsula, below the fall line of the rich Piedmont Plateau. Traditionally, demographic increases, decreases in seasonal nomadism, and a complexification (and resulting stratification) of society occasioned by increases in "down" (non–survival oriented) time have been viewed as the principal concomitants of a mastery of nature and the decrease in reliance upon opportunistic survival, that is, upon the gathering of foodstuffs provided fortuitously by nature.

However, the economic bases of, for example, the Fort Walton culture of the eastern Gulf coast (900 C.E.–Contact +), the St. Johns II culture of the north-central interior peninsula (750 C.E.–Contact +), and the Caloosahatchee culture of the southeast Gulf coast (500 B.C.E.–Contact +) contrast sharply with those of Mississippian groups farther inland.[5] In fact, those culture groups that constitute the exceptions to the imposed concomitance of agriculture-based economy and Mississippian social complexity all seem to have existed below the fall line of the Piedmont Plateau, along the Pleistocene-sand strands of the Atlantic Ocean and the Gulf of Mexico and across the relatively narrow southeastern peninsula of the continent.

Current archaeological research indicates that, rather than there being an increased reliance upon sedentary agriculture, the evidence for pre-Columbian maize agriculture in several of these regions is almost nonexistent.[6] Among the Timuguana, for example, researcher John Hann reports: "Horticulture seems to have made a greater contribution to subsistence for the westerners as a whole than it did for the easterners, some of whom may have been largely or even exclusively fisher-hunter-gatherers."[7] Nevertheless, among these there existed complex social hierarchies, mound-building traditions, and comparable iconographic institutions, even though the primary economic reliance was upon estuarine fishing, rather than agriculture. One group, the Calusa of the southwest peninsula, developed what appears to have been a very successful and lucrative regional economy centered on the harvesting and trading of sharks' teeth.[8]

Ultimately, adherents of Mississippianism included Native Americans from tribes widely variant in geographic areas and linguistic families whose primary commonalties were their broad contemporaneity and their acceptance of a body of beliefs and practices that, in its span of existence, spread farther, garnered more followers, and lasted longer than many of the significant religious and ideological movements of the modern Western world. At the same time, however, the tenets of Mississippianism were not universally accepted across the broad area of its impact. Thus, we might add to the list of (largely rhetorical) queries, Why did some peoples embrace the new ideology enthusiastically while others accepted only selected elements?

By the time the movement had reached and passed its zenith, approximately by the fifteenth century C.E., Caddoan-speaking tribes from today's Arkansas, Oklahoma, Texas, and Louisiana had accepted the Mississippian gospel. The Quapaw, a southern Siouan Osage people, and the Tcilokit (Cherokee), an Iroquois-speaking people whose territories ranged to the Atlantic coast, also accepted the teachings. Northern Algonquian-speaking tribes, such as the Illinois, Miami, and Shawanoe, and Catawban speakers of the Carolina piedmont accepted the teachings also.

One of the largest bodies of peoples to accept the Mississippian cosmogony was the broad range of Maskókî peoples in the southern and southeastern parts of the continent. This included tribes as geographically diverse as the Nétchez, Chactá, and Chicaça (Louisiana, Mississippi, and Tennessee); the Coça, Tusquege, Guale, and Yamásî (South Carolina, Alabama, Georgia, and Florida); and the Abalachi, Abalachicolo, Timuguana, Calusa, and Teguesta (lower Alabama, Georgia, and the Florida peninsula).[9]

Some contemporary linguistic researchers are unsure about whether the range of Maskókî speakers actually comprised a group of mutually unintelligible dialects or whether "by some means," the core Maskókî speakers had come to "dominate the linguistic map of the Southeast by A.D. 800," possibly through the use of a lingua franca.[10] However, several of the most basic drives in the human social repertoire also need to be discussed as providing the impetus for linguistic interrelations: the desires for sex and for territorial dominance, through warfare and trade, all of which function in cultures as elements of the discourse of power and will be discussed further. Irrespective of the impetus, it was the Maskókî peoples whose cultural success made them the principal disseminators of the Mississippian cosmogony across *La Florida*.

Mississippianism was manifested in a broad range of cultural and social traits and a material culture repertoire that exhibited variations across time and space but retained a significant degree of identifiability. Through analysis of material culture *sacra* or symbolic ceremonial objects, archaeologist Vernon Knight recently has identified a series of cosmogonic sets or "cult institutions" within Mississippianism that can be said to be principal indicators of its manifestations throughout the Southeast.[11] Knight's posited interpretation is considered by some to be an "alternate definition," but it has advantages that other, more simplistic and therefore obscurantist, interpretations do not have.[12]

Three cult institutions only are identified despite the fact that the number four has borne especial value among most Maskókî speakers historically as the number of power, that is, the number of completeness and symmetry.[13] However, two institutions actually may have been misperceived as one because of their particularly high degree of interrelatedness. For his purposes, Knight accepts an earlier definition of cult institutions that also has value here. They are "a set of rituals all having the same general goal, all explicitly rationalized by a set of similar or related beliefs, and all supported by the same social group."[14] As primary constituents of Mississippianism, they also help to delineate the symbolic dimension of the world of the Maskokálgî.

A "warfare/cosmogony complex" is identified as a single cult institution, even though it has two distinct elements that may be indicative of a complementarity of cosmogonic elements especially since one of its facets, a warrior cult, has maintained a principal and unique identity historically and continues to carry strong social value to the present. In its material culture manifestation, this complex is identified by a significant number of recurring motifs and symbols, all occurring on exotic and statused wares such as marine shells, copper, and imported stones. The symbology related to warfare includes images of "war axes, maces, arrowheads, highly abstract composite atlatl/bows, and specialized swordlike forms . . . and realistic representational art showing them displayed by elaborately dressed individuals."[15]

The second cosmogonic component of this complex includes a finite set of anthropomorphized animals and animalized human form representations that recur exclusively within this entire range of sacra. It is for this reason that Knight classifies this group of sacra together with the warfare complex. The possibility also exists, however, that the close associational value of these two sacral groups offers evidence of the high degree of in-

Some Native Tribes of Lower *La Florida* at European Contact
(Map by Synergy Design Group, Tallahassee, Florida)

tegration inherent in the circularity of Maskókî cosmogony. (See below for a discussion of circular and linear cosmogonies.) A teleological interpretation requires proof of complementarity; a circular cosmogony assumes it. Archaeologically, items in this range are encountered most often as grave goods, where the burials are spatially segregated not by sex, age, or occupation but, it seems, by "unilineal descent groups," undoubtedly Clans.

Another major element of Mississippianism well known among the Maskókî speakers was the communal construction of platform mounds. Despite the heterogeneity of external shapes and uses, Knight recognizes that their very construction was the manifestation of a Mississippian symbology that must not be overlooked. The importance of this symbology is most clearly emphasized in their internal structures. Rather than being a single construction, each mound is actually a series of periodic destructions and reconstructions characterized by ritualistic closings or cappings of the mound, often including the deposit of funerary wares, and the deposition of a new mantle of earth signifying communal purification and intensification of communal coherence. According to Knight, "This ritual behavior is entirely consistent with the most basic core metaphor of the great semiological complex of southeastern Indian cosmography."[16]

The tradition of mound building among the Maskókî speakers is one that also holds particular interest in this discussion of self-imaging and the continuity of objectification among their descendants. Platform mounds are intimately linked with the celebration and evolution of the major *búsketau,* or fasting rituals, of the Maskokálgî liturgical year, especially the Green Corn ceremony, which continues to be celebrated to the present.

The quadrilateral configuration of the mounds' platforms reaffirmed and reinforced the primacy of the number four and the teachings of the Four Teachers (see below), even as the Maskókî people placed it in obvious juxtaposition to the classic, round, ceremonial ground. The Spaniards immediately saw this space as analogous to their rectangular town plazas, because of its logistic centrality, its spacious character, and its importance in communal events, and thereby initiated the misconception that it was a "square" ground. Almost invariably, later European viewers couched their descriptions in terms of squares also.[17] However, it is important to realize that the current linguistic designator for this space in the Maskókî and the Hitchiti languages carries no significator for a "square,"[18] nor do we have any indication that their linguistic significators historically carried any such connotations.

The central, sacred fire of the ceremonial ground is laid out with four logs, radiating outward from a common center and forming a circle. The dances performed within its circle of light move around the fire in a circle, specifically counterclockwise, and the Clan camps that encompass the ground are distributed, ritually, in a loosely circular form. The whole is, consequently, infused with the semiotic power relationships of the circle and the square: the four-cornered circle.

The power of four is further reaffirmed in the historical and surviving grounds of the Green Corn ceremony, in which the cardinal directions are buttressed by ceremonial arbors for medicine makers and ceremonial leaders, warriors and other men, and women. The fourth "side" is toward the east, so that the sun may enter the ceremonial ground. Thus, the four corners of the mound and the arbors buttressing the circular ceremonial ground both couched public events in the discourse of the primary number of power, four, and engaged the power of the world's four cardinal points and the four elements, capturing and embedding them semiotically and ritualistically in the cosmogonic circle.[19]

As a facet of Green Corn ritual, the ceremonial ground still is periodically purified and closed, just as the earlier mounds were, generally in cycles of four years or multiples of four years, in medicine ceremonies involving spreading and burying the ashes of the sacred fire, sweeping the grounds, and capping the site by adding a new mantle of earth.[20] In symbolic deaths and rebirths, the peoples of the same fires—all peoples of the sacred fire—renewed and renew themselves as a coherent people and reaffirm their communal and individual commitments to the cosmogonic templates of the Maskokálgî.

The final pan-Mississippian element identified by Knight is "temple statuary." This discrete class of artifacts consists of male and female figures made of stone, wood, or ceramics and consistently presented in a highly conventionalized kneeling/seated "deathlike" position. From the existence of this class of artifacts is inferred an organized, exclusively male, priestly class, supervising maintenance of temples and ossuaries, funeral rituals, and sacred fires and functioning as mediaries between chiefly and community ritual affairs.

The term *priestly class,* however, tends to homogenize what was in actuality a heterogeneous range of practitioners, with individual specialties in a number of areas from funerary rites to herbal medicine to childbirth and divination.[21] In addition, we have no reason to believe that women, included in the representative icons, were not practitioners in various of these areas: they are to this day.[22] Further, it has been posited by an earlier researcher that these priests and icons were elements of a Mississippian cult of ancestors.[23] If so, then the priests, rather than just mediating between chiefly and community ritual affairs, were also the manipulators of a symbolic dimension wherein the entire community, including elites, together reaffirmed its continuity of existence within a discursive realm in which the past and the present unfolded into the future. This interpretation is much more consistent with a circular cosmogony than the antagonistic rhetoric of the simplistic priest-as-mediator paradigm and also is consistent with the role of the "medicine" practitioner today.

Knight's reinterpretation of elements of Maskókî culture has the important advantage of placing its southeastern manifestation firmly inside

"Their Idol." "Their idol . . . is four feet high and carved of wood.
Its head is like those of the people of Florida. . . . " Theodore
de Bry's 1590 engraving (plate 21) from the watercolor by John White
(published in Lorant, *The New World*, 267)

the larger context of pan-Mississippianism by superseding former analyses
that were based on the limited interpretation of specific sacra and their
symbology within the Southeast.[24] In this regard, his reevaluation is invaluable also because it lays the groundwork for a realignment of the basic paradigm within which later (seventeenth and eighteenth century)
Maskókî culture has been interpreted historically.

Previously, the beliefs and practices of colonial period Maskókî peoples
have been characterized generally as "attenuated, debased rudiments of a
richer and much more elaborate" Mississippian system, the earlier elements of which had been lost in the process of Conquest.[25] Knight concludes, rather, that the later, colonial period culture of the Maskókî speakers appears "to be *simple* transformations of the earlier institutional forms,
made under the burden of rapidly changing political, demographic, and
social realities of the European conquest of the continent" (emphasis
added).[26]

Although the process was hardly "simple," it was most certainly a transformation. In addition, although the speed of the process was increased, inevitably, by the expectations of the European Other and increased over time by additional introductions of disparate discourse sets (i.e., Spanish, English, French), it is important not to lose sight of the fact that all cultures evolve and transform within their own unique dynamics, and their transformations are always rooted in their own cultural antecedents. Therefore, change would have been inevitable even without the interposition of a separate and inimical culture. And change would have been impossible if the culture had not already contained viable templates for change that did not mitigate against the successful functioning of the culture.

Yet, while a recontextualization of Mississippian culture is critical to any real understanding of the historical process of survival, the rhetoric of Conquest that is used as the interpretational framework for Knight's model is problematic and, in that, it is also indicative of the misinterpretations basic to a Euroamerican locus of enunciation. Principally, the problems stem from the dangers inherent in any interpretational model that decontextualizes an integrated cosmogony as its constituent parts, thereby ignoring the synergistic dimension. Basically, this decontextualization occurs because the interpretational framework is inherently teleological; sociocultural elements are enunciated as oppositional rather than integrative (appositional).

Several examples will suffice. First is the consistent language of opposition used to designate cult institutions. As a basic tenet of the research, the sacra are grouped specifically to *differentiate* the secular and religious aspects of sociopolitical phenomena, rather than to place them in positions of interlocking and supportive circularity. A chiefly cult is "contraposed against" a communal earth/fertility cult, and a dyadic relationship is posited among cults, which wax and wane in power but only at the expense of the others.[27]

Then, the Maskókî speakers are characterized as "preliterate" peoples, a term used by other researchers as well, but one that implies a culturally deterministic evolution toward literacy, which implicitly is viewed as the sine qua non of self-imaging. Over a century ago, Albert Gatschet decried the tendency of researchers to cling to the erroneous belief that *quod non est in scriptis, non est in mundo.*[28]

Nonetheless, so strong has been the cultural lure of this ethnocentric belief in the overarching importance of literacy as the basis of cultural preservation that one historian recently has asserted it as a principal reason for Euroamericans' lack of information about the early history of the Southeast. "The native people of the South," he says, "have not told this story themselves because their sixteenth- and seventeenth-century ancestors were preliterate. Their ancestors' knowledge of the past was not written down, but resided in memory. By the eighteenth century, the Indians of the Southeast had lost almost all memory of the Spanish explorers and quite probably of their own ancient ancestors."[29] The implications of the several discourse sets contained in this statement are frightening. First, we are told that the burden of not having shared what remains of their cultural memory with the very people who have spent the past five hundred years attempting to subvert or obliterate it lies with the Native Americans. Then we hear explicitly stated and engaged the superiority of a literate culture over a nonliterate culture. Finally, the existence of coherent, memory-bearing Native American culture groups today is undermined, if not totally negated, by the arbitrary imposition of a cultural discontinuity. The legitimate domain of historical consciousness within an orally held and transmitted culture will be discussed further, below. Suffice it to reiterate that the discourse of each generation holds a historical present, and the burden of proof lies not with those who know but with those who would know.

Another expression of the teleological model is the continuing use of the designator "Conquest." As long as researchers continue to politicize Native American history by infusing discussions with the rhetoric of inequality of power, no meaningful realignments of expression will ever be effected. For the first two hundred years after Contact, at least, the Maskókî peoples were neither numerically nor politically subordinate to the Spaniards, despite constant attempts by the Spaniards to manipulate the Native Americans into a self-objectification consistent with subordination. Sufficient examples exist of the Natives' both enunciating and acting upon their own internalized autonomy to make clear their own self-imaging. Nor did the Spaniards imagine themselves to be in a sufficiently secure position—either numerically, politically, or even militarily—to make unilateral, large-scale decisions regarding the Natives' actions if the Natives chose, for whatever reasons, not to comply. As we shall see in the following chapters, Spanish rhetoric frequently was used to manipulate the locus of power even as the Spaniards admitted the inadequacy of their own attempts.

Despite the fact that some of his analysis still is couched in lineality, Knight's short reassessment of Mississippian symbology takes an important step toward reendowing the Maskókî speakers with their own cultural voice. For, as Knight concludes, "it is not really necessary to emphasize a distinction between political organization and the organization of cult institutions in the societies under consideration. These two aspects of social structure are so closely intertwined and congruent among ethnographically comparable complex societies that it makes little analytical sense to treat them as separate domains, except in the analysis of political office-holding per se. Mississippian institutional religion might better be seen as providing the *context* of Mississippian political power, along with the kinship system." To take this understanding to its inevitable conclusion, Mississippianism should, even more accurately, be viewed as constituting the context for the entire range of characteristics that provided, and continues to provide, coherence to the culture base of the Seminole and Miccosukee and Creek descendants of the Maskókî peoples today.

The "Maskókî" Construct

There is no reason to believe that the linguistically related tribes of the Southeast ever objectified themselves by a single name before the coming of the Spaniards, or even afterward during at least the first century of the European interposition. The word *Maskókî*, by which they have since come to be known, was not a linguistic product of the people to whom it referred. It was an applied term, generally "thought to have been derived from Shawanoe or some other Algonquian language, and to refer to swampy ground."[30] The original term *Maskókî* was therefore an impositional construct, being used as a designator by Native people who spoke another language. Many of its current bearers remember this.[31] All know that the word has no meaning in their own "Maskókî" language. But, like so many other linguistic adoptions, the word was firmly anchored in the lexicons and manipulated to conform to internal cultural standards, especially after it began to be modeled by English setters in the century following 1670. There is, however, no acceptable evidence to indicate exactly when the term was first applied or why it was internalized by certain tribes and not others. There are only small but important bits of evidence, some negative and some positive, to provide an explanation.

One negative piece of evidence is that the term *Maskókî* does not appear in the sixteenth-century Spanish documents. Because the Spaniards were quick to learn and record the names of almost all of the tribes with which they came into contact, the fact that it does not appear lends credence to the belief that it was not in use or, at least, was not in use in the lower Southeast where the Spaniards based their occupations.

The next piece of evidence is that the earliest written use of the term occurred in the late eighteenth century, in English documents. According to Alexander McGillivray, a politically ambitious mixed-blood and one of the first, in 1790, to make a documentary mention, "Tradition says the Muscoghis . . . came from the North West [(text unintelligible) and the English?] have called them creeks from the multitude of little rivulets abounding in the Country."[32] His summation is indicative of the prevailing usage in his period.

George Stiggins (1788–1845), a mixed-blood Nétchez and Maskókî, declaring his intention to "steer clear" of the usual "labyrinth of paradoxes" created by the annoying determination of white men to obtain information from Natives who would "recount . . . a fabricated tale" just to rid themselves of such impertinence, wrote only "the most probable side" of what he had learned from his Native peers. He wrote: "I can assert that it is not known by the Indians why the present assemblage of their tribes came by the appellation of Muscogee, [and] whether the Muscogee aborigines were destroyed or became extinct in the present tribes and only left their name at their extinction."[33]

The principal implication in both of these summations is that the term was in use within the indicated groups for some undetermined but lengthy amount of time prior to its being committed to paper. In addition, it was not necessary for the earlier holders of the name either to have been destroyed or to have become extinct, but only for them to have passed on their name to their descendants.

Nonetheless, the key to the reality of its origin may lie in the etymology of the word. Swanton's assignment of the word to Shawanoe, an Iroquoian language, indicates that we should examine contact points and periods between the two groups as a possible source of the word. First, topographically, the core settlement areas of the Maskókî speakers have been defined by non-Native researchers as having been along riverbeds and in river-confluence valleys with water access, on the interior of the southeastern Piedmont Plateau, much of which was certainly "swampy" ground.[34] On the Atlantic and Gulf coastal plains also, below the fall line of the Piedmont and including the peninsula, settlements frequently were established on hammocks that rose above swampy terrain, especially at the head of the peninsula in the region of the great Okefinocau Swamp.[35] These facts, then, resonate with the recurring question of where the Shawanoe speakers encountered the people whom they referred to as the Maskókî speakers who were living amidst swampy terrain.

In order to respond, we must revisit information concerning the presence of the Shawanoe people in the Southeast before Contact. At best, they have been viewed as ephemeral tribes, appearing much farther south than the core area of their later, historical-period descendants would indicate. In fact, the oral traditions of both the Shawanoe and the Seminole contain the memory that they had a home at one time in what is now Florida.

A United States Indian Agent to the "Shawanoese" in Ohio asked a tribal elder, in 1819, about the history of his people. He was told: "The Shawanoese—came here from West Florida, and the adjacent country. They formerly resided on the Suwaney River, near the sea. Black Hoof, who is eighty five years of age, was born there, and remembers bathing in the salt water when a boy."[36] Later, in Washington, D.C., in 1854, Buckingham Smith spoke to three "Shawnees" who remembered Black Hoof and elaborated upon his memories, corroborating them in fulsome detail.[37] Benjamin Hawkins, United States Indian Agent to the Creeks, whose information has much credibility, also said that, in 1798–1799, "Sua-wa-no-gee of the Chattahoochee river is inhabited by Shaw-a-nee and they retain the language and customs of their countrymen to the northwest."[38]

The Englishman Edmond Atkin wrote that the "Savanoes" were "stout, bold, cunning, and the greatest travelers in America," that their "origins are somewhat mysterious," and that, prior to the 1715 Yamásî uprising (in the Carolinas and what would shortly be Georgia), they lived on the "Savanoe" River.[39] The presence of the Shawanoe in the area has also led to a continuing controversy over the etymology of "Savannah," the name of the Georgia city founded by Oglethorpe in 1733, and "Suwannee," the name of the river that rises from the Okefinocau Swamp.

The Miccosukee Seminoles today retain an ephemeral image of the Shawanoe as "bogey men" who move silently through the forests and outside the campfire circles of the camps. According to Jumper family tradition, children who would not stay in camp at night and stay close to their families ran the risk of being taken by the "Shawanogałi," who "carried around big sacks and would put you in it and stuff your mouth full of that grey [Spanish] moss and carry you off!"[40]

Irrespective of these latter considerations, however, we can draw several tentative conclusions from the above information. First, some Shawanoe, at least, held cultural memories of their tribes' having lived throughout the lower Southeast in the early eighteenth century, if not earlier. This is, indeed, corroborated by the analysis of John Swanton, who cites English trade representative Henry Woodward's meeting at the present site of Augusta, Georgia, in 1674, of Shawanoe, who had been visiting Spanish San Agustín to trade.[41] Second, Woodward was in the Southeast only because the English had, just four years earlier, established Charles Towne in the Carolinas. That is to say, the permanent English presence in the Southeast began in 1670 and the designator "Maskókî" entered the English (not Spanish) lexicon after 1670. This indicates that the Shawanoe began to use their descriptor in the late seventeenth or early eighteenth century and the English learned it from them rather than from the "Maskókî" speakers themselves.

Because the term entered the written history of the United States through an English, rather than a Spanish, source, it was accepted, reiterated, ligitimated, and imposed upon members of the southeastern linguistic family. Next, however, we find that the designator was not applied generically across the Southeast. Only those Natives who shortly acquired yet another designator from the English, the so-called Creeks, were recontextualized as having been Maskókî. The Chicaça and Chactá of the Spanish documents received direct transliteration as the Chickasaw and Choctaw of the English documents. In the twentieth century, anthropologists and linguists recognize them as western Muskogean tribes, that is, as a western dialectical division of the Maskókî speakers, but they are not considered to be Creeks; they retain distinct, although frequently intersecting, identities.

There is no agreement among nineteenth- or twentieth-century Euroamerican researchers as to which tribes, specifically, constituted the total body of the Maskókî, just as there is no agreement on who, specifically, should be termed Creeks. This evidence only reinforces the fact that both designators were arbitrarily constructed and applied terms. There was no unanimity in the English selectivity and the confusion creates obfuscation to the present.

There is, however, some correlation among researchers concerning the core area of the Maskókî/Creeks, and there is also the important domain of self-imaging as carried by the Native people themselves today. The group being referred to by non-Native researchers is amorphous but centers on the remnants of the Coça province, one of the largest paramount chiefdoms in the Southeast (see Chapter 3), encountered in 1540 by the Hernando de Soto entrada and described by the survivors. (See Map 2 for the tentative dimensions of the Coça province.) This province was sufficiently large that it took the de Soto entrada twenty-four days to travel through it.[42]

In the process of the geographic migrations occasioned by the demographic impact of European pathogens, however, the coherent power of this great chiefdom was fragmented and its core elements relocated southward and eastward during the period 1540 to 1763, into areas that brought them into increasing contact with English traders from Charles Towne and Savannah from 1670 onward.[43] It is extremely important to realize, however, that the symbolic power of the chiefdom, which was couched primarily not in its politicomilitary might but in the cosmogonic significance of its sacred towns and the juxtaposition of those "power" towns, was not destroyed. That power, in the forms of social status, political precedence, and social weight within oral traditions, persisted into the nineteenth century and, in certain ways, to the present. The historical consciousness that continues to frame this rhetorical universe will be discussed further in later chapters. The past does, indeed, live within discourse.

Suffice it to point out now that four of these core or "power" towns of the Coça chiefdom are reported by Euroamerican researchers as having been the "founding towns" of the "Creek nation." One researcher reports them as Coweta, Cusita, Coça, and Apica.[44] In terms of the manner in which their significance was objectified by the peoples themselves, it is not necessary that they should have obtained their ascendancy solely as first or "founding" towns, however. Their status also obtained from their cosmogonic centrality in ceremonial and ritualistic terms; their number (four); and the power of specific individuals who resided in them, in terms of sagacity, heredity, and abilities to manipulate the mediated realm known to Euroamericans as "medicine."

Swanton lists Coweta as "one of the two great Muskogee tribes or towns. . . . According to tradition, they originally constituted one people with the Kashita [Cusita] . . . and after the separation [possibly in the late seventeenth century] [Coweta] became the head war town . . . just as Kashita became the head peace town."[45] Concerning Coça and Apica, Swanton reports the former as "one of the great original tribes of Muskogee [that], together with the Abihka [the eighteenth-century spelling of Apica], constituted the main representative of the Muskogee in the northernmost section of the old Creek country."[46]

Consequently, it may well have been the core components of the sixteenth-century Coça kingdom that were first encountered by a part of the

Shawanoe on their southward migrations, during the mid to late 1600s, and to which they applied the designator "Maskôkî." It was the critical elements of the province, the paramount towns, that maintained a coherent settlement pattern over the eighteenth and nineteenth centuries as the people moved southward and eastward. This probability is borne out in the imaging of another of the neighbors of the Maskôkî, the Tcilokit or "foreign speakers," called Cherokee by the English. As the Englishman Albert Gatschet recalled (above): "The Cheroki call all the Creek tribes Kusa-people."

However, the term *Maskôkî*, despite its internalization by the southeastern tribes and the fact that it has survived to the present within the cultural lexicon of these tribes, quickly became confused and obscured in the minds of Euroamericans after 1670 by the imposition of the arbitrary generic designator "Creek" by the English. In Chapter 9 we will place this change firmly within the larger recontextualizations imposed upon the historiography of the southeastern tribes by the documentary and interpretational dominance of the English over the past three-plus centuries.

The Maskokálgî

It was sometime after the mound building began among the Maskôkî peoples that the Four Teachers came among them. No individual names are known for them, but among today's Maskôkî-speaking Seminoles, they are remembered as *Hiya yálgî,* that is, People of the Light or Illuminators (from *hiyáyike,* light).[47] No one recalls where they came from originally, but the purpose of their coming is still known and many of their teachings are still remembered and revered by The People. It is recalled that they came from the four cardinal points, with the first coming from the north, which is still considered a directional source of primary power. The second came from the east, the third from the south, and the fourth from the west.[48]

The purpose of their coming was not to bring light in the physical sense but, rather, to bring enlightenment to the people. This enlightenment comprised four areas of knowledge. Thus, it was the Four Teachers who told the Maskôkî speakers, first and foremost, how they should relate to *Isákit' imisi* (from *isákita,* breath; life), the Giver of Breath.[49] "My god is not a white god, and he's not a white man," a medicine man explained to me recently. "The white man will never be my god. My god is god. And the woman is not my god. And my god is my own. I will remember him and do what he tells me. That's why the Seminole has been strong and has lasted for five hundred years."[50]

It was also the Four Teachers who brought the arts of healing that permitted the people to use the abundance of nature to the best possible advantage. Then, they taught the people all the ceremonies that must be performed in order to keep themselves wise and powerful and healthy, and, finally, they showed them the rituals, marked by the signs and images that were the symbols of their learning and their constancy.

This coming of enlightenment is the era that non-Native researchers who find its material remnants call Mississippianism. Among the Maskókî-speaking Seminoles, however, it is the term *Maskokálgî* that is used to indicate generally all of their cultural kin who adopted the Enlightenment of the Four Teachers. Therefore, the word has distinct discursive elements. It signifies not only the Maskókî speakers but also, rather more inclusively, the People of the Maskókî Way—the synergetic totality of adherents of the Four Teachers, including but not limited to the core Maskókî speakers, as contextualized by the Maskókî speakers themselves.

Consequently, the separate constructs must be applied very specifically in order to recapture their own specific intents and imports. The first comprises "Maskókî," the applied term that, as we have seen, indicates a people whose lives were conducted in the geographic context of watercourses, as well as a linguistic family in the broadest sense. From the viewpoint of non-Native researchers, this term has been used to indicate linguistically affiliated tribes historically and their linguistic descendants, from the Chactá of the Mississippi River to the Teguesta of *La Florida*'s southeastern peninsula. Some of these historical affiliations are still discernible from within the tribes today. For example, Seminole tribal members today frequently mention the close linguistic affinities that exist between Chactá and Mikísuukî and the relative ease with which the one may be understood by speakers of the other.[51]

The second construct, Maskokálgî, however, is a manifestation of the self-objectification of its bearers, as contextualized within their own cosmogony. It is invariably translated by Euroamericans only in its most simplistic element, that is, in terms of its linguistic components: the suffix *-algi* rendered as "many" modifying the linguistic differentiator "Maskókî." In this reading, however, the synergism of the larger, symbolic realm is ignored, to the detriment of the people who have infused it with living, discursive meaning for centuries.

Thus, we are reminded, yet again, that language is not synonymous with culture nor is it even, necessarily, a pertinent modifier of culture although it does serve as a mirror of its culture base. Neither is the material-culture repertoire dubbed "Mississippian" by non-Natives an adequate indicator of the culture whose cosmogony produced it. We must differentiate conceptually between the Maskókî speakers and the ideological adherents of Mississippianism or, more properly, the Maskokálgî, the People of the Maskókî Way. These concepts have been used indiscriminately by researchers, even though the dichotomy between the latter two is not forgotten by a number of today's Seminoles.

This is an important distinction because it is the distinction that the Natives themselves make and one that has been blurred consistently by Euroamerican interpretations that treat the two as synonymous in extent and in effect. In the sixteenth, seventeenth, and eighteenth centuries, however, dialectic boundaries among the various Maskókî speakers were sufficiently permeable to accommodate the increasing speed of geographic shifts occasioned by Euroamerican settlement and trading pressures. At the same time, the Maskokálgî cosmogony was sufficiently plastic to absorb external cultural pressures without disarticulating under their demands. Once again, the reality of the continuing existence of the Maskokálgî today as a discrete and coherent cultural group only reaffirms the process. As the old axiom reminds us, "The tree that bends does not break."

3 The Tree That Bends

Many of the early Americanists, especially . . . John R. Swanton . . . working
on the Southeast . . . also [Frans] Boas himself in his Northwest coast research, regarded the cultures they were studying as broken down, recover-
able only through memories encoded in discourse. For them, discourse was
a window to culture in a different sense; it was a portal through which one
could peer back into time, seeing amid the debris of the present world customs that had vanished, a way of life that had been eclipsed by European
culture. As one studies discourse today, discourse circulating in ongoing social life, it is all too easy to miss the important truth discovered by these
early Americanists. Discourse is in fact the means by which the past is kept
alive in the present, by means of which a culture is maintained. Without
that splendid, nostalgia-filled image of the past, culture is reduced to little
more than rote repetition. The truth that the Americanists found is that ancient times are alive in the present; they live in discourse.

—Greg Urban[1]

Power has to be analysed in terms of relations of power. . . . Power relations
can be analysed in terms of an apparatus (*dispositif*) [that is,] . . . a system
of relations . . . defined by a structure of heterogeneous elements . . . con-
sist[ing] in strategies of relations of forces supporting, and supported by,
types of knowledge. . . . [An] apparatus in its general form is both discursive and non-discursive, its elements being much more heterogeneous. . . .
Power in the substantive sense, *'le' pouvoir,* doesn't exist. . . . In reality power
means relations, a more-or-less organised, hierarchical, co-ordinated cluster of relations. So the problem is not that of constituting a theory of power.
. . . If power is in reality an open, more-or-less co-ordinated . . . cluster of relations, then the only problem is to provide oneself with a grid of analysis
which makes possible an analytic of relations of power.

—Michel Foucault[2]

The Cosmogonic Circle

The conceptual leap from an interpretation of culture as framed by the
discourse of a linear cosmogony to that in a circular cosmogony is an ex-

tremely difficult one, but attempt it we must, if we are ever to circumvent the transference of an alien, and frequently inimical, set of cultural values to our interpretations of a past not of our own making. Few studies have yet gone far enough in making clear this distinction.

For example, a recent interpretation by Nancy Farriss of Maya culture at the time of Spanish colonial rule goes far toward highlighting the organic nature of the Native Americans' "religious" structure and its ability to incorporate new discursive entities.[3] In this context, religion is treated "mainly as a social activity designed to keep the cosmos in operation and thereby ensure the continued survival of its human component."[4]

However, the use of the term *religion* and the treatment of its manifestations as independent social elements are still insufficient. There is no "religion," per se, in a circular cosmogony, and any discussion that removes religious-appearing elements from the larger cultural matrix in which they are embedded shreds the fabric of the Maskokálgî.

Farriss's method is to demonstrate the similarities between the Maya and Spanish Roman Catholic "religions." She suggests that we should "cease to see polytheism and monotheism as mutually exclusive alternatives" and view them, rather, as two different levels, "the parochial and the universal—within the public sphere of religion, which can coexist with each other." This approach is important in understanding *how* the Native Americans utilized their cosmogony to incorporate one set of the requirements made of them by the European Other. It still does not help us understand *why* they were able to make the incorporation. They were able to incorporate these requirements (to greatly varying degrees, as we will see) because a circular world view holds itself open to new possibilities while lineality excludes all that does not directly support it. The simplicity of the circular view is obvious, and deceptive.

A modern Seminole Tribe medicine woman explains the circular cosmos thus. "Imagine two turtle shells put together, one on top of the other, so that their undersides touch and together they make a whole circle. Don't think about those foolish stories of the turtle carrying the world on its back, because they don't make any sense. Those are white men's stories. The metaphor of the turtle shells is strictly to illustrate a concept. That's all. The upper or top half of the shells represents positive forces and the lower half, negative. But don't think that the upper and lower halves are any allusion to the sky and the places beneath the earth either. There is no 'heaven' or 'hell' here, just the potential for good or bad. And humans live in the middle, between the two possibilities. We all have the ability to choose, and everything that you choose is either good for you or not good for you. Those are the only choices. There is no 'sin,' and there is no 'right' or 'wrong.' The time of your death and the manner of your dying are already set when you are born. You can't change that. But how you get there is strictly up to you."[5]

That the cosmogony was objectified in exactly these terms prior to the interposition of the Europeans in the Southeast is not possible to state definitively. There are, however, sufficient inferences to be drawn from the domains in which the discourse of the missionaries was couched that we may learn many of the ways in which the objectification of the Native universe was engaged in daily life.

Francisco Pareja, OFM, proselytized among the Timuguana in the period 1595 to about 1626 and wrote the earliest surviving texts in any North American Native language. In his *Confessionario en lengua Castellana, y Timuguana,* published in Mexico City in 1613, he outlined for other Spanish Roman Catholic missionaries those ideological topics upon which they should question the Native converts most closely, in order to determine the state of their souls relative to the Roman Catholic parameters of "sin."

Numerous discourse sets, both Maskokálgî and European, are contained in his material or may be inferred from it. By the process of conversion, for example, the Spaniards sought to ideologically recontextualize Maskokálgî life within the power/control bounds of the Roman Catholic Church. Also, by recontextualizing meanings in order to introduce guilt and shame into the Maskokálgî social lexicon in areas where none had existed previously, they sought to manipulate these emotions in a public manner in order to anchor Native converts firmly inside the sphere of Spanish political allegiance. (See Chapter 8 for further discussion of these processes and their ramifications.) Therefore, by examining the topics that Pareja chose as most important to counter, we are able to identify some ideological elements of these natives' daily lives that conflicted most strongly with Spanish Roman Catholic ideology and that, consequently, can help us delineate what the Europeans saw as the cultural Other.

Two cosmogonic themes in Native life emerge clearly through Pareja's text. One is the profound degree to which the Natives viewed themselves as existing in a reciprocal (balanced) relationship with nature and all the elements of the natural world. The second is the tenuousness of that equilibrium; that is, the ease with which it could be disturbed by a lack of sufficient awareness and respect on the part of human beings.

Both of these themes are reiterated throughout the *Confessionario,* recast by the Spanish Roman Catholic as "superstitions," in an implied discursive if:then relationship. If, for example, one became ill and did not light a separate fire, then one would die.[6] If the fireplace popped, then it was a sign of war; if one did not spill out some of the broth when cooking the first deer killed, then one would not kill another.[7] The examples continue in this vein.

The particularly high positive social values assigned to certain areas of life are clearly illustrated by the numbers and weight of the negative values assigned to disturbances in those areas. The critical areas of food procurement—hunting, fishing, and gathering—are surrounded by numerous first-fruit injunctions all predicated upon propitiation of the sources, that is, upon maintaining reciprocity with nature. Likewise, the subjects of sexuality and procreation carry strong negative-value admonitions relative to a failure to maintain the cosmogonic equilibrium. (See Chapter 5 for further discussion of the roles of women in the Maskókî-speakers' societies and an examination of the manipulation of those roles by the Europeans.)

One further issue that is made obvious, not only by Pareja's questions but also by the broad social strata at which he directs them, is the degree to which this domain of Maskokálgî life referred to generically today as "medicine" permeated society at all levels. This point, in turn, reaffirms the inherently reciprocal and circular nature of the cosmogony. In her discussion of the Maya under colonial rule, Farriss divides their dealings with "the supernatural" into public and private spheres. We might more aptly see a reciprocal relationship of the Maskokálgî with all of the other elements and forces of the universe—a relationship that had to be maintained at all of the points of the human continuum from the smallest to the largest holding environment, from the purely personal to the communal, by the constant watchfulness of human beings and by the mediative effects of their positive actions.

This "medicine" domain was, and continues to be, broad and strongly valued, because its function was and is to serve as the medium of communication and interaction between seen and unseen forces in the cosmos. That is, it constantly recalibrates the society that, like the precise machinery that we understand so well today in a technological society, must have all of its parts operating in balance with reference to each other in order to function successfully. It was with the medicine domain in its most public or corporate expressions that the Spaniards—missionaries, administrators, and military—came into most frequent confrontation with the Maskokálgî.

Missionaries confronted the medicine domain as "pagan," "sinful," and "the work of Satan," because of their desire to effect an ideological change that they could measure only by externalities. Their inability to gauge the degree to which their prospective converts were internalizing what we now understand as a complete shift in cultural paradigms was a source of constant comment and frustration for them.

Administrators confronted the domain of medicine because both cultures politicized their metaphysical beliefs, albeit in differing terms, ergo an ideological shift would necessarily be embedded in a power shift. Finally, the military confronted it because, as they quickly discovered, personal medicine was at its strongest in the realm of the warriors and each military dispute was, for the Maskokálgî, a reaffirmation of power in both the metaphysical and physical sense, as well as a recalibration of social equilibrium.

Within the circular cosmogony, the equilibrium also is weighted differently from that within the linear model. First and foremost, the circular model is inclusionary rather than exclusionary. The philosophical and social ramifications of this view are myriad. All things not only exist in this model, but each also has its own right to exist. In addition, all things exist in complementarity to each other, rather than in opposition. The Giver of Breath and humans, men and women, and humans and nature all function in a symbiosis within which there is no need to "pit man against nature," to "wage the age-old battle of the sexes," or to face one's maker at such a relational disadvantage that one images one's self as "a mere flyspeck in the universe."

At the same time, a circular cosmogony does not impart a Pollyannaish view of the world in innocent and simplistic terms. The paradigm of circularity still includes personal and institutional dissension, warfare, deaths that do not occur in their own times, and any number of negative acts, such as the purposeful introduction of "bad" (harmful) medicine. Nor does inclusionistic circularity relieve any living organisms of the basic, repetitive labor of survival. It does, however, relieve humans of numerous complex interrelational antagonisms and functional oppositions that are the by-products of a Christian birth-by-sin (especially in the area of female-male relations), and it removes a teleologically oppositional framework that defers all pleasure to a world other than the current one.

In a complementary dimension, the circular cosmogony is expressed as the community and the circle of life that is created and perpetuated by the survival of the community. Indeed, within this framework, the community becomes the formalized metaphor for the circular universe, with the survival of the individual and that of the community inextricably bound, whether that communal construct is expressed by the extended family group (the Clan) or by a larger polity embodied in a village, in which several Clans live together. It is the inclusionary cosmogony that requires the completed circle of the community as its quintessential expression, while the exclusionary cosmogony reduces the symbolic dimension to the individual, whose solitary *telos* separates "him" from the very cosmos that gave "him" birth.

It is the reciprocal, or balanced, nature of the circular world that Euroamerican researchers have reported as the occurrence of red:white towns among the Maskokálgî. Generally explained simplistically as "war:peace" towns, there was actually a greater and more fundamental significance to their juxtaposition.[8] The color red does signify warfare and an overt state of belligerence, just as the color white does signify peace and the absence of belligerence, among the Maskokálgî and the Europeans. The symbolic realms are a great deal broader than those single facets, however. For example, Panther Clan today is still considered a red Clan because Panthers are traditionally medicine keepers who fight for the safety and health of the people.[9] In cosmogonic terms, a Maskokálgî red town was one in which the inhabitants bore a collective responsibility for maintaining the Old Ways of the Four Teachers. They preserved and conserved the medicine—the rhetorical and semiotic discourses that were the essence of their peoples' survival and success. Through their steadfast adherence to ritual and ceremony, they renewed the social contract with the unseen forces of creation, the contract that had been brought to them by the Four Teachers. Through warfare, they protected the contract. The concomitant white towns concerned themselves more with the fundamental pursuits of peace: social and civic administration and responding to the "talk," the expressed needs and concerns, of the people. Circumventing war and making peace were just two facets of the responsibilities of the white towns, but taken together red and white towns maintained reciprocity and balance.[10] Taken together, red:white towns constituted neither a dichotomy nor an antagonism. They constituted, rather, a reciprocity. In a reverberation of the two turtle shells, red and white spheres of concern and action interlocked the facets of the cosmos.

On the most personal level, this high degree of interrelatedness between the individual and the community functions to maintain an essential equilibrium within the community also. One Miccosukee Seminole explains: "My great uncle, my mother's mother's brother (I would call him my Clan grandfather), was the one who, by tradition, taught me. He was the one who showed me how the circles fit together and how my personal 'balance' influences everyone in the community—not just myself or the people in my house. Actually, it's a series of [concentric] circles, like a target. I am in the center, but I am not alone. The Breath Giver is there also and our relationship is the center. Then, the next circle is my personal relationship with a husband or wife. The next circle beyond that is my relationship with my children, and the outer circle is my relationship with my Clan and the rest of the community. I have to keep each one of those circles in proportion; if one gets too big or too little, all the others suffer. A change in one of them produces a change in all of them."[11]

This reciprocity of action and reaction is a primary concomitant of an inclusionary cosmogony and a facet of social equilibrium that functions as a mechanism of self-regulation in a society.[12] It is a facet of this cosmogonic equilibrium that is finally being recognized by non-Native researchers as the balance of "stricter determinism and apparently accidental development [which] are *not* mutually exclusive, but rather . . . more the rule in nature."[13]

Consequently, within a circular world, an unknown, cultural Other constitutes no ab initio threat to the basically inclusionary operational framework because that inclusionism imparts a degree of flexibility to the system that is not available to the same extent within a more brittle, linear construct in which the New constantly must be rationalized or rejected.

This, therefore, is the critically important basis of the survival of the Maskókî people as coherent cultural groups today. They have not been "destroyed" and "regenerated" as one historian characterized them.[14] Nor has their cultural survival been based upon "simple transformations of the earlier institutional forms."[15] Nor have they "lost almost all memory of the Spanish explorers and quite probably of their own ancient ancestors."[16]

Some contemporary anthropologists have even gone so far as to suggest the complete opposite of the argument advanced by this research: that the Spaniards confronted the Native Americans with realities that could not be encompassed by their world view and that that confrontation was the cause of a cultural collapse.[17] However, if the Maskokálgî had experienced cultural collapse, how could they also have survived as coherent cultural entities to this day? How could the United States government offer the irony of "federal recognition" to any southeastern tribes in the twentieth century if they had all collapsed in the sixteenth? One small example illustrates "reality" from a Seminole perspective.

In the 1820s, James Pierce, a Euroamerican, traveled in northern East Florida Territory and visited "Seminole" Indians whose village was in San Felasco Hammock (near present-day Gainesville). He recorded his experiences in an article about the new Territory of the United States, including an interview with the "chief" of the San Felasco Seminoles. "These Indians," he wrote, "do not appear to have a form of worship, but believe in a Supreme Being." He also reported, on the basis of further questioning, that "the chief had heard of our Savior, and his sufferings, but supposed he had been put to death by the Spaniards."[18] Pierce passed very little time with these Natives and still had no trouble realizing these elements of their traditional cosmogony. The comments of the "chief" indicate that these Maskokálgî had neither lost their culture to Spanish Christianity nor lost their cultural memory of the Spanish Others. Their memory lived in discourse.

The Maskokálgî had a cosmogony that, in its functioning, was viable, flexible, and successful for them. It was continuing to function successfully in 1825, and it continues today for many, not just despite the requirements placed upon them by the cultural Other, but because that cosmogony contained sufficient and significant mechanisms for coping with, and adapting to, externalities. The basic fact that descendants of these Maskókî peoples survive today as discrete and coherent cultural entities is, alone, sufficient proof that a significant proportion of that cosmogony survives also. Among the social strategies that comprised these mechanisms, discourse was a central element.

Finally, concerning life within circular societies, two further concomitants must be outlined. First, institutional, religious, and social power flowed along both horizontal and vertical lines but the mechanisms of horizontality were (and are) given far more weight than in linear-based societies. Second, this social horizontality, manifested as the institutionalization of individual prerogatives, was engaged within the Maskókî peoples' culture as a social dynamism that had the embodiment of much of its flexibility in the maintenance of social equilibrium.

Native American writers affirm the continued existence of this cosmogony today: "The necessary balances that have to be maintained between peoples in the community, and the community and the environment, are what constitutes 'government' in sacred aboriginal tradition."[19] In decision-making issues, for example, from the movement of camps, to warfare, to confirmation of leadership, the "talk of the people" was a major factor, and individual prerogatives—the right of the people, as individuals, to have their "talk"—were communally maintained.

The degree of autonomy inherent in the society of the Maskokálgî was also a facet of the gender system, that is, the social processes institutionalized for the relationships of the sexes. Unfortunately, this facet of their lives was subject to a great deal of obfuscation as it was filtered through an antithetical European, Christian, male value system. However, the documents of European interposition are punctuated with references to the love and caring that existed between husbands and wives and between parents and children, a fact that has been obscured by many modern researchers.[20] (The roles of women are discussed below.)

Individual autonomy was also visible as regarded the prosecution of war and the social status of warriors, since warfare functioned in such a pivotal role as a mechanism of social growth and recalibration among Native American groups. For example, the Spaniards with Hernando de Soto, on the first entrada to penetrate the interior of *La Florida*, from 1539 to 1543, noticed immediately that "the talk of the warriors was extremely important and carried much weight among them."[21] (Warfare and warriors are discussed below.)

In Euroamerican culture, in contrast, vertical power hierarchies predominated strongly, although horizontal channels certainly operated. Individual prerogatives frequently were subsumed by class and hereditary "rights" and by the superimposition of a "divine" authority structure as a legitimating force that was, itself, locked in a perpetual vertical power struggle with the secular hierarchy. The eventual replacement in the United States of elite rule by democratic-style mechanisms still, however, continues to assign primacy to "line" rather than "staff" authority, while the descendants of the sixteenth-century Maskókî speakers continue to assign significant social weight to the opinions and prerogatives of individuals.

The Dynamic Society

A major facet of the rhetoric of Conquest has been absolute reliance upon the concepts of cultural disruption, disarticulation, and destruction as the consequences of European interposition. These concepts, in turn, have much of their basis in the classic myth of a static Maskôkî world—indolent and unresilient, lacking the sociocultural vitality to recuperate from profound shocks, especially the shock of the demographic decline that was the concomitant of European interposition. But is this a representative view, or is it but another facet of cultural chauvinism?

The basic demographic picture is itself the subject of continuing controversies, with researchers placing population estimates at a low of about 50,000 for the area that is now the state of Florida and a high of 400,000 for the entire Southeast. The low estimate is based on documents produced by the Spaniards and illustrates another facet of Spanish manipulation of Maskôkî contextualization to European advantage, a process that will be discussed in detail in later chapters.

Briefly stated, however, Spanish sources tended to produce high estimates for mission areas across the northern peninsula where Spaniards were in more direct contact with Natives, where missionization efforts were most intense, and where reports of successful conversion of large numbers of Natives could be most politically beneficial. Conversely, Spanish reports downplayed or simply elided population estimates for Natives living beyond the control range of the missions and especially throughout the lower peninsula, where periodic missionization and colonization efforts were almost totally unsuccessful, where Spaniards were not in direct contact with the Natives of the interior peninsula, and where reports of large numbers of unconverted (therefore, uncontrollable) Natives would be viewed negatively by superiors.

The social value of such politically engaged estimates becomes particularly clear when one remembers that at no time throughout the entire Spanish colonial period in the Southeast did the number of Spaniards constituting the "conquering" force ever even approach, much less surpass, the number of Maskôkî peoples. At the high point of Spanish occupation of *La Florida,* in the third quarter of the eighteenth century, Spanish population totals would reach only about 2,700, while the Native American population across Spanish *La Florida* would still be or exceed 20,000.[22] Actual numbers of Europeans relative to actual numbers of Maskôkî speakers would make steady gains only after 1670 and the interposition of the English in the Southeast but, even so, demographics would not become a principal element of sociocultural power until the eighteenth century.

The high-end estimates of southeastern Maskôkî peoples are based upon recent calculations by demographer Henry Dobyns, who believes that the Southeast was a thickly populated portion of the continent. He places population density at 4.6 persons per square kilometer for the region along the Gulf of Mexico from the Attakapa people (of western Louisiana) eastward through the Abalachi territory of central *La Florida.* In the varied environment of peninsular *La Florida,* he concludes that population density was slightly higher, 5.72 persons per square kilometer, for a total population of 697,000.[23] This figure alone is over six times higher than that posited by John Swanton fifty years ago for the total of all the Maskôkî people, including the Chactá and Chicaça.[24] Dobyns reminds us, however, that although these assessments may seem high, the Native Americans could not have survived the epidemic ramifications of the introduction of European pathogens if their numbers had not been sufficiently high beforehand.[25]

In this, historian Peter Wood seems to concur when he calculates a demographic decline rate of 10:1, which still permits him to conclude a Florida (apparently not a *La Florida*) population of slightly under 20,000, even 170 years after the introduction of European pathogens. Wood also alludes to the problem of using Spanish estimations for peninsular populations when he concludes that "another *several thousand persons* inhabited the coastlines . . . further south [but were] *less familiar*" to the Spaniards (emphasis added).[26]

Spanish Roman Catholic Bishop Gabriel Díaz Vara Calderón, who toured *La Florida* missions in 1635, exemplifies the Spanish attitude as well as the irony of the traditionalist historic view. He rhetorically denigrated and dismissed these peninsular tribes, among whom the Spaniards had had little or no success with the conversion/subjugation process, when he described them as "savage heathen Carib Indians, in camps, having no fixed abodes, living only on fish and roots and trees."[27] His superciliousness would be ludicrous if it had not so often been taken seriously by successive Euroamerican researchers. In the first place, all *La Florida* inhabitants were objectified philosophically as "savage heathens" by the Spaniards unless and until they succumbed to the cultural suicide of conversion.[28]

Then, relative to the Native Americans who had accepted a primary (not a *fixed* but only a *primary*) residence under the watchful eyes of the Spaniards at the missions across the head of the peninsula, the Natives farther south on the peninsula certainly must have seemed untethered, but their itinerancy was not a sign of savagery, or of a lack of societal organization, or of a lack of "civilization." It was, rather, a standard element of their larger system of territorial ranging. (See below.) In the larger analysis,

Calderón's dismissal of the people whom he could not control says much more about Calderón than it does about the Maskókî people of peninsular *La Florida*.

All of the Maskókî peoples could have been characterized as having no fixed abodes, if they were seen only one time (as they were by Calderón) and were migrating among hunting and fishing camps or among ceremonial or Clan towns, and if they were judged by the standards of a culture in which attachment to the land and identification with a static corporate entity were of paramount value.[29] This migration, an integral feature of territorial ranging, has continued to be a basic feature of Maskókî life into the twentieth century, and its premise was neither random nor uncivilized, within its own context.

The documentary sources in each of the past five centuries are rife with examples of the constant movements of the southeastern Natives. A few examples from the sixteenth and twentieth centuries will suffice here. Historian Helen Hornbeck Tanner, in a recent work, highlights clearly the vitality and persistence of the travel, communication, and trade networks in use by the southeastern Natives, some "evident from the time of the mastodon to the present highway and railroad era."[30] Land and water trails connected the peoples of sixteenth-century *La Florida* with other Natives as far westward as present-day Texas and Mexico and as far northward as the Great Lakes region. The Spanish historian known as Barciá tells us that in the time of the coming of the Spaniards, the Calusa of the southwest peninsula were making dugout canoes large enough to hold eighty men and were traveling in them to Cuba.[31]

These trails were not fortuitous or directionless. They were rational, well-traveled networks of communications and trade associations that constituted regularly functioning elements of larger power networks within and among provinces. Nor were they discrete systems that declined in use with the passage of living memory. They were routes of interaction that were maintained over generations through purposeful replication of information.

Territorial ranging constituted a critical element of the dynamism that characterized the lives of the Maskókî speakers and one that has been almost universally downplayed or ignored in the historical analyses. Julian Steward lists intertribal trade and religious movements among the numerous agents that changed lifeways for Native Americans long before their encounters with Europeans.[32] Among the Maskokálgî, the list of cultural agents of change must also include the territorial expansions that were the explicit business of the elite warrior class and their sexual rangings in pursuit of extratribal wives, which were concomitants of the exogamous Clan system and, as such, the implicit business of the entire community.

In addition, the sociocultural ramifications of these territorial rangings must not be viewed as confined to trade, communications, warfare, and the exchange of women as discrete social elements because, in the Maskokálgî world, every template was interlocking with every other. Warfare patterns endured among the Florida Seminoles at least until 1858 and the end of the War of Removal. Among the Oklahoma Seminoles, they endured into the early twentieth century in intertribal conflicts and "uprisings." Echoes of these patterns persist to the current day among both groups, especially in the realm of war-related medicine and warriors' participation in extratribal warfare.

Hunting, communication, and trade networks have endured to the present. Seminole Tribal elders in Florida today still recall traditional seasonal rounds among the Clan camps and hunting camps of South Florida, which continued until Florida's open range laws of the 1940s destroyed much of their ability to support themselves and their Clans from the produce of nature. Among the Florida Seminoles, this change is recalled, profoundly, as "The Sad Time," when men began to sit around their campfires all day, with their guns across their laps, unable to support their families.[33] The social elements of territorial ranging persist to the present in Florida. Many Clans still recognize social responsibilities to make extended seasonal visitations to parallel Clan camps hundreds of miles distant and to send younger Clan members to stay with elder Clan relatives in order to receive traditional Clan information and instructions.[34]

Only quite recently, however, have some archaeologists begun to accept the concept of a mobile and dynamic Maskókî world and to urge their colleagues to "leave behind old notions of the Indians at peace with their world."[35] While societal dynamism and being at "peace" with one's world certainly are not mutually exclusive concepts, at least the reality is finally being addressed. As another researcher phrased it, "However stationary it may appear from the twentieth century, there was nothing static about this world."[36]

Numerous other elements constituted the basic components of this dynamic process. Extended food procurement, the earliest component of intertribal contact, facilitated extension of communication systems. Evidence of the facility of these communication systems may be found throughout the narratives of the chroniclers of the Hernando de Soto expedition in comments indicating how well and rapidly news of the Spaniards' coming traveled among the tribes.

Outgrowths of these food forays were wide-ranging trade networks, which were concomitantly buttressed by territorial expansions brought about by marriage alliances and by tributary alliances that were the results of the constant warfare that hallmarked the classic Maskokálgî. The communication lines mirrored the veins of power (tributary) networks, dialectic networks, and military alliance systems, and the fact that no research has thus far attempted to clarify these relationships is but one more evidence of their complexity, itself the result of their vitality.

For example, exotic raw materials and finished items that had their sources in the continental northeast and west, made from copper, galena, mica, and stone, traveled all the way to the Gulf coast and appear in peninsular archaeological sites regularly from at least 1 c.e.[37] Ritualized shapes and symbols tie these early peoples to an archaeological type site called the Hopewell-Adena Complex in Illinois—the source of a cosmogonic antecedent of the Maskokálgî.[38]

Marriage alliances and tributary status subsequent to military conquest solidified trade networks. Thus, Calus, the highest-ranking leader who dominated the lower southwestern peninsula of *La Florida* in the 1560s, surmounted the enmity between himself and the cacique of Teguesta, on the lower southeastern coast, by a marriage alliance that included tributary payments to Calus.[39] The title *cacique* is one that the Spaniards learned from Arawak speakers in the Caribbean and carried with them to *La Florida*. Garcilaso de la Vega, in "La Florida del Ynca," explained it thus. "This name curaca in the general language of the Indians of El Perú has the same meaning as cacique in the language of the island of Española and the neighboring ones, that is, lord of vassals."[40] In most Maskókî languages, the analogous term was *mikó*, or *mikî* (Mikísuukî), which did not indicate a "chief," as in the common European misconception but, rather, a "keeper" of the welfare of the people, whose responsibilities to the people were matrixed in reciprocity.

As a direct result of his military power, Calus also received tribute from the Jeaga and the Ais on the central peninsular Atlantic coast. An Utina leader in the northeastern headlands of the peninsula, whom the French recorded as Molona, told them that Saturiwa, his enemy, controlled thirty towns, ten of them through his "brothers."[41] By this term, Molona undoubtedly meant Clan "brother" or, in the English sense, blood cousin. The term and the relationship are still employed in exactly the same way today by Clan members.

Also included in the concept of territorial ranging were the social mechanisms for the increase and replication of Maskôkî town life, as well as for the replication of town life resultant upon natural deaths and disasters. The death of a particularly powerful practitioner of medicine, natural deaths in a family camp, or the destruction of a camp or town by lightening and fire would cause inhabitants to desert the site and reestablish themselves at another location. The destruction of a town as a result of warfare meant that survivors had to rebuild completely in a more secure location or move in with social affiliates.[42]

As we shall see in later chapters of this work, the process of relocating the residence of a leader or the site of an entire village was such a standard element of the social repertoire that it would be used repeatedly, throughout the Southeast, as a counter to the pressures of Spanish (and later English and United States) demands. Not even after 1858, when the United States ceased its Wars of Removal east of the Mississippi River, would this response to social stress cease to be employed by the Maskôkî peoples in Florida and in the Oklahoma Territory, nor would territorial ranging cease.

Demographic increases, concomitants of the ecological successes of the Maskôkî people, were the impetus for growing families to leave their birth towns and establish themselves independently. Well-established social mechanisms both permitted and facilitated this facet of dynamism, and linguistic conventions institutionalized it. Booker, Hudson, and Rankin remark upon the number of Maskôkî town names bearing the diminutive suffix -oci, which "was often used in the name of towns settled by individuals from other, established towns."[43]

On the opposite end of the spectrum of social approbation was the mechanism of ostracism and the instigation of new villages by expulsion. Individuals who disturbed the cosmic equilibrium jeopardized the harmony and security of all. The ultimate recourse for the society was to expel the offender, along with any who chose to support his (apparently, always "his") views or actions, thereby disassociating itself from the negative repercussions that were sure to result from the disequilibrium.

John Swanton, as a result of his interviews with Oklahoma "Creeks" and Seminoles in the early twentieth century, describes the *La Florida* town of Hilibi as reported "to have been built up originally of outcasts from other villages."[44] He identifies this town as the "Ilapi" mentioned by Rodrigo Ranjel as the town near the capital of Cofitachequi (at present-day Camden, South Carolina) where many from Hernando de Soto's entourage were sent to find provisions in 1540.[45] The same response mechanism was still in use in Florida in the twentieth century when the principal disturbance for which ostracism was imposed was consorting with Euroamericans against the specific admonitions of the Green Corn Council.

Ultimately, Spanish manipulation of population reports in their own cultural interests supports the earlier argument advanced in this work that the rhetoric of Conquest has been predicated not only upon the expectation of destruction but also upon the chauvinistic belief in the actual destruction of the Native Americans as well. As Dobyns concludes, the dramatic decrease in the population of Native Americans during most of the historic period "led Colonial and then national policy makers to believe that native groups would eventually vanish."[46] So sure were they that this would, indeed, be the case that United States history books have been written on that premise, and succeeding generations have reiterated the prophecy into fact. Such a belief has served a culturally chauvinistic end for, as Dobyns also states: "It would be difficult to overestimate the extent to which diminishing Native American numbers reinforced the European belief that the . . . invaders could make better use of the widowed New World territory than its aboriginal inhabitants had done."[47] For purposes of the present work, the estimate of 400,000 Natives across the Southeast is preferable to the lower estimates, because admitting the possibility of the significantly larger number impels us to reevaluate the culture-bound bases of our previous, lower estimates.

A further element of what might be termed the "disappearance model" of *La Florida* demographics is the inductive leap made by investigators when reporting the end of the First Spanish Period (1763), the close of the first chapter of Florida's Spanish colonial history. In fact, it is this chilling demographic assessment that has been reiterated time and again as the basis for Euroamerican belief in the literal extinction of the indigenous population of modern geopolitical Florida by 1763. Again, however, it is important to reexamine the context of this figure's source in order to realize how it has been misconstrued.

The First Spanish Period in *La Florida* ended as a result of the conclusion of the Seven Years' War in Europe (and its counterpart in North America, the so-called French and Indian War). *La Florida* was ceded to the English as part of the settlement, in exchange for Havana, which had been captured by the English during the war. In San Agustín, the principal political center of *La Florida,* Spaniards boarded ships for other Spanish-controlled settlements in the circum-Caribbean region. Political and civil officials, religious leaders, and almost every Spanish citizen left the territory rather than place themselves in the untenable position of coping with the antithetical incoming English, non–Roman Catholic, rule.

Approximately 600 Spaniards evacuated from Pensacola, plus 108 Christianized Natives. From San Agustín, 3,046 inhabitants departed, including 2,547 Spaniards, 315 black slaves, ninety-five free black persons, and eighty-nine Christian Native Americans.[48] Almost ninety percent of these people settled in and around Havana, Cuba, especially in the parish of Nuestra Señora de la Asunción in the Havana suburb of Guanabacoa. Some seventy-three families went farther, to establish themselves at San Agustín la Nueva in the Cuban province of Ceiba Mocha.[49]

This much is documentable fact: there were at least 197 Natives in *La Florida* who had been converted to Christianity and 197 of them chose to depart with the Spaniards. However, nowhere in the documents is there any indication that these were the *only* Christianized Natives remaining in all of *La Florida,* or even in that part of it that later became the state of Florida. Nor may we infer that these 197 were the *only* Natives remaining in all of *La Florida* or even in that part of it that later became the state of Florida, although this is exactly the inference that has been made.

In fact, the most conservative population estimates for the Native Americans remaining in *La Florida* at the time of the first Spanish exodus place the total at 700.[50] This might seem a negligible number, both culturally and genetically, except for two considerations. First, there are no credible reports of the numbers of Maskókî people living on the interior peninsula at this time; however, that no enumerations exist does not mean that no Natives existed. Second, even if this low estimate were correct, the number of survivors generally posited for the end of the Seminole War, in 1858, is less than half this number and the gene pool proved to be a viable one, nonetheless. Once again, we must focus on survival rather than destruction.

Nevertheless, this fragile detail has been parlayed by Euroamericans into the twentieth-century generic "fact" that all of the Native Americans in Florida became extinct by 1763 and the colony was left void of an indigenous population.[51] This, in turn, has been adopted as the moment of disarticulation upon which rests the accepted doctrine that the Natives who would enter the written documentary record at almost the same moment, as "Siminolies," were not native Natives but, rather, adopted children of newly recontextualized *Euroamerican* "Florida." In the crack between perception and possibility lies the truth.

The Oral Tradition

Cultures in which the entire responsibility for replication and perpetuation of the cosmogony is bounded by the ability of its members to hold its elements within the living memory of each generation, without recourse to written codification, embody a type of dynamism within themselves that is unique to orally codified cultures. This dynamism is both parent and child of the process: such cultures are constantly required to perform, at the same time, twin activities, regenerative and perpetuative. They encode and institutionalize a ritualized cosmic past that objectifies the culture, even as they reinvent and reinvigorate a social present that uses as its benchmark the very cosmogony that is constantly being reinstitutionalized. This is the process by which, within orally codified societies, "the reproduction of a structure become[s] its transformation."[52]

The purposes of the creation and recreation of a cosmic past are several. On a metadiscursive level, the continuity of the act vitalizes the society by reaffirming the reciprocity of its contract with nature (seen forces) and with a deity or deities (unseen forces). On an affective level, it creates positive bounds, institutionalizing those virtues that the society considers to be of highest value—that is, it idealizes the culture. It also embodies the negative bounds, either by explication or implication, that set the parameters of the idealization. Thus, implicit in the continuous replication is the blueprint for the replication.

The degree to which the cosmic past conforms from generation to generation is a correlative of the viability of the cultural value system within a given culture. The viability of the value system, in turn, is a function of the internal strength of the society's processes plus the impact of external (intersecting and/or competing) forces, that is, stressors, upon that society. The degree to which the cosmic past varies from generation to generation is also a function of the viability of a cultural system, manifested as its flexibility, that is, its ability to internalize new concepts without the trauma of a complete break with the formal template.

Because human beings are inherently incapable of functioning in an abstractly "pure" fashion, the cosmic past also serves as the template for the functioning of the system. That is, the concrete projections of the social present are also twins: processes and norms, the existence of which serves to (re)calibrate and maintain equilibrium within the society. Because the creation and recreation of a cosmic past establish both positive and negative bounds, the processual segment of the social present may unfold within a positive or negative framework at the functional level, but the result is the same at the metadiscursive level: norms are still established, revised, and reaffirmed.

This continuous process of reinvention and transformation takes place throughout each orally codified society. In order for the reciprocal interaction of the cosmic and the mundane (the concept and the concrete) to function properly, it is not necessary for the cosmic past to be static. In fact, in actual functioning, a static past would *not* serve. It is only necessary for any given generation within the culture to *perceive* it as static. Stability is in the eye of the beholder.

Within the Seminole culture today, the cosmic past is embodied in its creation story in the form in which it is recalled today, but that story does not necessarily have to conform specifically to the story as it was recalled in past centuries.[53] Nor is it necessary for the Seminole people to maintain only a single story. As tribal members reiterate constantly, "This is just the way I heard it—the way it was told in my Clan. But the Breath Giver told the story a little bit different to different Clans, and that's OK. They [the other Clans] have their way of remembering it, and we have ours."[54]

The cosmic past sustains power within the setting of an orally codified society, to a significant extent, through the apparatus of a Clan system. By the process of forming marriage alliances external to the range of biological kin available, families created extended living groups composed of biological and fictive kin called "Clans." In their social functioning, Clans constituted a complex evolution of the extended family group that had formed the basic unit of earlier, less complex, hunter-gatherer societies. In either case, however, the social focus was placed upon a corporate entity (the family and, then, the Clan), rather than upon the individual. The Clan, not the individual, was the embodiment of survival for a complete social unit because it carried within itself the blueprint for the replication of the society.

The Clan system meets Foucault's criteria for an apparatus because it consists of "strategies of relations of forces supporting, and supported by, types of knowledge . . . [and] in its general form [it] is both discursive and non-discursive, its elements being much more heterogeneous." The nature and functioning of the Clan system and the reciprocal nature of inter-Clan relationships make it an example of a positive processual segment among early Maskókî speakers. Fray Luís Gerónimo de Oré, OFM, noted, in the seventeenth century, of the Guale people of the peninsular headlands that "they consider themselves related provided they have the same names or lineage."[55]

George Stiggins (1788–1845), a half-blood Maskókî, explained the Clan system thus. "The strongest link in their political and social standing as a nation is in their clanship or families. By their observance of it they are so united that there is no part of the nation detached from another but [they] are all linked, harmonized, and consolidated as one large connected family, for by their family prescribed rules there is no part of the nation in which a man can not find his clansmen or their connection. . . . All the clans in the nation take their family descent from the mother, being of the same family as the mother, and can only take part with that family. The father and his clan or family are only the father family to the children and he and his clan or family have no legal say or interest in the children's family concerns."[56] It is important to realize that, almost five hundred years after its initial intersection by Europeans, the Clan system continues to maintain its centrality of function among the members of the Seminole Tribe of Florida, who continue primarily as an orally codified society.[57]

Among the Maskókî tribes, kinship was, and continues to be, transmitted through the mother and the maternal line.[58] Thus, a woman's Clan is transmitted to her daughters and her sons. Her daughter will, in turn, pass the Clan affiliation along to her own children. However, while a man will never relinquish his Clan entirely, the primary focus of his Clan duties and responsibilities will shift at marriage to the members of his wife's Clan. He will honor his wife's Clan grandmothers before his own and will relinquish them only upon divorce or the death of his spouse. Even then, the choice to return to his own Clan camp and duties will not be his own but, rather, will remain with the mother of his wife and with her aunts and grandmothers. *They* will return *him* to his birth family if and when they feel that it is appropriate.[59]

When the pool of marriageable partners was other family lineage groups within their own already established social system, Clan systems formalized networks of interrelationships among and between themselves that incorporated reciprocal expectations and responsibilities. Inter-Clan marriage was institutionalized as exogamous norms that created, in their functioning, a delicate balance between blood and fictive relations. Exogamous bounds formalized and institutionalized social relationships at the level of the Clan, the social unit that served as the basic corporate entity.

When the pool of marriageable partners was other tribes, the Clan system provided a strategy for incorporating the New or the Unknown into the Known and for perpetuating and expanding the population base, the social repertoire, and the span of territorial control. These same objectives functioned whether the tribe from which the marriageable partners were obtained was a willing reciprocant (as in the process of politicomilitary alliances) or an unwilling reciprocant (as in the case of militarily conquered tribes). The elastic Clan system provided the same network of interrelationships both within and among families and enforced the same corporate expectations and responsibilities. That is, two basic elements—creating processes and norms—remained the same.

Thus the Clan fulfills the requirements for a *dispositif* or apparatus. It comprises a system of relations formalized by the collective will of the society and defined by a structure of heterogeneous elements. Among those elements, one set that operates at both discursive and nondiscursive levels is the set of Clan totems. These are nonhuman entities, primarily animal. As their primary internal functions they both embody and impart assigned facets of individual personality as well as collective Clan character, thereby anchoring the people firmly to nature and reinforcing the power of the seen world.[60] In 1791, William Bartram described a ceremonial "square" at Atasi (Autose) and remarked that, on the walls of the buildings surrounding it were painted various animals, including a duck, turkey, fox, wolf, and buck deer, all with human heads.[61]

At the corporate level, totems differentiate among the various Clans, constituting and controlling the orderly functioning of the basic social system. At the cosmic level, the characteristics that they embody or are assigned are directly tied to a primary template of the cosmic past, the creation story. Creation stories, in turn, are mediative in nature and function; they are social bridges between the seen and unseen worlds and they "fix" the Clans in the formalized corporate structure, imparting status and legitimating social hierarchies that, in turn, establish and reinforce necessary relational strategies.

Herein lies a crucial element of cultural change over time relative to cultural stability: there perforce exists a point of diminishing cultural returns beyond which the innate flexibility of the system becomes the primary agent of its dissolution. The process of this change is embodied in both ongoing and discrete discursive events, where discourse is viewed in its broadest terms, as encompassing all rhetorical and semiotic utterances that, taken together, both recreate and delineate a network of relationships and a normative value structure.

That is to say, each orally codified culture also carries within itself its own point of diminishing returns, which may vary across societies. Within the Maskókî speakers as an orally codified and transmitted culture, the parameters for group maintenance have been carried as a significant element of the discursive body. Thus the oldest living Seminole Tribal member in 1990, Buffalo Jim, a respected medicine practitioner of long-standing repute, could tell an interviewer: "Two things will happen just before the end of the world. The first thing is that we will lose our language. That will be one of the signs. . . . And the second sign is that we will forget how to make our sacred fire."[62]

Greg Urban writes,

> Within a discursive community, an instance of discourse arises only against a backdrop of a continuing history of such instances, in relationship to which it can be situated. The actual situating is done subjectively, but it is based upon a vast range of historical experience with other instances, which are also part of the public circulation of discourse in the ongoing life of a community. . . . It is not that the meanings [of discourse] are necessarily shared, but that the collection of instances from which meanings are culled is publicly accessible. The collection forms the basis for recognizing interconnections, but the interconnections that are recognized may vary from person to person, depending in part on the degree and kind of access that they have had to the overall community history. Recent discourse studies seem to be suggesting, therefore, that shared meaning is a product of public accessibility rather than (or in addition to being) a necessary precondition for it.[63]

This then, for example, is a primary value of ritual and ceremony. They are an institutionalized font of public "instances." They provide the locus for shared access to meaning and, to the degree that that access is differential within the society, they form a reinforcement of differentiation in social structure. However, this reinforcement is not a one-way street; that is, it is not wholly impositional and vertical, as previous researchers have assumed.

The collateral value of rituals and ceremonies is as institutionalized singularities: events at which are created and recreated the social contract on its grandest scale—between the seen and the unseen facets of the cosmos. Each singularity (that is, each instance of ritual and ceremony), incorporates two communicative elements. The first element articulates what discourse analysts call a "world-to-words fit": the utterers (the individuals charged with iterating and reiterating the singularities) make promises to create a world that is presented in the words.[64] The second element, contributed by the respondents, is the assent to the contract, the imprimatur, as it were. A final element of the discourse is the psychological state, in this case, the state of belief, that binds the utterers and respondents in their renewed contract. This is the mechanical process by which the reproduction of a structure becomes its transformation.

Within this setting, the value of information changes in inverse proportion to access, so that the more esoteric the information the higher its social value in terms of transmissibility within an orally transmitted culture. Consequently, power may accrue to the holders and "keepers" of esoterica, but only in direct proportion to shared perception that a body of esoteric knowledge in fact exists; to a shared "collection of instances," or discursive utterances, "from which [shared] meanings are culled"; and to the corporate norms governing transmissibility.

Thus we find in 1566, in the land of Escampaba, called by the Spaniards the land of Calus or Carlos, that the Native leader Don Felipe (whom the Spaniards have renamed and put in power) tells Fray Juan Rogel, SJ, about information that "he and his forebears, the kings, held guarded in their breasts and that they did not communicate . . . to anyone except to their successors."[65] In addition, Rogel affirms that, in their public ceremonies, "even in the very idolatries . . . the vassals maintain that they know nothing about what they adore or about the cult of the idols beyond that which the king and the head shaman (*hechizero mayor*) tell them."[66]

As a result of this process in continuous (and continuing) action, we find the Frenchman M. Le Page du Pratz, in 1763, observing the Nétchez in Louisiana. He comments that, as they are an oral society, they transmit "the remembrance of any remarkable transactions" by constant repetition. "Consequently many of the youths are often employed in hearing the old men narrate the history of their ancestors, which is thus transmitted from generation to generation. In order to preserve their traditions pure and uncorrupt, they are careful not to deliver them indifferently to all their young people, but teach them only to those young men of whom they have the best opinion."[67]

In terms of durability, esoteric information creates and reinforces group uniqueness, and discourse is the vehicle for its replication and perpetuation. However, the uniqueness of the status group that holds the esoteric information is neither an end in itself nor a wholly discrete element when it occurs within a circular cosmogony. The strong tendency on the part of non-Native viewers to report or discuss it as such constitutes a classic reductio ad absurdum.

As Foucault clearly sees, power in the substantive sense—that is, unconnected power—does not exist. The existence of power indicates that a grid of relations exists. All power is relational. In the case of the Maskokálgî, the power that accrued to the status group that held the esoteric information was, just as was their statused social position, an assigned power. It was de facto if not de jure their part of a social contract, the other part of which was the acquiescence and participation of the rest of the society in this relational system. Together, not separately, they constituted a grid of power relations. Together they maintained a reciprocal power system that held the cosmos in balance.

In addition, irrespective of the fact that much specific, esoteric, ritual knowledge was lost or transformed with the deaths of the knowledge holders, others arose who were willing to fulfill the social contract. Also, irrespective of the fact that much ritualized knowledge has been lost over the centuries, the process of information loss or transformation has not been the critical element of cultural continuity. As long as the individuals have arisen who have been personally inclined or chosen to fulfill the contract by taking on the roles of information holders, then the cultural template has remained intact. And that cultural template has not depended, and does not depend, upon linear confirmation. The template exists in the heads and hearts of the people and requires no books or documents to be transmitted from generation to generation. It is transmitted in discourse.

Now we have two critical parts of the answer to the question, How have the Maskokálgî survived almost five hundred years of contact with, and stress from, Euroamericans and still managed to remain a discrete and coherent cultural entity? They have done it, first, because their template was the process and, second, because the process was not dismantled or destroyed just because so many Maskókî peoples' lives were lost during the continuing story of contact. Such is a part of the manner, then, in which discourse circumscribes the circle.

4 Geography, Society, and Continuity

It has been argued that it is almost impossible to use a direct historical approach to work backward from the well-documented eighteenth-century tribal societies . . . to their prehistoric chiefdom forebears. . . . The only useful approach is to look at the southeastern Indians at the dawn of contact through the eyes of the early Spanish explorers of the sixteenth century. Once an understanding of that period is reached, it can be useful as a baseline to work both backward into prehistory and forward to link up with the documented societies of the eighteenth century.

—Marvin Smith[1]

Redefining the Discussion

From the discussions in the preceding chapters, we now see that it is no longer sufficient to amass narrative data concerning the Maskókî speakers, as if the physical dimensions of their lives, alone, were enough to give us a clear understanding of the rhetorical and semiotic dimensions. Nor can we—the We who were and remain the cultural Other—accomplish this end merely by finding new questions to ask, at least not as long as the new questions are born of old discourse and rhetoric. At the outset, we must recontextualize our particularist domains of interest to include the entire southeastern locus. We must see the Maskókî peoples not as physically, ergo culturally, isolated tribes, ripe for Conquest by our culturally and numerically superior antecedents but, rather, as a coherent holding environment, comprising a broad range of vital and dynamic power systems and networks over space and time. Within this environment, some Maskókî tribes were more economically and politically engaged than others, as well as being more politically advantaged. The numerous shared meanings of their rhetorical universe made their relationships transparent, however. Beyond all else, we must cease to manipulate their past for them by transferring to them the teleological expectations and limitations of their cultural Other.

Then, in order to perceive the cultural continuity of the Maskókî peoples of the Southeast, we must do several things more. First, we must describe the social geography of the major Maskókî tribes at the opening of the sixteenth century and learn what we can about the fluidity of their lives. Then we must be able to demonstrate the geographic dimensions of their dynamism over time, in response to both intrinsic and extrinsic motivators, which were the necessary concomitants of social reamalgamations and which link the southeastern peoples together with their descendants.

Finally, we must be able to clarify effectively the dichotomy between cultural change and social change; the latter not necessarily affecting the former. That there is cultural continuity seems obvious, despite continuing emphasis in the literature on cultural dissolution or decline. The existence of the so-called Seminoles as a coherent and discrete cultural entity today offers prima facie evidence of a significant degree of continuity, but for researchers still mired in the rhetoric of Conquest, that continuity may be less than obvious.

When a Vantage Point Becomes a Disadvantage

Two lacunae in the documentary process give the occasions for much confusion. One is the connection, or perceived lack thereof, between the Maskókî tribes whose demographic decline and geographic shifts were occasioned by the initial impact of European pathogens, which impact was felt throughout the sixteenth and early seventeenth centuries, and the "emergence" of recontextualized Creeks, Seminoles, and Miccosukees in the eighteenth century.

These Maskókî peoples' pasts were rhetorically manipulated away from them by Anglo-Saxon Euroamericans in a direct and concerted effort to disarticulate them from their physical and philosophical equity in the land: equity, that is, both in the conceptual sense of a personal and communal framework and in the physical sense of a circumscribed tenureship. The resulting disempowerment consequently undermined their social coherence sufficiently that subsequent Euroamericans, already predisposed to perceive discontinuity, could both perceive and treat them as *novis personae* with only minimal vested interest in land proprietorship.

Although the value of land and proprietorship were of more centrality to the English colonists and subsequent United States citizens than they had been to the earlier Spanish settlers, these disparate foci each had a negative impact upon the Native Americans. Prior to 1670, this negative impact was constrained solely by the economic and ideological abilities and interests of the Spanish Crown in sending soldiers, settlers, and supplies to *La Florida*. Thus, of all the entradas effected by the Spaniards prior to permanent settlement in 1565, no establishment lasted for more than a few months, and no establishment that lasted even that small amount of time was farther inland than a few leagues. Also, none of their establishments were in the interior of the *La Florida* peninsula.

Even after the settlement of Santa Elena and San Agustín, the Spaniards never accumulated either a sufficient population or sufficient funding from the Crown to populate the interior of the upper Southeast or of the lower peninsula substantially above and below their "power corridor," the mission/rancho line from San Agustín westward into Abalachi (see Chapter 8). Thus, despite sporadic reports gathered from peninsular Natives who constantly were traveling across the areas, or the reports of specific military reconnaissance parties, the Spaniards never were in direct day-to-day control of the Southeast's interior or of the interior of its lower peninsula or even in direct day-to-day contact with those inhabitants. Consequently, we must cease to accept Spanish assessments of these areas as definitive and treat them instead as no more than what they really are: highly politicized and self-serving statements of particularist interests.

Following 1670 and the establishment of a permanent English presence in *La Florida,* the documentary record of the Maskókî peoples began to be written in English as well as Spanish. However, during the ensuing three centuries, the rise of England as a world power would coincide with the decline of Spain in the political arena. In North America, the increase in the number of English colonies and their concomitant demographic increase would coincide with the decrease of Spain's physical presence. Along with the physical increase of the English presence in North America came the ideological increase of anti-Iberianism and the increase of anti-Spanish rhetoric, concomitants of the Black Legend.[2]

Consequently, the Euroamerican view of southeastern Native American history quickly would come to be espoused exclusively by English speakers and continuously reaffirmed by increasing numbers of like-minded settlers with increasing numbers of economic and ideological demands and with the military technology at their command with which to enforce their own particularist viewpoints. These peoples rapidly displaced many of the Maskókî peoples from their ancestral domains across the Southeast and set in motion a new series of periodic geographic shifts during which the Maskókî people reeled back and forth across the Southeast in dizzying, kaleidoscopic fashion.

Herein lies a critical point of Euroamerican misperception. English speakers, who were in fact "discovering" many of these Native Americans for the first time in the eighteenth century, were doing so only within the processes of claiming land, establishing boundaries of politicoeconomic control, and reckoning potential degrees of resistance to settlement from Native American occupants. As a direct consequence, their philosophical domains of interest coincided principally with the physical boundaries of their political domains of interest, and these geographic domains of interest did not prove to provide sufficient impetus, or impetus of sufficient duration, for settlement of the interior peninsula of *La Florida* until well after Spain relinquished control of the Floridas, once and for all, to the young United States, in 1821.

That is to say, English colonists of the area they named "Georgia," for instance, were principally interested in the boundaries of Georgia at any given time and in those Native Americans who occurred (not owned or inhabited land, or resided, or claimed ancestral homes) within their own Euroamerican spheres of political, economic, and military interest. The realities of the Native Americans, whose lives had been spent in territorial ranging irrespective of the impositional borders of a Georgia or *La Florida* or Carolina, were, for all practical purposes, an irrelevant factor in the Colonial equation. In addition, the writings of those few observers to whom the memories of individual Natives might be of interest had little or no bearing, ultimately, upon Euroamerican "laws" or "boundaries" or property "rights," despite the fact that these memories connected the Natives to geographic areas that crosscut international land claims and confirmed a physical equity in the land centuries—millennia—longer than that which Euroamericans had amassed.

That much of the information amassed in the past century concerning these peoples has come from archaeologists also has exacerbated this perceived discontinuity of Native American occupation. One archaeologist explains it thus. "Why has the decline of chiefdoms brought about by European [that is, Spanish] contact been so little studied? Archaeological sites in the Southeast that produced early European [again, Spanish] artifacts were often mistakenly given eighteenth-century [that is, English] dates; indeed, there is still this tendency on the part of some. Only recently have the artifacts typical of the early historic period been recognized."[3]

What this researcher is leaving unsaid confirms the cultural biases outlined above. The tendency of Euroamerican researchers to use later, English, occupations as the baselines of North American historical-occupational interpretation rather than earlier, Spanish, contacts has left the Southeast missing almost two hundred years of its history. Reestablishing this history, through an examination of the centers of interaction between the Native Americans and the Spaniards, is the sine qua non for understanding the history of the southeastern United States.

The second lacuna in the history of the Southeast, in reality a subset of the first, is defined by the peninsula of *La Florida* and the relationship between its original Maskôkî peoples and those same later-recontextualized peoples. Was the peninsula actually depopulated by disease and warfare by 1763? Were, then, those recontextualized Seminoles and Creeks who would, by the close of the United States's eastern Wars of Removal in 1858, have their territorial ranges reduced to the frontiers of the Florida Everglades and the reservations of the Oklahoma Territory, composed entirely of Maskôkî people whose earlier lives and heritages had anchored them solely to areas outside of the peninsula?

Although the evidence is not completely unambiguous, the burden of proof must shift from the Native Americans, who hold their past within their present, to the Euroamericans who clearly have a strong vested interest in denigrating and disregarding that past. Some Miccosukee-Seminole Tribal elders today recall the memories of their grandparents and great-grandparents regarding the presence of their ancestors on the peninsula. It is their memory that the Seminoles were not driven into Florida by the pressures of United States soldiers and settlers. Rather, they recall that their ancestors had been migrating southward toward the lower reaches of the peninsula for all time because their medicine people always had told them that *ichî bolán*, literally "the nose of the deer," or the pointed tip of the southeastern peninsula, was the place where they would ultimately find refuge and peace.[4]

Obviously, this viewpoint differs radically from that of English writers, to whose advantage it was to divide the various elements of the Maskôkî peoples, even by the use of subversive methods to foment discord among them. It was a classic "divide and conquer" technique that they used, but the English underestimated many of the Maskôkî speakers and their sense of their own prerogatives, by at least as wide a margin as did the Spaniards.

Early in 1764, with the transfer of what was left of *La Florida* to the British pending, Captain Bentura Díaz wrote to the governor of Cuba that "the savages of this nation [i.e., the tribes surrounding Pensacola] do not respond to acquaintance, compulsion, promises or obligations."[5] What Captain Bentura Díaz was recognizing, in his own self-serving way, was that even after two centuries of European pressures, many Maskókî speakers still operated from their own matrix image of themselves as autonomous agents. The power still had not shifted.

At the same time, however, the Euroamericans were well on the road to institutionalizing their own preconceptions and expectations. It was more convenient, for example, to image the Maskókî speakers as discrete groups bearing no elements of interconnectedness. It was this psychology that would generate the arbitrary and generic "Creeks" and, then, divide these "new" peoples still further into "Upper" and "Lower" factions. It is this psychology, in addition, that would arbitrarily impose the unrealistic designators "Miccosukee" and "Seminole" upon peoples whose own realities had long become irrelevant in Euroamerican minds by this time. John Stuart, British Indian Agent for the Southern District, explained this classic "divide and conquer" strategy to Lieutenant Pampellone, who was departing for St. Marks on the Gulf where he would take command.

> It will undoubtedly be detrimental to His Majesties service, that too strict a friendship and union subsist between the different Indian nations within this department; it is therefore incumbent upon us by all means in our power to foment any jealousy or division that may subsist between them. But this must be done with great delicacy, and in such a manner as not to awaken the least suspicion in them that we have any end of view to answer by it.[6]

Even archaeologist Charles Fairbanks, whose report on the origins of the Seminoles, prepared almost two centuries later, would be used by the United States Land Claims Commission to counter a multi-million-dollar suit brought by the Seminoles of Florida (which the United States ultimately would lose), admitted the part played by the English in manipulating twentieth-century perceptions of the Seminoles' cultural history. In commenting upon Stuart's instructions to Pampellone, he stated: "It seems probable that this policy was continued to the point of emphasizing the differences between the Lower Creeks in Georgia and those in Florida. Thus it seems that the formal separation of the Creeks and Seminoles is, in part at least, a result of English intrigues."[7]

In his cultural civility, Fairbanks is being overgenerous. He also has fallen prey in his assessment to part of the error he wished to dispel, because he has obscured the origins of both groups by the use of the English generics "Creek" and "Seminole." He and other twentieth-century Euroamericans would compound the disassociative myth about the Maskôkî speakers of the Southeast by recording the Seminoles as having originated completely outside of modern Florida and as having been pushed southward from Georgia and Alabama into Florida and all the way into the Everglades by 1858—that is, only *after* Euroamericans had confirmed themselves as the a priori possessors of this portion of the United States. Change, however, is in the eye of the beholder. The differences between the Maskôkî peoples of the sixteenth century, inside and outside of twentieth-century Florida, and their nineteenth- and twentieth-century descendants are more apparent than real.

What's in a Name?

We will never know, in full detail, the demographic extent of the Maskôkî tribes that dotted the Southeast at the time of the coming of the Spaniards. That this is so is the result of several factors. First, the complete body of orally transmitted information held by the Maskôkî speakers in this regard never was shared with Euroamerican recorders. Second, the numbers of Spaniards who came to *La Florida* in the sixteenth century were too few, relatively, to explore the entire Southeast and record the names and principal locations of all tribes for themselves, even assuming that the Maskôkî peoples would have, in every instance, shared it with them. These are obvious circumstances.

A third factor, however, is less obvious. It was never really possible to record a complete picture of the tribes because, at any moment, that picture might be changing. More important, twentieth-century interpretations of the histories of the tribes elide significant elements of those histories by failing to address the system of discursive naming strategies of the Maskôkî speakers. A wealth of information concerning power networks is embodied in these strategies and can be revealed when they are examined. This approach is exceedingly complex but relatively untapped. No attempt will be made here to uncover all of the specific relationships; only the broad nature of the systems will be described and several pertinent examples offered indicating the value of the process.

Beginning at the communal and state levels, it was part and parcel of the dynamism of the Maskokálgî that multiple naming systems were in use at the same time for the same polities, and the referent system was situational. Names—of social landmarks, of villages, of tribal enclaves and their capitals, and of territorial ranges—all fixed their foci in the eyes of the beholders in the most utilitarian manners; that is, in manners that most facilitated the multiple reciprocal interactions of all of the elements of the societies that created them. People and villages might be called after their individual leaders, whose names in turn might or might not change from generation to generation. Landmarks might lend their names to the people who lived near them, irrespective of language or leadership. Or the people of one polity might use differing names for themselves or their neighbors depending upon the context of the power relationship. Garcilaso de la Vega, in his rich narrative of the de Soto entrada, explains quite clearly that "in many parts of this great kingdom [of peninsular *La Florida*] the lord and his province and its principal pueblo are called by the same name."[8]

This system was antithetical to the well-established Iberian system of place naming as separate from leader identification. The practice of positioning individuals relative to their communal polities, however, did exist within the Iberian social lexicon, and it was a point of pride to be associated with a successful and favored corporate polity.[9] The Spaniards understood this system (ergo, Juan Ponce *de León*, Pedro Menéndez *de Avilés*, etc.), but it was a concomitant of this pride that town names changed little or not at all over time.

Helen Nader, in her review of the Castilian system of corporate entities and the Crown's sale of status within its absolutist matrix, reaffirms frequently the attachment of the Spaniards to their towns. She concludes: "When the conquistadors described their travels through dense jungles, over some of the most impressive mountain ranges known to man, and across some of the world's greatest rivers, they talked in terms of moving from one town or city to another. As Lombardi noted, 'They cross mountains and discover great rivers, but their motion, their decisions, and their goals seem regulated more by the presence or absence of Indian towns, the distance to previously established Spanish towns, or the possibility of supporting a new Spanish center, than by the existence of geographic obstacles.' The conquistadors described the Indians in terms of their relationships to towns. . . . They described the Americas in terms of Castile, as a patchwork quilt of municipalities."[10]

Consequently, the multiple reference systems in use in this new world seem to have confused or eluded the Spaniards collectively and many of the individual recorders specifically and, thus, we are sometimes left today with a dizzying array of tribal and/or place names that may or may not designate the same people.[11]

A people might also come to be known by their neighbors, whether friends or enemies, or by a geographic or topographic designator that had nothing to do with a leader, the base language or dialect, or any social determinant. Thus, in 1823, a leader would appear at the talks with United States representatives at Moultrie Creek as "Econchatti micco," from which we learn that his people's nuclear territory was, topographically, one of *ekan chatî* or "red earth" as expressed either by themselves or by Maskókî-speaking neighbors. The name says nothing of the people themselves, however, nor are we at liberty to assume that they are a wholly new and distinct tribe simply because they appear at some point designated by a name not mentioned in earlier centuries.

Names might be imposed upon a people from without, based upon some perceived characteristic or historic event. Thus, the Yamásî bear a name indicating a "tame people" in the Maskókî language. Because this designator predates the distinctly untame uprising of the Yamásî against the English in 1715, we may infer that the Maskókî speakers from whose language the word *Yamásî* emanates had some older reason for imaging them as such, undoubtedly a cultural memory of war and Conquest. Consequently, it is left for non-Native researchers to use the name as a clue and not neglect the search.

Within the Maskokálgî cosmos, the multilayered flexibility of naming was not haphazard. It was the intellectual child of a social and cultural system that reiterated its success daily in its continuity. For example, the names indicating a specific tribe and the inhabitants of an entire region might be the same in situations in which it was useful for the name holders to create and sustain power connections for their own benefit. In other cases, the names indicating a certain geographic group, that is, a tribe and/or region, might be different depending upon the source of the information and the perceived social utility of the utterance.

Thus, for example, when the Gentleman of Elvas wrote in the sixteenth century of the "country of Coça" he described it as "thickly settled in numbers and large towns, with fields in between," indicating that he was actually describing a political entity of significant proportions.[12] When the Spaniards finally reached the large town that bore the same name as this "country," that is, Coça proper, its capital, it is plain that their inclusive term indicated both the inhabitants of a socially powerful town of Maskókî speakers and the significant number of individuals living in towns allied with, or tributary to, the main town of Coça.[13]

In fact, Coça, the capital, was the political and military nexus of a social network so large that it took Hernando de Soto and the members of his entrada twenty-four days to march through it: twelve days to reach its capital and another twelve days to reach its southernmost town.[14] At an estimated speed of twenty to twenty-four kilometers per day, this indicates that the chiefdom of Coça ranged across at least 240 to 288 kilometers.[15] Concomitantly, so great was its social position among all the southeastern peoples that, three hundred years later, when the power of the capital's control mechanisms had degraded as a ramification of natural attrition and European pressures, and its tributaries had amalgamated or spun out from the core area, its Iroquoian-speaking neighbors still imaged all of the Maskókî as "Kusa People" and fixed them by that name in their discourse.[16]

The tributary and attendant towns and villages within the politicomilitary orbit of power towns also had their own discrete names, which were also relative and dynamic and were imaged variantly from within their specific societies. The Spaniards would take pains to record many of these discrete designators and even to explain some of the Maskókî peoples' taxonomic systems. The Spaniards' interests, however, as mentioned earlier, were not in social science or even in taxonomy per se but, rather, in knowing their potential enemies, identifying potential converts, and assessing potential labor pools.

Some towns and villages were designated relative to the name of the principal leader of each, while others might bear a straightforward reminder of an event or carry some landmark or topographic descriptor, as a utility for travelers, traders, and war parties. Thus, for example, those whom the Spaniards recorded inclusively as the "people of Coça" might also be, exclusively, the people of Apica.[17] In the sixteenth century, this already had long been a powerful town. Part of its name may have meant "to go before" or "go out in front" (that is, to go in advance of the others), indicating that its people were among the earliest of their cultural kin to reach what would become Coça territory. Some Seminoles today, both Maskókî and Mikísuukî speakers, translate it thus.[18]

According to a belief told to Georgia Governor James Oglethorpe in 1735 by Chekilli, the Apica were among the four tribes that migrated across the Mississippi together and joined the Coça who, apparently, had already moved westward from Tcilokit-controlled territory. The other three were the Cusita, Chicaça, and Alibamo.[19] In 1800, Tussekiah Micco told United States Indian Agent Benjamin Hawkins that the Cusita, Chicaça, and Coweta tribes had migrated eastward together and found the Apica already living on the Coça River.[20] In either scenario, their name fixed the Apica permanently in cultural precedent as a high-status group.

John Swanton does not translate "Apica" but, rather, refers obliquely to George Stiggins and dismissively to a "folk explanation" that referred to "a supposed event in the past history of the tribe."[21] Consequently, if the respected researcher John Swanton were to be taken as a definitive source, a tribe whose history is valuable to understanding the history of all the Maskókî peoples—and a part of whose history is embodied in its name—would be ignored. George Stiggins, a half-blood Nétchez and author of *Creek Indian History* (written prior to 1836), who traded between Maskókî speakers and the Spaniards of *La Florida,* says that their name is a referent to their use of a dialectical variant, and this might explain another facet of their history.[22]

Stiggins cites a cultural memory among the nineteenth-century "Abeka" people that they lived, before the coming of the Spaniards, in "Coosawattee" or Coça Old Town, in the territory of the Tcilokit. However, the dialectical variant to which he ascribes their name seems to be Western Maskókî or Chactá.[23] None of these assertions actually conflict, however, because no time constraints are placed upon their occurrence. If the Apica people moved eastward even slightly in advance of other affiliated tribes, they might well have stopped at one point in or near territory controlled by Tcilokit people. The word *Cherokee* itself is an English transliteration of that Maskókî word, indicating simply "foreigners" or "people who speak a foreign tongue."[24]

However, by the time de Soto entered *La Florida,* the Apica had removed as a result of conflicts with these Tcilokit to "Coosa Tul-muchessee" [*Coça tal ima chisî*] or Coosa New Town, on what has come to be called the Coosa River. Archaeological evidence indicates that the location of this town was at present-day Rome, Georgia.[25] Their language had long since merged with that of the numerous Maskókî speakers but they had obtained and held a social position of honor among the people of Coça territory, whose politicomilitary prowess had brought them to a position of hegemony in the region. Their unique designator, "Apica," however, fixed them for all time in relation to their own past.

In other words, their name not only embodied their social power but also served to recapture that power, for succeeding generations, as long as the name remained. And remain it did, in the person of a living leader who also carried their past in his name. If that leader managed to acquire the power of personal status, in addition to the powers of historical and hereditary status, then the positive benefits of his association with the people increased, and the social utility of preserving his name increased as well.

Shortly after the entrada of Tristán de Luna passed, in 1560, the current leader, Apica, and at least some of his people moved southward. By 1715, they had relocated in what is now south-central Alabama. Stiggins says that during his own lifetime they lived in "Abekochee" [Apica cî] or Little Apica, indicating by apposition that there had been, at some point, a big, or at least a bigger, Apica.[26]

Most researchers cease their interest in Apica and the Apica people there, but, interestingly, further references exist. In 1765, when La Florida had been reduced in territory to relatively little more than that of Florida today, the new English proprietors of East and West Florida met separately with leaders of regional Maskókî tribes. The English were interested neither in converting nor in marrying the Natives, but only in regularizing land ownership, ergo the power to access land without the costs of conflict. In 1765, West Florida officials met at Pensacola with "the chiefs and warriors of the Abekas and Tallapousses,"[27] indicating that the Apica were ranging across the Gulf coastal plain that would become lower Alabama and northern Florida.

There is no direct evidence at this time that these same Apica people were moving their principal camps into the Floridas, but there are interesting and frequently overlooked pieces of evidence that underscore the durability, flexibility, and power of naming as a discrete discourse set. One piece of evidence concerns the powerful Maskókî leader, Apica, whose name would become a household word in the United States during the Second Seminole War. His power in war medicine, which is to say in manipulating the cosmogonic forces to the support of warfare, which was also a principal concern of the medicine practitioner, would make him the mentor of outstanding warriors and the nemesis of every United States soldier who served in the Florida Territory for almost two generations. In his name and person were embodied the orderly and systematic transfer of power from generation to generation, within a setting that permitted society to "recapture" the status of public respect and cosmogonic proficiency that had accrued to all of his predecessors. And it was as simple as retaining and reassigning a name, within the parameters of the Clan.

In Maskókî, Apica and his people were Apicalgî; in Mikísuukî/Hitchiti they were, collectively, Apikáłî. Apica, Apicalgî, and Apikáłî were poorly transliterated by Euroamericans as "Apiuki," "Abiuki," "Abeukî," "Arpiuki," and "Arapieka," the English *r* being wholly introduced and the *p/b* being inserted interchangeably. Underscoring the social connection between Apica and Abiuki is the fact that his principal war leader (a position usually called "sub-chief" by Euroamericans) was "Coosa Tustinugger," that is, a *tastanakî* or warrior who had strong war medicine, from Coça, indicating either the capital or the territory of which Apica had been a statused part.[28]

Often in the nineteenth century, Apica's identity was obscured still further and denigrated by the Euroamerican application of a totally unconnected pseudonym, "Sam Jones," applied to him by the officers of the United States military at Fort King (Ocala), Florida. A Captain Galt, who saw him selling fish to the soldiers and could envision no other reason for his entering United States military establishments than that the Native American liked money, wrote a parody on a popular poem, "Twas Dunois the Brave." Galt wrote instead, "Twas Sam Jones of Sandy Hook fisherman of New York," and his fellow officers arbitrarily cloaked Apica in yet another layer of obscurity.[29]

However, within the name of this single individual, there exists an excellent illustration of the flexibility and strength of a public discourse network that embodied the power to draw an unbroken thread of the Maskokálgî past into any Maskokálgî present. It was a method of fusing the positive forces of the seen and unseen worlds and harnessing that power for the continuous good of the community.

The flexibility of this naming system was manifested by its internal functioning not only during times when there were no direct, outside stressors upon the social system but also during times when there were. An excellent example of the adaptation and internalization of non-Native expectations is visible among the Escampaba people of *La Florida*'s southwest peninsular coast. The accuracy of López de Velasco's nationalistic synthesis is belied by a reinterpretation of the documents, but he does confirm the fact that Escampaba's naming system was flexible enough to accommodate change.[30] The fact that the change was only cosmetic, and did not have any substantial effect upon the basic belief systems, is evidenced by the later actions of the Spaniards themselves. When they first entered Escampaba's capital in 1566, the Spaniards used much force to impress the Natives of Spanish power. As a grand gesture of diplomacy, the

Escampaba leader offered vassalage to the Spaniards, had tribute brought to them ceremonially, and apparently took on the name of their great leader, Carlos (Carlos Quinto), which he heard as "Calus," because his language lacked the European *r* sound. The Spaniards honored their own pronunciation and continued to refer to him as Carlos.[31]

In 1567, when the Spaniards finally realized that Calus was actually resisting their domination, they made the ultimate power move: they killed him, despite the fact that he was a very powerful and popular leader among his own people, and replaced him with a more pliant member of his own Clan, whom they unilaterally renamed "Don Felipe." The new puppet cacique feared constantly that he would be killed by the people he ruled as a result of their strong dislike of him and his obsequiousness to the Spaniards.[32] As it turned out, his usefulness to the Spaniards diminished and they killed him instead.

However, despite the Spaniards' attempts to impress the Calusa with their power and to manipulate leadership and dominance, it was the traditional naming system that survived. In 1612, Spanish ships from San Agustín visited the Calusa and learned that seventy villages still were reporting to a leader named "Carlos," probably the Clan nephew of the earlier powerful and popular leader whose personal attributes had not been forgotten by his people.[33] As Fray Oré realized, names institutionalized kinship.[34]

Western Christian Europeans developed an analogous system in their reapplication of male names in the form of "el Mozo" or "Junior," but these generally have not extended beyond the fourth or fifth generation and they originally were based on the desire to preserve economic power (as distinct from other types of power) within an emerging sixteenth-century system of primogeniture.

The visibility and centrality—hence, social power—that accrued to the individual, accrued to his Clan as well. The social parameters of naming discourse sets were the hereditary limits of the Clan. In yet another expression of the centrality of the Clan, principal male leaders were permitted to procreate within its bounds, together with the principal transmitters of the Clan, the leaders' biological mothers and sisters. This discourse set, that of designating official physical partners, buttressed the naming discourse set in order to institutionalize certain facets of power within certain Clans. Contrary to the interpretations of some Europeans, the process of sibling marriage was not a right but, rather, a requirement of leadership: the same basic element of reciprocity of rule that was expressed later by Europeans as noblesse oblige, but one expressed within social power parameters antithetical to those of European Christianity.

Thus we see that, in the larger sense, naming among the Maskókî peoples served essentially the same purpose that it serves among non-Native cultures to this day, but on a much more socially powerful and far-reaching level: names "essentialize interconnections."[35] Naming is a metadiscursive practice that "require[s] ethnographic investigation as part of the social circulation or life of discourse more generally."[36] In the largest sense, naming is an essential element of the discourse of power because it embodies the power to name, which contains the power to fix a public image to such a degree as to form and institutionalize public perceptions.

In the case of later Maskókî:Spanish power discourse sets, the prerogative to name would take on new and profoundly significant dimensions in relation to the imaging of the Maskókî peoples by Euroamericans. In the most specific sense, however, naming discourse contained an element of flexibility within the Maskokálgî world that it did not within the Euroamerican world. Linear cultures place high value on stability as an element of control. Circular cultures embrace fluidity and change, as essential elements of all existence.

5 Power and Gender

I have served in these provinces of Florida . . . since the adelantado brought me as a soldier, and in this time I have suffered hunger, nudity and much misery, not because the land is so bad as they hold it to be, but due to the poor government it has had, and because their resources were little to conquer so many people and such a great land.

—Bartolomé Martínez, 1577[1]

Matriliny Versus Matriarchy

Among the Maskókî speakers of the Southeast, the apparatus of social power was composed of a more or less coordinated cluster of relations, its parts being both discursive and nondiscursive and heterogeneous. These clusters were made of power spheres that included both men and women and used strategies that required the participation of both sexes and the strengths of both sexes. The resultant gender system, therefore, had its own internal coherence and obviously operated successfully within the culture that created it, because many of its parts remain within the cultural repertoire of its descendants today.

Its principal grid of relations was the Clan, a relational system regulated by both a set of nondiscursive elements, that of genetics or chance, and a set of discursive elements, the institutionalized social discourse between women and men that channeled its continuing existence. Within this apparatus, the accident of birth and the social processes of formal pairing and of adoption were formalized into relations of power by a set of complex social rules regulating intra- and inter-Clan functioning.

The centrality of the Clan to the social matrix of Maskókî life has been mentioned repeatedly in this work. On the physiological level, its functioning vitalized both private and public relationships, making viable what would most certainly otherwise have been sets of closed and overworked gene pools. On the social level, so central and viable has been the mechanism of the Clan among the Maskokálgî that it has survived to the present among the Florida Seminoles not just in name but with a significant number of elements functioning.

It survives among the Seminoles of Oklahoma also, but has been meta-morphosing gradually over the past century and a half since Removal into a "Band" system. This latter is, in reality, merely an accommodational mechanism by which transported southeastern Maskókî peoples absorbed the expectations of the United States government with as little disturbance as possible to their already heavily stressed Clan/relational power grid. The effects of Euroamerican expectations are visible, however. (See Chapter 8 for discussion of the current Clan system.)

In the functioning of the Clan, we find the most visible evidence of the integral roles of women in maintaining equilibrium within the Masko-kálgî cosmos. This relationship of the sexes, or social construct of gender, is a facet of the Maskókî peoples' self-imaging that has been distorted con-stantly in the process of Euroamerican reporting.

As Gerda Lerner reminds us in her seminal work on the creation of pa-triarchy: "Sexual attributes are a biological given, but gender is a product of historical process. The fact that women bear children is due to sex; that women nurture children is due to gender, a cultural construct. It is gender which has been chiefly responsible for fixing women's place in society."[2]

Layered upon the roles evolved for women historically from within their own cultures are those assigned to them through the filtering of the cul-tural Other. In the case of the Maskókî people, not only has the story of women's roles in society gone largely undiscussed but, further, their imag-ing in the secondary research has been particularly resistant to change. They have been portrayed consistently as minor recurring themes, always subordinate to the politics and warring of men, at best. At worst, they have been depicted as dehumanized war booty, child factories, work slaves, or items of sexual currency and intercultural barter.

An excellent example of the way Europeans imaged Native American women, even before sufficient Europeans had met them to make their own biased judgment, is contained in the remarks of Amerigo Vespucci, who both shocked and titillated his audience when he told Europeans that In-dian women were "very libidinous, *yet* they have bodies which are *tolerably* beautiful and cleanly." The women were also so "lustful" that *they caused* the genitalia of their husbands to "swell up to such a huge size that they appear deformed and disgusting; and this is accomplished by a certain de-vice of theirs, the biting of certain poisonous animals. And in consequence of this many lose their organs which break through lack of attention, and they remain eunuchs" (emphasis added).[3]

The objective of this discussion is not to argue for total equality of the genders among the Maskôkî speakers. Not only did such not exist, but also it did not need to exist for the Maskokálgî to function. Nor should the Clan system, with its emphasis on the transmission of hereditary kinship solely through the female line, be assumed to imply a matriarchal system, although both academic and nonacademic observers have made the short inductive leap from matriliny to matriarchy repeatedly over the centuries without ever developing any clear standards of definition. Lerner, however, explains the dichotomy clearly.

> I think one can truly speak of matriarchy only when women hold power *over* men, not alongside them, when that power includes the public domain and foreign relations and when women make essential decisions not only for their kinfolk but for the community. . . . [S]uch power would have to include the power to define the values and explanatory systems of the society and the power to define and control the sexual behavior of men. It may be noted that I am defining matriarchy as the mirror image of patriarchy. Using that definition, I would conclude that no matriarchal society has ever existed.[4]

Lerner and many other researchers also concede that considerable controversy exists among social scientists over how to categorize any given society. Eleanor Leacock, in describing the high status of Iroquois women, cites as evidence of matriarchy the fact that they held authority in major areas of group life.[5] Other researchers have viewed the same evidence but do not conclude that Iroquoian society was matriarchal. They cite the fact that Iroquoian women were never "chiefs" or political leaders. The high status of the women they attribute to a unique Iroquoian situation based upon their exploitation of a particularly rich environmental niche.[6]

The status and functioning of Maskôkî women contradict several of these conclusions. Among the Maskôkî peoples, women held power through numerous formal and informal channels, even though their power still did not equate with that of men. John Swanton, after examining much historical information, a great deal of it contradictory in its praise or condemnation of the ways Maskôkî genders related, concluded the following.

> [T]he hard life of Indian women . . . was not usually considered hard by them but as the customary and essential, and it was in large measure but their share of a life which was harder all around than the lives of many civilized [*sic*] human beings. . . . It was not just [i.e., fair][,] then[,] to condemn the Creeks on account of some of their customs or

to praise them overmuch on account of others. But, abstracting the [gender] customs themselves from the people, we may say that those of the Creeks were upon the whole on a distinctly higher level than the customs of most of the hunting tribes of American Indians and indeed than those of most of the agricultural tribes about them.[7]

Making allowances for the cultural chauvinism to which even Swanton was not immune, we may draw several important points from his remarks. First, value judgments have value only when they have cultural relevance. This would be too obvious to be stated here if it were not so often forgotten by researchers. Second, even drudgery and subordination are relative. Finally, although Swanton singles out the core Maskókî speakers, the Coça people, from among the Maskokálgî, he still accords gender, the relations of the sexes, a "distinctly higher" status among them than among other Native Americans. The status of women was intimately related to, although not wholly dependent upon, the existence and functioning of the Clan system. It will be important not to lose sight of this reality during the subsequent years of European impositional constructs.

A division of labor existed between the sexes, but it was couched not wholly in the discourse of subordination. Rather, it resided principally in the discourse of separation of spheres. Based primarily upon the high social value of warfare and professional soldiering among the Maskókî peoples, women's spheres were complementary rather than antagonistic. Anderson and Zinsser view the evolution of female subordination within a culture as a response to the development of intergroup competition and warfare resulting from stressful ecological and social circumstances.[8] They cite the ancient Greeks as an example, because they were a warrior culture.

The Maskokálgî were a warrior culture. Archaeologically, their warfare complex is iconographically rich and its rise is accepted as a basic element of the rise of Mississippianism. Agriculture, often cited as the prelude to patriliny, was an important element of subsistence among the Maskókî people who lived above the fall line, but among those of the Atlantic and Gulf coastal plains, fishing had more significant value.

Europeans who reported women as the drudges of daily life were not wholly incorrect.[9] Drudgery was a facet of their spheres of action. At the same time, Europeans who reported on the caring and genuine affection that existed between the sexes certainly were correct even though the Maskókî people generally were not known for their public displays of affection.[10]

Among the material culture remains of Mississippianism, archaeologists find temple statuary representing both males and females. This has led Knight to posit that there may have existed an "authentic cult of ancestors."[11] However, whether the statuary represented deities or ancestors, the reality remains: women were included in the range of venerable images. And although venerability confers only a limited type of power, it belies total subordination.

In addition, sufficient examples of women as tribal leaders exist over both time and space in *La Florida* to make it clear that their positions were not wholly subordinate. The Spaniard Juan Pardo, sent out from Santa Elena by Don Pedro Menéndez de Avilés in 1566–1567 to explore the interior to the westward, encountered villages "where I found many Indians and women chiefs."[12] A cacica of Cofitachequi, whom de Soto and his men had encountered over a generation earlier, is an obvious example of a powerful woman leader. The capital of the territory was the town of Canos (near present-day Camden, South Carolina). Although it appears that several languages were spoken within the power sphere of Cofitachequi, Maskókî was pervasive and the iconography of the territory was clearly Maskokálgî.

Before the Spaniards arrived at the town where she was quartering, she had been informed of their coming. When they arrived, she treated them courteously and welcomed them with gifts from the stores of the town, and possibly even from the graves of the people. The Gentleman of Elvas, who accompanied Hernando de Soto, said of the Lady of Cofitachequi: "We traversed her lands for hundreds of leagues, in which, as we saw, she was very well obeyed, for all the Indians did with great efficiency and diligence what she ordered of them."[13]

Although the Gentleman's pronouns create a certain ambiguity, it also appears that this Lady of Cofitachequi was only the aunt of the official ruler of the territory, who was also a woman, and that this Lady was only visiting a town that happened to lie on the path of the de Soto entrada. She was there in the highest official capacity, however, to "execute justice on certain of the principal men under command of the ruler who had rebelled against her and kept the tribute."[14]

Thus we see that, inside a very rich environmental niche such as Cofitachequi obviously was, the matrilineal descent system was functioning, and a woman, or possibly two women, were occupying positions of power to which accrued many or all of the appurtenances of male power. Not only was the Lady of Cofitachequi wielding delegated judicial power (from the actual cacica), but she also may have been wielding supreme personal power over life and death. She commanded deference and respect from the people. She also had the authority to command labor and direct local resources. It is very tempting in this instance to infer that a real matriarchy was in existence in Cofitachequi. However, a larger understanding of the shared power concept of gender, inherent in the reciprocity of a circular cosmos, leads back around to the conclusion that matriliny is not synonymous with matriarchy. On the other hand, neither does patriarchy, couched in a circular cosmogony, totally preclude female power.

Wives, at the highest levels at least, had at their disposal the power of influence if not the power of direct authority. It was the wife and three daughters of Hirrihigua, a cacique of the southwest peninsula, who convinced their husband and father not to kill his young Spanish captive, Juan Ortiz. Garcilaso de la Vega, el Ynca, reports that Hirrihigua permitted himself to be swayed by their pleas on two occasions, because of his great love for them.[15]

The system of obtaining formal partners ("marriage" in European terms) offered variety for men, and under certain circumstances, for women. As I have mentioned earlier, male members of Clans carrying hereditary leadership were expected to choose first or primary mates from among Clan women. In that way, leadership remained in the control of a specific Clan. However, this system did not close the status ranks entirely. Secondary wives frequently were offered by tributary villages in order to increase the value of alliances.

Wives also were obtained through warfare and kidnap and, although such certainly did not automatically confer status, neither did it always constitute a condition of slavery. The Timuguana of *La Florida*'s northern peninsula obtained wives from neighboring tribes by kidnap, and it was considered a great victory. The Timuguana warriors, reported Richard Hakluyt, particularly esteemed this method of securing wives, "for afterward they marry these virgins and love them above all measure."[16] Calus (Escampaba) was planning to marry the daughter of Oathchaqua (on the peninsular east coast, near Cape Canaveral). Her father was taking her to him, with her entourage, when they were attacked by a party of Serrope and taken by them as wives. The Serrope regarded it as a great victory.[17]

As regards these women taken in war, there is a further facet of their role that bears discussion, principally because it previously has not been considered. Descriptions of this element of Maskokálgî life state the reality with no commentary on the social ramifications of such actions, but ramifications there were, and they had a bearing on several aspects of life. First, whether these women captives entered their new tribes singly or as groups, their cultures, languages, social customs, arts, and all the myriad elements of their societies that they carried within themselves also transferred with them to be incorporated, subtly, into their new society of residence. These women were significant indicators of the dynamism that hallmarked the Maskokálgî. Even though they were not in social positions from which to exert a major influence upon their new culture of residence, they were in perfect positions to insinuate new ideas, methods, and languages into the larger repertoire.

The successes of the Maskókî speakers in war and commerce within what was clearly a multilingual setting have led some current researchers to suggest the possibility that a lingua franca was in use across the Southeast.[18] However, the necessity for such a linguistic amalgam, as separate from the base Maskókî language, is obviated by an institutionalized influx of women into the towns, who were bringing outside language skills with them as a standard part of their social repertoires. Further, the same researchers themselves admit that a number of the most successful southeastern towns and chiefdoms appear to have been multilingual in their daily functionings, thereby further precluding the need for a lingua franca.

Other facets of the values of women among the Maskokálgî include their recorded missions as observers, as go-betweens in war, and as facilitators of diplomacy. It is undeniable that the records of the entradas also indicate that women were given by the male leaders of towns to the Spaniards to function as bearers of burdens and as sexual objects for the soldiers, and this reality seems to offer evidence of the low social value of women among the Maskókî people generally. It is highly possible, however, that there was another reality in play, as in so many other areas of the Maskókî peoples' lives.

The Spanish documents are filled with reports of the constant conflicts between the Spanish Roman Catholic culture and that of the Maskókî peoples concerning sexuality and the practices of sex. The Spaniards deplored what they chose to see as promiscuity, perversion, licentiousness, and wantonness verging on depravity in the sexual frankness of the Native Americans, not only in *La Florida* but also in other areas of the Americas as well. Despite the well-documented dichotomy between law and practice in many areas of Spanish sexuality, and perhaps because of the preoccupation of Roman Catholicism with controlling the sexuality of women, in the eyes of the European Spaniards the Native women could only be virgins or whores, and the entire sexual mores of the culture could only be predicated upon a Satan-inspired blindness.[19]

However, the major elements of this "theory of retroactive consent," that is, the Spanish Roman Catholic belief that Native Americans who obviously had strayed from their proper *telos* would thank the Spaniards later for being forcibly returned to it, have finally been discredited. It is no longer acceptable among rational academics to view Native cultures as aberrations, and human sexuality is certainly a basic and valid part of human culture, regardless of any parameters established for it within a culture. Consequently, it is possible that among the Maskokálgî, women could be sent away with the Spaniards not because they were of little value but because they were of sufficient value that their going might appease a cultural Other with the demonstrated power to inflict grave harm upon all the Maskókî people, not just the women. Further, the Spaniards' sexual requirements might not have been viewed as profoundly onerous, in and of themselves, by female members of a group whose sexuality was bounded differently and laden with less-negative values than that of the Spaniards. This is not to say that there were no negative attributes associated with the Spaniards' taking of females; these were numerous. However, the negative attributes were couched in the rhetoric of direct power over the entire tribe and the seemingly arbitrary contravention of the cultural rules of warfare.

As we see, then, it is critical to a new understanding of the Maskokálgî that women be afforded their legitimate role in the creation and continuance of that culture. That place may be understood as subordinate to the role of men in certain areas, but not in all areas and not automatically in areas analogous to the roles of Spanish Christian women. "[S]eparate status or activities do not determine the status of women or their relationship to men."[20]

The Horizontal Analytic: Public Power

A direct extension of the Clan relational system was yet another system—the relational system or apparatus that formalized the ways in which humans functioned as an element of the larger world around themselves, a world composed of visible and invisible elements and forces. The intersection of these planes of existence—the personal, the public, and the cosmic—was the nexus of the seen and unseen worlds and, together, they created a multidimensional sphere of existence—a circular cosmos—of which the Maskókî peoples were a part and within which they functioned as the Maskokálgî. However, the public sphere in society is always an outgrowth of private relational systems and responds, in positive or negative ways, to that personal system of interrelations.

As Foucault tells us, power in the substantive sense does not exist. It is, rather, a coordinated cluster of relations. In the case of the sixteenth-century Maskókî peoples, this cluster was formed of concentric overlapping spheres of authority and responsibility spanning both temporal and spiritual realms. The stable functioning of the Maskókî universe was dependent upon maintaining an equilibrium among these spheres, as has been discussed earlier. Each individual—male *and* female—bore responsibility for maintaining this equilibrium. This is what Fray Pareja demonstrated for us when he cited numerous instances of actions by which individual Native Americans could destabilize their world. It is also evident from the explanations provided by twentieth-century descendants of these peoples that this reciprocal cosmogony constituted, and continues to constitute, the critical matrix for the functioning of the individual within the larger society.

Certain individuals within each town, however, bore particular responsibility by virtue of their having been born into Clans—not merely families—with especial assigned responsibilities, or by virtue of their evinced and acknowledged prowess in certain areas, or by specific assignment. In all such cases, the temporal and spiritual spheres had as their nexus a single individual or Clan-related individuals, whose responsibilities were assigned and confirmed by common consent and whose concomitant authority was constantly subject to public accountability.

Much has been made by non-Native researchers of the "political" structure of the Maskókî speakers, ostensibly in attempts to understand the structure of the culture and the functioning of its societies in general, both before and after the coming of the Europeans. In effect, however, these attempts have served principally as ways of rationalizing Maskókî culture within the evolutionary trajectory of Euroamerican culture, in order to interpret it within the cultural parameters of the Euroamerican locus of enunciation. This basic fallacy has led to numerous misunderstandings.

The misunderstandings begin with the discursive premise. In the models created, for example, by Fried and by Service, and more recently by Wright and by Scarry, the concept of "political" power and access to it are central to the arguments.[21] Even more fundamental, the very definition of "Mississippian societies" is predicated upon "political organization" as a key characteristic.[22] However, the compartmentalization of "political" power as a discrete element of social infrastructure really works best only within a compartmentalized (i.e., linear) culture. Within an integrated (i.e., circular) culture, the act of segregating political power from other facets of social power discursively limits its realm of meaning significantly. In order to reevaluate the process with any degree of reality, we must define a new "grid of analysis which makes possible an analytic of relations of power."

To underscore this segmentation, in all of the current models, the grid of analysis is so structured that access to political power is restricted or completely closed. Scarry, following Wright's model, posits a "chiefly class." Within this class, each "family" has "widespread marriage ties with other elites, forming alliance networks that are unlike those of commoners. The elite will be more closely linked to each other than they will be to their subjects."[23] We have already seen, however, that the central element of the Maskokálgî was the Clan, not the family. Also, we have broadened our understanding of the functioning of the Clan by reincorporating the power spheres of women, both inside and outside the Clan, into the larger social functioning.

In a recent work on the Savannah River chiefdoms, David G. Anderson has become one of the first to posit a new understanding of the "elite-commoner" social dynamic. He concludes: "How commoners fit into the administrative and political life of southeastern Mississippian society has received little investigation. Typically assumed to be pawns of the elite, with little say or influence, the commoners may actually have had much greater power, particularly in local matters. Some form of communal decision making almost certainly had to characterize every Mississippian community, if for no other reason than to provide assent to the decisions of the elite."[24]

What Anderson is pointing out, quite accurately, is the reciprocity of rule that was an intrinsic characteristic of the Maskókî circular cosmogony. Increased reciprocity is, in turn, a concomitant of increased emphasis upon horizontality of the power structure within such a world view. Don Felipe of Escampaba defended his marriage to his biological sister by saying that his people demanded it and that he could not fail them.[25] In the social power structure of Timuguana leaders to the north, a 1564 observer noted that "if there is anything of a serious nature to be taken up, the king summons Iaruas, that is, his priests, and elders, from each of whom he

"A Council of State." Theodore de Bry's 1591 engraving
(plate 29) from the *Brevis narratio* of Jacques le Moyne

(published in Lorant, *The New World*, 93)

seeks [an] opinion, one at a time. Indeed they reach a determination about
nothing whatsoever without first convoking several councils, and they deliberate thoroughly before they reach a decision."[26]

Sixteenth-century Spanish observers automatically transposed a European hierarchical system onto this power structure, in which they had only
a cursory and particularistic interest. In their contemporary European
monarchical states, with their temporal drives for consolidation of power
intensified as they were by the parallel and competing spiritual and temporal power spheres of the Roman Catholic Church, the Divine Right
principle of rule determinedly accentuated verticality of authority.

In fact, in the Spanish principalities of the later fifteenth century, verticality of power had so restricted social mobility that the breaking of
those restrictions, as engendered by the metaphoric leap across the Atlantic
in 1492, is viewed by many current investigators as one of the most salient
consequences of settlement in the post-Columbian "new" world. Small
wonder, then, that sixteenth-century Spaniards should transfer, transpose,

and superimpose their own social value system upon a culture so radically different as to be beyond their comprehension.

The ruler of a powerful Maskokálgî town, with tributary towns in its power orbit, obtained his or her power base by virtue of having been born into a specific position in a specific Clan. In addition to birth, however, succession had to be confirmed by the Clan and by other tribal leaders. The documents also provide sufficient evidence that hereditary heirs could be displaced by stronger family rivals.

The birth position that allowed an individual to succeed to power usually was that of the eldest son of the eldest sister of the previous ruler. It could, however, be the eldest daughter of the eldest sister, as is evidenced by the fact that some head towns had women rulers, such as the famous cacica of Cofitachequi of de Soto's accounts and the cacicas of Santa Catalina and Tulafina (1695).[27]

Rather than being the holder of solely "political" power, a temporal ruler also held spiritual power—twin vestments that made each leader a nexus of the two worlds and publicly reaffirmed his or her unique responsibilities to uphold the temporal-spiritual reciprocity that was the fulcrum of the cosmic balance that constituted the matrix of positive communal continuity. In the case of some adherents of the Maskôkî Way, the apparatus was transparent. For example, Monsieur le Page du Pratz, the Frenchman who established an excellent rapport with the Nétchez of lower Louisiana, reminds us that, more than two hundred years after the interposition of the Europeans, the Nétchez, a western Maskôkî-speaking tribe, still continued to vest twin powers in their supreme ruler. In 1763 he reported on the death of "the *Great Sun,* who is at the same time chief priest and sovereign of the nation."[28] After death, his bones reposed within the temple. During his reign, eight priests had assisted him in the daily rituals that propitiated the cosmic forces.

Among other of the Maskokálgî, the nexus was also transparent, represented, for example, by the assignment of responsibilities to elites whom the Spaniards sometimes described generally as "principales" and "caciques" and whom they observed as primary- and secondary-tier leaders. Fray Pareja underscored their twin temporal-spiritual roles when he differentiated questions for them concerning first-fruit ceremonies, control of granaries, the propitiation of intangible growth forces, and malfeasance by physical abuse of subordinates.[29]

Of course, Pareja's purpose in delineating these activities was to recouch

Native action and meaning within a Roman Catholic context and, consequently, to shift the power source to a Spanish god whose force was manipulated by the Spaniards. In this, the Spaniards achieved only limited and temporary successes in the century and half during which they were the principal Europeans with whom the Maskókî peoples had contact. The English, who interposed after that time, were not interested principally in ideological shifts but, rather, in economic exploitation of the Maskókî peoples.

The basic power paradigm imposed upon the Maskókî speakers by Euroamerican researchers concerns the evolution from what are called simple, or pristine, chieftainships to paramount, or complex, chieftainships.[30] Simple chieftainships are defined as "small regional polities commanded by hereditary elites."[31] Complex chieftainships were tiered power structures in which one or more towns were involved in a reciprocal power network with one or more larger and more successful towns.

Success, however, in Maskokálgî terms, was not a direct correlate of success in European terms, nor was success based principally upon an agrarian economy as is often accepted in current research. Among the Spaniards (and the other western Europeans), the success of a town was predicated specifically upon agricultural and pastoral success, the numbers of workers tied to the land and landowner, commercial proliferation, security from military attacks, and the success of elites in manipulating influence into preferment, all within a strongly vertical power structure that ran upward, from *comunero* to monarch and god.

Among the Maskokálgî, the success of a town was in direct proportion to the ideological values of its Clans, their ability to manipulate the temporal and spiritual realms to the advantage of the people, and the prowess of their warriors in the single most important Maskokálgî enterprise, warfare. Swanton summed up this reality succinctly when he wrote: "[S]ocial advancement and the whole structure of the state was dependent on war to such a degree that a complete account of the institution involves an almost complete account of the Creek [*sic*] social system."[32]

The essential nature of the town as a cluster of groups that came together to make medicine—that is, as a network of discourse sets cooperating in a concerted effort to manipulate temporal-spiritual forces—is revealed in the language. The root *tal-* and the word *talwa* in Maskókî embody the cosmogonic essence. Some current researchers have come close to understanding this when they explain the etymology of the word thus.

"Creek [sic] is the only Muskogean language in which the meaning of the root tálwa has been extended to mean 'town.' " In Hitchiti, Koasatî, and Chactá, the cognates comprise the meanings "dance" and "sing." So, "for Creek speakers, it would seem that a ritual concept [of] 'those who sing together' was extended to mean 'a town, a polity.' "[33]

It would be more accurate to say that "Creek" is the only Maskókî language in which the meaning has been made transparent. Among the Maskokálgî, neither singing nor dancing serves purely social functions. Both are basic elements of making medicine and both require the central power element, the fire. People who sing and dance together are people who come together around one fire—the same fire, as in a *búsketau* but especially in the liturgy of the Green Corn. Only those of the same town may enter the ceremonial ground to dance and sing around the sacred fire. Outsiders enter by communal permission only. Thus, those who dance and sing together are, by definition, people of the same fire and the same town.

Among male Maskókî speakers, individual ability counted for a great deal and was the vehicle by which the parameters of social power spheres could be permeated. The civil and the military were the twin power spheres that were bound together by the mediative sphere of medicine. Among female Maskókî speakers, the avenues to social power were attenuated but not less real. The mediative realm was the most accessible, but civil power also was available in certain instances to those whose birth within power Clans gave them additional impetus.

The Maskokálgî Way of War

Warfare operated within both Native American and European cultures as a high-value social mechanism during the sixteenth century, but it was predicated upon different objectives and prosecuted in very disparate ways, to a great extent because of the relatively increased horizontality of the Maskokálgî power structure that was its matrix. Swanton understood the centrality of warfare when he wrote: "[W]ar among the southern Indians was a social institution and warlike exploits [were] necessary means of social advancement."[34]

What he did not understand, of course, is that among the Maskokálgî, every facet of life was a social institution, and all existed for the same overarching purpose: to keep the cosmos in balance, in turn keeping the people surviving and prospering. But balance, within a circular cosmogony, must not be construed as, or equated with, stasis. Neither the anthropological theories of functionalism, which depict the world as a perfect balance, nor the conflict theories, which view conflict as the tension that binds societies, apply exclusively here. Both are necessary to maintain equilibrium.[35]

Conflict "recalibrates" the circular society; it reconfigures the society in response to disruptions engendered by actions—appropriate or inappropriate within the parameters of a given set of social norms—on the part of human beings. In relation to warfare among Spaniards and other Europeans whose society was bounded by the requirements of a linear cosmos, warfare among the Maskokálgî functioned in a more "pure," or abstract, sense. However, the clash between the two power systems was at least as bloody in the physical sense as it was profound in the abstract sense.

Spaniards, especially Castilians, steeped in the Crusading mentality of the Middle Ages, viewed their leap across the Atlantic as a direct extension of their crusading zeal. The military metaphor for the acquisition of converts to the Roman Catholic faith, the "Conquest of souls," included the distinct possibility of the physical Conquest of bodies as well. This was especially utilitarian when couched within the rhetorical context of the philosophy of the "just war," which circulated during the rhetorical and theological debates over the true nature of the *indios* and which consumed the first half of the sixteenth century.

By means of their metadiscursive manipulations, Spaniards recontextualized the use of power (physical force) to convert peoples, whom they saw as having been led away from the true path of Catholicism by Satanic forces, within a "consent in retrospect" realm. The real utility of this viewpoint lay in its concomitant, however: conversion was only one's entree to salvation, whereas death—later, or sooner—was its sine qua non.

Over the centuries following European interposition, Maskókî tribes would adopt European warfare technology, to a limited extent (for example, the gun would eventually replace the bow and arrow completely, but the Maskókî people would never become dependent upon the horse to the same extent as the Europeans, or even to the same extent as other Native American tribes). They would conform to European warfare tactics only when it suited their own purposes to do so, and Euroamericans would transfer their own value structures onto these actions. (This, for example, is the impetus for the myth that was introduced in the nineteenth century of a "Creek Confederation.") The underlying principles of warfare among the Maskókî people, however, would remain unchanged for as long as men

"Setting an Enemy's Town on Fire." Theodore de Bry's 1591
engraving (plate 31) from the *Brevis narratio* of Jacques le Moyne
(published in Lorant, *The New World*, 97)

of the Maskokálgî could find any field upon which to practice their ages-old and highly valued skills.[36]

The concept of warfare as defined in European terms as a prolonged conflict incorporating a series of battles predicated upon a long-range strategy and prosecuted using a series of short-range tactics to achieve limited objectives did not exist among the Maskókî peoples. The various chronicles of the Hernando de Soto entrada, for example, make clear that war for the Maskókî peoples was, rather, a state of belligerency between specific leaders and towns that was marked by periodic surprise hit-and-run attacks, the purpose of which was to destroy an enemy village, kill its warriors, and capture and incorporate its women into the dominant society.

States of belligerency, based upon intertribal territorial struggles, breaches of social conduct, and long-remembered instances of each, were factors of everyday existence for the Maskókî people. However, rules of conduct and prosecution, firmly embedded in the cultural matrix and the network of social discourse sets, described its parameters and institutionalized expectations. For at least the first four centuries following European interposition, until 1858, the Maskókî people continued to operate principally within these parameters, incorporating European technology into a framework of traditional Maskokálgî values, expectations, and rewards.

A reason, although apparently not the basic reason, the idealization of warrioring has retained such a high value among Maskókî peoples over the centuries is its intrinsic relationship to medicine, that power sphere uniting the seen and unseen forces of the cosmos. In a classic Maskokálgî circle of power relations, Maskókî warriors were practitioners of medicine. Their personal abilities and learned skills in the realm of war medicine enhanced their fighting skills, which, in turn, increased their abilities to protect the people. The more they engaged their medicine skills in the welfare of the community, the more accolades and honorifics they potentially received from the people, and the more opportunities the town acquired to put its war medicines to positive use.

The town's medicine bundle, described in European Christian terms as an "ark" by the eighteenth-century observer James Adair, was the central repository of the power items from which both combatants and noncombatants drew strength.[37] Its power sustained the town in the most basic cosmogonic sense. Its existence was the physical and metaphysical embodiment of the contract between the Maskokálgî and the Giver of Breath.

Individual Clans and towns had discrete medicine bundles, but allied towns also drew upon the powers of practitioners in central medicine towns, who held especial powers. However, by the late seventeenth century, as the Maskókî towns began to be moved southward and eastward and to fracture into constituent Clans under the new pressures of English settlements and trade expectations, medicine bundles were moved away from their central power sources, the practitioners of the medicine towns, and towns were forced to rely more heavily upon the mediative skills of individual practitioners.

The power of the bundles was renewed each year as a culmination of the Green Corn ceremony, one of the four principal elements of the Maskokálgî liturgical cycle and the only one that survives to the present. The centrality of the medicine bundles, therefore, is reconfirmed by their continued existence, in both Florida and Oklahoma, but their contents today have little to do with war and are focused almost exclusively on the health and cultural continuity of the people.[38]

The bases of warfare were not arbitrary, in the largest sense. They were formalized as breaches of etiquette, vengeance for aggravations, and premeditated acts of aggression designed to evidence military prowess and provide opportunities for the towns to protect and aggrandize themselves and, at the same time, for the warriors to aggrandize themselves as well, to the credit of the town. Spaniards frequently confirmed the power of influence exercised by the warriors beyond their own specific values to the communities within warfare, even as the archaeological evidence outlined earlier in this book constitutes the physical evidence of the high social value attached to being a warrior and the broad range of icons buffering and affirming warriors as statused individuals.

However, even though the rhetorical and physical discourses of war were accorded high value among the adherents of the Maskókî Way, the lives of the people were equally bounded by the discourses of peace and stability by which the New was incorporated and anchored. Warfare was not the default state of society; peace was.

Fray Alonzo Gregorio de Escobedo, writing in the first decade of the seventeenth century, said that the greatest ambition of "all" Native men was to become warriors.[39] His comments should not be accepted without reservation, however. All of the games of the young men were modeled on physical prowess, such as was necessary for warfare, but boys practiced to become hunters of game as well. Warriors received the best food available, better than that of women and children and noncombatant males, but this was not because the warriors used the power of their status to take what the rest of the people begrudged them. It was, rather, because the mentalities of the towns placed the positive values attendant upon being a warrior near the apex of their collective social value structures. Warriors were the physical and psychological shields that protected the existence of the people in each town. When especially dangerous conditions existed, women, children, and noncombatants slept in the center of the town and the warriors camped around them, to shield them physically.

Caciques were, as stated earlier, the physical nexus of civil, spiritual, and military power, but they were also a part of a reciprocal power structure and, as such, subject to the requirements and expectations of the people whose cosmos they manipulated. Before the decisive battle of Mabila, as Hernando de Soto readied his men for battle, the cacique of the town, which was allied with powerful Tascaluça, was beseeched by his warriors not to submit himself to the battle. According to the Spaniards, who learned of it later from Mabila women who were captured there, the Native

"Exercises of the Youths." Theodore de Bry's 1591 engraving
(plate 36) from the *Brevis narratio* of Jacques le Moyne

(published in Lorant, *The New World*, 107)

men reminded the cacique that "matters of war and victory were a haz-
ard of fortune."[40] Consequently, he should leave command of the battle to
others, in order that those who survived would still have a leader. After
some discussion, the cacique acquiesced to their entreaties. In the course
of the day's events, it was wise counsel.

Warfare, obviously, was a basic element of statecraft. When the Serrope
warriors stole away the daughter of Oathchaqua, whom Calus was planning to marry, the Serrope regarded it as a great victory. Calus was a re-
nowned warrior himself and the loss of so dear a prize was surely a double,
perhaps a triple, loss to him: he not only lost a political alliance cemented
by marriage ties but he also lost status as a result of a successful attack
aimed at him personally. We have no way of knowing whether Calus and
Oathchaqua's daughter knew or cared for each other personally or whether
theirs was to be a marriage of state, but perhaps he lost honest affection
as well.

As a result of the importance of warfare as a political tool, researchers have a difficult time defining the physical frontiers of various complex chiefdoms among the Maskókî tribes. Not only were some "border towns" undoubtedly multilingual, which may imply multiculturalism, but also they were frequently in danger of falling prey to territorially ambitious neighbors. Coça, the power town of that complex chiefdom, may have held sway over Talisi, a smaller town to the southwest in 1567. "At the very least, it is clear that Coosa was not the unchallenged chief of Talisi," researchers conclude.[41] A regional conspiracy "does not prove that these towns were paying tribute to Coosa, but it does clearly indicate that, even in 1567 they were capable of joining forces with Coosa against an outside aggressor."[42]

The ability of the Maskókî people, as towns or as individual war leaders, to take independent action should come as no surprise now that the horizontality of the power structure is clear. One of the paths to status among the Maskokálgî, for both men and women, was heredity, without doubt, but there were others as well. Age conferred a certain status for both sexes. In addition, we have seen that abilities as a mediator of cosmic forces, that is, as a practitioner of medicine, conferred status. Oratorical skills and prowess as a warrior were excellent paths to visibility. Regardless of the path, the Maskókî Way prized individuals who committed themselves to the honor of the Clans and the welfare of the town. Warriors were in an excellent position from which to move in several interlocking spheres.

War leaders gained status by performing successfully, in accordance with sociocultural expectations, but their rewards were very much at the discretion of the people. No honors were automatic and none were necessarily permanent or even indicative of permanent rank. Status, signalized by honorifics (titles), by awards of feathers and metal and shell gorgets, and by scarification in ritualized patterns and colors, might be withdrawn and removed as a result of later actions considered to be breaches of public trust. At the most, they were signs of influence rather than affirmations of permanent rank. It was not unusual for unscrupulous warriors, ambitious for recognition, to scarify themselves without the sanction of the community's power structure. In these cases, ceremonies of public defamation reasserted and reaffirmed the unilateral power of the community to confer and confirm status.

Torture and death were the fate of those who fell in battle. Enemies' bodies were dismembered and their parts carried back to the towns as trophies. This was a common practice in the sixteenth century and it was still a feature of warfare in the eighteenth century.[43] Prisoners were tortured, and the women of the victorious town, many of whose partners had been

"How Outina's Men Treated the Enemy Dead." Theodore de Bry's 1591
engraving (plate 15) from the *Brevis narratio* of Jacques le Moyne
(published in Lorant, *The New World*, 65)

lost to them in the action and all of whose lives had suffered the impact of
the belligerence, performed the tortures. However, women also served as
arbitrators and diplomats, a reminder that gender assignments were separate and not in all areas subordinate for women.[44]

Warfare tactics varied somewhat according to the abilities and inclina-
tions of the war leaders but certain commonalties still existed. The French
cartographer, Jacques le Moyne de Morgues, who accompanied René de
Laudonnière to *La Florida* in 1564, noted of two powerful leaders from the
northern peninsula: "When Saturiba went to war, his men followed him
in whatever order they happened to be. But his enemy Holata Outina . . . ,
who was more powerful, both in the number of his men and in wealth,
than Saturiba, marched his forces in regular ranks like an organized
army."[45]

II Enter the Spaniards

6 The Entrada Model in the Southeast, 1510–1565

[Hernando de Soto] knew nothing either of the islands or the land of the North [*La Florida*], knowing only the method of government of Pedrarías, in Castilla del Oro and Nicaragua, and of Perú, which was another manner of dealing with the Indians; and he thought that [experience] from there sufficed to know how to govern here on the coast of the North, and he deluded himself, as this history will relate.

—Rodrigo Ranjel[1]

Eastern North America as a whole is an excellent area in which to test the anthropologist's hypothesis that differences in Indian-European relations are due largely to different responses to differing Indian cultures; or conversely, the historian's hypothesis that differences in colonial relations are largely due to differing European policies and actions and institutions.

—William Sturtevant[2]

The exploration and settlement of *La Florida* proceeded in two distinct phases, each incorporating its own unique set of characteristics. In the Entrada Phase, from 1510 to 1563, Spanish explorations proceeded on the Spanish new world model. However, the responses of the Maskókî peoples to the Spaniards' presence were drawn directly from within their own experiences with the Spaniards in *La Florida*, while the Spaniards brought to their *La Florida* entradas baggage from experiences in other parts of the new world that they were exploring and settling.

In the expansionist Settlement Phase, from 1565 to 1763, the Spaniards' cumulative experiences with *La Florida*'s Maskókî peoples reconfigured both the actions and interactions of the Spaniards with the Native peoples, creating a unique environment for the Spaniards. For the Maskókî peoples, the Settlement Phase increased sociocultural pressures significantly but their social repertoire of actions and interactions only broadened, as the

Maskókî peoples incorporated whatever they saw as viable tools of protectionism into their classic social repertoires. The intrinsic culture of the Maskókî peoples, however, remained the same.

During the Entrada Phase, the Crown repeatedly offered the standard rewards and concessions of power to the succession of men who attempted to establish a permanent Spanish presence: tax exemptions; power to hold and grant land; an *adelantazco,* which included civil power, the power to make certain appointments and grant some preferments, and, sometimes, the power to pass on a remunerative title for inheritance as well; and, most important, the power to create a *mayorazco* (an entailed estate), which would protect the royal concessions and consolidate wealth and preferments for one's family in perpetuity.

As the Conquest of the mainland of the Americas proceeded, from 1519, and as the body of information concerning the lands along the northern and eastern Gulf coast grew, the settlement of *La Florida* soon included the objective of linking the two Spanish realms, Nueva España (Mexico) and *La Florida,* by an overland route protected by a fortified line of missions and settlements. This plan never materialized, although the Spaniards tried repeatedly. The Spaniards did explore much of the Southeast, however. They learned a great deal about what they could expect from future investments. They fended off English and French attempts to supersede Spanish claims, and they effected a number of small settlements that, ultimately, failed. It was a valiant and amazing effort, but the resources that the Spanish empire chose to commit to this purpose proved insufficient for them to dominate this vast portion of North America and overcome the considerable resistance skills of the Native Americans, especially the Maskókî peoples.

It was in the same year that *La Florida* entered the Spanish lexicon, in 1513, that Pedro Arias de Avila, or Pedrarías Dávila as he was commonly known, was given superiority over Vasco Nuñez de Balboa at Darién and Castilla del Oro (Panamá). His appointment was all a part of the control system that the Spanish monarchs had already used many times before in the process of claiming the Americas and, more often than not, successfully. It would be Felipe II's strategy in *La Florida* as the Crown sought to recoup control of the colony much later in the century. Even as the monarchs granted titles and concessions to one explorer, ostensibly opening to him vistas of power and preferment, they set a curb upon his ambitions by granting overlapping or directly competing powers to yet another explorer or to a Crown official, essentially placing the two powers in antagonistic postures and allowing them to fight out the details of the limits of their own powers and authority. Above all, however, for all of the *capitulaciones* (capitulations) and *asientos* (assignments of rights) it provided, the Crown pursued its *Real Quinto,* its Royal Fifth of the profits, with greater or lesser success but regardless of who won, lost, died, or lived.

Pedrarías exercised almost unbridled physical and emotional power in his governance of Castilla del Oro. His heavy-handed treatment of the Native peoples was brutal and effective. His methods brought him into constant competition and conflict with Balboa, whom he finally ordered executed in 1519. Pedrarías moved to Nicaragua as governor in 1527 and died there in 1531, but his governmental methods did not die with him. He had not given them birth and so they lived on in other Spaniards.

Spain's New World Matrix

The movement of the Spaniards to an Atlantic world that they saw as "new" was an ideological and conceptual leap that virtually dwarfed its geographic concomitant. It has been posited by some researchers that the centuries of intercultural relations, both positive and negative, between the Spaniards and the Moors on the Iberian peninsula had sufficiently prepared the Spaniards to deal, conceptually, with the existence of the cultural Other. This is too simplistic an assessment, however.

The discovery of *La Florida* by the Spaniards during the first half of the sixteenth century proceeded as an integral and inevitable part of Spain's exploration of its new world of natural and human treasures. On their entradas, however, the Spanish explorers carried with them not only their matrix Iberian expectations, but also all of the intellectual and ideological by-products of their ongoing American learning experiences as well.

In 1510 and 1513, when the earliest contacts with the southeastern peninsula of North America were made, Fernando II still ruled Spain.[3] By 1516, however, the Crown had passed to Carlos I, son of Queen Juana (daughter of Fernando and Ysabel, and called "La Loca") and the Habsburg Felipe I ("The Fair"). Carlos I, under whose aegis the Spaniards would invest, but fail to settle, North America, was a crusader in the quintessential Iberian sense of the word.

As the maternal grandson of Fernando and Ysabel, the royal pair who had married clandestinely (for love) and fought off their own families and countrymen for the first decade of their partnership to hold on not only to their relationship but also to any semblance of a kingdom as well, Carlos inherited a passion for conquest. Fernando and Ysabel had extended their military and political domination to all of the Moorish polities on the Iberian peninsula by 1492 and had secured from the Roman Catholic papacy the invaluable *Patronato Real*, the concessions that financed much of the development of their kingdoms.[4] The remainder of their lives (until 1516 and 1504, respectively), would be spent in integrating the economic power of the Roman Catholic Church into their secular regime, reformation of the clergy, and the ethnic cleansing of their realms.

As the secular power of the Roman Catholic Church grew in Europe, and especially in Spain, church policy toward non-Catholic neighbors hardened into intolerance. By 1492, the Moors and Jews, who had proven themselves to be viable, and valuable, commercial allies to the Iberians during the earlier centuries of *convivencia*, had, in the main, proven intractable in the face of increased Spanish demands for assimilation. Unwilling to give up their social, commercial, and religious freedoms to the Spaniards, thousands of Moors and Jews exercised a cultural option and began a mass exodus to Africa and western Europe, the lands from which so many of their ancestors earlier had come to Iberia. Those who remained converted to Catholicism—some from genuine conviction and others from fear or opportunism, but the contributions of these "converts" to the vitality of Spanish life were nonetheless real.

Carlos I of Spain was the legatee of this powerful combination of Habsburg militarism and Spanish Catholic zeal, and it was he who would take Iberian power to the zenith of its Golden Age. As Carlos V of the Holy Roman Empire (from 1520), he would complete the application of the *Patronato* to the Iberian peninsula and consolidate the transfer of Spanish power to the Americas. His administrative abilities, especially as juxtaposed against the micromanagement style of his son and successor, Felipe II, were forceful and direct.

However, the people with whom the Spaniards would come into contact on the other side of the Atlantic Ocean were, in every sense of the phrase, products of a different world. The Native Americans, although many were seafarers within their own continental spheres, and even though their social repertoires contained centuries of travel models, inhabited territories that they imaged as having been theirs, exclusively, from time immemorial. Their creation stories, their ancestors' births, and their lives were all vested in these lands. Unlike the Jews and the Moors, the Native Americans did not envision emigrating in the face of any pressures because their cosmogonic matrix did not include an image of immigrating.

In the case of the Seminoles and Maskókî peoples, still today they consider Euroamerican scientists' stories of intercontinental migrations to be unacceptable. Their creation stories principally image the people as having been created in the Southeast, literally out of the earth. Their images of interactions with strange lands required the strangers to come to them, not vice versa. Indeed, many Seminoles today have received the traditions from their grandparents' grandparents that Euroamericans are white skinned because they are made of the sea foam of the ocean that cast them up on Native shores.[5]

As long as the Spaniards were exploring only the islands of the circum-Caribbean, and confronting only those Carib and Arawak peoples whose levels of cultural sophistication they perceived as far less than their own, their collective ability to deal with a cultural Other presented no insurmountable problems. Their discoveries prompted introspection, but this did not apply to the Americas, however, principally because the perceived dichotomies among the Spaniards', Jews', and Moors' culture bases were far smaller (especially after the centuries of the *convivencia*) than was the perceived dichotomy between the Spaniards' and Native Americans' culture bases.

However, the Spaniards did have an ideological model for dealing with individuals whose spiritual concepts differed from their own and whose culture base, although shockingly new, they could image as shockingly inferior. The model for the former event was the Roman Catholic philosophy of "conversion." For the latter, most convenient were the social and economic models for dealing with slaves, as a group, although the concept of slavery in the Spaniards' world was not attached to color or geographic location. When, in the wake of the initial contact, Queen Ysabel decreed Indian slavery per se to be unlawful, as African slavery per se was unlawful on the Iberian peninsula, the Spaniards still relied upon those classic models of conquest: that is, upon conversion and upon slavery, as mediated by the rationale of the "just war." These philosophical models were not unique to *La Florida*. On the contrary, they were integral elements of the Iberian cultural transposition. Consequently, an understanding of their value in Spanish culture is critical to an understanding of the Spanish experience in *La Florida*, in both phases of interposition.

Conversion

Roman Catholicism's philosophical journey from the secular to the religious—from the Aristotelian philosophy that formed many of its basic tenets to the ideology as refined by Isadore of Seville and Thomas Aquinas—had provided the Spaniards with certain strategies for incorporating the conceptually "new" into what had been, in the minds of its Greek propounders, inherently a rigid and closed ideological framework. As a result of the philosophical manipulations of Isadore and Aquinas, it was no longer necessary to be born into the system. The closed element of the Greek in:out polarity was softened in Christianity by a permeable frontier, rhetorically constructed as "conversion," a useful tool for overcoming the obstacle of increase by birth alone. The rigidity of dogma, however, remained.

Power, in organized religious institutions, is based upon economic wealth, which is, in turn, based upon the emotional and economic commitment of increasing numbers of institutional members. A system that provided for increase solely through the slow and relatively haphazard process of birth was doomed to limited power. The mechanism of conversion radically increased the potential rate of acquisition of members/power. When Roman Catholic theology added the mechanism of conversion to the philosophy of inherent "rightness" of ideology, the possibilities for increase of numbers made a quantum leap. Not only *could* nonbelievers be brought into the system but also they *should* be brought in because the ideology was uniquely "right." This mechanism of manipulated belief and inclusion would become the paradigm for all of Western Christianity.

With the discovery, in an unexplored world, of a radically disparate ideological Other, however, the shock of the new impelled Iberian Roman Catholicism—the zenith of European Catholic fanaticism—to begin a rapid and desperate introspection for some internal mechanism that would permit the incorporation of the "Indians" into a system far too rigid to simply permit them their own, separate existence. It was not necessary to look far. It is, however, to the credit of the Iberians (as opposed to the English, French, or Dutch, ultimately the other colonial super powers) that they chose to look at all.

The definition of Right depends, for its existence, upon the definition of Wrong, just as Good exists only contrapuntally to Evil. Aristotle's linealism set all "Natural Men," as he styled them, on a long, straight road to reunion with the perfection of the *Primum Causam*—the Prime Mover, their stated creator. Aquinian linealism institutionalized the journey as a road filled with obstacles placed in the path to enlightenment by evil diversionary forces. Roman Catholicism further refined the processual philosophy with the theory that human beings—if they were, indeed, human beings or Natural Men—could be diverted from the path to salvation by evil, and they could be returned to the path by Roman Catholicism. Conversion was the bridge.

Throughout the first half of the sixteenth century, debate continued among Spanish legal and theological scholars over the exact nature of the Crown's responsibility to the Indians and the Indians' exact abilities to recognize the rightness of Spanish Catholicism. The University of Salamanca was the epicenter of this debate. From there was propounded the critical argument that might be termed "the concept of retroactive consent." Together with the concepts of conversion and the just war, it constituted the intellectual matrix of the Spanish explorers. As Anthony Pagden explains it: "Any man who is capable of knowing, even in retrospect, that something is in his own interest may be said to have consented to it, even when there is no question of his having exercised any freedom of choice."[6] As an outgrowth of the debates, and with an unmistakable degree of irony, the Spanish Crown adopted as its official policy toward the Native Americans a degree of inclusion and recognition of rights that was unmatched in the later official policies of the English and the French.

The Just War

Although the Spaniards went to great lengths of rationalization and justification to place the Native Americans within the framework of their own (the Spaniards') ideologies, their policy of inclusion did not preclude the use of force under any circumstances. Slavery was an unnatural state but could be justified on the basis of military conquest, refusal to accept Roman Catholicism, or, as in the specific case of the Native Americans, if the people in question were found guilty of practices (such as cannibalism and sodomy) that mainstream Spaniards considered to be violations of the wishes of their god.

Concomitantly, Crown policy did not contain any absolute mechanism by which it might definitively control the actions of its representatives and subjects thousands of miles away. The magnificently elliptical response made to the monarchs by a Spanish new world official, "*Obedezco, pero no cumplo*" ("I obeyed, but do not comply"), contains the heart of all that the

Spanish Crown sought to preclude in its management of lands thousands of miles distant from its physical control. On the other hand, given the strong impetus of personal aggrandizement and profit that motivated not only the Spaniards but also all of the European newcomers, Spain's processes of introspection and intellectual rationalization were unique and did produce a significant degree of legal constraint among its American subjects.[7] There remained, however, very definite limits to the degree of cultural toleration that could be generated by an inherently exclusionary ideology. At these limits, the Spaniards inserted their conceptual just war.

Cristobal Colón configured the European reception of all the Native Americans with the word images that he drew for Their Most Catholic Majesties, Fernando and Ysabel, in his formal report of 1493. He portrayed them as possessing of neither iron nor steel, "nor . . . fitted to use them." They were "handsome" but also "guileless and . . . generous." They held no ideological "creed but neither [were] they idolaters," for they believed that all things came from the heavens (he believed), including the Europeans. He saw them as intelligent, good navigators, and possessing a single language. He noticed very quickly that some men, seemingly as a perquisite of leadership, had multiple wives, and he saw "work" as more the province of women than of men. He also noted the ascendancy of communal over personal property.[8]

These word images from Colón fed the superciliousness of Europeans, beyond Spaniards, who imaged themselves as both unilaterally powerful and unilaterally right. Within the Iberian culture lexicon, the inherent inferiority of the *indios* turned their guilelessness and generosity into ignorant, childish naiveté. Their awareness of an unseen world became a vestigial confirmation of their having once been on the True Path. Their basic intellects, navigational skills, and linguistic abilities only reassured the Spaniards and later Europeans that the Indians could be bent to more enlightened purposes, even as the same elements confirmed their inherent inferiority within the Spanish and European cultural hierarchies. Consequently, following the initial period of exploration and introspection, the information that the legatees of Colón received reaffirmed their own collective sense of righteousness and rearmed the Iberians with a moral rectitude that would, ultimately, surmount all philosophical quibbles.

What the Europeans chose to see as the complete dominion of Indian men over Indian women led them to the operative assumption that the Christian superstructure of a paternalistic gender system could be superimposed quite neatly over the Native gender system. Repeated Spanish remarks about social realms in which they chose to see female licentiousness, concupiscence, and overt lust, reinforced in the retelling by European cosmographers, appealed to the repressed sexuality of Christian males who frequently and brutally enforced their own desires on Native women, whenever Native power networks coincided with their own agendas or military ascendancy permitted.

This ubiquitous and unrelenting power discourse, coupled with significant military power and the willingness to use it in pursuit of a disparate agenda that was, itself, born of a totally disparate cosmogony, was what Rodrigo Ranjel referred to as Pedrarías Dávila's "other manner of dealing with the Indians." Colón practiced it. As Carl Ortwin Sauer stated, Colón's Indian policy was "simple, rigid, and [ultimately] unworkable. . . . The heritage of his mistakes continued long after him."[9] That heritage continued in *La Florida* for at least a century. It could be argued that it has continued to the present.

The *La Florida* Model

All of the *entradistas* of the first, or exploration, phase of *La Florida* settlement were, directly or indirectly, parts of Cristobal Colón's Americas legacy. This legacy consisted of two major elements: first, the a priori imaging of the cultural Other as profoundly subordinate in all ways, social and cultural, and second, the inclusion of the ultimate negotiating tool, the use of main force not excluding destruction of life as a choice of first resort, in their bid for power. The unnamed slavers who reconnoitered the coast in 1510, creating the impetus for the profoundly negative receptions that would be accorded future Spaniards by southern peninsular Natives, were moving northward, systematically, as a part of Colón's Americas legacy, decimating the Native populations of the Caribbean islands by their raiding.

Juan Ponce de León, the first Crown-licensed explorer of the Southeast, had sailed with Colón on his second voyage and had been a leader in the 1504 War of Higüey and the violent "pacification" of the southern peninsula of the island that the Spaniards named Santo Domingo. Further, Ponce de León had learned first-hand from Fray Nicolás de Ovando, *comendador* of the military order of Alcántara and governor of Santo Domingo and Española, the values of punitive reprisals and preventative military actions to forestall real or imagined threats of uprising.[10] These rationalizations introduced a useful model for neatly skirting the Crown's slavery injunctions.

In 1513, Juan Ponce de León was given the first royal *asiento* to explore the Atlantic and Gulf shores of the land that he arbitrarily named *La Florida*. Ponce de León explored along the lower shores of the eastern peninsula, rounded the tip, and moved up the west coast, possibly as far as today's Tampa Bay. His contacts with the Natives were limited but negative. In a day-long battle, the Spaniards took four women and four men as prisoners, and the Escampaba people drove the Spaniards back with a display of strong defensiveness, covering the water with a rain of arrows.

This concerted military action on the part of the Escampaba, later known as Calusa, remained a critical factor in the inability of the *entradistas* to explore fully or settle *La Florida* during the first half of the sixteenth century. In other words, the willingness of the Maskókî peoples to make their own use of the ultimate negotiating tool, main force, in order to maintain their prerogatives, frustrated the will of the Spaniards who had imaged themselves as the preeminent holders of the ultimate negotiating tools.

The Spaniards operated from the ideological premise that their cultural superiority inherently included military superiority and the power to remake these people in the shape of Iberian discourse. Almost three hundred years later, the Spaniards still would be complaining of the unwillingness of the Maskókî peoples to internalize a manipulated ideological matrix in order to coincide with the Spaniards' imaging (see Chapter 8). In addition, the discourse of thousands of the Maskókî peoples, as pronounced in both their words and actions, still would remain firmly embedded in their own imaging and cultural matrix, irrespective of various Euroamerican socializations.

Following the official establishment of their claim in 1513, other Spanish explorers focused their attention on the potential of *La Florida,* and all of them reached its shores as veterans of the Americas experience. That is to say, they brought conceptual models for interactions with the cultural Other that ran the entire colonial gamut from emotional conversion to death. These models were neither entirely secular nor entirely religious, because their twin motive forces were so firmly engaged—both consciously and unconsciously—in the Spanish mentality as to be inseparable for any significant purposes or periods of time. Thus the concept of conversion can be viewed, in a broader context than that typically imparted by a uniquely religious reference, as a rhetorical twin concept within the cultural reference system; that is, religious conversion and cultural conversion went hand in hand.

As a result of these twin reference systems of cultural and religious conversion, the Spaniards valued the land they found in *La Florida* in relation to its arability and the lucrative natural resources that it might produce. They valued the inhabitants of the land for their sheer numbers and their physical ability, in direct relation to their potential as the labor force that could make the riches of the land accessible to the individual Spaniards and the Spanish Crown (frequently in that order). They valued the Natives in inverse proportion to the resistance that would have to be overcome in order to apply Native labor to the land. And they valued Roman Catholicism as the ideological matrix that was the font of their rightness and served as the key to a relatively nonviolent subsumption of these new peoples into their ostensibly supercedant secular and ideological systems.

Relativity was the key to viewing the Roman Catholic conversion process as nonviolent because, by the sixteenth century, neither the ideological matrix of Christianity nor the philosophical application of the conversion process inherently required nonviolence. This view was maintained despite periodic reaffirmations by Ysabel and by her grandson of their commitments to the ethical treatment of the *indios*. However, if reunion with the Prime Mover was the teleological objective of Christianity, then physical death, sooner or later, was the sine qua non of obtaining that objective. Death before conversion was a lamentable loss of a prospective soul, but death after conversion only sped up an eminently desirable process.

During the first entrada into *La Florida,* however, conversion was not the primary objective, just as it had not been in the earliest entradas elsewhere in America.[11] It was inherently a utilitarian concomitant nevertheless; utilitarian in that any disposition toward Catholicism that could be created among the Natives ultimately would be reflected in efficiency of settlement and lower costs. The more the Native peoples found rationales to accept the rhetorical tenets of Spanish Catholicism, the more they would internalize the rhetorical universe of Catholic Spaniards.

From 1521 (the time of Ponce de León's second voyage) onward throughout the exploration phase, the *La Florida entradistas* offered the Maskókî peoples a set number and range of usable rationales to effect their acceptance of the Spaniards and of Roman Catholicism. They repeatedly ran the gamut of these with each new group that they encountered until one of two results was obtained. Either one rationale or combination of rationales succeeded and the Spaniards gained ascendancy (but not necessarily control) of the group, or none of the rationales worked and the Spaniards searched for a more pliant group. The impetuses for acceptance of the rationales spanned a continuum from nonviolent to totally violent, including negotiations leading to emotional conversion (frequently based on the power of signs and wonders); philosophical conversion (a sincere, internalized, ideological shift); conversion by duress (the result of the fear engendered by implied force of any kind); and conversion by fear (the result of direct, applied force).

In the early days of the Americas interposition process, the Spaniards relied heavily upon the violent end of the continuum, and the *entradistas* of *La Florida* were the products of this mentality. Regardless of whether one accepts all of the allegations of Bartolomé de las Casas, his summary of Spanish methods in America retains its validity: there were far too many who were "foolish and cruel and greedy and vicious."[12] However, as Hernando de Soto's secretary, Rodrigo Ranjel, cogently observed, these methods were not as successful in *La Florida* as they had been in other areas of the Americas.

In a second attempt to settle his grant of peninsular *La Florida*, Ponce de León made a final voyage to the lower west coast in 1521. His desire to invest the coastline was rejected by the Natives (probably the Escampaba again), and they drove him off. The cumulative baggage of the Spaniards' past failures to seek a common ground with the *La Florida* Natives in their negotiations was weighing down each successive contact. The Spaniards failed at this negotiation completely, and his try cost Ponce de León not only his economic investment, but also his life. As Carl Ortwin Sauer summed it up, "Ponce de León [destroyed] Puerto Rico, but then [he] tried it once too often on the tougher natives of [La] Florida."[13]

In that same year, however, two Spanish slavers, Pedro de Quejo and Francisco Gordillo, encountered a Native land farther north, on the Atlantic coast, where word of the Spaniards had not yet reached. They reported this land in such glowing terms that their sponsor, Lucas Vásquez de Ayllón, took the story to Spain in 1523 and told it to his friend, Pietro Martire d'Anghiera (Peter Martyr).[14] Martyr's account of "Chicora," together with the stories that Ayllón told, gave rise to a legend of a "New Andalucia" in the Southeast, filled with all the natural abundance of its Iberian counterpart. It would lure the French and English into direct competition throughout the sixteenth and seventeenth centuries with the Spaniards for that part of *La Florida* that lay between thirty-two and thirty-nine degrees north latitude.[15]

The Natives encountered by the Spaniards on this unofficial entrada were Catawban speakers, possibly "proto-Cherokee" as one historian terms them.[16] Their territory (near present-day Winyah Bay, South Carolina) lay along a cultural frontier with Maskókî peoples. Once again, the Spaniards' new world Entrada model was employed, to the ultimate detriment of Spanish aims. Quejo and Gordillo at first traded with the Native people, then used the trust that they had thus engendered to lure some of them aboard. About sixty men and women were forcefully abducted from their families' land. Half died at sea. Of the rest, taken to Santo Domingo, most died of disease or privations. A few escaped to the island's interior. The slavers attempted to justify their actions to the Crown's representatives by alleging that the Natives were cannibals and sodomites, thereby invoking the rhetoric of the just war and slavery. Then, to ameliorate their actions, they promised to return the Native peoples to their home as soon as it became convenient.[17] Only one, recorded as Francisco or "El Chicorano," ever saw his people again, however. Ayllón took him, as a personal servant, to Spain and then back to *La Florida*'s upper east coast.

In 1525, Pedro de Quejo again reconnoitered on Ayllón's behalf and returned to the people of "Chicora." Only with great difficulty were they persuaded that he would not kidnap any more of them, and he assuaged their hostility with more trade goods and promises that those taken from them would soon be returned, even though he knew full well that this could not be so.[18] The Natives had not forgotten their lost relatives, and they would not forget the lies of the Spaniards, regardless of the ameliorating lure of trade.

In 1526, Ayllón himself mounted an expedition to *La Florida*. The Chicora survivor, Francisco, was with him. Ayllón carried six hundred persons in all, including seamen and civilian men, women, children, and black slaves as settlers. Dominican friars accompanied this expedition. As soon as they reached the Chicora area, Francisco "El Chicorano" and several other Natives fled, never to be seen by the Spaniards again. Despite Ayllón's assertions that Francisco had been converted to Roman Catholicism and that he had been as loyal to Ayllón as a son and had been treated as such, Francisco obviously did not see his own position as being so desirable.[19] His family and his land meant more to him than whatever passed for kind treatment at the hands of the Spaniards, and his conversion by duress obviously was never internalized.

The frequent inability of the Spaniards to manipulate anything deeper than externalized belief among the Maskókî peoples, or to gauge degrees of their internalization of Spanish Catholicism, would continue to plague their relationships with the southeastern Natives throughout the entire colonial era. Ultimately, it would be the Maskókî peoples' trump card in all negotiations with these persistent and destructive cultural Others. However, within the rhetoric of Conquest, Spanish righteousness would clothe Spanish lies in the service of successful negotiation in the garb of justifiability. Meanwhile, Maskókî duplicity, in the service of negotiating survival, would ever be imaged as Satan-inspired, pagan barbarism.

Eventually, after exploring a portion of the Atlantic coastline of *La Florida,* Ayllón's *entradistas* established the colony of San Miguel de Gualdape (on what is now the Georgia coast) in an area that was not densely settled by Natives. The colony lasted for three months. Basic causes of its failure were typical: the discomforts of the heat and the insects, of which there was a superfluity, and insufficient food and resources (fish were plentiful but, somehow, the Spaniards were too weak to catch them). Dissatisfaction grew among the settlers and one faction chose to impose itself upon the Natives. They moved to a nearby village, uninvited, and, uninterested in their hosts' concepts of hospitality, quickly wore out their welcome.

Garcilaso de la Vega reported their fate some years later, as he heard it from a survivor. The Natives, it seems, perceiving no value in negotiating with people whose actions they saw as beginning at a place beyond the bounds of legitimate negotiation, treated their guests with great hospitality for four days (the ritual number) and, then, slew them all. Next they attacked the Spaniards' small coastal settlement and destroyed it as well. The survivors—not including Ayllón, who had already died in *La Florida*—escaped to Española.

Gonzalo Fernández de Oviedo, in his *Historia general y natural de las Indias,* concluded, just as Ranjel and other observers had, that the Spaniards erred in believing that they could treat the *La Florida* Natives in the same high-handed manner as they had those of the Caribbean. The Maskókî people were still too bellicose, and too much their own masters, to succumb to superciliousness and a little trade. Furthermore, with centuries of a Mississippian warrior heritage to draw upon, the Maskókî peoples would continue to image themselves as maintaining their military options throughout the entire colonial period. Consequently, the negative reports of the Ayllón survivors diminished Spanish hopes of finding their "New Andalucia" in *La Florida,* and the experiences of the subsequent entradas would do nothing to revive those hopes.

The grant obtained by Pánfilo de Narváez, Ayllón's old enemy, in 1526, to explore the northern Gulf coast and all of *La Florida* (still considered a peninsula) was more productive, in terms of information about conditions in *La Florida*. It still failed to plant a settlement, however, and did nothing to give the Spaniards a positive image in the eyes of the Maskókî people. Narváez landed an army of four hundred, with forty horses, near Tampa Bay, with the objective of exploring the land from the peninsula westward to Nueva España. He marched northward, becoming the first recorded European to go into Abalachi territory, where illness halted his trek.[20] He ordered boats built to continue the trip by water, but lost almost all of his men to the sea. Only five, including Alvar Núñez Cabeça de Vaca, survived and, after eight years of captivity among (Texas) Natives, they reached Mexico in 1536. Narváez himself had disappeared.

Cabeça de Vaca wrote of his fascinating experiences with the Narváez entrada and also told Spaniards that *La Florida* was the richest country in the world. However, he turned down an opportunity to return, with Hernando de Soto, and it would be left to the de Soto expedition (1539–1543) to give Europeans their first detailed account of the interior of the Southeast, including first-hand accounts of some of the most complex Native societies on the northern continent. As one historian has observed, "by 1535, the largest unexplored part of the Americas was North America."[21]

In terms of their attitudes toward the Natives whom they encountered and their treatment of them, Narváez and de Soto were both further elements of the Colón legacy. The hostility that they encountered on the part of the Abalachi peoples was a direct counter to the power that the Spaniards sought to wield preemptively. Their strategies were predicated upon a determination to move through new territories as expeditiously and safely as possible; in other words, with as much logistical support from tribal stores and as little resistance from tribal members as possible. The Spaniards' willingness to incorporate into the negotiation the entire range of negotiating tools, from discussion to destruction, had some limited effectiveness in terms of their own topographic progress (that is to say, in the short run), but was eminently ineffective in terms of ultimate Spanish settlement of the Southeast (that is to say, in the long run).

Stories of the white men and their strange, irrational, and destructive ways were permeating the Southeast, traveling along the trade paths from village to town and across tribal territories, and the Spaniards stepped ashore to the results of their own publicity: villages deserted by Natives who chose not to even deal with the strangers; roadways blocked by the military autonomy of powerful Native leaders; guarded rhetorical negotiations predicated on mistrust; and, everywhere, purposely misleading and erroneous information designed by the Natives to rid themselves of the Spanish presence as quickly as possible. It was not the Natives who were the interlopers here.

Ironically, Fray Bartolomé de las Casas, the great polemicist, apparently respected Cabeça de Vaca and used his account of the Narváez entrada as illustrative of the possibility of *peaceful* settlement. Even Hispanic historian Rolena Adorno accepted Cabeça de Vaca's narrative as successful because it "took a counter-conquest position." Cabeça de Vaca, he claims, approached the Natives "unarmed" and "advocated peaceful conversion of the natives and demonstrated that good treatment of the Indians produced results that served both the well-being of native populations and the economic interests of Spaniards."[22]

Cabeça de Vaca did, indeed, advocate peaceful interactions with the Natives and, with the strength of the Narváez entrada diminished by attrition, he found himself in numerous situations in which a modicum of cultural sensitivity became a survival tool. However, the overall realities of the Narváez entrada could be described as "peaceful" only in the eyes of the most ardent Hispanophile. Narváez and his men debarked to a purposely deserted village and found that the people deserted their villages regularly as a power stratagem, in order to deny their enemies logistical support. The Spaniards had no interpreters. They captured Natives and demanded maize. They high-handedly burned personal properties, including ceremonial items with high social value. They routinely took Native hostages and forced them to serve as bearers, and they attacked villages (which would have been difficult if they actually had been "unarmed"). They capitalized on occurrences of nature, seeing themselves as favored by their god with miracles and the Natives as naive and ingenuous. Much more than any example of the possibility of peaceful conversion, the Cabeça de Vaca narrative is an excellent example of the caution that must be exercised by modern researchers who might confuse cultural chauvinism with historical reporting.

Hernando de Soto and his five hundred to seven hundred *entradistas* (accounts disagree), including soldiers and some women, were a larger and infinitely more destructive force in the Southeast than the Narváez force had been. With horses, pigs, and myriad supplies, they marched up the peninsula and, ultimately, across what are today nine southeastern states. "De Soto had better scouting [than other explorers had had on their entradas] and an efficient policy of moving from the central town of each [province] to that of the next, a technique probably learned in Central America," writes historian Paul Hoffman.[23] The term *efficient*, however, deserves discussion.

De Soto and his entourage stopped at or near Native villages and, in the classic model, forcefully took hostages whom they used as bearers, guides, and translators from one village to the next. Women of the various tribes were forced to serve the men as personal servants and as sex partners. De Soto's men plundered villages and towns, respected neither human life nor property if either impeded their objectives, and used displays of force as the ultimate negotiating tool to an extent unparalleled in other *La Florida* entradas.

With the Battle of Mabila (in present-day southern Alabama), on October 18, 1540, Native disgust with Spanish demands reached a climax, and de Soto's men demonstrated the full extent of the force that they were willing to employ to get their own way. Despite the severe physical damage inflicted on the Spaniards by the highly developed fighting skills of the cacique Tascaluça and his Mabila warriors, that some of the Spaniards escaped with their lives was a victory of sorts. The Spaniards required twenty-eight days to recuperate.

Furthermore, despite the inflated Spanish report of over three thousand Mabila killed, the Mabila people continued to exist as a coherent social group for at least another two hundred years, until 1763, after which time they ceased to be mentioned in Euroamerican documents. Even so, we must not take this as evidence that they ceased to exist as a people.[24] In addition, despite the physical damage inflicted upon the Mabila people by the Spaniards, other tribes continued to exercise their own prerogatives and to aggress the foreigners and reject their pretentious demands.

In 1549, the Europeans were once again denied entry into *La Florida,* again by the Escampaba of the southwest peninsula, who obviously imaged themselves as maintaining their entire range of prerogatives. Fray Luís Cáncer de Barbastro, a Dominican and a veteran Americas missionary, was one of the exceptions to the entrada mentality, who believed that his only hope of converting the Natives lay in contacting people who had not already been antagonized by the Spanish willingness to negotiate with force of arms.[25] However, his pilot ignored his direction to find a new port of entry for *La Florida,* one that word of the Spaniards' methods might not have reached, and, instead, entered a familiar one. The Escampaba perceived no value in hearing European talk. Further, all of Cáncer's good intentions were insufficient to overcome the power of the entrada image that had been so forcefully created in the minds of these *La Florida* people. The Escampaba lured him to the shore with feigned interest in his prayers and trinkets, kidnapped his companions, and, eventually, killed him as well.

In 1559, Tristán de Luna y Arellano transported to *La Florida*'s shores the largest entrada thus far and the first to specifically intend settlement. Once again, as in earlier expeditions, Luna y Arellano himself and many of his *entradistas* were veterans of other settlements in the Americas and holders of the classic entrada mentality. The group, consisting of fifteen hundred soldiers and settlers, was attempting to fulfill what originally was a Nueva España plan to plant missions on the Gulf coast. Quickly it had evolved further, into a design for a line of fortified settlements that would link the Atlantic coast with Nueva España. However, the matrix issue for the Spanish Crown in the settlement of *La Florida* was the growing settlement competition from the French and a current French-Spanish diplomatic stalemate over territorial limits in the Americas.[26] To forestall French incursions, especially into North America, Spain needed actual physical settlements rather than bold political claims.

Luna landed at Bahía Filipina del Puerto de Santa María (Mobile Bay), moved on to Santa María de Ochuse (Pensacola Bay), and searched inland from there for the paramount chiefdom of Coça, which de Soto survivors had described as rich and well stocked. Instead of wealth, they found the land much changed. They found that many of the formerly populous, thriving villages were empty and deserted. The Natives told them that the people had died of disease. What remained unchanged, however, were the interactions of these Colón legatees with the Natives whom they did find. The Spaniards still took by force whatever they could not obtain by other types of negotiations, and they still disdained any meaningful semblance of equality in dealing with the Natives.

The Luna y Arellano entrada had internal problems of leadership, however, and, by 1561, had failed in its purpose. Angel de Villafañe was sent from Nueva España to replace Luna y Arellano. Villafañe had modeled his attitude toward the American Natives in the Darién fleet of Pedrarías Dávila and in the "pacifications" of the Natives in Nueva España. He left fifty Spaniards at Ochuse (Pensacola) Bay, and the rest of the Spaniards retreated to their well-established base of settlement and supply in Habana and Nueva España to regroup. However, a renewed attempt to settle *La Florida,* this time aimed at the Atlantic coast and the area of Santa Elena (between thirty-three and thirty-four degrees north latitude), also failed. Villafañe encountered no acceptable site, in all his reconnoitering, for the purposed settlement.

Two further Spanish attempts were made to effect a settlement in *La Florida* in the period 1560 to 1563, but each was also unsuccessful. Martín Díaz (1560) was obstructed from reaching land by bad weather. Lucas Vásquez de Ayllón the Younger (1563) may have been trying to enrich himself rather than to settle *La Florida,* as he promised the King, but underfunding and mutiny destroyed his emigrant group before it even reached *La Florida*'s shores.

It was at this point, with no Spanish settlement effected in *La Florida* even after slightly more than half a century of exploration, that the Spanish Crown paused in its attempts and the Entrada Phase closed. The sum of the reports on the potential value of *La Florida*'s land, resources, and labor was inconclusive, at best, and highly negative, at worst. However, the French, acting upon their diplomatic policy of "effective occupation," were actively seeking out their own potential settlement sites in *La Florida* and this competition, ultimately, would spur the Spanish Crown to mandate one final attempt.

In addition, while Spaniards had been seeking out new sources of revenue and souls in their new world, the Crown increasingly had been turning its crusading zeal inward, into Europe, to maintain control over its previously conquered souls and sources of revenue. The ideological challenges of Protestantism had evoked a rapid, prolonged, and expensive military response that had required Carlos V and, after 1556, his son and heir Felipe II, to guard jealously the national resources. The matter of *La Florida*'s claim to those precious resources would have to be held in abeyance—but not for long.

The Maskókî Art of Negotiation

Of the two converse paradigms, the anthropological and the historical, posited by Sturtevant and quoted at the opening of this chapter, it is the anthropological that has the most to offer in terms of our understanding of the negotiations taking place between Spaniards and the broad spectrum of Maskókî peoples in the Southeast in the sixteenth century. Rodrigo Ranjel saw it; Oviedo realized it; and we must as well. The willingness of the Spaniards to resort, all too rapidly, to the ultimate negotiating tools did not allow achievement of the purpose for which these

Table 1

Negotiating Range of the Maskókî Peoples

1. Diplomatic negotiations
    a. Rhetoric of peace
    b. Alliance (nonmilitary, voluntary)
2. Nonviolent displays of power
    a. Panoply as power
    b. Power discourse
    c. Feint/attack (as power display)
3. Unarmed resistance
    a. Flight (as a denial of logistical support)
    b. Deception
    c. Disdain to fight
    d. Suicide
4. Acquiescence under duress (fear/force)
5. Alliance (military)
6. Armed resistance
7. Aggression

tools were intended. Over the ensuing century and a half, the Spaniards modified, or, at least, attenuated, their responses to *La Florida*'s peoples, in order to accommodate the unique circumstances with which they were confronted.

Thus the historian's converse hypothesis, that differences in colonial relations are largely a result of "differing European policies and actions and institutions," is also accurate, but only as far as it goes, because the impetus for the change came not from any unilateral desire on the part of the Europeans themselves but, rather, from their confrontations with peoples whom they could not conquer so easily. With either paradigm, however, we still fall short of creating a representative picture of the Maskókî peoples' interactions with the Spaniards for one fundamental reason: both hypotheses reempower the Native implicitly, but not explicitly.

It is important to understand, as far as possible, the reality of the Maskókî peoples' range of negotiating tools throughout the Entrada Phase. Diplomatic negotiation, consisting of nonviolent discussion and the possibility of bilateral decisions, was always an option for the Natives. Conversely, the maximum negotiation, based on the unilateral introduction of physical violence and the willingness to end lives, remained an option for the Maskókî people as well. In fact, the range of negotiating tactics available to the Natives never actually changed throughout the entire first Spanish colonial period.

This realization is critical to an understanding of the actions of the Maskókî peoples, because it directly contradicts the image of diminishing alternatives that has been perpetrated by Spaniards and perpetuated by succeeding Euroamericans. Sometimes, the diplomatic alternative was successful, such as at those times when the European intruders left a Native group, taking with them nothing more than a small supply of food, freely given. At other times, the diplomatic alternative gained Native war leaders a negotiated temporary military alliance, as a result of which Spanish soldiers went into battle to support Native objectives. Sometimes, diplomacy was not successful, such as those times when the Spaniards preempted dialogue with attack. However, the range of possibilities remained the same.

At no point during the Entrada Phase did the Natives fully see—nor could they have foreseen—that their contacts with the Europeans were not isolated instances. That is, the Maskókî peoples had no way of internalizing the knowledge that there were powerful and populous polities living beyond an ocean who were able and willing to commit tremendous human and economic resources, over an extended period of time, to effect total dominion over the Native Americans and their territories. This was to their advantage, however, because, despite the fact that the Spaniards attempted, regularly, to impress this *on* them as a reality and to impress them *with* this (Spanish) reality, and despite the fact that a limited number of individuals undoubtedly came to accept the Spaniards' assertions *as* reality, the overall attitude of the Maskókî peoples did not change. Their world was their own, and their prerogatives remained their own.

This was clearly visible in the actions of the tribes as well as in their reactions to the Spaniards' range of negotiating tools. Their actions and reactions were all indigenous response mechanisms. They hardly could have been anything else, particularly at this early phase of contact. That is to say, in every instance in which the Native peoples interacted with the Spaniards, they did so in the currency of well-tested combinations of traditional responses drawn directly from their own social repertoires.

Even though the demands of the newcomers may have been extraordinary in terms of the Natives' previous experiences, the actions of the Natives were all composed of ordinary elements, and these were not uniformly capitulations to Spanish pressures. Every type of response was firmly anchored in the cultural matrix and informed by a unilateral assumption of the inherent transcendency of its symbolic universe. Furthermore, as facets of Native negotiation, the responses relied upon the inherent flexibility of the Maskókî culture to incorporate the New.

The negotiating postures utilized by the Maskókî peoples clearly fell into several categories, examples of which abound in the rhetoric of the Spaniards. The most pacific end of the negotiating spectrum may be characterized as a diplomatic negotiation, in which two autonomous negotiants met each other with no expectations of losing significant prerogatives. In these encounters, the southeastern peoples showed signs of amicability and a willingness to interact with the newcomers on nonconfrontational terms. First meetings between Natives and Spaniards, for example, frequently were characterized by wholly diplomatic negotiating postures.

De Soto's *entradistas,* in but one example, "entered a large province called Coça. The Indians came out to receive them peaceably and treated them in a very friendly manner, giving them [of their own volition] provisions and guides for their march from one pueblo to another."[27] Admittedly, Coça was a large, wealthy, and powerful polity that may be judged, even at this later date, to have had little to fear from the strangers. However, its actions were not unique among those of the Maskókî peoples. Later in the Spaniards' ramblings, the cacique Ycasqui informed de Soto's party that he had been hearing about them for a long time and was sufficiently impressed with the reports that he wanted to preclude war.[28] Although in this case the Spaniards ultimately used their own deceptions to manipulate Native belief systems, the fact remains that the Natives clearly operated from their own decision-making base.

Cabeça de Vaca found Natives who actively and publicly commiserated with him and his companions over their misfortunes, solely because the Natives' own social traditions required such commiseration as a responsibility of friendship.[29] Cabeça de Vaca found "kindness and good will" among many of the Natives with whom he and his *entradistas* interacted.[30] Cabeça de Vaca's general summation, concerning all of the Natives whom he encountered east of the Mississippi River, indicates quite clearly the autonomy that they valued. He saw that "whoever would fight them must be cautious to show no fear, or desire to have anything that is theirs; while war exists they must be treated with the utmost rigor; for if they discover any timidity or covetousness, they are a race that well discern the opportunities for vengeance, and gather strength from any weakness of their adversaries."[31]

As a subset of diplomatic negotiation, the Maskókî peoples were willing to appease or accommodate the Others, even to the temporary expedient of acquiescing until such time as they might regain their own prerogatives by whatever means necessary, including deception and the application of force. Within Maskókî society, there was no onus attached to the use of deception in gaining one's objectives in antagonistic negotiations. Such an ability marked intellectual cunning, which was an added virtue in a warrior who already possessed military cunning. Needless to say, the Spaniards perceived the actions of the Natives as reprehensible, while they characterized their own deceptions as necessary means to positive ends.

The Maskókî peoples, for their part, frequently saw in the strangers and their unique military weaponry the possibility of buttressing their own authority over tributary or antagonistic tribes. Warfare was the principal business of the Native men and they sought military alliance with these Others whenever they believed that they might use such an alliance to their own successful ends. As de Soto's *entradistas* passed the cacique Guachoya, for example, the people awaited the Spaniards on the river and importuned them to make war on Guachoya's nearby enemies, promising the Spaniards military support. De Soto declined, fearing a trap.[32]

In 1564, however, the Timuguana leader, Outina, negotiated a military alliance with the French troops of René de Laudonnière against Potanou, a nearby rival leader. Outina consulted with his seer, who informed him that the numbers of the enemy were great and, consequently, Outina considered discarding his war plan as unworkable. The French commander disparaged him, however, accusing him of "lacking courage and of being a poor leader."[33] The rhetorical challenge was successful. The French, willing to take the front lines of the battle in order to impress foe and ally alike, tipped the balance of the fighting and the enemy was routed. However, the French commander, not understanding the warfare system of the Natives, expressed "great wrath" when Outina left the field, considering his point made and uninterested in pursuing the victory further.

The Maskókî people were very aware of the value of panoply and display and preemptive negotiating strategies. Panoply and ceremony remain central elements of power negotiating to this day. Whenever the Native leaders had sufficient opportunity to prepare for their initial encounters with Spaniards, they prepared themselves with ceremony, panoply, and whatever degree of pomp their material culture resources could support. They did this for exactly the same reasons as did the Spaniards: to indicate and illustrate power and to exercise dominance in the ensuing negotiations.

On October 31, 1528, as the Narváez *entradistas* negotiated with Natives for an exchange of prisoners, the leaders of the tribe appeared in court attire. The Spaniards were, indeed, impressed and described them as "comely and of more authority and condition than any we had seen before."[34] De Soto and his entourage were met by many ceremonial groups. For example, a cacica was brought out to meet them "with much prestige," carried on a litter covered with white cloth. She spoke to de Soto with "much grace and self assurance," but when she gave him a string of pearls that she took from around her own neck, Rodrigo Ranjel assumed that she did it only to ingratiate herself with the governor.[35] He could not have conceived of the possibility that she might not have considered it necessary to ingratiate herself with de Soto.

The Spaniards, being far from home, deep in a potentially hostile land, and usually outnumbered, purposely chose as their principal negotiating posture a bold attempt to create a climate of fear whenever possible. When a messenger from the powerful lord of Tascaluça approached de Soto's camp at Talisi (in Coça), de Soto told his men that "those on horseback should gallop, and sound the trumpets (more to impose fear, than to make ceremony with such a reception)."[36] The Natives, he found, were capable of using exactly the same strategy. They stalked his company, attacked at hours considered dishonorable in European warfare, and generally harassed the Spaniards with hit-and-run tactics that denied the Spaniards the option of direct confrontation.

When diplomatic negotiation and panoply failed, and the prospect of military victory seemed limited, the Natives attempted to appease the volatile Spaniards, at least as far as necessary in order to regain their own power position. They acquiesced to demands for bearers and women, gave canoes and corn, built or lent shelters, and generally attempted to encourage the marauders to move on. On other occasions, the Natives burned their own villages, destroyed their granaries, and deserted an area in order to deny logistical support to the Spaniards.[37] As has been discussed earlier, this mechanism of vacating a village or town site was a well-established feature of the social repertoire and probably was associated, in this instance, with a realistic view of an imbalance in military potential.

In a large number of instances, however, the Maskókî peoples and their neighbors were perfectly willing to resort to negotiation based on direct force, just as were the Spaniards. The main differences in the two approaches to force lay in the facts that, first, the Maskókî people employed hit-and-run tactics that were not a part of the classic European military repertoire, and, second, unlike the Spaniards, they attached no stigma to departing the field of battle if the odds appeared unfavorable for any reason. These elements of the militaristic warrior mentality of the Maskokálgî retained their strength into the twentieth century, until the time when Maskókî people began to enlist in the United States military establishment and to submit to a more Euroamerican mentality in regard to warfare.

War parties attacked principally in the middle of the night, reserving the element of surprise as much as possible. However, they also exercised their options of aggression by going out to meet the Spaniards and doing battle with them, or by just goading them with hit-and-run attacks to take the measure of their ability and willingness to respond, at any juncture at which success seemed feasible or critical.[38]

It is undeniable that the fire power available to the Spaniards, in the form of the arquebus and the crossbow, was a technological advantage of no small proportions. Not all of the southeastern peoples were awed by their advantages, however, and this factor must be kept in proportion in evaluating power discourse also. Cabeça de Vaca wrote: "So effectual is their maneuvering that they can receive little injury from cross bow or arquebus; they rather scoff at them; for these arms are of little value employed in open field, where the Indians move nimbly about."[39] Nor did the Spaniards receive full value from the hot, heavy armor that they had transported across the ocean. The power and precision of the *La Florida* warriors' arrows, especially cane arrow shafts tipped with chert projectile points, rendered the Spaniards' metal shells less than satisfactory as protection.[40] In conjunction with the southeastern heat and the fact that reflected sunlight on burnished metal made the Spaniards walking targets, the armor became almost a liability. Spaniards soon discarded their metal jackets for quilted cotton "armor" that they acquired from the Natives.[41]

In the open, where crossbows and arquebuses had diminished effectiveness, horses were important in creating in the minds of the Maskókî people not only doubts about their own abilities to protect themselves adequately but also questions about the sources of these extraordinary items. Doubts are the seeds of fear. Cabeça de Vaca reported: "Everywhere else [i.e., in the open] the horse will best subdue, being what the natives universally dread."[42] Nonetheless, the fact remains that the Native people continued to aggress and resist and exercise the full range of their prerogatives despite the fact that later Euroamerican historians have chosen to characterize them as demoralized and having diminished alternatives.

In the case of the horse, we must also remember that the Maskóki people never formed a social preference for its use in the way that southwestern Native peoples did. They would tend herds of the descendants of the horses brought by the Spaniards but would prefer cattle and pigs and would not become horsemen in the manner of the Plains Natives. What may well be one clue to the Natives' imaging of the horse in the Southeast is still available today. Seminole elders recall that the old name for horse is simply "big deer," or *ichî chobî* (Mikísuukî) and *icho thlocco* (Maskókî), and that their ancestors used these terms before they borrowed the word *caballo* (Mikísuukî, *cawayî*, and Maskókî, *coäko*) from the Spaniards. In other words, the Natives imaged the horse in terms of an already known entity rather than a potentially frightening unknown entity. Certainly, the terrain over which the Maskókî tribes ranged did not always facilitate the use of the horse. Swampy, low-lying areas provided little advantage to horseback riders. It appears that the Maskókî peoples knew this all too well.

Even Stones Have Virtues

No discussion of the negotiatory discourses that took place between the Spaniards and the Maskókî people would be complete without including some mention of the impact of signs and wonders on the balance of power. This is not an element that properly can be included in the classic range of negotiating tools, since signs and wonders may or may not be elements that can be included in the negotiation and manipulated at will by either party. From the Spaniards' point of view, signs and wonders were an opportunistic element of the negotiations. From our point of view, they are another of those elements of southeastern history that has been the occasion of much confusion and denigration of the Natives over time. From the Maskókî peoples' point of view, we must discover what they really were, and are.

In the category of signs and wonders we must place such events as sick Natives getting well shortly after the Spaniards prayed for them or made the sign of the cross over them.[43] In other events, lightning might strike a ball game pole in a village of recalcitrants, moving them to view the Spaniards in a more friendly manner, or a Spanish-planted cross might be thought to bring rain.[44] These are but a few examples of myriad instances in which power in the seen and unseen worlds seemed to merge for a specific instant.

The Spaniards were themselves Roman Catholics and adherents of a religious belief system that holds among the most basic tenets of its credo many signs and wonders, such as human resurrection after death, a virgin conception, and the ritualized transubstantiation of bread and wine into human flesh and blood at the instigation of a specially designated priest. However, as we have discussed earlier, Roman Catholicism cloaked itself in a righteousness that sought to retain power unilaterally, by constantly seeking to remove or denigrate the power of every other belief system.

In the case of the Maskókî people, the Spaniards characterized their every reaction to unseen forces as emanating from one of two sources. If the reaction paralleled any segment of the belief structure of Roman Catholicism, and could be manipulated to its ends, then the source of the reaction was declared to be the Roman Catholic god (for example, in the events mentioned above). If the reaction was not parallel, then its source could only be Satan and the confusion produced by his misleading power. In one collateral example of a nonparallel response, the French members of the Laudonnière entrada, products of Roman Catholicism, used the negative explanation on the Timuguana leader Outina when he consulted his seer before committing himself to battle against a powerful enemy.[45] Regardless of its source, however, the instances of most signs and wonders became occasions for the issuance of some opportunistic power rhetoric by the Spaniards, and, in many instances, the rhetoric had, at least partially, its desired effect. It promulgated fear or awe or devotion in the minds of the Natives, which permitted the Spaniards to effect a power shift away from the Natives' own social hierarchy and toward a Spanish social hierarchy.

Because the power of signs and wonders was predicated upon unseen forces, and because their influence was not always visible but depended for real efficacy upon the durability of an internal shift that could not be directly controlled, their impact was difficult to gauge. The most profound impact could be the basis of a true "conversion," an ideological shift of potentially permanent duration. Even at its least profound, however, the impact could create a mentality of fear and submission that also could be useful to the Spanish cause, although this mentality would be of unpredictable duration. The chasm that lay between the two extreme possibilities proved to be one of the Natives' many advantages.

However, another, and much greater, advantage that accrued to the Na-

"Outina Consults a Sorcerer." Theodore de Bry's 1591
engraving (plate 12) from the *Brevis narratio* of Jacques le Moyne
(published in Lorant, *The New World,* 59)

tives was that imparted by their circular cosmogony, and for this advantage
the Spaniards had no intellectual frame of reference or interest. Cabeça de
Vaca reported an exchange with some of the Natives in the Southeast that
illustrates this point well. At one point, the Natives wished the Spaniards
to assist them by curing the sick. The Spaniards laughed at them and de-
murred, saying that they had no training or art in such matters. So the Natives exercised their prerogatives and withheld food from the Spaniards—a
potent weapon—until they should acquiesce.

> Seeing our persistence, an Indian told me that I knew not what I ut-
> tered, in saying that what he knew availed nothing; for stones and other
> matters growing about in the field, have virtue, and that passing a peb-
> ble along the stomach would take away pain and restore health, and cer-
> tainly then we who were extraordinary men must possess power and
> efficacy over all other things.[46]

Non-Native researchers almost uniformly have dismissed this type of
discourse set as "magic" or "witchcraft."[47] The true beauty of this state-

ment, however, lies in the recognition that it is an obvious product of a circular cosmogony. It is clear refutation of the Conquest rhetoric that depicts the cosmogony of the Maskókî people as brittle and closed. That short-sighted view images the Spaniards as having confronted the Natives with a reality that could not be contained in their world view and that, somehow, caused their cultural collapse.[48] The reality was exactly the opposite and if social scientists are not saying so with conviction yet, at least they are moving away from the classic Conquest model.[49]

The circular cosmogony is inclusionary to a degree impossible in the linear construct. The fact that the Maskókî peoples could include within their operative world view the daily interaction of the seen and unseen and the manipulation of both of those worlds was unprecedented within the systemic parameters of linealism. Roman Catholic priests were merely the mediums who channeled forces that they did not command. Among the Maskokálgî, seers and shamans moved between the two worlds and manipulated the forces themselves.

In the interactions between the Maskókî and the Spaniards, an understanding of this dichotomy is important because it opens the door to our understanding of the prerogatives that the Maskókî peoples retained, even under the pressures of European interposition, and of the flexibility of a Native belief system that could incorporate the New without having to dismiss the Old.

During the entire Entrada Phase in *La Florida,* when the Spaniards had almost exclusive access to the Maskókî peoples in the Southeast, they did not accumulate sufficient demographic numbers or numbers of arms to enforce their ideological dominance upon the people to a degree consistent with their own (the Spaniards') propaganda. Despite the Spaniards' comings and goings, the Natives continued to exercise their entire range of prerogatives throughout the period. With the settlement of San Agustín, in 1565, would come an era of radically, but selectively, increased social and cultural pressures on the Maskókî peoples. Even so, however, their range of negotiating tools would remain the same and their sociocultural range of responses would remain couched in the same matrix. Their cosmogony, flexible and absorbent, would endure.

7 El Sombrero de Tres Picos

> The essential purpose ... [of the establishment of San Agustín was] to found viable agricultural settlements. As in Spain, the farmers were to cluster around villages; the town was to be the spearhead for the advance of Castilian civilization.
>
> —Eugene Lyon[1]

> The next daye in the morninge, being the ffirst of Maye, we assaied to enter this porte.... We perceived a good numbre of the Indians, inhabytantes there, coming along the sandes and seebank somewhate nere unto us, without any taken of feare or dowbte.... And as I began to go towardes [their leader], he sett fourthe and came and received me gentlye and [rose] after there mannour, all his men following him with great silence and modestie, yea, with more than our men did.
>
> —Jean Ribault[2]

The cumulative image of *La Florida* created in the minds of the Iberian Spaniards as reports of the entradas spread was not uniformly positive. De Soto's men had discounted the possibility of large profits. Cabeça de Vaca reported the natural beauties of the land, but the costs—human and economic—to both entradas to obtain that information were undeniable. Consequently, reports of the many natural beauties of *La Florida* notwithstanding, the potential for profits seemed too low relative to the labor- and capital-intensive efforts that would be required to realize those profits. In particular, the Natives were viewed as too bellicose. Too many times already they had killed Spaniards and rejected the gospel of Roman Catholicism. It appeared that *La Florida* would be neither a fertile field of souls nor a rich land of quick profits.

Both of these considerations weighed heavily on the new king, Felipe II. In 1556, his father had abdicated the Spanish Crown in his favor, although Carlos's Germanic kinsmen would not give Felipe the Holy Roman Emperorship as well. Carlos V retired the field, as it were, defeated. Felipe II inherited the largest empire in the history of the Western world and enough problems to fill that empire. He had Protestant wars in Europe,

Native rebellions in the Americas (not to mention ambitious and avaricious Spanish subjects there as well), and bankruptcy at home; Spain's sea-veins madly pumped American gold and silver into their mother country in a determined effort to save the Spanish body politic.

However, in the years after 1492, Colón's path to Spain's new world had expanded into Europe's superhighway. Despite what Spain saw as its a priori rights to settlement and exploitation, and despite the decisions codified in the Treaty of Tordecillas and the Papal Donation of 1493, which definitively divided the discoveries between Spain and its earliest rival, Portugal, the other powers of Europe were not willing to stay out of American waters or out of the race for the Americas' vast potential profits. In the final analysis, these concerns turned out to be decisive factors in Spanish settlement efforts in *La Florida*.

By the sixth decade of the sixteenth century, Spain's most irksome rivals were the French and the English—but especially the French—both of whom were responding to the twin European beliefs that there was a river that began somewhere on North America's Atlantic coast and gave access to the Pacific and that southern Spain's parallel latitudes in the Americas would be rich and fertile lands.[3] The French, in particular, also had rationalized Spain's rhetorical claims to *La Florida* with their own counter-rhetoric, espoused as the doctrine of effective occupation.[4] By the 1550s, the French had published sufficient reports of their explorations along the Atlantic coastline to permit them to justify extending their American claims southward from forty degrees south latitude to what is now Cape Florida.

In the highly politicized French model, all territories not physically occupied by the Spaniards were not considered to be Spanish properties, Spanish claims and papal bulls notwithstanding. In other words, regardless of what Spain claimed as her territory, in the final analysis all that really mattered was what she could hold, and this, more than any other reality, was the one that would guide the European fate of *La Florida* for the coming two and one-half centuries, until 1821, when Spain would no longer be able to hold any of it.

For the Maskókî peoples of *La Florida*, however, this was truly a foreign reality, in every sense of the word. European observers and Euroamerican historians certainly have sought to impose it upon them over the years and certainly have filtered their history through it ad absurdum. However, there is no reason, beyond the dictates of cultural chauvinism, to believe that the Abalachi or the Escampaba/Calus or the Teguesta or the Coça gave

way so easily to an image of a land divided—to a "Conquest" subordination that deprived them of their ancient prerogatives and their freedom of
movement and required them to commit cultural suicide in exchange for
cast-iron pots and hatchets and the dictates of a pale, white *dies irae.*

Even in the mid-seventeenth century, at the zenith of Spanish pressure
(the period that twentieth-century Euroamerican historians have named
the "Golden Age" of the Spanish missions), the majority of the Maskókî
peoples still would be configuring their actions within their own universe
and expressing their responses in the context of their own domains of interest. And when, in 1717—a full two centuries after the Europeans began
their negotiations with the Maskókî peoples—a Spanish official would
characterize the descendants of the same peoples as "children of self interest," he would be more correct than he knew. What he would fail to ap-
preciate was that he was also a child of self-interest, but within a separate
realm of interest. In addition, his willingness to condemn the Natives for
their unwillingness to part with their reality would be excellent evidence
that they had not, indeed, done so.

During the 1550s and 1560s, a period of particularly intense French
competition, the Spanish Crown lost ground in the Caribbean and the
south Atlantic and sought to regain it at the treaty tables of Europe. In
the assessment of one historian, by 1556 Spain "had almost lost control of
the waters of the Caribbean and of [Habana] . . . , the assembly point for
Spanish ships returning to Europe with the treasures of the Americas."[5]
Spain's plans for a coherent defensive line across *La Florida* to Pánuco in
Nueva España and across other parts of the Americas had not yet been
realized, as evidenced in the failures of the *La Florida* entradas. As a result,
the silver *flotas* were being required to convoy along the main commercial
routes, the most dangerous of the sea-lanes and the very routes used by all
of Spain's enemies.

Iberian interest in *La Florida,* because of its strategic position, revived.
Dr. Pedro de Santander, a King's *veedor* (inspector) on his way to Nueva
España, outlined five reasons the Crown should reinvigorate its efforts to
settle *La Florida* and, in so doing, echoed the growing sentiments of his
countrymen.[6] Security for Spanish shipping was his first priority, followed
by the need to occupy the land effectively and preclude occupation by
other powers. Then, Spanish occupation would, obviously, expand the
Spanish empire, provide new souls for conversion to Roman Catholicism,
and open new fields of potential profit for those Spaniards who had not yet
found wealth in other parts of the Spanish colonial Americas.[7] These were

excellent rationales all, but His Most Catholic Majesty would require one more "push," from other sources, before *La Florida*'s settlement would take on sufficient import for him to commit to it Spain's precious resources.

The Spanish Beachhead

In 1562 and 1564–1565, the French provided the push. Three entradas established short-lived garrisoned settlements on the Atlantic coast of *La Florida*, under Jean Ribault at Port Royal and René de Laudonnière at the mouth of the River of San Juan or, as the French called it, the River of May (now the St. John's River). These they effected even as French and Spanish diplomats negotiated nonintervention in Europe and Ayllón readied his (ultimately abortive) Santa Elena entrada.

For the next two decades Spain and France would compete for a foothold in the Southeast, and the Spaniards would prevail. As is so often the case, ultimate Spanish success would not be based upon European diplomacy or royal mandates but upon the human element at the lowest common denominator: at the interactive level of human being to human being, in the heat and mosquitoes and hurricanes of peninsular *La Florida*, where Native American, Spanish, and French powers met.

The individual who finally negotiated the feat that no previous Spaniard had been able to effect—the safe establishment of a permanent Spanish presence in *La Florida*—was Pedro Menéndez de Avilés. Menéndez was Spain's premier seaman, a Roman Catholic of devotion almost equal to that of his employer, Felipe II, and a member of a large and highly ambitious family. In critical ways, Menéndez was the first of *La Florida*'s *asiento* holders who was not a Colón legatee. For the Natives, however, he was only, in the final analysis, a single island of plausibility in a sea of negotiatory treachery.

A native of the Iberian province of Asturias with noble family connections, Menéndez had demonstrated the outstanding nautical abilities that made him so useful to his king in encounters with French corsairs in the north Atlantic. That is to say, he had gained his reputation by dealing with other Europeans, according to classical rules of warfare, rather than with Native Americans according to "just war" rationalizations.

This is not to say that the possibility of using the just war concept would remain beyond Pedro Menéndez, who, in fact, would attempt later to apply it to the Ais peoples of *La Florida*'s eastern peninsular coast. In 1571 he and his companions had a narrow escape from the peremptory challenges of the Ais after a shipwreck near Cabo de Cañaveral. In the face of such outright power as the Ais presented, Menéndez would have had them all declared slaves so that, within his own rationalized universe, he might use retaliatory force to capture them and sell them in the islands to recoup his expense of Conquest. After a year and a half of consideration, however, Felipe's Consejo de las Indias denied his petition.[8] Menéndez complied with the decision.

In 1550, Spain's Casa de Contratación, its Indies House of Trade, gave Menéndez license to take two ships to Tierra Firme for trade. However, French corsairs again threatened his country's profits as well as his own and Menéndez sought and obtained a position as captain general of the Crown's Indies fleets. From this powerful and lucrative position (in terms of access to trade and contraband), Menéndez gained both revenues and enemies. The Casa charged him and his brother/partner with smuggling. However, his friends and family connections ultimately prevailed. This was crucial to Menéndez, whose forte was and remained sea operations and military command. The complex intrigues of the land-based court with its competing family interests were forever detrimental to him.

Felipe had taken him, among his guard, to England for the prince's wedding to Mary Tudor, the eldest daughter of Henry VIII. Afterward, Menéndez stayed in Europe to fight more Frenchmen in the waters between England and Flanders, further entrenching his position by filling supportive posts with family members and providing invaluable safe escort for the moneys that supported the Spanish victory over the French at St. Quentin in 1557. For this last service, in particular, he was rewarded with personal honors from the English Catholic Queen Mary and the Spanish Catholic King Felipe II. As a result of the victory, the Spaniards and the French made European peace, at Cateau-Cambrésis, in 1559. The issue of effective occupation of the Americas, however, remained unsettled despite intense negotiations.

By 1562, King Felipe was in an extremely difficult position—even more difficult than usual. A second marriage alliance, this time with the French princess Elizabeth of Valois (the tragic Mary Tudor had died in 1558), had not tempered French aspirations in North America. Also, the Spanish treasury was recovering again from bankruptcy; even American gold could not offset the costs of the Protestant wars in Europe and military losses to the Barbary raiders in the Mediterranean.

The Americas were pumping blood into the Iberian body, but, as physical extremities of that body, they were constantly attempting to exercise far too much independence. Despite efforts to maintain strict controls on the individuals who were permitted to emigrate to the Americas, and strict controls on Felipe's subjects once they were in the Americas, the proximity of natural treasures and the possibility of preferment and wealth that would have been unattainable in the closed social system of Spain made the risks of disobedience to royal authority acceptable, even exciting. In contrast to many who flaunted Felipe's will, Menéndez was a king's man—a little smuggling and a lot of family loyalty notwithstanding.

When Ayllón's mandate to settle and fortify Santa Elena went unfulfilled, Felipe almost despaired of settling *La Florida* and he found little reason to do so either. In 1562, the French Huguenot admiral, Gaspard de Coligny, sent Jean Ribault to reconnoiter and settle in *La Florida*. He established a colony at Port Royal, essentially the area of the Spaniards' earlier Santa Elena, leaving thirty men to their fate.[9] After mutiny and near starvation, the survivors were rescued from small sailing craft by Englishmen and taken to England. The colony had lasted one year.

Finally, Felipe determined to make one last attempt. This time, he asked a man whom he considered both an excellent seaman and a trustworthy vassal, Don Pedro Menéndez de Avilés, to end the French pretensions by establishing a Spanish presence. However, by the spring of 1565, before Menéndez could supply himself and depart, word of another French entrada spurred the Crown to add troops and monies to the expedition.

René de Laudonnière had led the second settlement attempt, in 1564, and Jean Ribault returned to supply him in 1565, on exactly the same day on which Pedro Menéndez finally arrived to (successfully) drive the French out. The second French voyage established a fortified colony at the mouth of the River of May. It lasted for barely thirteen months.

On all of their voyages the French interacted directly and, for the most part, peacefully with the southeastern Natives; certainly more peacefully than did the Spaniards, on the whole. Although they shared with the Spaniards a willingness to resort to force as a standard element of negotiation, the French exercised force with less frequency. However, despite certain short-range differences in their approaches, the long-range objectives of both European Christian groups were the same.

René Laudonnière, decrying the cruelties of the colonizing methods of the Romans in the introduction to his *Three Voyages*, explained more than he realized. After staining their rivers and lands with the blood of the foreign peoples whom they had sought to conquer militarily, he said, the Romans had found their own country overrun and destroyed by the foreigners. "These results, I say, are contrary to the rewards received by those who are only interested in the public good, that is, in the universal well-being of the people, and try to bring unity one with the other, more by foreign commerce and communications than by military measures, *except when these foreigners do not want to pay attention to their obligations which are so beneficial to them*"[10] (emphasis added).

This is simply the Roman Catholic concept of the just war, in its commercial guise. The Natives were expected to know, intuitively, that their best interests lay in complete capitulation and cooperation with their cultural betters. If they did not "pay attention," then "military measures," that is, force and violence, were justified. Laudonnière continued, listing the objectives of the French monarchy in exploration and settlement. "So, monarchs have sent out enterprising persons to establish themselves in distant lands to make a profit, to civilize the countryside, and, if possible, to bring the local inhabitants to the true knowledge of God."[11] Indeed, the Timuguana were still trading with the French until at least 1580.[12]

However, in addition to France's overtly commercial realm of interest, here we see also that the differences in contact approaches and negotiating postures among the western European powers were more of emphasis than of objective. Among the French, commerce was of the first importance and religious conversion was an option. Among the English, as discussed earlier, land ownership was paramount, commerce was its natural by-product, and religious conversion was largely irrelevant. Among the Spaniards, Conquest of land and Conquest of souls melded perfectly in a crusading ideal that had all the Christian earmarks of an Islamic jihad. Among all three, however, death remained a viable negotiating resource.

The episodes of Menéndez's arrival at the head of *La Florida*'s peninsula just in time to confront Ribault's ships, his establishment of San Agustín (on August 28, the feast of St. Augustine, bishop of Hippo), his subsequent forced march through a hurricane to destroy the French Fort Caroline, his sea chase southward to capture shipwrecked escapees, and his execution of almost all of them have been told and retold in fascinating detail, by contemporaries and historians alike.[13] Within seven short weeks, Menéndez was the European winner in the battle for "possession" of *La Florida*. Spain announced her victory to the world. What had been merely a philosophical reality became an operative reality for the Spaniards: but not for the Natives.

Settlement and Cultural Transposition

Menéndez worked swiftly and well to establish a family base of wealth on his *asiento* lands. The harbor and land that Menéndez sighted on the feast day of St. Augustine had all the characteristics of a useful military base, but it was not his intention for it to become a capital city as well. It was the much-touted Santa Elena that was his first choice for *La Florida*'s capital. Santa Elena would become the centerpiece of the *mayorazco* or entailed estate that Menéndez would be permitted to create, in order to protect his concessions and family accretions, as well as the Atlantic anchor for the long-envisioned military chain of fortifications connecting Pánuco in Nueva España and *La Florida*, which he intended to make a reality.

For several reasons, however, predominantly including Native resistance and Spanish mutinies, Santa Elena proved not to be a viable colony, whereas San Agustín survived. Even as the two small military colonies (or presidial colonies, as one historian characterizes them) struggled to maintain the Spanish presence, they also struggled to establish a negotiating posture with the surrounding Natives. This negotiation, which lasted as long as the Spanish presence in *La Florida*, has been periodized by several researchers relative to various facets of its existence and the presence of the Spaniards.

Sturtevant cites periods of Exploration, Co-existence, Missionization, Depopulation, and Diplomacy, focusing on the interactions of the Spaniards and the Native Americans.[14] Bushnell, always directing our attention to the Spaniards and their colonization efforts, divides *La Florida*'s existence into periods of *Adelantamiento*, Nearer Pacifications, Farther Pacifications, Building of the Castillo, and the Walled City.[15] Only in a reference to Sturtevant's Co-existence period does she mention a process of negotiation, in which "the Spaniards and Indians attempted to influence each other's behavior through trade, diplomacy, and war."[16] This process of mutual influence, however, was ubiquitous throughout the periods that I call, simply, the Entrada and Settlement phases. The process did not begin and end in one, short, arbitrarily defined period. From the point of view of the Maskókî peoples, only the frequency and intensity of the negotiations varied over time.

The Spaniards imaged themselves as overlords of the land that they claimed and named *La Florida*. Pedro Menéndez envisioned Santa Elena as his capital and San Agustín as a flourishing tributary in his province of "Oristan": two rich seaport cities to anchor the wealthy estate of a seafaring man and his family. His plan was hardly overambitious, for the most part, given the bountiful returns obtained by other Spanish entrepreneurs in the Americas. Inevitably, however, in the business of adventuring, the highest yield attaches to the highest risk.

The part of Menéndez's plan that was overly ambitious was his basic assumption that a land with no proven major deposits of natural resources to draw settlers, but with a large number of openly antagonistic prior occupants to repel settlers, could be made sufficiently attractive through the force of his own will and the strategic use of his family's venture capital. Possibly the land could have been attractive: *if* enough of the maintenance costs could have been shifted to the king's treasury without shifting control as well; *if* a critical mass of colonists could have been found; and *if* the Natives had been less their own masters and more predisposed to internalize Spanish hegemony along with Spanish Catholic ideology, instead of determinedly choosing life, liberty, and the pursuit of quality trade items.

That is not to say that some of the Maskókî peoples did not, to varying degrees, internalize religion and culture along with the trade items. However, when we look at the Maskókî-Spanish negotiation in its totality, we must keep in mind the realities with which the Spaniards dealt daily and not merely the elements of the story that seem to support foregone cultural conclusions. For example, it is important to recall that, because the Spaniards withstood and fended off numerous diplomatic and military assaults upon their imaged overlordship of *La Florida,* they did, in fact, remain the sole Europeans in direct and continuing contact with the Maskókî peoples for the first 160 years of European interposition.

As we have seen earlier, however, at no point did Spanish demographics even approach, much less equal, those of the Maskókî peoples, except in very limited areas and at very limited times. Consequently, rather than widespread contact and control, over the duration of their unilateral tenure the Spaniards managed to effect only the creation of what may be termed a "power corridor" across the head of the *La Florida* peninsula. This corridor, the primary axis of which was the chain of missions that spread westward from San Agustín through the province of Timugua and, finally, into but not through the province of Abalachi, was neither continuous nor stable, but within its confines, the Spaniards were able to exert greater influence on the Natives' imaging of themselves than in any other area of *La Florida.*

Other realities bore upon the degree of influence, however. First was the fact that the influence was continuing, but not continuous. Severely limited military and logistical support, and insufficient supplies and numbers of missionaries, together with inevitable and continuing military challenges by the Natives, made it impossible for the Spaniards to physically saturate the corridor, much less the entire territorial range of *La Florida*. In addition to all of these elements, the Spaniards' internal power struggles, occasioned by civil, military, and religious competition for the limited resources and for access to the Native labor pool, hampered any concerted and long-term use of those resources (see below).

Second was the fact that, throughout the period, the Native peoples continued to exercise their prerogatives to physically quit the Spanish sphere of influence, Spanish admonitions and threats notwithstanding. They defected from missions, from villages, from employment at *ranchos* (fortified ranches) and *haciendas* (farms), and from civic work projects and bearer assignments. All of these considerations will be discussed at greater length in the next chapter; suffice it to say here that the Spaniards had ample evidence of the precariousness of their ability to exert influence over the Natives and demonstrated as much in their actions and official reports.

As a further example of the realities with which the Spaniards dealt, we must consider the military and political exigencies of their own world, beyond their negotiations with the Maskókî peoples. Their ability to negotiate unilaterally with the Natives ended abruptly in 1670. In that year, the Spanish and English Crowns concluded the Treaty of Madrid, by which Spain bowed to international pressures and recognized long-standing English claims to the "Carolina" Province, the southern border of which was set at the Savannah River, deep inside *La Florida* and a mere 175 land miles up the Atlantic coast from the Spanish guns at San Agustín.

After the English established a southeastern base of operations at Charles Towne, the freedom of the Spaniards to pursue their own agendas with the Natives was severely impaired by the necessity to outbid and outnegotiate the English, whose national coffers had not been so radically depleted as had those of the Spaniards over the preceding half century. English traders began to move into the interior of the Southeast with all deliberate speed, sealing their commercial negotiations with increased qualities and quantities of trade wares and turning the formerly bilateral negotiations into trilateral talks. Moreover, the trade wares of the English included guns, an item the Spaniards had long been loathe to furnish to tenuous Native allies.

This latter point is particularly important. Let us look at that fact from the reverse and, thereby, add emphasis to another important Spanish reality. During the entire first century and a half of their relationships with the Maskókî peoples, the Spaniards did not hand out weapons, broadscale, to the Natives. Despite the rhetoric of Conquest that civil and military officials used, and despite the thousands of ostensibly true converts of whom religious officials boasted glowingly, the obvious inference is that the Spaniards, who knew the immediate reality behind their own rhetoric, knew full well how little confidence they could place in their vaunted Spanish "control." However, in 1565, with a Spanish settlement finally a reality—two settlements, in fact—and Menéndez's grand plan for *La Florida* only just beginning to unfold, the promise of Native control was still alive.

The Three Corners of the Spanish Hat

There still continues a debate over whether *La Florida* should be termed a colony, a military presidio, or a maritime presidio,[17] but the discussion actually hinges on matters of degree as much as substance. *La Florida* was a colony with principal military importance, or a military station that had a degree of colonial enterprise greater than has been heretofore believed. Its citizenry included troops trained for action on land, as well as those trained for engagements at sea, and all of the civilian components without which no military establishment would survive, in the sixteenth century or today.

As Eugene Lyon has concluded, Menéndez planned to establish a marquisate for himself and his family, based upon viable agricultural settlements. If these settlements had to be guarded by military forces while they took root, this was simply a means to a rational end. No Spanish colonial enterprise had become a flourishing, lucrative colony solely on a military basis.

However, irrespective of how we ultimately characterize *La Florida* in relation to other Spanish colonial enterprises, we must look beyond these concepts to recontextualize *La Florida,* in its larger Iberian cultural aspects, as a sociocultural entity cut from the same cloth as all other Spanish transpositions. The traditional view of *La Florida* as a poor and languishing semiforgotten outpost of empire must be left behind, in favor of opposite and compelling realities that have become obvious as more documents have been reviewed.

According to Lyon, San Agustín and the Spanish power corridor composed "an ethnically diverse community widely engaged in trade and the production of commercial crops." In this regard, he summarizes, *La Flor-ida* was "a culturally rich and complex society, rather well-equipped and supplied for its tasks of colonization and for the implanting of Castile in North America."[18] Consequently, he concludes, "The traditional view that Spanish Florida languished as a poor garrison settlement thus has become more of a hindrance than a help to understanding the colony's role."[19]

The triple imperatives of the Spanish Crown were the same, whether we discuss colonization in the so-called "core" areas of Spanish settlement (Nueva España and Perú) or in the cultural outposts of the Spanish empire. In every instance of Spanish interposition, cultural transposition was the sine qua non of colonialization, and Spanish culture of the late six-teenth and early seventeenth centuries was a figurative three-cornered hat, its salient points comprising the state, the church, and the military. The military conquered, the church subverted and converted, and the state managed.

In imaging the Spanish hat, however, it is important to keep in mind the nature of the Spanish monarchy and its embracing of the church and the military, not as equal allies of the state but, rather, as its tools of state pol-icy.[20] The *Patronato Real* gave the Spanish monarchy the responsibility to champion the Roman Catholic Church but, more important, it gave the monarchy the justification to control many of the internal workings of the Iberian church, along with significant portions of the copious monies that flowed through it. With the use of these incomes to pay soldiers and sail-ors, as opposed to earlier decentralized royal practices of imposing troop levies on individual noble landowners, in this period the Crown began to shift military allegiance away from the independent elements of the no-biliary establishment and toward a dependent relationship with a central monarchy.

In sixteenth-century Europe, this concept of a centralized military es-tablishment was just beginning. However, the requirements of quantum expansions in Spain's *ultramar* empire meant that, in Spain, the task of centralizing military authority had to proceed in tandem with the tasks of creating a dependent nobility, consolidating monarchical power, and con-solidating revenues that would be critical to the process of solidifying loy-alty among the military. That the Spanish monarchy managed such a feat, and managed to keep the corporate polity that it created from fragmenting into a thousand autonomous pieces across space and time, is remarkable.

Without argument, the participation of the state in the constitution of the cultural platform was a relatively new facet of Iberian life, but its emergence was nonetheless real and powerful. Only with the marriage and sub-sequent politicomilitary struggles of Fernando and Ysabel had a coherent Spanish "state" begun to emerge from the regional and autonomous pow-ers of the Iberian noble provinces. When Carlos I melded to his title that of the Holy Roman Emperor, the additional power and visibility gained for "Spain" an external image of institutionalized solidarity that proved al-most too costly to maintain internally. So, to a great extent, because of the economic costs and social requirements of majesty, coupled with the overarching need to centralize control of strongly independent polities, the prerogatives of nobility on the Iberian peninsula were being inexorably subsumed by the state. Furthermore, despite the sociocultural and eco-nomic latitudes provided by the opportunities of Spain's new Atlantic world, which threatened to facilitate a revival of noble autonomy, the Spanish Crown, under Carlos I/V and his son, Felipe II, retained and staunchly defended its centrist position.[21]

The trajectory of *La Florida*'s sociopolitical evolution followed the (by 1565) classic pattern. The settlement was created as an *adelantamiento*, that is, as a proprietary colony with a significant degree of autonomous power delegated to the *adelantado* or *asiento* holder, yet even before the death of the *adelantado* the Crown slowly began to bolster the powers that it did reserve to itself and to recoup those that it had earlier delegated.[22] By 1570, the process of recovery had begun with the establishment of an annual *situado* for the support of the royal troops stationed in San Agustín.[23] By the end of the second "life" of administrative authority promised to Menéndez in his *asiento,* which was claimed by his son-in-law, Hernando de Miranda, the Spanish Crown moved to begin making ap-pointments of governors itself, and by 1577 the Crown's process of recov-ery was complete. By that time, however, the nobility understood as well as did the Crown how limited were the potential profits to be realized from *La Florida* and what were the real benefits to be gained by its support. The best that the Spanish Crown could hope for as a return on its investments in *La Florida* was an increase in military security for its *flotas* or treasure fleets, an objective of no inconsiderable value; an increase of souls for its ideological harvest; and economic returns of any kind that might offset even a portion of its immense outlay for military defense.[24]

In 1602, however, even these possibilities still seemed doubtful given the tenuousness of San Agustín, and the Crown considered, for the last time, moving the colony farther northward. The final decision to maintain it was

Table 2
Population Estimates for *La Florida*, 1565–1763

Period	Estimate	Population	Area
1510	200,000	Native Americans	Lower *La Florida*
1580s	150	Soldiers	San Agustín
	240	Women, children (including < 100 black persons)	
1597–1602	15,000	Native Americans	Timugua
1608	30,000	Native Americans	Abalachi
1633	16,000	Native Americans	Abalachi
1689	3,380	Native Americans	Timugua
	9,600	Native Americans	Abalachi
1702	1,500	Total population (Spaniards + black persons)	San Agustín
	8,000	Native Americans	Abalachi missions
1715	3,700	Native Americans	Peninsular *La Florida*
1763	800	Total population (Spaniards + black persons)	Pensacola
	350	French	Mobile
	700	Native Americans (no reliable count for the southern peninsula)	Peninsular *La Florida*
	3,046	Total population (2,547 Spaniards + 315 black slaves + free black persons + 89 Christian Natives)	San Agustín & environs

Estimates for European, Euroamerican, and black populations are fairly reliable in all years. Estimates of Native American populations are a compilation of documentary and archaeological information.

predicated, once again, upon the military strategy of the location as a base for protection of Spanish shipping and the feasibility of using it as a point of entry into the interior.[25]

Corporate Structure

As Lyon writes, "It is clear that Spanish Florida, like Jamestown and Plymouth, suffered its starving times in the early times of the colony. It is also true that the colony shrank from its initially proposed dimensions, and [after 1574] lost to some degree the expansionist drive which characterized it under Pedro Menéndez. It is certainly less clear that there was parallel shrinkage of the cultural matrix carried forward from the sixteenth century.... [I]n cultural as well as economic terms, sixteenth-century Florida was far richer than we have been led to believe."[26]

At no time in its Spanish colonial history was *La Florida* ever self-supporting. However, in terms of the economic base of the colony, San Agustín "was probably as well supported as any Spanish garrison town in the sixteenth through eighteenth centuries."[27] The annual *situado,* or allowance, was computed on military *plazas,* that is, upon the officially allocated military strength of the garrison. Thus it was to the benefit of the governor to keep troop strength up, on paper, and to lobby for increases in the military establishment. Several useful research sources have become available recently that cover the internal workings of the *La Florida* economy and its close relationship to the economic concerns of the Spanish Crown and the economic vicissitudes of the Spanish viceroys in the American colonies.[28] They outline a colony whose economic fortunes rose and fell in direct relationship to the interests and economic fortunes of its Iberian source.

The *situado* was a major element of the "royal economy," the funding package that was the direct link between *La Florida* and the Spanish Crown and the most direct method of Crown control. *Situado* funds paid, broadly, for rations, wages, munitions, and bonuses. In the cases of the regular clergy (those living within an ordered rule, such as the Jesuits and Franciscans) and secular clergy, the Crown's *situado* paid each an alm or stipend, plus "alms for habit and sandals."[29] The individual alm was equal to the wage paid to one military *plaza,* or place (one soldier).[30] By 1616, there were thirty-seven Franciscans in Florida. In 1648, the official number of allotees was raised to seventy, but there is no reason to believe that seventy friars ever served in *La Florida* at any one time.[31]

Missionaries served in *doctrinas* or mission centers, where, with the permission of the cacique, they lived and where a church was established, and in *visitas* or Native villages, where they visited and where there probably was a church. Beyond that, they made stops in various villages, again with permission, and remained there for some weeks or months, sometimes succeeding in gaining converts and sometimes not. Researcher John Hann has identified 108 missions, of varying durations, ultimately created by the Spaniards during their first occupation.[32]

In each instance, Native labor was key to the success of the mission, from the Spanish point of view. On March 18, 1520, Carlos V had ordered Natives in the Antilles freed from the *encomienda* system as the Spaniards holding the *encomiendas* died.[33] *Encomiendas* were land grants that included the "right" to command the labor and tribute of the Native groups living on the land. In return for their labor, the *encomendero* agreed to be responsible for the Christian education and care of the Natives. The king's abnegation of the *encomenderos'* concessions, however, was principally a step toward the Crown's reclamation of its own rights in the newly settled lands. Always fearful of conceding too much power to others, the Crown preferred that Native groups should remain under its own direct control, rather than under the control of private individuals who could divert tribute payments.

In 1542, the Crown attempted to extend its control of Native labor and tribute to the mainlands of the central and southern Americas with the promulgation of its New Laws of the Indies. The attempt was singularly unsuccessful. By that sixth decade of entrenchment, Spanish colonists in their new world were in a position to shift the balance of power, slightly, away from the Crown. Henceforward, the Crown would continue its policy of control principally by undermining individual powers through judges and administrators whose official allegiance was to Spain rather than to themselves or to the *encomenderos*.

In *La Florida, encomiendas* were not granted during the Entrada Phase, while so much about the land was still unknown. There is little reason to believe that the Spaniards, with no more military power or logistical support than they had, could have enforced them among many of the autonomous Maskókî peoples, even if the Crown had granted them. In 1573, Felipe II, son and successor to Carlos V, would promulgate new *Ordenanzas* specifically permitting *encomiendas*, as an important source of revenues for the Crown.[34] However, the 1565 *asiento* with Don Pedro Menéndez de Avilés, by which *La Florida* was finally settled, made no mention of the privilege one way or another. Ostensibly, it was left to the will of Menéndez to carve out a profitable niche for himself if he found conditions of land and labor to be favorable.[35]

A subject of much dissension and ill will as the Spaniards moved their negotiations beyond the environs of San Agustín was Native labor levies and the larger power system of *repartimiento*, the partitioning of Native labor forces among Spanish recipients by Spanish authorities. Used successfully throughout most of the Spanish colonial network from Nueva España to America del Sur, labor requirements were first placed upon *La Florida's* Guale peoples, who had passed through the "wars of fire and blood," which the Spaniards had used to crush their 1597 uprising.[36] In

1600, Governor Gonzalo Méndez de Canzo required Guale people to labor in the rebuilding of San Agustín after a fire. Once the precedent was established, the labor not only of the Guale peoples but also of the Timuguana and the Abalachi peoples in their turns would be demanded by the Spaniards in the fields, in civic projects, for the bearing of burdens overland, and in the domestic service of civil, military, and religious administrators. In 1647, interim governor Francisco Menéndez Márquez reacted to an uprising in Abalachi sparked by incessant Spanish labor demands by demanding a regular labor *repartimiento* from both pro- and anti-Spanish Natives.[37] Horses were scarce in *La Florida* and were allocated to elites, both Spanish and Native, but not to Natives generally; consequently, as one Spanish treasury official bluntly stated it, "until mid-century the most common pack animal in Florida was still an Indian."[38]

However, in this as in other instances, the Spaniards would be forced by the determinations and abilities of the Maskókî peoples to temper their demands and make the best of the realities that the Natives imaged and enforced. Despite the basic and critical value of Native labor in other Spanish colonies, none of the Spaniards' "jointly cherished expectations [of establishing labor-intensive levy systems] could be realized without satisfactorily resolving the relationships with the present occupants of Florida."[39] This they would never completely accomplish.

During the seventeenth century, when Spanish movement across the northern peninsular power corridor was at its peak, fragmentation of Native villages was occurring at a more rapid rate than ever before in *La Florida*. In response to increasing Spanish demands for labor, Guale, Timuguana, and Abalachi Natives comprising labor levies were called away from their families and required to live in labor camps, from which some defected and in which others did not survive.[40] Further, as a result of the traditional movements required by deaths (in this case, intermittent epidemics) and the pressures engendered intermittently by insufficient food, Native men began to move about as individuals, independent of their families and towns, seeking work from the Spaniards. These *cimarrones* lodged themselves in established social niches as day laborers in construction or as contract laborers on Spanish *ranchos* across the head of *La Florida*'s peninsula. Hundreds more, at least, created places for themselves in marginal enterprises such as charcoal burning or supplying wild game, baskets, or pottery to the Europeans.[41] Despite their best official efforts, Spanish administrators were never able to contain or control this group, and there is no reason to believe that their descendants could not have survived at least until 1763, reforming as affinity groups across the very areas where the English would find them as "Seminoles."

Typically, labor demands by Spaniards and Native responses fell into a few distinct categories. Foremost, the Spaniards could make no demands until they had effected some understanding with a cacique or micco, usually in a verbal agreement of *amistad,* or friendship, that included mutual benefits. Again, within the traditional matrices of the Maskókî peoples, reciprocity was basic to any interaction.

The benefits to the Spaniards typically included permission to plant a cross in the village and to send missionaries, in order to preach their opinions of the value of the Roman Catholic cult; broad access to village laborers, both male and female; expectations of military alliance or, at least, of access to military intelligence; and access to village produce, enhanced by European technology provided by the Spaniards. The benefits to the Maskókî peoples included payments in the form of limited types of European tools, textiles, and miscellaneous trade goods; expectations of a military alliance in times of attack by Native or European enemies; and access to whatever miscellaneous elements of Spanish culture they chose to view as useful.

"Every condition that made pacification difficult was present in Spanish Florida. As a result, the colony would never lose its character as a military outpost," concludes Amy Bushnell.[42] However, by the very nature of its principal value to the Spanish Crown, as a guardian of the Plate Fleet routes, neither could *La Florida* afford to lose its military character. Nor would the Crown, with no more to gain from *La Florida* than it already had, risk scarce resources on it.

Bushnell continues:

> Indians who could not be pacified by the sword, the gift, or the gospel shared certain characteristics. Typically, they were seasonal nomads, indifferent to the sacraments and unwilling to settle down in farming villages on the Mediterranean model. They had a high regard for individual liberty and governed themselves by consensus rather than coercion. Finally, they could not be quarantined from contact with Spain's European rivals.[43]

The critical point that Bushnell misses is that *all* of the Maskókî peoples whom the Spaniards sought to subject fit this description, even those whom the Spaniards succeeded in bringing under their hegemony. Consequently, we cannot theorize that it was the same sociocultural matrix that provided the impetus for some Natives to succumb and for others to resist. All of the Maskókî peoples ranged over territorial hunting and warring grounds. None of their societies had ever included farms "on the Mediterranean model," nor were any potential benefits of such new methods necessarily obvious to them. Individual liberties were a hallmark of the strongly horizontal power structure of all of the Maskókî peoples. Finally, given the choice between government by consensus, in their own model, and government by coercion, as Bushnell characterizes the Spanish model, the choice was, indeed, quite clear to the majority of the Maskókî people.

8 Fear as the Forerunner of Faith

They deprive us of every vestige of happiness which our ancestors obtained
for us, in exchange for which they hold out the hope of the joys of heaven.
In this deceitful manner they subject us, holding us bound to their wills.
What have we to hope for except to become slaves? If we kill them all now,
we will throw off this intolerable yoke without delay. All they do is repri-
mand us, offend us, oppress us, preach to us, [and] call us bad Christians.
                              —Juanillo, cacique of Guale, 1597[1]

Indians as a rule are better friends to the French, who let them live in freedom, than to my people and the religious who restrict their way of living;
and the French can accomplish more with them in one day than I in a year.
                    —Pedro Menéndez de Avilés to King Felipe, 1571[2]

In sum, the study of missionization must proceed from an analysis of both
societies in contact. When this is done . . . the emphasis shifts from a
schema where passive, pagan people trade their benighted condition for
civilization and Christianity, whenever the missionary impulse becomes
sufficiently strong, to an explanatory model that takes account of a continuous, coherent exchange between the traditional local religions and the immi-
grant religion.

                                            —Gary B. Nash[3]

Cultural Attrition Versus Cultural Collapse

The Maskókî peoples of the Southeast passed through two separate, major
periods and types of profound cultural stressors in their passage from the
sixteenth through the eighteenth centuries. During the first of the two periods, the Entrada Phase (1510–1563), the primary types of pressure were
two. First and foremost was that occasioned by the effects of European
diseases inadvertently introduced by the Spaniards. As no respecters of
age, intellect, or status, these accidental pathogens frayed many of the
power networks that had constituted the warp and weft of the Natives' social fabric. This stress is undeniable, but its effects must not be overesti-

mated. This stress, at least as much as the second type of cultural stressors—the presence of the Spaniards and their insistent proselytizing and politicizing—required the survivors to draw upon the resources of their well-established social repertoires in order to rearticulate themselves time and again.[4]

The severity of the physical impact of these insidious European pathogens was obvious to the Spaniards and has been discussed earlier in this work. There is little contention among modern researchers that, over the course of the sixteenth century, at least, previously unknown illnesses struck down thousands of Maskókî peoples, as well as peoples beyond the members of the Maskókî cultural family.[5] What does remain contentious, however, is the subject of the sociocultural impact of the demographic losses.

If disease is no respecter of age, sex, or status—and it is not—and if the individual Maskókî losses to diseases in the Entrada Phase included many who were holders and carriers of specialized and privileged social information—and they surely did—is it then appropriate to conclude that these losses precipitated a "collapse" of Maskókî culture?[6] Or is this conclusion one more inductive leap that has passed into popular myth as an element of the Conquest rhetoric that continues to disarticulate and disempower the Maskókî peoples?

First, we must realize that Maskókî culture could not have collapsed, in the literal or figurative sense of the word, or the Spaniards would have experienced no coherent resistance from the Native peoples after 1565, as they sought to extend Spanish hegemony beyond the very limited village confines of their own effective occupation. Further, if demographic shock had, indeed, precipitated cultural disintegration, then we should expect to find the Maskókî peoples, at least, among the southeastern Natives, wandering and culturally incoherent by 1565, with their social networks nonfunctional. Such certainly was not the case, however.

Demographer Henry Dobyns, in an effort to shift historical focus toward the severity of pathogen impact upon Native Americans, makes an inductive leap when he posits that "aboriginal lifeways for the Native peoples of North America clearly terminated with the large-scale depopulation caused by the initial smallpox pandemic in 1520–1524. Those peoples cannot be considered to have continued their prepandemic ways of life unchanged and unaffected by a massive loss of manpower."[7] However, the two conclusions are at odds. There can be no argument that the losses of "manpower"—which included woman power—affected the

Maskókî peoples in far more than the obvious demographic sense. However, Dobyns himself goes on to point out what he sees as a "conceptual error" among those researchers who assume that precontact Natives held static lifeways until the coming of the Europeans: "Aboriginal ways of life influenced by entirely American causes changed for many Native American peoples long before they ever saw a European or an African."[8] Among these causes he cites intertribal trade and "religious" movements.[9]

His points are well taken but do not go far enough. No sociocultural entity is static. Maskókî peoples had been changing within their own cultural trajectory before the arrival of the Europeans, and they continued to change afterward. They continue to change to this day. As but one example, it is apparent from archaeological evidence that Maskokálgî rituals already had begun to decrease in complexity prior to European interposition.[10] So, although it is undeniable that the losses of members because of the effects of epidemics placed severe short-term stresses upon the Maskókî societies in addition to requiring long-term adjustments to the losses of collective memory and place holders, we must be careful not to leap to the conclusion that these stresses disarticulated their social systems to such a point that they became nonfunctional and easily conquered. In order to do so we would have to assume that the cultural templates of the people were so unsuccessful and brittle as to give way under the demands of the Other, and such certainly was not the case in either the Entrada or the Settlement Phase of Spanish interposition. On the contrary, it was the coherent resistance of the Maskókî peoples, well documented by the Jesuits, the Franciscans, and the Spanish civil and military establishments, that constituted a major, and perhaps decisive, impediment to any reality of Spanish Conquest in *La Florida*.

The most documentable response of the Maskókî peoples to the initial impact of the pathogens was the process that one researcher has referred to as "settlement amalgamation" but could be termed more appropriately as the establishment of affinity groups.[11] This was a direct recourse to traditional social customs that were, themselves, facets of the dynamic template that had long hallmarked the Maskókî peoples and has been discussed earlier in this work. Once again, there is no reason to believe that this process began only with the coming of the Spaniards or, conversely, that the coming of the Spaniards was such a definitive event as to mark the process as a terminal one for the Maskókî peoples.

In this process, individuals who found themselves living in a world knocked out of balance by untimely deaths and the losses of individuals who functioned as social connectors, reestablished their equilibrium within the bounds of long-established social templates of authority and succession. What other response was there to which they would have had recourse except one that had functioned so well for so long?

Within this template, lines of authority and responsibility, well delineated, long tested, and flowing strongly through the Clan system, permitted the survivors to shift their social networks to affinity groups. These groups, composed of parallel Clan members from other towns and villages within the same power constellation, became surrogate social networks. In addition, the survivors relocated themselves to their parallel affinity group, consequently re-placing themselves in the larger society and regaining an acceptable and functional level of equilibrium.

The Seminoles of the present day retain essentially the same system, which is still functioning, along with adjunct systems. Members of one Clan in Florida consider themselves to be brothers of the parallel Clan in Oklahoma and transfer host duties, ceremonial and ritual relationships and responsibilities, and requirements of respect and deference to each other.[12] As an example of an adjunct system of affinal transfer, when the existence of a Clan becomes endangered, either through untimely loss or natural attrition among its female holders, it can be "adopted" into an affinity group so that its members do not lose their sense of place in the larger social system.

In this adjunct network of affinal transfers, within the past century in Florida, Bobcat Clan has been adopted into Panther Clan, and Wolf Clan has become a part of Bear Clan. As an example of inverse functioning, Tahkóshat Clan, which was for some portion of the nineteenth century a part of Otter Clan because its own numbers of women had fallen unacceptably low, recovered sufficiently by the late nineteenth century to resume its functioning as a discrete Clan within the Tribe, and it continues so today.[13]

The individual and collective templates for social relationships have not fallen apart over the years with the deaths of responsibility holders. Their duties have been transferred, in as orderly a manner as possible, so that equilibrium could be restored as rapidly as possible and continuity protected. Even if we stipulate that the loss of esoteric information held as a facet of the collective social power base may have been significant and real, we must realize that, as discussed in earlier chapters, this loss should not be viewed as definitive; in order for the social system to continue to function successfully, it was not necessary for exact information, or even complete information, to be transferred from generation to generation. It was only necessary that there should be a shared body of beliefs, confirmed by public instances, and a collective acceptance of those beliefs institutionalized as a template that could serve, as it were, as a fountain from which all might draw and drink. One excellent and still highly visible example of such an instance is the Green Corn ritual, discussed earlier, at which so many of the public and private templates were, and are, reconfirmed. Thus, the formation of affinity groups that took place as a direct response to the demographic decline that followed as the wake of contact was also a survival strategy that provided cultural continuity and reestablished social equilibrium and should not be equated automatically with profound cultural decline.

As regards the process of relocating villages, seasonally, ceremonially, or permanently, this too was a standard element of the Maskóki social repertoire that obviously had been called upon long before the arrival of the Spaniards and their pathogens. At the most basic level, that of food gathering, whole segments of villages relocated, seasonally, to a fixed round of living sites. As another instance, when individuals died of natural causes, their houses might be burned or at least deserted, and the surviving Clan members would relocate to a sufficiently distant location.[14] A young man of a powerful family, who was not in line to inherit leadership, might choose to start his own village within the power constellation of his parent village, or a man who was exiled from a tribe because he had occasioned some major disruption of the equilibrium might begin a new settlement with any members of his Clan who would be willing, or required, to go with him.

A significant body of archaeological evidence highlights the process of village relocation over the three centuries following Spanish interposition. Once again, however, we must be careful not to taint the process, in retrospect, with impositional and chauvinistic brittleness. Some of the principal towns of the powerful Coça province, for example, made obvious shifts to the south and east in the period following initial Spanish contact.[15] In addition, the numbers of those towns decreased as disequilibrated survivors reestablished their equilibrium in affinity groups.

Archaeologist Marvin Smith has demonstrated this process for the Ocute province of *La Florida*'s central interior (now north-central Georgia) and has reached conclusions that are far more consistent with the social templates of the Maskóki peoples than are those reached by Dobyns. Dobyns sums up features of Native response patterns to "depopulation," asserting that survivors amalgamated in environmental niches that were more productive than their former sites and stating that responses to biological trauma included, among other things, "rapid changes in many conventional understandings formerly shared."[16] Smith, however, demonstrates, with the upper branch of the Oconî, among others, that geographic relocation did not necessarily equate with social dislocation, and he finds continuity in these people, who later became known to Europeans as the Ocutî, from the period of de Soto's entrada at least until the Yamásî War, in 1715. The processes of naming and name variability have already been outlined in this work. A change of names, when the rationale behind the names is not clear, cannot be taken as any definitive indicator of a change in the peoples holding the name. The name might reflect a change in caciques, or a change in geographic referents, without any cultural or social changes in the people themselves.

By 1565, the Maskókî peoples had recovered sufficiently from the initial demographic shock and social trauma of the new pathogens as to have amalgamated in functioning affinity groups. Moreover, their elastic social networks, which intrinsically incorporated the requirement of continuity in response to social stressors, had permitted new individuals to fill the positions of cacique, *iniha, tanákî,* and others, in their villages in order to correct a damaged system and recover control, thereby reestablishing equilibrium. Their cosmogony had not been lost and their dynamism still propelled them. If this had not been so, the Spaniards would have had no cacique or *iniha* or *tanákî* in any village to describe.

In but one instance, Dobyns himself posits this process of amalgamation in action as an alternative, but then he opts for the conclusion that supports his thesis, that settlement amalgamation was the result of pathogen impact rather than part of a traditional response pattern. In discussing the Potano, who were Timuguana tributaries centering in the northern interior peninsula of *La Florida,* he seeks to correlate Spanish accounts that place their number of warriors at 10,000 in 1539 and 2,000 between 1562 and 1568. Either, he posits, the Potano population had declined by a factor of five to one over the intervening period or "if population had not declined, then the Potano polity of 1539 had split, or towns of the 1539 chiefdom had been annexed by neighboring polities by the 1560s."[17] In the light of traditional Maskókî social templates, this latter possibility makes at least as much sense as the specious assignment of all change to demographic, ergo social, loss. It reminds us once again that population reports for peoples not within areas of direct Spanish contact should not be accepted automatically as proofs of Native depopulation.

Anthropologist John Worth, in discussing power shifts among Guale towns, apparently in the aftermath of the Guale uprising of 1597, begins to outline the dynamic of amalgamation at the village level. He recognizes the continuity of some village names throughout the seventeenth century, because their continuity was contained in the passage of hereditary titles. Further, he realizes, these leaders maintained their own discrete constituencies, even within the larger populations of towns. "What changed during the early 17th century," he concludes, "was not so much the overall sociopolitical organization of [the] Guale and Mocama [tribes], but the distribution of population across the landscape. Specifically, while outlying satellite villages did not completely disappear, they seem to have physically relocated to central towns, where they apparently maintained a distinct identity within the general population of each town."[18] This view certainly is more consistent with Maskókî social functioning, historically and currently, than a model of haphazard amalgamation. Once again we see that the Natives maintained a significant degree of internal order.

The First Negotiations

In the Spanish Roman Catholic world, proselytization and Hispanicization were inextricable elements of military and political interposition. Pedro Menéndez de Avilés may have seemed a realist when he admitted that the French could establish more peaceful and successful negotiations with the Natives in *La Florida* than he because they did not proselytize (at least not in *La Florida*), but his realism still was bounded completely by his Spanish Roman Catholic cosmogony, for he also believed the ultimate good—the *telos*—of the Natives' souls was "salvation" by a Roman Catholic god. In addition, in the long run, this eventually would serve his own objectives and those of his king as well. Consequently, he supported the tentative movements of the first of the *La Florida* missionaries toward the Natives living beyond the immediate areas of Santa Elena and San Agustín.

These earliest Settlement Phase attempts to convert the Natives were, on the whole, negotiative failures. The reasons behind these failures, and later failures by other Europeans in other areas of North America, are finally becoming clear. As researchers Gary B. Nash and J. Frederick Fausz have pointed out regarding the English proselytizers in the Northeast: "We are beginning to comprehend that Christian missions 'are, and always have been, revolutionary enterprises, demanding that the non-believer commit cultural suicide,' and that missionaries worked within a system of colonial belief and behavior that stressed above all the need to destroy Indian autonomy and to vitiate Indian power."[19] As we have seen in earlier chapters, this ideological matrix informed the policies and actions of the Spaniards, in general, as well as it did those of the English proselytizers, specifically. However, at this point, the power and autonomy of the Maskóki peoples of *La Florida* had been neither vitiated nor destroyed, and it would not be, at least through 1670.

Historian John Hann views the missionization efforts in *La Florida*'s Settlement Phase history as having occurred in four periods, at least from a historiographic perspective. The first, from the late 1560s through 1587, comprised "tentative and mostly unsuccessful attempts ... about ... which little is known."[20] About the second, from 1587 to 1616, as the Roman Catholic friars moved northward and eastward across the province of Guale, and westward into the immediate environs of Timugua, more is known. However, the results were very tenuous and, by this second and the third generation of missionization activities, many of the Natives had reached the end of their patience with incessant Spanish demands. In Timuguana in 1584, and in Guale, in 1587 and again in 1597, they exercised their own options to end the tiresome negotiations by killing a number of the missionaries.

In the third period, from 1616 to 1655, missionization activity was more tolerated by the Natives of peninsular *La Florida* than it had been at any time during the preceding century and a number of missions were established, generally spreading westward from San Agustín across the province of Timugua and into Abalachi (to the environs of present-day Tallahassee). Further, the Spaniards themselves felt that the missionaries were at their most enthusiastic during this period and worked with more alacrity and determination than during earlier or later periods.

Our knowledge of the missions during this period is limited, however, to an incomplete 1655 list of those *doctrinas* at which friars were stationed, and obviously many missions were short lived. Given the violent reactions of the *La Florida* Natives to the high-handed demands of the Spaniards, it appears that the missionaries stationed themselves in villages where they were asked to preach and where the Natives seemed willing to tolerate them and declared them missions until such time as they began to make significant inroads or wear out the patience of the host tribe. If the latter occurred, they moved on to any other village or town that seemed potentially less volatile.

The best-known period of missionization was, of course, the latest and, as history would have it, the last. This was the period from 1655, the zenith of what since has been dubbed (by the cultural Other) the seventeenth century's "Golden Age" of proselytization in *La Florida,* until 1704–1706, when the missions were destroyed by English attacks that drove into the heart of peninsular *La Florida.* Including those ephemeral missions established during the Entrada Phase, and others abandoned or moved, there appear to have been a total of 128 *doctrinas* (mission centers), *visitas* (villages, sometimes with churches, visited by friars), and villages where priests or lay brothers lived in the *La Florida* provinces of Guale, Timugua, and Abalachi between 1566 and 1706. However, we must also remember that, throughout the whole missionization era, only seventy friars ever were authorized by the Crown to serve in all *La Florida,* and it is not known whether the total ever reached that number.[21]

During the Settlement Phase, the work of attempting to Christianize *La Florida*'s peoples was undertaken first by the members of the Society of Jesus (Jesuits), beginning in 1566. Pedro Menéndez, as a result of the friendship he had formed with the Jesuits at their monastery of La Cartuja in Sevilla, had requested of the king and of the Society of Jesus general Francisco de Borja that they be given the mission field of *La Florida.*[22] However, by 1572, almost as quickly as they had come, the Jesuits abandoned their work among the southeastern Maskókî peoples on the grounds that the Natives were too nomadic and not inclined to stay at missions and that the cruelty of the soldiers created an animosity among the Natives that could not be overcome.[23]

The dynamism of the Maskókî peoples as they ranged across hunting territories and shifted their camps from one seasonal center to another has been discussed earlier in this work. The Jesuits, apparently, expected to find sedentary and docile Natives, awaiting the command of the "true god" and ready to throw off their centuries of functioning cosmogony at the moment when an obviously "right" alternative appeared. However, the observations of the Jesuits must be taken, also, as a reminder: first, the tribes *were* dynamic and not in a state of shock from pathogenic trauma and, second, their social systems not only were not in shock but also were continuing to function sufficiently well that they could repulse the negotiative advances of the Other in a coherent and—most important—successful manner.

As regards the Jesuits' secondary reason for their failure, the theme of negative competition between the religious and the military establishments in *La Florida*, this would quickly become a recurring one and ultimately would fill reams of letters and reports to the king and the *Consejo de las Indias* (the Council of the Indies, created by Carlos V in 1524 to oversee Spain's *ultramar* policies). The immediate occasions for the competition would range from internal bickering over territoriality, to demands for access to Native labor, to greed for the profits from Native labor, to a real competition for the limited economic resources provided by the Crown.

David Hurst Thomas, in surveying the Spaniards' internecine power struggles, also recognized larger background issues. "Such disputes over military and religious priorities reflected deep-seated differences in perception about the true role of the mission system: as strictly agent of the [Roman Catholic] Church or as an ingredient of a presidio system designed to conquer and safeguard new frontiers."[24] If Spanish *La Florida* officials were conflicted over these twin objectives, however, they were only reflecting an ambiguity that began with the monarchy and permeated Spanish society over issues that no true Spaniard could fully separate.

Irrespective of these larger issues, this constant competition became a significant element in the failure of the Spaniards to live up to the king's expectations in *La Florida*. In addition, because they were neither culturally collapsed nor powerless, the Native peoples found ways to take advantage of the Spaniards' internecine squabbles and make them tools of survival. David Weber understands this concept and concludes: "Whatever their spiritual successes, then, missionaries failed to advance permanently, defend effectively, or Hispanicize deeply Spain's North American frontiers of the seventeenth century. . . . The mission did not fit Bolton's model of a successful 'frontier institution,' and it failed in large part because Indians did not wish it to succeed."[25]

After 1565, Menéndez sailed along the Atlantic and Gulf coastlines of *La Florida's* peninsula, searching out sites where he might plant the seeds of Hispanicization, in the form of a small group of soldiers, blockhouses and housing, and a Jesuit or two, in villages where they did not appear to be immediately threatened. In the short seven years of their presence in *La Florida*, the Jesuits lived and preached in ten or, possibly, eleven locations (including one five-month attempt in what now is called the Chesapeake Bay region).

In five of these locations, open hostility and attacks from the Native peoples curtailed proselytization more rapidly than in the others, which were all eventually abandoned because of lack of success, although some of the areas were later reinvested by the Franciscans. In only one instance did any of these missions achieve any permanence. That one was the mission of Nombre de Dios, which was, literally, under the guns of the various fortresses of San Agustín.

The attitudes of the Jesuits and their trajectory of approach are obvious in the meager surviving documents. They first approached the village or town leader and concentrated much of their effort on him or her, on the premise that the power of the office and the example would have significant influences upon the townspeople. As was discussed earlier, however, they erred grievously in assuming that they could transfer their own cultural templates directly onto the Natives.

Fray Juan Rojel, in one of the richest of all the *La Florida* documents (in terms of ethnographic data), describes the ineffectiveness of his efforts to "undeceive" the Escampaba/Calusa of their "errors and idolatries and evil customs and wicked laws."[26] As historian Eugene Lyon has concluded: "It . . . became clear that the Indians might be willing to accept the Christian God as a coequal or even superior deity in their pantheon, but that claims for exclusivity on behalf of [that Christian] God would meet dogged opposition."[27] Where the intellectual Jesuits relied upon argument, the industrious Franciscans relied more upon physical labor, but both relied upon fear as a prime motivator.

The Order of Friars Minor, commonly known as the Franciscans, took over the missionizing process in *La Florida*, arriving first in 1572, just two years before the death of Menéndez and three years before the outbreak of the first regional uprising, in the province of Guale (today's southeastern Georgia), which took the Spaniards four years to quell. A second uprising, in 1597, sent Natives migrating to nearby islands in resistance, and the coastal missions went into a long period of decline.

Although Guale and coastal (Georgia and South Carolina) missions continued to exist into the seventeenth century, the axis of primary interaction shifted from north-south to east-west. After 1595 the Franciscans began to experience an increased degree of acceptance among the Timuguana tribes in the area in which San Agustín was located and to push westward across the northern portion of that territory and, after 1633, into the center of the Abalachi province, which would become the western frontier of the missions of *La Florida*.

The Franciscans' discourse with the Natives of *La Florida* had a consistent design and therefore a consistent shape, which becomes readily transparent in the documents. In order to preconfigure negotiations in a favorable light (to themselves), the Spaniards used panoply, exhibitions of military prowess, and an abundance of trade wares as power displays and lures. Careful always to characterize their powers as delegated, not self-generated, they assigned the illusion of even greater power to the unseen monarch over the sea whom they served and to the supernatural deity whom he served and to whom he attributed his power. In this manner they sought to add fear to their negotiating toolkit and tip the balance in their own favor before the long-term elements of the negotiation even began.

Juan Pardo, the Spanish military officer sent out from Santa Elena, in 1566 and in 1567, on surveying entradas into the interior of *La Florida*, during which his *entradistas* reached present-day Tennessee, provides one indication of the psychological process of manipulation that the Spaniards sought to effect as their initial imaging by the Native peoples. In every town and village, Pardo's interactions were formulaic. He had the inhabitants called together (always noting this action, as if their actions were solely his to command) and made them a speech. "I talked to them about God and His Majesty, just as I was ordered to, and they replied that they were ready to obey His Holiness and His Majesty."[28]

Whenever possible, the Spaniards entered a town in panoply to display as much wealth/power as they had available. Then, they offered their respects to that particular town's cacique or cacica, and the *hombres principales*, and distributed gifts as a further power display. Then, after food and courtesies, they introduced the threat of physical force by assigning submission requirements, based on the demands of an even more powerful master than they themselves: the king whom they served and who would send more enforcers if his demands were not met. Then, they raised a cross, assigned power to it by venerating it, and pronounced themselves to be factors of the supernatural power it symbolized. They encouraged the Natives to join them, couching the invitation in terms of their (the Natives') own protection, asked the Natives to swear fealty to the twin forces of king and god, and left the cross standing in the village as a tangible reminder of their expectations. Later, as the Spaniards began to recognize the high-value associations of semiotics among the Maskokálgî, they placed greater and greater social emphasis on the cruciform, assigning to it power in their stead.

If the tribal members complied with their immediate demands, the

Spaniards frequently executed formal treaties and departed, chauvinistically satisfied that a real understanding had been reached and real changes had been effected.[29] It served neither the interests nor the egos of the Spaniards to consider that the Natives merely might have been obliging them, as host duties, or responding out of short-term curiosity or, even, that the Natives might have been willing to negotiate some sort of reciprocal tribute arrangement, if these new Others also met the Natives' own expectations of reciprocity in interpersonal relations. However, reciprocity did not inform the Spaniards' cosmogony as it did the Natives'. The Spaniards presented their demands as unilateral and binding.

Distribution of gifts, or, more accurately, bribes, was meant to serve the same purpose of luring the Natives into compliance and submission. Fray Escobedo, OFM, wrote of his expedition to Guale in 1597 with Fray Chosas that the missionaries and soldiers carried gifts for the Natives of Castilian wool blankets, knives, fishhooks, scissors, glass beads, sickles, and hatchets "so that these uncivilized people who served the Devil would be properly impressed by the wealth and strength of Spain."[30] The gambit did not always work, however. The Jesuits had tried to use the same bargaining tool, to no avail. Fray Rojel had reported to a brother Jesuit that "although the king . . . left off coming [to religious instruction] because of being so busy with and involved in his idolatry, they [the rest] learned the prayers well while the handouts lasted and they were already beginning to believe the things that I was telling them. But when the handouts ended, they all took off."[31] Obviously, the friar was deluding himself, along with any uncritical reader, when he boasted that the Natives had been accepting his dicta as truth.

Once they had gained the initial interest and attention—no matter how potentially short-lived—of the Natives, the missionaries' next step was to couch their discourse selectively in the rhetoric of fear and submission, introducing the possibility of pain into areas of the Natives' world where none had existed before. Fray Francisco Pareja, OFM, who served in *La Florida* longer (1595–1626?) than any of the other Franciscans during this second mission period, has left us with significant examples of the central discourse of Spanish negotiations and the patterns in which that discourse was applied. In one typical comment, Fray Pareja reported to the king: "If there are people rebellious at conversion—I can say that after I preach about the pains of hell and the joys of heaven they have converted."[32]

In the earlier stages of the negotiations in *La Florida*, the missionaries delivered their harangues through interpreters who were sometimes members of their own company or Spanish soldiers who evidenced an aptitude for languages, sometimes Natives with a language aptitude, and sometimes Natives from *La Florida* or other areas of the Americas who had been kidnapped on earlier entradas and purposely taught Spanish, on the premise that they also would have a natural affinity for Native languages. The Franciscans, however, placed emphasis on learning Native languages themselves in order to embed dialogues in familiar rhetorical patterns, and over the second and third mission periods, many of them would gain great proficiency with the various dialects of the Maskókî linguistic family.

However, the Spanish documents are full of references to Native interpreters, who also made convenient scapegoats when negotiations failed. Fray Juan Rojel failed, reported Fray Escobedo, because he did not speak the language and his interpreter, misunderstanding him, offended the Natives by what was said.[33]

La Florida governor Méndez de Canzo (1596–1603), explained a typical system to the Crown. Concerning the Native provinces surrounding San Agustín he wrote: "Counting this city's province . . . , all the above mentioned provinces must have caciques numbering more than fifty. There are a great number of caciques subject to these head caciques. There are five different languages spoken in these provinces and the people of one tongue do not understand those of another except by *atequies* [interpreters]. To this effect I ordinarily have and raise in my house Indians from each province for the purpose of language."[34]

As it happened, Fray Pareja himself had an excellent aptitude for languages and quickly learned to communicate with the Timuguana without an interpreter. In fact, he acquired such facility as to write a grammar and vocabulary, a catechism, and a guide to confessing in the Timuguana language—the earliest extant books in any North American Native language.

Thus, through their own words and the words of their interpreters, the Spanish friars systematically recontextualized external facets of the Natives' lives as "sinful" and as the work of the devil. Since no template for "sin" existed within the Maskokálgî cosmogony, the word did not carry as negative a value for the Natives as it did for the Spaniards, in whose cosmogony it constituted a benchmark. Therefore the element of European-style fear, the classic Roman Catholic attachment to sin, was stressed in constant admonitions about hellfire and damnation. In this way, the proselytizers could express and reinforce a negativity that was specifically constructed to weaken the Natives' belief systems by adding a fear-laden alternative, so that it then could be superseded by the salvational power construct of Roman Catholic and Spanish belief systems.

However, the efficacy of this system, of course, was principally an exponent of geographic and cultural proximity. Consequently, the Spaniards placed emphasis on coercing the Natives into fixed living centers, where the influences of the civil, military, and religious establishments could be brought to bear upon them unremittingly. Pareja reported that Natives at the mission centers were religiously observant, attending mass when it was celebrated, reciting the Divine Office, and congregating for feast days, for Holy Week, and for the Confraternity of the True Cross. However, "in the territories of the interior, they go to mass only every two years or so."[35]

The Spaniards realized that they had little hope of influencing, let alone effecting change among, the *La Florida* Natives, whose numbers and territories were far greater than their own, unless the Spaniards could accomplish two prerequisite objectives. First, each group of prospective converts had to be persuaded to give up a central element of their dynamism that was, in practice, a central element of their autonomy. That is, they had to be persuaded to relinquish the seasonal round of multiple living sites that had served them so well for so long, in favor of living in one, fixed, location. In this way, even a small number of Spaniards could have a greatly increased effect upon them and could sustain that effect in daily proximity.

Then, concomitantly, the Spaniards' abilities to convince the Natives to remain in a single location depended directly on their abilities to achieve the second prerequisite objective: to persuade the Natives that some substantial benefit accrued to making such a significant social change. In this facet of the ongoing negotiation, the Spaniards used twin, classic, negotiating ploys, which would today be characterized, simply, as a "carrot and stick" approach.

They demonstrated to the Natives that a distinct advantage accrued to their acquiescing to Spanish demands and remaining in a fixed location, that is, the advantage of the new, technological base to which the Natives would have access, provided in the forms of caring, protective, missionaries to teach them high-yield agricultural methods, provide European material culture items, and arrange access to a world-wide Spanish supply base. At the same time, they demonstrated to the Natives that a distinct *dis*advantage accrued to their failing to acquiesce to Spanish demands. This disadvantage lay in the prospect of social disruption and death occasioned by civil and military confrontations and physical destruction. Thus the missionaries tried to set themselves up as the keepers of the "carrots" and the Natives' main line of defense against the governors' "sticks."

However, once again, it is important to reiterate that this negotiating technique had very real limits and very real pitfalls. The Spaniards would have liked to have been able to spread their influence over a much larger physical area than the actual physical area over which they could spread their troops, but this hope was only chauvinistic, not realistic. Fray Pareja knew, as did the rest of the missionaries, that the greater the physical distance the Natives lived from the Spaniards' sociomilitary "epicenters," the less control the Spaniards realistically could hope to exercise.

Further, the Spaniards weakened their own potential for effective use of the system by their almost continuous squabbling over who should hold the carrot and who should wield the stick at any given time. In one example of many, Fray Baltasar López, OFM, informed the Crown, in 1602, that conversion lagged because the governor was not playing his part. He reported that the numbers of converts would increase "if the governor would punish and threaten [them]. The priests [could then] be merciful to the natives so the Indians could love them more and minister to them. So if Your Majesty would order [the governor] to support and favor this cause, it would grow and be more effective in winning souls for heaven."[36]

However, in 1657, when Governor Rebolledo made an official *visita* to Abalachi, his obvious agenda was to depict the Franciscans as the wielders of the stick. The Abalachinos had risen up against the intrusive Spaniards in 1647, because of excessive labor requirements and low or no pay, coupled with constant Spanish attempts to restrict their social traditions. The official report of the 1657 *visita* is so formulaic as to make transparent the governor's agenda. In town meetings with civic leaders across Abalachi, not a single negative action is attributed to the Spanish military establishment. Conversely, in every town, the Franciscans are denounced by Native speakers for forcing their people to work without pay and exercising arbitrary and excessive acts of anger upon the people, beating, kicking, and whipping them without cause.[37] Further, the friars prevented the Natives from selling their manufactured items to the soldiers, only so that these men of god could reserve the profits for themselves, by buying Native goods low and selling high to the soldiers.[38] At San Juan de Aspalaga mission, the report continued: "The Indians strongly asserted that they were not slaves and should not have to submit to such indignities. They especially resented this treatment because they were Christians and had obeyed all the Father's orders."[39]

In each village where they gathered, the *visitador* asked if there were murderers, acts of immorality, or persons keeping concubines. The response was always negative. In each village, the Natives were proud to feed the soldiers and work for them. And, in almost every village, caciques brought up their desire to have the *visitador* reconfirm the caciques' power and control in their towns, and the *visitador* obligingly complied. As a result, the governor felt himself officially vindicated: a classic, and obviously prearranged, win-win negotiation.

However, beyond the immediate and overt politicization of power, once again the problem of long-range authority turned upon the classic axiom of effective occupation: what you do not physically occupy, you do not really control. The Spaniards knew this, although they spent inordinate amounts of time attempting to shift blame whenever controls failed. The Natives knew it too, however, and those who lived beyond the effective reach of the Spaniards' carrot-and-stick influence—that is, outside of the Spaniards' power corridor—clearly demonstrated their knowledge by their abilities to finesse, ignore, or repulse unacceptable negotiations.

Even at the height of the seventeenth century, when Spanish negotiations were at their most successful, the Spanish sphere of influence lay within the bounds of the mission power corridor, which began at San Agustín, the fortified nucleus of *La Florida*. Beyond those bounds, on the south, lay the entire peninsula of *La Florida*, where early Spanish efforts to outnegotiate members of the Calusa and Teguesta power constellations had failed and where Spanish supply lines would be stretched to their maximum extent.[40] It would be 1697, and then again 1743, before more missionaries would be available to try again in this area and, then, they would be dispatched directly from Cuba rather than from San Agustín.

Meanwhile, to the north of Spain's tenuous power corridor lay the entire interior of the Southeast and the thousands of Maskókî peoples with whom Spain also would fail, because a lack of soldiers and logistical support would make it too risky for the Spaniards to split their limited resources and stretch their lines of support thinly enough to reach these areas. In this interior, the stresses of epidemics would be stronger than those occasioned by the expectations of the Spanish negotiations. Indeed, as archaeologist Marvin Smith sums it up: "Outside of areas of prolonged European-Indian contact, for example [in] the interior Southeast, acculturation had virtually no influence."[41]

Within the corridor, however, it was the Natives who did internalize the shift in cultural paradigms and who did become Hispanicized to any extent, and consequently dependent upon Spanish protection, who paid the greatest price for their shift. It was they who would suffer the most in the second part of the European Settlement Phase, after 1670, when they became the least-autonomous elements in the political and military clashes between the Spaniards and the English.

Concerning the impact of Spanish negotiations upon the peoples of *La Florida*'s southern peninsula, John Hann reports of the Calusa: "Throughout those two and one-half centuries [of the Entrada and Settlement phases] the Calusa were remarkably consistent in remaining totally impervious to the several missionization efforts directed at them, even when the mission efforts were launched, supposedly, at the request of the Calusa themselves. The Calusa are notable as well for the survival of their faith in their own belief system, which lay behind their disinterest in the new religion brought by the Spaniards."[42] Obviously, the Calusa were not the only *La Florida* peoples south of the power corridor to resist the transparent blandishments of the Other, or all of *La Florida*'s southern peninsula would have become a Spanish tributary, but the Calusa seem notable principally because a degree of documentation exists for them that does not exist for their neighbors.

As a result of the carrot-and-stick psychology, the Natives who succumbed to the coercion of the Spaniards and relocated physically to mission sites were available for more prolonged attacks on their belief structures. In addition, they were physically weakened by constant demands for their physical labor, and for the proceeds of that labor, not to mention by the physical pain of beatings for infractions of the many rules.[43]

As another facet of their constant attempts to negotiate control, the Spaniards, themselves the authors of a highly stratified society shaped around a strongly vertical power structure, dealt first and principally with the caciques and *hombres principales* among those whom they sought to influence. The Spaniards assumed that, as leaders, these individuals had the unilateral power to effect change among their people. The Spaniards had no understanding of, or interest in understanding, the dynamics of a horizontal power structure and, so, failed completely to understand when caciques argued that they could not acquiesce to Spanish demands because to do so would be to contravene the will of their people or fail to meet their expectations. The result of this would have been to seriously disrupt the equilibrium of the entire Maskokálgî universe and risk dire and terminal repercussions. This was particularly so in the cases of short-term negotiations. That is to say that the Spaniards had a much better chance of effecting their objectives and "winning" the negotiation when they negotiated from a large, fixed power base such as San Agustín or a fortified mission where military ascendancy had already been asserted, or where the demographics approached equality or superiority. In the case of small contingents of friars and soldiers, obviously outnumbered and poorly supplied, the lure of a Spanish god with little power had little appeal.

Consequently, those Maskókî peoples who succumbed to Spanish demands and made the most changes in their sociocultural bases were those who lived in the closest proximity to the largest constellations of Spanish culture elements. The dynamic behind this reality is critical to our understanding of the whole Native American–Euroamerican negotiative process. The Spaniards, as the first of the Europeans and Euroamericans to negotiate with the Native Americans of *La Florida* and North America, were asking (and often demanding and frequently coercing) the Natives to "commit cultural suicide." And, by the time the missions were destroyed by the English, many thousands of them had.[44]

However, the underlying dynamic of this process was the dynamic of *reciprocity,* the benchmark of the Maskokálgî cosmogony: anything given up had to be replaced by something of equal value, so that the cosmos would remain in balance. For the vast majority of the Maskókî peoples, the ones who did not succumb to the powerful inducements of fear and trade goods, neither the Spaniards nor the English nor any other Euroamerican group ever managed to offer anything of a value equal to that of their own successful system. In addition, even among those who made the external changes demanded by the Spaniards, many changes did not become permanent because the lack of value received became apparent. The Spaniards could neither judge nor measure nor even anticipate this reality, and to it can be attributed the ultimate failure of the Spanish negotiations with the Maskókî peoples, all their damage notwithstanding.

In his review of English proselytizing among the Natives of the land they called "Virginia," Gary Nash grasps several considerations concerning Native-English negotiations that are analogous to these important considerations concerning Native-Spanish negotiations. One is the centrality of demographics to the process of conversion and another, even more important, is the force of a successfully functioning cosmogony. He states, "When the Powhatan Confederacy was at least as strong as the Christian invaders, no amount of proselytizing could make a headway against a belief system that functioned admirably from the Indian point of view."[45] John Smith, founder of the Virginia colony, put it even more succinctly, and realistically. Not until "their Priests and Ancients have their throats cut," he said, was there any "hope to bring them to conversion."[46]

"That missionary success depended upon prior political domination [i.e., demographic and/or military domination] is rarely recognized in the historical literature on conversion," Nash continues, "which almost uniformly implies that indigenous people were simply waiting to be converted or that lack of accomplishment in this endeavor represented inadequate efforts on the part of the European community. This is to adopt the ethnocentric viewpoint of the early propagandists who insisted that 'savages' wanted to be converted because 'they groane under the burden of their bondage of Satan.'"[47]

Nash further compares studies of the conversion process among the Oglala Sioux and the Algonquians and concludes the same thing. Military and demographic superiority were essentials to a successful European negotiation. Epidemics were an element of the overall process, but only one element. Conversion came only if, and not until, "communal integrity had been compromised step-by-step . . . and sources of collective identity and individual social stature had been destroyed."[48] Even then, conversion was not necessarily total and the "praying Indians" often conformed outwardly but "inwardly preserved most of their traditional belief systems."[49] These conclusions certainly are borne out by the negotiative process as it was played out in *La Florida* between the Spaniards and the Maskókî peoples.

During the third period of the missionization process in *La Florida,* from 1616 to 1655, the Franciscans moved conversion westward across the northern peninsula. It was the period of their greatest zeal and the period when the groundwork was laid for the benefits that would be reaped at mid-century. First the Timuguana near San Agustín and on the St. Johns River received missionaries, then the *Timucua Alta,* that is, the Utina and Ustaqua, in the triangular region circumscribed by the Suwannee, Aucilla, and Santa Fé rivers.[50]

After 1633, the Abalachi people in the panhandle and present-day lower Alabama asked to receive missionaries. There, Spanish conversion and expansion would be ended, in the years 1704 through 1706, by the destructive raids of the English from the north and east. However, in the seventeenth century, the only full century of direct interactions and negotiations between the Spaniards and the Maskókî peoples, we may obtain an excellent and intimate view of the discourse of each of the participants in this high-stakes negotiation.

The Spanish Crown envisioned all the Natives of *La Florida* as constituting a "Republic of Indians" with which it could treat diplomatically, on European terms, at least in the abstract.[51] Native leaders were afforded certain types of deferential treatment under Spanish law, just as elite Spaniards were. The Spanish social system, which relied so heavily upon a vertical hierarchy, transferred its vertical power imaging to the Natives as well: "As vassals of the King of Spain, chiefs were the indispensable link between Spanish authority and Indian converts."[52] These leaders were singled out for intensive negotiations, given special bribes, and officially told that they would be exempted from certain forms of labor and punishments. In this manner, the Spaniards thought to shift their allegiance away from their own people and toward the Spanish power structure. At the same time, their children and heirs frequently were forcibly separated from them and sent away to Spanish schools, to be indoctrinated into Spanish culture. The obvious message to the caciques was that their power was tenuous and to be preserved only at the price of their allegiance to the Spaniards.[53]

In fact, the caciques who participated in the system did provide tribute laborers for civic projects in San Agustín, bearers for transport of goods between the capital and the towns and villages along the power corridor, ranch and field hands for the cattle ranches and the wheat fields of Timugua, and other services, but the caciques did not do this out of love for the Spaniards. Each fiscal year from 1593 onward, the Spaniards allocated funds—the *gastos de indios* or Indian expenses—to reward "friendship" and services rendered by allied caciques and to entice the gentile caciques to ally. Once again, however, a critical dichotomy existed between the way the Spaniards viewed the transaction, that is, as one-way, vertical largesse, and the way the Native mind viewed the transaction, that is, as a two-way, horizontal facet of reciprocity. Royal treasury officials complained, in 1627, that caciques "stalked into town as though [it were] they [who] were collecting tribute 'and that is what they call it.'"[54] The caciques were upholding their part of the reciprocal arrangement, and they expected the Spaniards to uphold theirs.

However, despite a veneer of deference, the willingness of the Spaniards to introduce fear into the negotiation or to resort to high-handed, impositional decision making whenever they felt they had sufficient power to do so was all too obvious. Despite assertions that they did not meddle with Native successions and that they consulted with the caciques and *hombres principales* on decisions concerning their own peoples, the willingness of the Spaniards to ignore their own assertions whenever power was in the balance is all too clear in the documents, and it was eminently clear to the Natives.

Therefore it follows as no surprise that it is also clear from the documents that Native leaders did not always image themselves as "good vassals," even if they had professed conversion and allegiance. When "gifts" were withheld or not available, for instance, the true nature of the Natives' imaging of themselves becomes transparent. At those moments, it becomes possible to see that the Natives saw themselves as equal participants, with the prerogative to withdraw their "loyalty." If Spanish demands became excessive or if the Natives simply tired of hearing them, they struck at the Spaniards militarily and ended the negotiation, at least temporarily and, sometimes, permanently as, for example, in military attacks on the Atlantic coastal islands, the lower peninsula, and the interior of the peninsula's headlands in almost every decade of Spanish interposition.[55]

Spaniards retaliated for Indian attacks with crop burnings, sentences of forced labor, and hangings, all in the name of "pacifications." Bushnell concludes that despite these power displays, the Spaniards did not destroy the legitimacy of Native succession.[56] This conclusion is simplistic, however. The Spaniards did not disrupt Native leadership successions among those Natives within their sphere of influence, whenever an intact tradition was most advantageous to the maintenance of Spanish control. However, the Spaniards did not hesitate to disrupt traditional leadership successions among Native converts, if they had the military power to buttress the change, when it came to practices that contravened Spanish or Roman Catholic law. Excellent cases in point were the rights to leadership of those caciques who maintained the tradition of polygamy and those who condoned dancing or ball playing, all of which were firmly embedded in the cosmogonic matrix of the Maskokálgî. These practices agitated the Spaniards constantly but served as instances of public utterances by which the Native people reconfirmed their cultural articulation.[57] The Spaniards were threatened by whatever they could not control or manipulate.

Although the Spanish systems of forced labor requirements, in the forms of the *repartimiento* and *encomienda,* were never institutionalized in *La Florida* to the extent that they were in larger Spanish settlement areas of the Americas, Spanish demands for access to Native labor were nonetheless real and nonetheless onerous to the Native peoples. The Royal Spanish *Ordenanzas* of 1573 permitted *adelantados* to make *repartimientos* or allocations of Native laborers from each village and to grant *encomiendas* or land grants, which included access to Native laborers on that land, to individuals in areas apart from the colonial core.[58] It was also expected that the governor would require tribute from any caciques who entered vassalage agreements.

In areas such as Nueva España and Perú, where there was a greater population density of both Natives and Spaniards, as well as a much more intense competition for more abundant natural resources, the system that was used by the Spaniards was more codified and enforced than in *La Florida,* where the vast areas beyond the Spaniards' power corridor could offer refuge to Natives who chose to reclaim their own prerogatives by escaping to affinity groups or to the wilderness.

However, in numerous instances, among those Natives who inhabited Spain's power corridor, the missionaries not only succeeded, but also succeeded to a sufficient degree that individuals began to model themselves on the Spanish culture and also to denigrate those of their tribe who clung to their "old ways." Bushnell points out that, as the seventeenth century progressed, proselytizers did not enter a village to begin their work without the express consent of the cacique. Again, however, we must keep the picture in balance. No amount of Spanish cooption of the Native leadership could ever totally offset the fact that Natives who did not wish to be converted to a system of Spanish slavery, both ideological and physical, always maintained the option to defect—and they exercised it, too. They are spoken of in the documents, constantly, as *fugivitos, infieles,* and *cimarrones,* the latter term in particular an important clue to the process taking place, as will be discussed in the next chapter.

In 1647, Spanish governor Francisco Menéndez Márquez subjected all of the Abalachi Natives, Christianized and non-Christianized alike, to the *repartimiento,* saying that the Christian Natives were nearly used up in the other provinces. However, many of the Natives deserted their villages and roamed as a free labor force, going from ranch to ranch, rather than permit themselves to be subjected to the labor levy.[59]

A form of *repartimiento* required the Natives to work on civic and private projects, such as the military fortifications of San Agustín and the fortified cattle ranches of the interior, but customary usage required some reciprocity in dealing with the Natives. When the governor called for laborers, they were to be provided with passage money and provisions and given gifts when they arrived at their destination. Both Natives and

missionaries complained loudly when they considered the labor requirements excessive, but conditions were not always mitigated, as we have seen
in the meetings with the *visitador* in 1657.

La Florida came to depend upon the agricultural by-products of the
missionization effort, specifically the Abalachi missions, both in terms
of the human labor force that they provided and in terms of indigenous
agricultural products and Spanish-introduced varieties. Corn, hogs, beef,
hides, tallow, fruits, and fowl, among other things, not only augmented San
Agustín's supplies but went to the markets of Cuba as well. A major ex-
port from Abalachi, however, was its people. It was more densely populated
than other Native regions, and the Spaniards' labor requirements took a
heavy toll there. In 1676, a generation after Governor Rebolledo's *visita*
found the missionaries solely responsible for the Natives' problems, Fray
Alonso Moral, OFM, who had served for thirty-three years in *La Florida*'s
missions, described in graphic detail the lives of many whom we will never
know as individuals.

> All the Natives of those provinces suffer great servitude, injuries, and
> vexations from the fact that the governors, lieutenants, and soldiers
> oblige them to carry loads on their shoulders to the Province of Apa-
> lachee and to other areas and also to bring loads from those regions to
> the fort of St. Augustine. And it usually happens that to enhance their
> own interests they pretend that this work is in Your Majesty's service,
> without paying them what is just for such intolerable work. And if now
> and again they give them something for that reason, it is a hoe or an ax
> or a cheap blanket or some other thing of such slight value to pay for
> their work, which involves carrying a cargo on their shoulders from the
> fort to the Province of Apalachee, which is eighty leagues distant, and
> the same return. . . . And in addition to this, in order to employ them
> further, they detain them in St. Augustine for as long as they wish . . .
> with very short rations, such as giving them only two pounds of corn a
> day and giving them for pay, at the most, one real for each day of work,
> which sum is usually given them in the form of old rubbish of little or
> no value or utility to them. Add to this the further vexation or injury of
> being snatched by force from their homes and villages, not only for
> tasks at the fort but also for work for private citizens, and this in the
> rigor of winter (when they come naked) or in the middle of summer,
> which is when they are most occupied in the labor of their crops on
> which solely depends not only their sustenance and that of their wives

and children but also the victuals necessary for the relief of the garrison. . . . Each year from Apalachee alone more than three hundred are brought to the fort at the time of the planting of the corn, carrying their food on their shoulders for more than eighty leagues with the result that some on arrival die and those who survive do not return to their homes because the governor and the other officials detain them in the fort so they may serve them and this without paying them a wage. . . . This is the reason according to the commonly held opinion that they are being annihilated at such a rate.[60]

9   Children of Self-Interest

[The Indians are] children of [self] interest, they seek and receive, here they
do the same and all appears little [to them.]

— Spanish governor at Pensacola to the Spanish
governor at San Agustín, July 24, 1717[1]

That same day, before the council began, I asked the . . . chief [of Coweta],
by what reason were the English in his town, with so much liberty and so
much license. . . . He turned to me to say that he had not invited them, that
they had come of their own accord. . . . I replied . . . that I would use force
on him who would put unwelcome strangers in another's house. . . . The
most he [finally] did was to bow his head and shed tears. After a short inter-
val he replied to me that I was as white as they were (the English) and that I
should reach an agreement with [them].

— Lieutenant Diego Peña to the governor of San Agustín,
Antonio de Benavides, September 28, 1718[2]

The policy of the Indians is Simple and Plain. Tis confined to the Securing
of their personal Safety, a Supply of their Wants, and fair Usage.

— Edmond Atkin Report[3]

Beyond its ostensible domain of interest, the welfare of the Natives, Fray
Moral's letter, which graphically illustrated the lives of the mission Natives of
La Florida and with which we closed our discussion of missionization, also
makes transparent other discourse sets that are pertinent to the larger sociopolitical condition of *La Florida* in the later seventeenth century. Competition
between governors, who held military as well as civil authority and maintained their power base at San Agustín, and the Franciscans, whose power base
was dispersed along the mission corridor, increased radically during the last
decades of the seventeenth century. Each used official rhetoric to frame the
other as a malefactor and to lay claim to the demographic and economic power
base that the missionized Natives constituted. In retrospect, Spain's objectives

would have been far better served if the Spanish factions could have clung to the realities of their common cause.

Without a doubt, however, another facet of this conflict was a reflection of the larger, and rapidly changing, colonial competition, over which the *Floridanos* had no control. Even as the Spaniards sought to solidify their internal influences among the Natives whom they had persuaded to remain within the mission corridor across the head of the peninsula, the external parameters of their negotiations were changing. Since its establishment, the tiny presidio of San Agustín had withstood English challenges and had paid the price of international rivalries, rising like the phoenix from its own ashes. However, the pace of English settlement attempts had increased from the first decade of the seventeenth century, and the English had begun to interpose in other Native-occupied territories along the north Atlantic frontiers of Spanish-claimed *La Florida*.

Their Plymouth (1607) and Jamestown (1620) settlements had little impact on the greater Southeast, initially. As early as 1629, however, while the Spaniards were still negotiating with Native peoples on the sea islands of Guale and in the riverine villages of Timugua, the English king Charles I granted to his own subjects lands running east and west from ocean to ocean and north-south from thirty-six to thirty-one degrees north latitude.[4] Not only were English views of North America as nebulous as those of the Spaniards, but also English attitudes toward effective occupation were obviously the same as those of the French: what the Spaniards had not settled, they did not hold.

Although no portion of this grant was actually taken up, in 1663 the English king rewarded it, in expanded form, and the Lords Proprietors of an English province of "Carolina" became Spain's new neighbors in *La Florida*. They were hardly good neighbors: the expanded grant included lands southward as far as twenty-nine degrees north latitude, that is, below San Agustín. In 1670, the Spanish Crown negotiated a compromise at Madrid that confirmed the rights of the English to settle, but only above the Savannah River. It was the best that Spain could effect, but it was only a rhetorical respite for *La Florida*.

Quickly, in that same year, the English established a settlement at Charles Towne, and very shortly, from this base, English agents began moving westward and southward among the Maskókî peoples, into the interior of *La Florida*. Charles Fairbanks declares this establishment of the Carolina colony to be "the major event in the history of Spanish Florida."[5]

While it is certainly inappropriate to continue to define the Spanish history of *La Florida* in English terms (as we have discussed earlier in this work), the gravity of the moment is nonetheless reconfirmed in Fairbanks's statement.

As a direct result of English entry into the negotiation, the nature of the power relationships and the tenor of the discourse between the Spaniards and the southeastern Natives changed completely and irrevocably. From 1670 onward, the negotiative process became multilateral rather than bilateral; the weight of cultural stress upon the southeastern Native groups became profound; and the number and types of cultural stressors exercised upon them increased exponentially. The combination reached the zenith (or the nadir, depending upon one's point of view) of its impositional weight in the first half of the eighteenth century. The situation exploded into warfare, not once but in a chain of bloody confrontations, and the explosions sent tribes and fragments of tribes ricocheting all the way across the Southeast and into the Caribbean.

That any Maskókî survivors managed to realign themselves in affinity groups and carry forward not only their individual lives but also their collective cultural lives in the Southeast from that point to the present is nothing short of miraculous. Their survival as coherent groups, and as holding communities for the cultural templates and social systems that had served them so well for so long, only reconfirms the validity and viability of those systems and reminds us, yet again, that we must search for the mechanisms of their survival rather than invent the mechanisms of their destruction.

The strategy of the English in *La Florida* was clear and forceful: the Natives were warriors, and the English wanted to manipulate their power to the benefit of incipient English mercantilism. In addition, their discourse was not couched either primarily or secondarily in the rhetoric of conversion. This was no discourse of salvation, with its requirement of cultural suicide. Nor were the English interested in philosophical supercedence of the Maskokálgî, that is, of the cosmogonic matrix of the Maskókî peoples' culture and societies.

In fact, they were not specifically interested in the people, per se, at all. The mercantilistic English began a discourse of economics with the Maskókî peoples that would, in the long run, wreak more social havoc among them and their descendants than had the devastating pathogens of the previous century. However, we still must separate social from cultural effects. Land was the principal focus of English economic demands:

colonization affirmed it; Crown-sponsored militarism enforced it; and the highly lucrative, and destructive, deerskin and slave trades exploited it.

Clearly, the elements of the cultural and social pressures to which the Maskókî peoples were subjected by the Spaniards were fundamentally different, both in form and intensity, from those to which they were subjected by the English. At the basis, both European powers believed themselves possessed of a superior religion, which possession buttressed their right to rulership. However, although the *asientos* frequently highlighted the centrality of religious conversion in Spain's settlement process, the English Crown felt no such ideological compunction.[6]

Even as English monarchs asserted rule by virtue of their "especial grace," that is, by divine right derived directly from their god, just as did other western European monarchs of medieval and early modern periods, this grace implied no mandate to proselytize. It did, however, confer an a priori right to rule, and, to the English, rulership entailed dominion of the land rather than of people. This mentality is clearly demonstrated in the letters patent granted by Elizabeth I, which repeatedly mandate that the recipient "discover, find, [and] search out" lands that also repeatedly are described as "remote, barbarous, and heathen," in order to "have, hold, occupy and enjoy" not the peoples but the "soyle of all such lands" as they may discover.[7]

To the Spaniards for whom, as we have seen earlier, the concepts of economic and ideological Conquest were twins, commercial success included—nay, required—philosophical complicity (at least). In order to facilitate this paradigm shift, the Spaniards had tried to keep those Natives who succumbed to their initial negotiations unarmed, on foot, and bowed by the guilt and fear of Roman Catholicism, as methods of maintaining influence from an unequal demographic base.[8] The English, on the contrary, began to negotiate reciprocal nonaggression pacts with interior Maskókî peoples, by the terms of which the English would supply guns and horses and quantities of attractive trade goods and the Maskókî tribes would provide slaves to work "English" lands, in addition to supplying the deerskins that formed a significant feature of the base of a lucrative, colonial English economy.[9]

A number of the Maskókî tribes allied themselves with the English and agreed also to protect the advances of the English into the interior, not only against the hostilities of nonallied tribes, but also against the retaliation of the Spaniards. From the Native point of view, this was an excellent no-lose negotiation: those tribes that allied themselves received access to a new technological base that could provide the winning edge in traditional intertribal belligerencies. If the new white Others defeated Native enemies of the English-allied tribes, then their enemies lost, and the Maskókî tribes that had agreed to work with the English won too. If the new white Others fought the old white Others (the Spaniards), then no matter who lost, the Maskókî tribes still won because they had one less white enemy. The English unleashed a firestorm across the Southeast.

Agriculture had never been the principal business of the Maskókî peoples: warfare had. Basic and critical social templates concerned the functioning and ramifications of warfare in society, and these templates interlocked with every other template. Linear documentation produced by the Spaniards during the Entrada and first Settlement phases of their interposition among the Maskókî peoples illustrates clearly their concerns with pacifying the bellicose Natives, partly by settling them in population centers accessible to Spanish religious and military powers.

From these culture bases, the Spaniards sought to break the militaristic traditions of the Maskokálgî, first, by eliminating the belligerence of their converts and, then, by protecting their converts from the classic belligerence of surrounding "infidel" or "pagan" tribes.[10] The documents contain numerous references to diplomatic missions by which the Spaniards sought to negotiate peace between and among belligerent infidel and converted tribes and the Spaniards.

These references also reveal to us several important processes beyond the obvious. For one thing, they confirm, consistently, the dynamic nature of the Maskokálgî world. Not just territorial hunters, not static agriculturalists, and not isolated polities, the tribes perpetually recalibrated their cosmic equilibrium in conflict. From genetic revitalization to the semiotics of power at the broadest community level, warfare fueled Maskokálgî society. The people drew upon it as one of the most tangible and dependable fonts of utterances from which they renewed their social compacts. The Spaniards, realizing, at least, the propensity of the people for belligerence, had tried to suppress it. The English, chauvinistically thinking to control it, virtually gave those Maskókî tribes that allied themselves with the English carte blanche.

Furthermore, beyond the dynamism of the surrounding tribes, the documentary references to warfare remind us that this element of dynamism could not have existed among the peoples as a unique or isolated element. Social evolution, of which warfare was but one motive force, was an ongoing part of the lives of the peoples with whom the Spaniards were negotiating. Certainly, then, beyond the power sphere of the Spaniards there must have been an equal or greater amount of evolution among the peoples of the peninsula and the interior. Caciques died and were succeeded and many tribal designators changed. Military, tributary, and family alliances shifted. Clans grew or decreased in population and tribes grew or declined in power. In addition, women, as leaders, diplomats, and conquest wives and slaves, transmitted alternative templates of social actions. Some of these evolutionary processes took place within sight of the Spaniards, and some did not. Consequently, it becomes important to recall that although we cannot always "see" social evolution in the documents this does not mean that it did not take place.

Here, therefore, we must take up also a change that appeared to take place but, in reality, did not. It was a change in the Maskókî peoples that was far more apparent than real, because it was a change wholly manufactured and manipulated in the minds—and documents—of the English, who interposed into the Maskókî-Spanish negotiation from 1670 onward. This "change" was the arbitrary construct of the misnomer "Creek" and the myth of a "Creek Confederation."

The act of naming is also the act of creation and the "right" to create is inherently the assumption of a profound power: "Name-giving is a powerful activity, a symbol of sovereignty."[11] It is an exercise in intellectual objectification, but objectification not within the context of the named. It is, rather, an exercise embedded wholly in the cultural context or particularist agenda of the group or individual exercising the assumption of the power to name.

Within the context of the Spanish-Maskókî negotiations, the Spaniards had assumed the right to name, as power-bearing agents of their deity. Village names were ritually subsumed by Roman Catholic saints' names, to attach them to the power of "mother church." By the ritual ceremony of baptism, the quintessential rite of passage in the process of conversion, the Spaniards had symbolized the cultural suicide that they had demanded of those Natives who wanted access to the power constellation the Spaniards represented, that is, to any or all of those things that the Natives perceived as material culture or sociocultural benefits of Hispanicization. Within the rite of baptism, they had unilaterally assigned Spanish names to converts, thereby stripping away (from the Spaniards' point of view) not only the individual but also the entire cosmogony that had existed in "paganism," replacing it and him or her with a "new" person clothed in Roman Catholic redemption. However, the Native peoples did not always attach to the discourse of conversion and the symbology of baptism the profound social values that the Spaniards attached to them. And their actions during the initial stages of this later Spanish Settlement Phase, certainly from the 1670s to 1704, provide us with very clear evidences of the Native reality in opposition to the Spanish reality.

The English, again, initiated no coherent discourse of conversion. Nor did they indulge in the semiotics of individual name changing as a signal of cultural conversion at the individual level. Their interest in the Maskókî peoples was not operative at the individual level, nor were they even specifically interested in the Maskókî peoples, as such. In the pursuit of economic success and military security in their colonial enterprise, the English rhetorically homogenized and obliterated the Maskókî tribes, by intellectually burying them under an arbitrarily imposed and fictitious name, to wit, Creeks.

The name was a corruption of that first applied in the late seventeenth century by the English specifically to those collective villages of Maskókî peoples living on the creeks tributary to the Ocmulgî (Ocmulgee) River (in present-day lower Georgia). These peoples appear to have been members of the Otci'sî tribe and, so, the English called them "Ochisi Creeks" and, within a generation, dropped the Natives' non-English designator in favor of the single English word.[12]

Further, as the use of the English word *Creeks* became entrenched among English speakers, its application increased and became generic. By the early 1700s, English traders and officials were obscuring the realities of all of the Maskókî tribes by assigning to them fictive memberships in geopolitical polities that they (the English) designated as the "Upper Creeks" and the "Lower Creeks." This designator was also fictitious and based solely upon the occurrence of their towns and villages either above or below the geographic fall line across what later became Alabama and Georgia. Even though this geographic designator has been applied time and again by Euroamerican researchers as if it were a social marker, it has no social validity within the Maskókî world. However, in the western European world, with its classic tradition of *quod non est in scriptis, non est in mundo,* these arbitrary, obfuscating, disarticulating, and disempowering aliases were institutionalized in the English documents. As a consequence, they have become the default usages of the Euroamerican peoples who later created United States history in their own image and likeness.

Who were these "Ochisi Creeks," in their own reality, if they were not the generic Creeks of the English? What may we learn from their own realities that might have applications to a twentieth-century understanding of their cultural descendants? Although the designator "Creek" was an invention, the peoples whom it designated were not; their realities still retained the constructs of earlier centuries, when the Spaniards had known more specifically the names by which they defined themselves and had recorded many of them in their own terms.

John Swanton indicates, with plausibility, that the word *Otci'sî* is a Hitchiti-language word "applied particularly to the Muskogee."[13] If this is correct, then the Hitchiti, themselves members of the Maskókî linguistic family, were using the name generically and the Spaniards were accepting it specifically. The Otci'sî were the Ichisi/Chisi/Achese of the de Soto chronicles, inhabitants of an independent town by Spanish description at the moment of the Spaniards' passage, but physically adjacent to the large Ocute province (to the northeast). To the north and west of both of them lay the even larger, wealthier, and more powerful Coça province, which was also a member of the Maskókî linguistic family.[14] In fact, the Coça power constellation contained the core towns of the Maskókî peoples, the elder towns of their cultural matrix, and the keepers of their most powerful traditions in medicine. To the south, west, and east of the Otci'sî lay further provinces of Maskókî peoples, also members of the old linguistic family and who also had their own mutually unintelligible members of that family already by the sixteenth century.

It is in description of all of these Maskókî peoples that Swanton applies the term *Creek Confederation,* the adoption of which by many other Euroamerican researchers has been the occasion of so much more misunderstanding. The first and foremost problem with this designator is that it uses the fictitious name *Creek,* when it could just as easily retain the Native word *Maskókî* and, with it, some semblance of Native reality. Then, there is the problem of the uppercase letter *C* in *confederation,* which implies some formal entity that is not substantiated in the European documents or in Maskókî tradition. Finally, there is the problem of the word *confederation* itself and the concept that readers infer from it. In the use of this descriptor, there is the concomitant implied image of a clearly agreed-upon contract, whether of written or verbal rhetoric is immaterial, as a result of which two or more polities enter into a compact or an alliance either in support of each other or of some enterprise. Further, its application imparts an image of a people, although widely scattered, acting in concert with their mutually agreed-upon aims. All of this clearly is not the case.

Swanton declared, for no apparent reason, that "when we first hear of . . . [the] Muskogee tribes . . . [that is, in the sixteenth century,] [t]he Confederation evidently existed in some form at that time."[15] Swanton does not mention as much at this point in his text, but he relied extensively upon George Stiggins's account of Maskôkî history. Stiggins, himself half Maskôkî, may have promulgated the error that has been so long perpetuated by Euroamerican researchers. He wrote of a "Creek or Muscogee body," composed of "tribes who retain their primitive tongues and customs."[16] Further, he declared, with an obvious degree of boosterism (although he fought with United States troops against his Maskôkî kin in the Creek War of 1813–1814): "These tribes are inseparably united by compact and consolidated by individual and national interest."

However, there was no "confederation" that united the Maskôkî peoples, certainly not in any documentary sense and, apparently, not even in any discursive sense. If there had been, as but one example, Alexander McGillivray (1759–1793), who wanted so much to unite the Maskôkî peoples in written compact *and* concerted action against the Euroamericans, would not have encountered so much difficulty in doing so.[17] Indeed, archaeologists have begun to question this chimerical "confederation" as well. Marvin Smith, Vernon Knight, and Sheree Adams discount it, at least as late as 1700.[18] However, although there was no confederation in the sense of any concerted agreement or action, there were nonetheless some agents that defined the Maskôkî peoples as a coherent group, at a much greater level than that of concerted action, or else we would not be able to speak of them as a people.

What did exist, above all, among the Maskôkî peoples was a set of cultural templates or commonalties that anchored the Maskôkî firmly in their Maskokálgî heritage. However, as we have already seen, the larger belief system of which the Maskokálgî, or People of the Maskôkî Way, were a coherent part, and which we may designate as Mississippianism, was not unique to the Maskôkî peoples. It did, however, find unique expressions among the Maskôkî peoples. Then, the fact that their languages appear to have emanated from a common source also marks them but, as we discussed early on in this work, language is neither synonymous with culture nor is it a definitive indicator of culture. Our constant reminder of this reality is the common motive force of warfare, which divided rather than united the Maskôkî peoples at the tribal level. Within and among the Maskôkî peoples, however, we also can recognize those shared symbolic dimensions, such as warfare and medicine to name just two, with analogous realms of meaning that contextualized them in a shared universe. However, none of these factors either requires or even implies unanimity of thought or action on any specific subject. Perhaps that is what George Stiggins meant to say.

La Florida's Eighteenth-Century Metamorphosis

In 1672, the Spanish Crown, recognizing the radically increased vulnerability of *La Florida,* with only its single wooden presidio (its ninth) as its primary defense, finally sent funds for the construction of a stone fortress to protect San Agustín and the inland provinces. A labor levy of three hundred Natives per year was exacted from the three provinces of Spain's mission corridor to support the civic projects in San Agustín, especially the construction of the new fortress, El Castillo de San Marcos.[19] Although the construction ultimately took over two decades, its presence proved invaluable to Spain's maintenance of its increasingly tenuous hold on a highly circumscribed *La Florida.*

By 1674, the English had agreed to supply guns to the non-Maskókî Chichimeco, or Westo as the English renamed them, whose territory lay north of Spanish-influenced Guale, so that they might create a military buffer for the English.[20] In addition, by 1680, English-allied or instigated Maskókî tribes began to harass the western end of the Spanish mission chain, in the very heart of *La Florida.* John Worth concludes, cogently, that in the entrance of the Chichimeco peoples into the lower Southeast we finally begin to see the impact of the more northerly English settlements. Propelled by English commercial pressures for slave trade, and emboldened by supplies of English weapons, the Chichimeco were but the harbingers of more intense English demands for slaves and deer hides. As various of the Maskókî tribes allied themselves with the English, and turned their new weapons on their own cultural kin to the south and east, a degree of internecine warfare was precipitated that was far more intense than anything the Maskókî peoples had theretofore experienced.

The last four decades of the seventeenth century were a time of peril for the Spanish mission Natives of Guale province particularly. Not only did they begin to experience the pressures created by the English settlement of the Carolina province, but also the growing English establishment in Virginia, even farther north, produced an impact upon *La Florida*'s outliers that was negative in every way. John Worth's excellent assessment of the role played by the territory that would, after 1733, be called Georgia, makes it clear that this area was a critical ground for the amalgamation of one of the affinity groups that would shortly go together to the southwest, across the crown of *La Florida*'s peninsula, as a free (undominated) people who spoke of themselves as *yat'siminolî* (in Hitchiti) and *istî siminolî* (in Maskókî). The word and the concept still exist today in both Seminole Tribal languages.

In his *Struggle for the Georgia Coast*, Worth describes the process taking place in the 1670s by which the name *Chiluque* (Tcilokit) may have come to be applied to Natives living on the barrier islands around Santa Elena.[21] In this region, known to the Natives as Escamaçu, in 1672, a Spaniard described an individual Native as a "Chiluque," and modern researchers still are casting about for an understanding of this word, or the new tribe that it may represent. Worth correctly explains, however, that the etymology of the word is core Maskókî and that it was applied to any people who spoke a language foreign to the Maskókî speakers. Thus it came to be applied, at about the same time, to the foreigners who lived on the northeastern borders of the core Maskókî, the old Coça kingdom, and to individuals taking refuge among the mission Natives at Santa Elena.

Worth continues: "Such a possibility would indeed be consistent with the interpretation of the old province of Escamaçu/Santa Elena being a haven for refugees from a variety of regions, most or all of which *came to be known as* Yamasee Indians. Nevertheless, whether these Chiluque of Santa Elena were identical with, part of, or distinct from the emerging Yamasee confederacy is presently unclear based on existing documentation" (emphasis added).[22]

However, there are, indeed, further bits of information to be gleaned here. First, as we have discussed above, we must abandon the use of the term *confederacy*, which too often obfuscates when applied to the southeastern Natives. In the late seventeenth and eighteenth centuries, some of the Yamásî peoples supported the English, raiding with them into Spanish power spheres. Others supported the Spaniards and took refuge under what appeared to be their protecting mantle, near San Agustín. The refuge was illusory, but the fact remains that there was no unanimity of political thought or objectives among the Yamásî peoples.

There may also have been one other element that constituted a bond among the Yamásî, and the clue to it may come from the word itself. *Yamásî* is a Maskókî phrase meaning "tame, or tamed, people" and it is still in use today, as a term of derision. Because the epithet was applied to individuals at Santa Elena as distinct from the term *Chiluque*, this seems to be an indication that Maskókî speakers were making the assessment and that the "tamed people" were representatives of tribes who were not considered to be foreign speakers. Thus, rather than a discrete tribe or an allied group of tribes and peoples acting from an overt, agreed-upon palette of attitudes and actions, what we may be seeing in the Yamásî is the amalgamation of a constellation of tribes, carrying within them the imprint of some much earlier shared experience or defeat. Otherwise, more likely, the use of the derisive designator "a tamed people," which actually had applied earlier to a core group of peoples defeated by some Maskókî tribes, may have been in the process of expansion at this time of increasing *cimarronaje* to include any Maskókî tribal remnants or individuals who permitted themselves to be "tamed" by the Spaniards. That is, by going in to the mission sites to be controlled by the Spaniards, they lost the collective power and visibility that attached to a strong cacique and a strong town, and the other Maskókî speakers derided them for it. If this is indeed the case, then it also explains one more point, that is, why there should suddenly seem to be so many Yamásî in relation to the other tribal peoples. They appear particularly, in the middle decades of the seventeenth century, throughout the peninsula of *La Florida* and in what seems to be disproportionately high numbers. Perhaps it was not that the tribe was growing but, rather, that the currency of the epithet was growing. This possibility still does not tell us by whom or when the original carriers of the epithet were "tamed," but it does remind us of the historical value and validity of Native naming systems and our need to pay them closer attention.

In addition to the external English impetus, another critical but separate, internal, reality was converging with Spain's fears regarding its dwindling sphere of influence. The underlying realities of the paper wars between the Spanish civil/military authorities and the missionaries were becoming all too apparent and were taking their toll upon many of the missionized Natives. Over the second half of the seventeenth century, the Spaniards' inland advance slowed and stopped in western Abalachi. As Bushnell phrases it, "the three Florida provinces of Timucua, Guale, and Apalache seem to have reached the saturation point in conversion by the mid-1640s."[23] More accurately, the Spaniards had reached the limits of their physical and ideological span of control. Only radical demographic increases could have helped them regain their impetus, but Spain's human and economic resources were needed, more and more, elsewhere in her colonial empire. By the end of the century, the mission Natives were complaining loudly and repeatedly about the failures of the Spaniards to abide by Native expectations of reciprocity.

Clear pieces of evidence of this process at work are provided by Don Patricio and Don Andrés, the caciques of Ivitachuco and San Luís, respectively, in Abalache, who wrote repeatedly to the Spanish Crown, petitioning because "justice is not administered to us."[24] It was not law that was the prime concern of the Natives, it was justice. Time and again, the Spanish officials at the mission village required domestic services of the Christianized Natives, mistreated them physically, and paid them nothing. The civil/military authority required Native tribute labor to construct not only public defenses but personal residences as well, and their new residences literally crowded the Natives out of the village. The Natives from San Luis, the caciques said, had consequently withdrawn one league into the woods. Many fled the mission altogether, some going as far as Guale province. The Spaniards, it appears, paid lip service to redress but, ultimately, changed nothing. The Natives stored up their grievances, along with anxieties at a world out of balance.

By 1702, another negotiant entered the bargaining in *La Florida* or, rather, re-entered through another port. After some years of attempts to plant a colony along the Gulf coast, in a concerted effort to use and control the Mississippi River, the French established a settlement at Mobile, inside *La Florida*. This posed a serious threat to the recently re-established Spanish presidio at Pensacola, Spain's only effective occupation beyond the mission corridor. By 1717, the French would penetrate the territories of the Maskókî tribes as far north as the traditional Coça province. There they constructed a "factory," a fortified center for the collection of Native-supplied deer hides and other manufactured goods and the distribution of French trade wares, on the Coça (Coosa) River. They called their factory Fort Toulouse. The Natives called it *Franca choka chula*, "French treaty house" (from the Maskókî *chokó*, "building or house," paralleling Mikísuukî *chikî* or "chickee" as English speakers misspell it, and *chóka*, "a writing or paper," as a treaty). It was there that Andrew Jackson would force upon the Maskókî tribes, friends and foes alike, the single largest land capitulation in southeastern history, as a reparation for the Creek War of 1813–1814.

The interposition of this third negotiant had one direct and one indirect effect upon *La Florida*, but both were ultimately negative for the Natives and the Spaniards. The French used the negotiating strategy of setting one tribe against another so that they could control both. In the lower Gulf region, this sent infidel tribes moving directly eastward toward Abalachi. In the northern reaches of "Louisiana" the great Nétchez tribes rose up against the French, and from the western and northern reaches of core Maskókî tribal territories, some of the adjacent Koasatî, Chactá, and Chicaça began to migrate eastward into the old Coça province and, indirectly, to pressure the core Maskókî tribes, which were already pressed from the north and east by the English.

Over the first half of the eighteenth century, these *La Florida* tribes would suffer severe economic hardships as they overhunted their traditional ranges to satisfy English demands for deerskins and their own desires for English trade wares. The pluralities of tribal males began to neglect warfare for deer hunting and to neglect hunting deer for hunting other Natives, as the English demand for slaves increased. Consequently, other and concomitant pressures would stress their social systems as natural cycles of use and distribution of resources within the tribes meshed more and more erratically with the social requirements of maintaining cosmic equilibrium. These pressures were felt by the Maskókî peoples of *La Florida,* from the old Coça province to the sea islands of Guale, and from the province of the Alibamos to the bleak *cayos,* which the Spaniards called *los martires,* off the southern tip of the peninsula.

It would be very easy to interpret these pressures as the death knell for the Maskókî peoples and simply to reiterate the rhetoric of Conquest that has buttressed Euroamerican chauvinism for so long. That coherent tribes of descendants of these proud and resilient Natives still exist today impels us, however, to seek further for the process by which they survived the destruction that the Euroamerican documents proclaim.

Caught between this English- and French-instigated southward press of the Maskókî tribes, which tribes themselves were stressed by English demands for deerskin trade goods and slaves and the territorial clashes among the Native tribes and, in growing numbers, the *cimarrones* and migrant groups south of them, were the missionized Natives of Spain's power corridor. By the nature of their cooption into the missionization process and by periodic Spanish reprisals, they had been denied much of their access to their concerted power to offer resistance. Within two generations of the interposition of the English into *La Florida,* not only would they lose another degree of their autonomy, but many would lose their lives as well, as Carolina's Colonel James Moore smashed at the loose line of Spanish power in *La Florida,* the missions, in 1704 through 1706.

One important facet of their autonomy the Maskókî peoples would retain, however, and one they exercised repeatedly throughout the entire two and one-half centuries of Spanish negotiations, was the option to quit the negotiations and place themselves physically beyond the Spaniards' sphere of discourse and power. As we have seen earlier, the problem (for the Spaniards) of *cimarrones*—Natives who simply left their power corridor and, apparently, their entire sphere of influence—was an old and continuing one. During the second half of the seventeenth century, the Guale, Timuguana, Abalachi, and other Natives whose lives centered within the Spaniards' power corridor began to exercise this option in growing numbers. These *cimarrones* would re-ally themselves in affinity groups throughout *La Florida*'s peninsula and beyond Spanish control and, although the English would anglicize the epithet that the Spaniards had applied to them, these generic "Siminolies" would still be Abalachi and Abalachicolo and Chatot and Potano and Guale and Hitchiti, and Yamásî and Yuchî, and many more: some were moving southward ahead of Euroamerican advances, but many had traversed and hunted the peninsula for a century and two centuries, and more.

Spanish *Cimarrones*

The etymology of the nineteenth-century generic designator "Siminolies," precursor of today's "Seminoles," is a subject that few Euroamerican researchers choose to confront. Most unilaterally conclude that, in some form, it carries the implication for today's Seminoles of a person who is "wild" or a "renegade," that is, actively running away from something—presumably from the possibility of a civilized, Euroamerican, life. Florida State Chamber of Commerce rhetoric affirms this simplistic separatist vision, without explanation, of a people at once homogeneous in their own society and heterogeneous in the voluntary seclusion of their Everglades existence, thereby once again neatly sidestepping any involvement with, or responsibility for, the Euroamericans' obscurantist vision. However, as in so many other instances, the realms of meaning embodied in the name are much richer and more historically engaged than the simplistic fiction. The key to uncovering the meaning of the term *Seminole* in all its historical richness lies in the discourse of the Spaniards and the Native Americans of the circum-Caribbean.

First, it is useful to note that the word does not appear in the earliest official Spanish lexicon, the 1611 *Tesoro de la Lengua Castellana o Española,* compiled by Sebastián de Covarrubias Horozco. Its earliest documentary use was in the *Historia* of the Spaniards' new world written by Fernández de Oviedo, in 1535, where it appears as a descriptor of an *indio cimarrón o bravo* and *puercos cimarrones o salvajes*.[25]

In his 1926 work *Hilfswörterbuch für den Amerikanisten,* Georg Friederici defines it as an American borrowing thus:

> [C]imarrón, çimarron . . . , maroon; Wild, ungebändigt, entlaufen, flüchtig; Es toda cosa huida y retirada; simarón, que era él que huia ó ausentaba del dominio ó señorío de su dueño; hombres y animales indómitos, plantas silvestes.[26]

Joan Corominas, in citing the word in the *Diccionario Crítico Etimológico Castellano e Hispánico,* assigns its etymology to America, but explains that the prefix *cima-* is of obscure American origin, while the suffix *-arron* occurs frequently in Castellano, in combination with numerous and varied root words.

The Real Academia Española's *Diccionario de la Lengua Española* still carries the word *cimarrón* and defines it thus:

> Cimarrón, na (De cima.) adj. Amér. Decíase del esclavo que se refugiaba en los montes buscando la libertad. 2. Amér. Dícese del animal doméstico que huye al campo y se hace monteraz. 3. Amér. Dícese del animal salvaje, no domesticado. 4. Amér. Aplícase a la planta silvestre de cuyo nombre o especie hay otra cultivada. 5. R. de la Plata y Urug. Dícese del mate amargo, o sea sín azurcar. 6. Fig. Mar. Dícese del marinero indolente y poco trabajador.[27]

The fact that the first printed use of this word occurred relatively early in the exploration phase of American interposition admits the possibility that the Spaniards coopted a word from one or more Native American languages, possibly Arawak. At least one commentator assigns the source to La Habana.[28] As the final entry above indicates, however, the term has many uses, of which some apply to humans and others to plants and animals. The most important thing that it illustrates, however, is that the definitions all are bound by a concept rather than by a race or by any specific sociocultural group. The word *cimarrón* images a realm of meaning that is one side of a dichotomy of existence: the *out* side. However, rather than in the Spanish or English sense of a fearful people, escaping from their proper place, the phrase has been internalized by its bearers in the sense of an indomitable people who choose not to permit themselves to be controlled or domesticated by any others. They image themselves as a people who have steadfastly maintained freedom of thought and action and refused to accept a restricted life or to submit themselves involuntarily to the dominion of another. Both the Maskôkî and Hitchiti, or Mikísuukî, languages in use among the Seminole people today still contain parallel significators that speak to this characteristic of indominability. Furthermore, in neither language is the significator used by the people to image and embody themselves as a discrete group. In other words, the word carries only the lexical weight that it carries in English: that of an adjective, not a noun. In Maskôkî, the term is *istî siminolî*, and in Hitchiti the term is *yatî siminolî* or, in its vernacular contracted form, *yat'siminolî*. Both terms are most frequently translated by English speakers today as "wild" or "renegade," but such usages are reductionist, at least, and depend for their symbology entirely upon the locus of enunciation.

A typical early application of the term was to slaves who refused to remain under the control of Spanish masters. Among Spain's American colonies, African slave revolts began almost as early as slavery itself, so the term has had long use. Slaves rose up on the island of Santo Domingo in 1522 and in Nueva España (Mexico) in the following year. In 1526, the first slave insurrection in North America occurred, in the short-lived colony established by Lucas Vásquez de Ayllón the Elder (near what is now called Sapelo Sound, in Georgia). African slaves revolted in Cuba in 1530 and also in the five-year-old capital of Columbia, where the city was destroyed. Despite the fact that the Spaniards meted out the harshest of punishments to rebellious slaves, they continued to risk life and limb to live in freedom. Successful runaways formed communities that the Spaniards referred to variantly as *cimarrón, palenque,* or [cim]*marón* (in English, *maroon*) towns.[29]

In *La Florida*, the Spaniards' documents make it clear that the term also was being applied to the Maskôkî peoples. At least as early as 1635, a Spanish soldier in *La Florida* recalled having been sent, in 1622 and 1623, to recover from the missions of Guale and San Pedro de Mocama fugitives whom he referred to as "*Indios Simarrones.*"[30] The usage appears again in 1655 letters.[31]

In *La Florida, cimarronaje,* or the movements of individuals beyond the Spaniards' sphere of power or influence, became more and more commonplace throughout the seventeenth century. Bushnell, speaking of the mission corridor, concluded: "None of the Spanish, whether friars, soldiers or settlers, could solve [La] Florida's almost unmentionable problem: the Indians were dying off. The earlier they had been converted, the sooner they were gone. The eastern part of Timucua, once the most populous part of the ecumene, was so depopulated by epidemics *and emigration* that it could not even provide the ranchhands for the Spanish and cacique-owned cattle ranches now [in the 1670s] occupying its old fields. . . . [La] Florida had become a hollow peninsula" (emphasis added).[32]

This statement is instructive. The implication is that the Natives who were running off were running northward, off the peninsula. There is no definitive reason not to believe that many were migrating southward, however. True, there were no major sources of English trade wares to lure them there before the turn of the century, but there were almost no Spaniards there either. By the second half of the century, there seem to have been labor shortages in Abalachi as well as in Timugua. Pearson surmises that the 1656 uprising in Tumugua may have occasioned the departure of many Natives from the path of the Spaniards who were sent to quell them.[33] Moreover, juxtaposed to the notices of *cimarronaje,* we also find evidence that Native peoples who chose to leave the Spaniards did not leave *La Florida* "a hollow peninsula."

Sergeant-Major Domingo de Leturiando, who made a *Visita General* to Abalachi in 1677–1678, spoke with caciques and *hombres principales* in villages throughout the province and told them, repeatedly, that they were not to admit "wandering men" to their villages. He said, specifically, that there were "large numbers" of these wanderers and that they should be required to show a permit from Spanish authorities before being admitted. Again, during the *Visita General* of Captain Antonio de Arguelles to Guale in the following year, it was noted that the cacique of Santa Catalina mission was experiencing problems caused by wandering males, some single and some married, but all disruptive.[34] Obviously, there were numerous individual Natives in the *La Florida* wilderness whom the Spaniards could neither control nor count. By the early eighteenth century, their numbers would only be greater.

Bushnell writes, "In the early 1700s, Indian commoners took advantage of Florida's war with Carolina to abandon their towns and chiefs altogether. The Spanish retained effective control only of St. Augustine, which became an entrepôt of intercolonial trade."[35] By the year 1701, also, the term *cimarrón* was still current among the Spaniards, and many independent Natives to whom it referred were living in the area of the La Chua *ranchos,* in what is today Alachua County on the north-central peninsula.

Chua, as the Timuguana called the area, or *la chua,* with the Castilian article affixed, was and remains a unique geological area of *La Florida's* north-central peninsula. Its karst topography facilitates the formation of sinkholes that permit standing waters to disappear periodically and create a vast prairie. *Chua,* the graphic Timuguana signifier for this area, imaged a bowl with a hole in the bottom, in other words, a vessel that would not hold water. It was in this area that the Spaniards made their largest land grants, not only to Spaniards but also to some Native caciques as well. These grantees established fortified cattle ranches, at least as early as the mid-seventeenth century, and hired or blatantly coopted the labor of Maskôkî peoples from numerous surrounding areas to tend herds of cattle and other domesticated animals.

John Hann quotes San Agustín governor José Zúñiga y Cerda as instructing Joachín de Florencia, who was to lead an expedition southward from San Francisco Potano into Mayaca and Jaroro territory in the interior peninsula, to "spend some time in the woods and environs of the La Chua Hacienda 'to clear the land of *yndios cimarrones . . . ,* who had been wandering in them *for some years'*" (emphasis added).[36]

In a further event that conjuncted with this fact, the destruction of the Spanish mission corridor opened the peninsula to incursions by Maskôkî tribes whose traditional territorial ranges long had been around and above the corridor and to English agents bent on wreaking havoc among Spanish power networks across the head of *La Florida's* peninsula. "A possible explanation for the rapid spread of violence [in the peninsula] is that some of its perpetrators had already established themselves in [La] Florida to some degree prior to the destruction of the missions in 1704," Hann surmises, because, he notes, "surprisingly, the first repercussions were felt as early as 1704."[37] Given the number of *cimarrones* who had gone into the *La Florida* wilderness over the preceding half century, conflicts seem less surprising. So, the evidence may be circumstantial, but there is a significant amount of it. First, we find repeated references to *La Florida* Natives who had been quitting the Spanish power corridor over a period of almost fifty years. Then, we find the term *cimarrón* continuing to have currency throughout the period, in a time and place that was critical to the incursions of English speakers into territories where Spanish previously had been the only documentary language. These English speakers, and writers, set the stage for the transliteration of Spanish discourse systems into English discourse systems and for the documentary metamorphosis of *cimarrones* into Seminoles, but not until after 1763.

In all of these instances, the term *cimarrones* is being applied to Maskókî peoples whose territorial ranges included the area that is twentieth-century Florida, regardless of the specific villages in which they might have been born, the Spanish Roman Catholic missions that they might have left, the Maskókî languages that they might have spoken, or other discrete designators by which they might have imaged themselves.

Undoubtedly, if the term was in common usage among the Spaniards whose discourse was directly with the Maskókî speakers whose ancestral territories were inside or across the borders of what later became the Euroamerican state of Florida, then it was a familiar one to them and could easily have been internalized by them or, at the very least, sufficiently recognized by them as to provide the basis for their affirmation when the term was heard and arbitrarily borrowed by the English.

The first documentary use of the English transliteration of *cimarrón* appeared in 1771, only after the Spaniards had been politically and physically supplanted and Spanish *La Florida* had become the much-reduced English territories of East and West Florida. No official documents had been produced in English in *La Florida* prior to 1763 because no official English documentarians were available to produce them. However, in 1771, English Indian Agent John Stuart wrote to General Thomas Gage, from Mobile, that a Native informant "acquainted me that the Seminoles or East Florida Creeks had frequent intercourse with Spaniards at the Havannah by means of fishing vessels which frequent the Bays of the western side of the Peninsula."[38] Although Stuart characterized the "Seminoles" as Creeks, he characterized them as Florida Creeks and, by this period, the English were using the term *Creeks* generically for numerous Maskókî tribes.

Finally, we must remember that the word *cimarrón* was always an epithet, the descriptor of a *process* and not specifically of a *people*. In fact, both the Mikísuukî speakers and the Maskókî speakers among the Florida Seminoles today still retain the transliterated significator in their vocabularies in just this sense. In addition, at least one family of Maskókî speakers even retains the word *lachua*, with the pre-Spanish Timuguana significance of "a little pot with a hole in the bottom."[39] Above all, we must realize one thing further. The fact that the term only appeared in English for the first time in 1771 does not mean that the people to whom it referred only appeared for the first time in 1771 or that they were entering an area that had no American geopolitical significance for them for the first time. In both figurative and real terms, Maskókî history certainly did not end with the Spaniards, and Seminole history did not begin with the English.

A Defining Moment in *La Florida* History

The European history of the Southeast during the first half of the eighteenth century is well known, both in its English and its Spanish facets. The War of the Spanish Succession, centered in Europe, provided the impetus for another Spanish-English clash in *La Florida,* in 1702. It was the largest and best-organized challenge to Spanish occupation that the English had yet mounted and it was only the new stone fortress at San Agustín and the forceful *La Florida* climate that preserved Spain's tenuous foothold.

Colonel James Moore brought English troops and English-allied Maskókî warriors southward, by land and by sea, into the very presidio of San Agustín. After fifty-two days of siege and bombardment, only twenty buildings of "little consequence" were left standing.[40] The Spanish defenders of the town, fighting from behind the covert way and the ramparts of the Castillo, held out until an emergency call to Habana brought a relief ship up the leeward side of San Agustín's barrier islands and an approaching *huricán* drove the English besiegers back to their homes—but not for long.

The English, even more prescient than the Spaniards in their military matters, and more aggressive, determined to strike out at what they clearly realized as a triple threat to their nascent colonial establishment in the Southeast. Colonel Moore, in his report to the Lords Proprietors of Carolina on his successful raids into Abalachi in 1704, laid out the English position very clearly. "Before this expedition," he wrote, "we were more afraid of the Spaniards of Apalatchee and their Indians in conjunction [with] the French of Mississippi, and their Indians doing us harm by land, than of any forces of the enemy by sea. . . . [But] Apalatchee is now reduced to that feeble and low condition, that it can neither supply St. Augustine with provisions, or disturb, damage or frighten our Indians living between us and Apalatchee, and the French. In short, we have made Carolina as safe as the conquest of Apalatchee can make it."[41]

Through a comparison of the Spanish and English reports of this defining moment in *La Florida*'s history, more of the realities of the Maskókî peoples' world become apparent, separate from the manipulated world that the Spaniards sought to create in their documents. The Spaniards had spent 139 continuous years negotiating with the Natives to secure not only their economic support and military alliance but also nothing less than a total shift in their cosmogony as well. Reports to the King and to church officials outside of *La Florida* had been filled with images of thousands of happy Natives submitting themselves to the will of "mother church" and flocking to baptism in true conversions. The reports also contained news of Native uprisings and defections, of course, and the need for constant vigilance over their Native "children." Overall, however, they sought to create and reinforce an image of successful negotiations, wherein the Spaniards won more rounds than they lost and life, no matter how hard (for the Spaniards), was still better here than in other parts of the Spanish colonial empire (for the Natives).

As a result of these documents, some historians have been led to accept the manipulated Spanish image and to conclude, as in one (albeit extreme) example, that "to Spaniards, Florida must have seemed like a native Utopia by comparison to other colonies. In . . . [it] the goals of peaceful evangelism were largely met. Indian slavery was stymied; Indian lands did not suffer alienation; Indian lives were not shortened by service in mines or manufactories. . . . Cooperative, convent-trained chiefs supplied friars, soldiers, and settlers with plentiful labor and low-priced products. The natives, in turn, received the gifts of heavenly salvation and earthly sanctuary, plus the material benefits of clothing, iron tools, and useful plants and animals."[42] It would not be hyperbole to say that, in 1704, Colonel James Moore staged a referendum in Abalachi on the "heavenly salvation and earthly sanctuary" offered by the Spaniards, and the Spaniards lost.

However, the accounts of the Spaniards concerning the destructions in Abalachi highlight only death, destruction, tortures, and the carrying off of the Native peoples into slavery.[43] Moore's accounts highlight the destruction and, in addition, the numbers of Natives who not only chose to leave the missions rather than fight but also chose to leave the Spanish sphere of influence entirely and migrate northward with the English, voluntarily.[44] Still, for reasons of diplomacy, delicacy, or disinterest, Moore does fail to report the tortures traditionally practiced in warfare by his Native allies.

Both accounts, however, admit that a significant number of Natives neither died nor were taken in slavery nor left to seek their fortunes with the English. Many of the Abalachi survivors, for example, migrated westward to the French at Mobile, where their descendants remain to the present.[45] Boyd, Smith, and Griffin conclude that "it is likely that many had [prior to 1751] returned to their original home."[46] Many others, in addition to those who voluntarily moved toward Carolina with the English, went eastward to the Spanish missions of Guale. The Christianized Abalachi who chose to remain under the control of the Spaniards were resettled near San Agustín and are visible in the mission documents until 1726, when their number was given as forty-two.[47] We must remember, however, that this small number accounts *only* for those who placed themselves under the control of the Spaniards and not for all of the others who had left the missions over the preceding decades.

Moore's attacks on the missions and *ranchos* did not begin and end in a single year, nor was he the only assailant of Spanish power. The history of this entire, final segment of the Settlement Phase (1670–1763) could be chanted as one long litany of attack and counterattack.[48] British attempts to take San Agustín were costly and destructive, but all failed. San Agustín became the military staging post for attempts to oust the English, first from the Carolinas and then, after 1733, from Georgia. The Spaniards were not successful in any of their sorties but, at least, they proved repeatedly that they would not allow the presidio to be taken at little cost. *La Florida*, however, they could not wholly save.

After 1670 and the entrance of the English, the history of the Maskókî tribes of *La Florida* begins to diverge from that of the Spaniards. This is not to say that their story is better told, after this point, in relation to the story of English settlement. The events that were set in motion by the interposition of the English took on a life of their own. However, the willingness of the English to supply the Maskókî warriors with the technological accoutrements of war, and their encouragement of intertribal warfare as a means of deflecting the Natives from the English and shielding their colonies from the Spaniards, showed what can only be described as a profoundly callous disregard for human life, effective though it was.

The Spaniards continued to try to protect the converted peoples who remained within their mission provinces, but of those who still inhabited the peninsula they had no control and only limited knowledge. Guale was extremely vulnerable by the end of the century, and survivors from at least fifteen discrete settlements had taken refuge at three coastal missions by the 1680s.[49] Increasing harassment of the Abalachi missions by Abalachicolo warriors, whose traditional territories centered on the Chattahoochee River (in territory that would remain a part of European Florida for another century), threatened the Abalachi missions. In attempts to reach out, northward and westward, beyond the Abalachi terminus, the Spaniards negotiated with the Abalachicolo tribes between 1679 and 1681 and raised the troop strength in Abalachi in 1682. Nevertheless, English traders reached the Apalachicola River by 1685 and began their own, frequently successful, negotiations. By the last decade of the seventeenth century, English agents had reached the Mississippi River, the French had invested the Gulf, the Spaniards had reinvested Pensacola, and the Maskókî tribes between the Gulf and the Chattahoochee River were in almost as much furor as their cultural kin to the northeast.

The Spaniards sent out emissaries to discover which way the political wind was blowing and found it blowing from three directions at once. In addition, neither Spanish promises, threats, bribes, nor appeals to past loyalties could make the Natives commit themselves to anything that reassured the Spaniards. Factions, frequently composed of young warriors anxious for the honors of war, were forming within towns. The horizontality of the Maskókî power structure had always allowed for independence of thought and was even flexible enough to permit factions to break away as a facet of the formation of new towns. However, for many towns, factionalization was taking place more rapidly than it would have in the course of natural attrition and more rapidly than demographic rises based on births or the capture of women could compensate. Ultimately, many tribes, as discrete polities, would cease to function at the tribal level during this process. Again, however, it is important to remember that this evolutionary paradigm was not new to the Maskókî peoples. Only the speed with which it was beginning to happen was new.

Old caciques tried to control their young, headstrong warriors, but the lure of warfare was sometimes too strong. If they could reach consensus in their towns, many wise leaders tried to play one group of white men against another, in the hopes that the tribe would be left alone. As the "emperor" of Coweta told the Spanish envoy in 1718, the Spaniard was as white as the Englishmen so he should reach an agreement with them and, the inference was, leave the Natives out of it. This ploy seldom worked for long.

To meet the constantly increasing demands of the English factors for raw materials, in the form of deerskins, to drive the engines of mercantilism, the Maskókî peoples began to deplete many of their basic food supplies and destroy the ecological balances of many of their territorial ranges. Regardless of the ecological price that the tribes were paying for the skins that the English demanded, however, the regime and prices that the English traders continued to offer for the precious skins were so poor as to be insulting to the tribesmen and, in 1715, the Yamásî of Carolina rose up against the English. Verner Crane believes that the philosophical power behind this uprising may actually have been the Maskókî tribes.[50] If the Yamásî really were "tame people" who were, consequently, looked down upon by the Maskókî whose towns bordered the Yamásî settlements, and if they were also, as it seems, in physical proximity to the Abalachi who recently had been so poorly used by the English, then the impetus for their volatility becomes transparent.

Tribes that had only a few years earlier left the head of *La Florida's* peninsula at the destruction of the missions and moved northeast toward the English were now propelled back into their "ancient seats." Of course, no amount of inducements on the part of the Spaniards could persuade them to resettle the actual mission sites, "since the country had been so entirely cleared that there was no game, and the domestic animals having been destroyed during the war," and since the spirits of the dead were (and still are) considered by the Maskókî to be potentially malevolent.[51] Captain Daniel E. Burch, United States Army, over a century later interviewed a Creek man "of great age" who purported to recall the destruction of San Luis mission. He confirmed that "[no] Indians lived near St. Louis [San Luis] until the forests grew up. The Indians have preserved a superstitious story, which keeps them at a distance from St. Louis. . . . They cannot be prevailed upon to accompany the whites there, even to show the place."[52] The Spaniards, and later Euroamerican historians, have chosen to see this temporary abandonment as the creation of a permanent void across what would more than a century later become north Florida and, drawing a retroactive line across the peninsula, also would chauvinistically exclude the Maskókî tribes, who had roamed back and forth across the whole territory for centuries, from consideration as members of the Seminoles of Florida.

In the wake of Moore's destruction, the Spaniards at San Agustín retrenched. They resettled the missionized Natives in areas closer to the presidio and tried to reestablish previous routines of work and prayer; they had little else to offer. However, the events of 1715 further disrupted Spanish attempts to recreate a favorable balance of power within their sphere of influence. The Natives whose towns and villages were disarticulated by the Yamásî War began to migrate southward and westward into the peninsula, nearly outstripping the ability of the officials and friars to cope. Attempts to negotiate with an almost daily stream of new residents, Christian and infidel alike, sometimes failed. At least two dozen tribes, with their various languages, were represented in the reduced missions. To the Spanish missionaries, it was only "babble."[53] In addition, the lands to the south of the old mission corridor were in a state of flux as well, as were the lands to the north.

In 1717, the Spanish governor at Pensacola wrote to the Spanish governor at San Agustín that seven caciques, from the Talasi, Tequipache, and Talapuse tribes, had been sent to Nueva España to visit the viceroy. This was done as a symbolic power display in order to maintain the tenuous military support of the Indians in *La Florida*. The governor of Pensacola reminded his superior that this was very expensive, but necessary, as the Indians were "children of [self] interest, they seek and receive, here they do the same and all appears little [to them]."[54] That is, they constantly negotiated among those who pressed them to obtain the most favorable deal and had no allegiance other than to the source of their own best interests. In this they were no more self-interested than the European powers who sought to belittle them with their chauvinistic imaging of the Natives as children.

The Spaniard, frustrated, was condemning the Natives for their failure to form ideological bonds to the Spanish cause, even though such bonds would surely place their people in the unpleasant and untenable political and military position of forming a human buffer between the Spaniards and their British and French opponents. From the Spanish point of view, this made them selfish children. From the Natives' point of view, this was rational self-preservation.

The Natives who had not fallen under the sway of Spanish Catholicism did not hesitate to retaliate immediately if their negotiating terms of full reciprocity were not met, by any European party.[55] Even many of those who had remained at the mission sites had done so only as long as they retained access to European material culture wares and to the supplies upon which the Spaniards had sought to make them dependent by discouraging their territorial rangings. In the 1730s, Spanish officials remonstrated (the only power they had) with the missionized Natives at San Agustín, in the very heart of *La Florida* Hispanicism, for their overuse of rum. The Natives retorted, from their own consciousness, that "if it were a bad thing to get drunk the King would not give them aguardiente."[56] After all of the years and money and lives that the Spaniards had allocated to negotiating cultural change among the *La Florida* Natives, their power still was more vaunted than real. Spanish officials admitted that, even among those Natives living within the physical sphere of Spanish force, in the environs of San Agustín, "these miserable natives are as heathen as if they had not been born in a land of Catholics."[57] However, the La Florida peoples still knew that it was their own land, and not the land of the Catholics.

Consequently, they felt no compunction to remain when the ratio of Spanish trade to Spanish propaganda became sufficiently unfavorable. In 1736, for example, ostensibly Christianized Natives left Spanish hegemony, both ideologically and geographically, when a viable alternative presented itself. They transferred their allegiance to the British, because the British offered them arms and more trade goods and did not require them to commit cultural suicide in order to get those things. Baptized Natives simply struck themselves on the forehead saying, "Go away water! I am no Christian!"[58] Clearly, the La Florida Natives saw themselves as retaining prerogatives of personal and tribal action, even after 226 years of collective knowledge of the Spaniards' ability and willingness to utilize the entire gamut of force elements to gain total control.

Without a doubt the most fiercely independent—or, the Spaniards would say, recalcitrant—of all the tribes with which they negotiated were the Calusa and the tribes of their power constellation in the southern peninsula. These same people who had been the Escampaba of Menéndez's days, and whose cacique had taken the Spanish royal name, Calus, had institutionalized the power associations of that name by conferring it on descendant caciques for almost two hundred years. However, it was not power by association that they sought; rather, it was the enhancement of their own self-imaged power. In the 1740s, together with descendants of Teguesta's people, and the Natives of the cayos, they still continued to resist, absolutely, Spanish demands that they relinquish their cosmogony in favor of a Roman Catholic world in order to obtain Spanish goods or military support.

The composition of the world around them had been altered significantly, even though they had steadfastly resisted permitting their own world view to change. No longer undisputed lords of the peninsula, their territories had been invaded by other tribes, carriers of the same warrior template as they possessed, and determinedly seeking territories where no white men challenged their autonomy.

The Calusa and their affiliates negotiated with the officials of Cuba regarding the possibility of leaving the peninsula, and several hundred did leave, only to encounter new illnesses on that island that ended their lives there.[59] Those who could not or did not go, and who numbered in the thousands according to the Spaniards, refused determinedly when confronted with the nonnegotiable requirement of the Roman Catholic Spaniards that they effect a total paradigm shift in exchange for Cuban-Spanish aid.[60] The friars, realizing the true nature of the Natives' realms of interest, ended the negotiation.

In their report on the Natives of southern *La Florida* and the *cayos,* Franciscans Joseph María Monaco and Joseph Javier Alaña of Cuba admitted very bluntly what they were up against in dealing with a people whose self-imaging had retained its own centrality. In the clearly enunciated realm of interest of these *La Florida* people, we may or may not be seeing an extreme case, but we surely are not seeing a unique case. The people still followed their traditional seasonal patterns of territorial rangings, which the friars chauvinistically characterized as "rootlessness" and assigned to "indolence." The possibility of lifeways that did not include ambition in the Spanish style was beyond these propagandists.

They reported, with eminent clarity:

> The reception that they gave us was very rude. . . . [A]ccording to their way of thinking, this matter of becoming Christians has no other significance than the receiving of the sacramental water with these conditions [for doing so]: that, without their doing any work, the king our lord is to support and cloathe them; . . . the superstitions that they are full of are to be allowed to remain in place; and last, in the teaching of the children, no punishment at all is to be used. [This was] the first condition that the chief proposed to use in the name of all. . . . Their bold proposal of these conditions is born of their being convinced that in admitting our religion in any manner, they are doing us a great favor. They went so far as to say to us that if they were to have to build a church in their village, we would have to pay a daily wage to the Indians, and that if Spaniards were to have to come to settle they would have to pay tribute to the cacique of the lands, which belong to him, he said, and not to the King of Spain.[61]

Ultimately, neither the peninsular Natives nor the vast majority of the Maskókî peoples of the Southeast would negotiate with the Spaniards on any terms that included relinquishing their cosmogony. That cosmogony comprised a viable constellation of templates that had served them well for hundreds of years (at least) and the Spaniards never offered them anything to replace it that was of equal value.

The radical increase in intertribal warfare precipitated by the entry of the English into the *La Florida* negotiation was, ultimately, more destructive demographically than the ideologically weighted negotiation instigated by the Spaniards, which sought to destroy the Maskókî peoples culturally. Without argument, thousands of *La Florida*'s women and men succumbed to the destructive blandishments of both negotiations. However, ultimately, the surviving Maskókî peoples of the Southeast, both those whose lives before the coming of the Spaniards had centered on the peninsula and those whose lives had not, retained the central autonomy of their own self-imaging throughout their long and arduous negotiations with the Spaniards. The cosmogonies that enfolded them and sustained them throughout the centuries of pressures from the cultural Others were stronger and more viable than any proffered alternatives. They were strong enough to permit the people to incorporate useable cultural borrowings and to manipulate those extracultural elements into shapes that they could anchor firmly within their own matrix. This is the reality of the survival of their descendants to this day.

Spanish Coda

What the English were unable to achieve by force, they finally achieved by negotiation. Spanish *La Florida* ceased to exist politically in any size or shape in 1763, when Spain relinquished her interests east of the Mississippi River to the British as a result of the treaty that closed the Seven Years' War in Europe. The English had captured La Habana, and the Spanish Crown, weighing its importance against that of troublesome *La Florida*, agreed to a trade. The *Floridanos* even exhumed some bodies rather than leave them to the tender mercies of their long-time enemies, the English.

As for all of those reported thousands of *La Florida* Natives whom the Spaniards had cajoled, coerced, and threatened into trading their world view for that of the Spaniards, a pitiful few remained in the final analysis. Of those who had negotiated away their self-images for a manipulated Spanish vision, most had paid with their lives for trusting the Spaniards to protect them. Thus, in 1763, after all of their negotiations, only eighty-six Natives left *La Florida* with the Spaniards.[62] Furthermore, of all of those thousands of Native peoples whom the Spaniards never had been able to seduce with iron pots or hatchets or an imagined god, the most advantageous political rationale was to write them off officially as "savages," elide them rhetorically, and desert them militarily.

The central issues remain, however. The interests and actions of the

Spaniards did not drive the Maskókî peoples to forget who they were. Neither did their own desires to obtain European material culture items ultimately lead the Maskókî peoples to relinquish their entire cosmogony in exchange. Ultimately, the critical elements of the template for the functioning of the Maskokálgî were carried in the minds and hearts of the individuals, and the Maskókî peoples did not cease to exist as a result of their first two and one-half centuries of negotiations with the Europeans.

The change of European flags in 1763 and the physical departure of the Spaniards were of minimal consequence, per se, to the Maskókî peoples. The diseases of the sixteenth century, the material culture lures of the seventeenth and eighteenth centuries, and the episodes of violence of 1704 and 1715 had had more negative impacts upon them than a mere change of flags. The flags marked the end of an era only in terms of the parties to the negotiation.

However, at least this relieved the Natives of the concerted pressures of the conversion process. With the end of the mission chain had come the end of the Spaniards' strongest phase of religious proselytization. When the Spaniards left *La Florida* in 1763, their leaving simply removed one party from the table, but the culturally related Maskókî peoples remained, their cosmogony still visible. Bushnell says that when the Spaniards departed *La Florida*, "It seemed as though the heathen and the heretics had won." [63] From the point of view of the departing Spaniards, that may well have been so. From the Natives' point of view, however, it may well have seemed that it was the heathens and the heretics who had finally left.

10 Conclusions:
The Past as Prelude

> I know that most men, including those at ease with problems of the greatest
> complexity, can seldom accept even the simplest and most obvious truth if
> it would be such as would oblige them to admit the falsity of conclusions
> which they have delighted in explaining to colleagues, which they have
> proudly taught to others, and which they have woven, thread by thread, into
> the fabric of their lives.
>
> —Leo Tolstoy[1]

> Within twenty-five years [of the Creek War of 1813–1814], the entire family
> of red men, Creeks, Cherokees, Chickasaws, Choctaws, and Seminoles, were
> swept away from the South and either buried under the ground or banished
> to the remote western country beyond the Mississippi River.
>
> —Robert V. Remini[2]

> In Indian Territory, later Oklahoma, the Confederation took on a new form
> as the Creek Nation, and preserved its identity until 1907, when the Creek
> population was theoretically merged in the general population of Oklahoma.
>
> —John R. Swanton[3]

For many years, those of us southeastern historians who were raised on the
English view of United States history have sought to shift our field of vision
to include and understand the Spanish experience in the Southeast, which was
the earliest European national experience in North America. As this present
work demonstrates, however, effecting this shift in interpretational paradigms
has been such an important and worthwhile endeavor that even those of us
who have accomplished it (and this certainly does not include all Americanists, or even all historians of the Southeast) have stopped short of a further
objective that might have offered the ultimate viewpoint from which to examine our formation as a North American people. That is, we have stopped
short of interesting ourselves in the viewpoint of the Native Americans who

used this land so successfully for so many years before the arrival of any Europeans and whose experiences in the process of European colonialization shaped, to a significant extent, the trajectory of that process.

This is not to say that Native American voices have been excluded from research efforts in southeastern European history. They certainly have not, as the citations in this work attest. However, in the words of an old Spanish aphorism, "Everything in life depends upon the color of the glass through which one is looking." In this case, we have long viewed the Maskókî peoples of the Southeast through an English-colored glass and, viewing through this glass, we have arbitrarily and unilaterally formed the expectations that have shaped most of the interpretations that we have embedded in our own cultural matrix concerning them.

Recently, some few researchers have begun to view the Maskókî peoples of the Southeast through a Spanish-colored glass, invoking the rhetoric of Spanish Conquest within contexts that seek to impose European expectations of destruction and disappearance retroactively to a period before the interposition of the English. By this process, the writers situate an Iberian construct within the matrix of the American experience. In neither case, however—in neither the English nor the Spanish paradigm of successful cultural transposition—have the Maskókî peoples of the Southeast been viewed or described through any glass of their own color. It is hoped that the present work effects some small shift in that direction.

There are several different approaches by which the current work might have been undertaken. A detailed examination of the specific sociocultural processes of the Maskókî peoples before, during, and after Spanish interposition certainly could have been in order. The objective of such an approach would have been to bring to light the myriad cultural continuities that marked the survival of the people and to place their social evolutions in perspective relative to that survival. The problem inherent in this approach would have been the continuing lack of a viable conceptual foundation upon which to base it. Another approach would have been to track several of the more visible tribes through the process of negotiation, synchronically and diachronically, although this would have been more tenuous given the discontinuities in many of the documents and would have served the overall process poorly.

The approach that I have chosen has been to conduct a conceptual reappraisal of the interpretive process by which we, as social scientists, have judged the Maskókî peoples and unilaterally have embedded them in the historical matrix of a Euroamerican nation not of their own making. In order to do this, I have focused on some of the elements of the major constellation of myths that have informed Euroamerican imaging for three hundred years. The objective of this work has not been to effect a change in the historical view of events but, rather, to effect a change in the application of historical glasses through which we view these events. In simplest terms, the objective has been to demythologize the past of a people whose primary birthright is their own humanity.

Who were the Maskókî peoples who met the Spaniards in southeastern North America in the sixteenth century? Were they semi-isolated, static tribes of sedentary agriculturalists whose cultural framework and social systems were so unsophisticated and brittle that European interposition could shatter their world completely and permanently? Or were they, alternatively, groups of phoenix-like resurrectionists who could suffer crushing fragmentation and rise, in new plumage, from their own ashes?

The reality is that they were neither. The reality is that they were something far more complex and far stronger than any of the traditionalist Euroamerican images have ever indicated. They were tens and hundreds—perhaps thousands—of individual tribes, networked together in cultural kinship by greater and lesser elements of a coherent cosmogony. From the elements of this cosmogony they derived templates for social functioning that operated with greater and lesser degrees of success, within an unlimited number of their own discrete but analogous and compatible social systems, for centuries, at least, before the coming of Europeans.

These templates rose and fell in value of utility over time, according to internal trajectories of growth and change that were tied solely to the larger interrelationships of all the templates within the world of the Maskokálgî. In this, they were not different from other cultures. The template constituted, in fact and in practice, networks of power relationships: Foucault's *dispositifs* or apparatuses. The structure of heterogeneous elements that defined them, both discursive and nondiscursive, became transparent in the strategies of relations of forces supporting, and supported by, the various types of knowledge bounding, and bounded by, the apparatus.

For example, in the inner workings of the Clan, the strategies of relations were composed of types of knowledge that placed each Clan in a functional position relative to the seen and unseen worlds, as well as relative to the complete range of the animal world, and relative to both the public and private worlds of communal and familial interactions. Any abstraction of power in the substantive sense was obviated, as it must be. Sufficient were the human-generated clusters of organized, hierarchical, coordinated relations. The analytic of power was encoded in the template. The existence of the descendants of the Maskókî peoples today, as discrete and coherent cultural entities, affirms the viability of the cosmogony that gave rise to those templates.

Taken as a whole—and they must be viewed holistically in order to be discussed realistically—the Maskókî peoples constituted a power system and a loose network of cosmogonic adherents whose language occupied at least as much territory as, and possibly more than, its military frontiers did. Once again, however, we must recall that language neither confines nor defines culture. Rather, it is only a single variable that we use for the sake of convenience and have permitted to pass into myth. Its negative value lies in the fact that it is so convenient that it frequently is misused.

Nor may we continue to speak of a Maskókî "confederation," even with a small letter *c*. This is an example of another misused convenience that has passed into myth. The Maskókî were dynamic and evolving people, and a principal element of that dynamism was the freedom of its individual elements to evolve individually within the cosmogonic power networks. In order for us to perceive coherence at the largest cultural level among the Maskókî peoples, from the perspective of five hundred years, it is not necessary that that same perception of coherence should have informed the daily interactions of the people. Further, it is not possible to impose order retroactively, although Euroamerican researchers certainly have tried.

In the centuries prior to contact, the Maskókî peoples had embraced and enriched an already rich and complex cosmogony that, in a form that social scientists have since from the Euroamerican point of view labeled "Mississippianism," had begun to pervade the lives of the people across the Southeast. As we saw in Chapter 2, the teleological antagonisms transferred to the Maskókî peoples by a linear Euroamerican culture do not stand up under revisionist interpretations when Maskókî culture is reembedded in its own circular cosmogony. Within a few hundred years after the coming of the Four Teachers, the preponderance of Maskókî tribes in the Southeast had embraced the tenets of their teachings and had, in fact, made those teachings the fabric of their lives. The Maskókî peoples became, in their own imaging, the Maskokálgî or the People of the Maskókî Way. Their belief system incorporated multiple templates for successful integration of all available cultural and social domains of interest. From physical birth to physical death, the templates provided parameters for contextualized functioning. In addition, between the finite worlds of physicality and the infinite worlds of cosmic elements and forces, the templates provided a smooth and integrated interaction that placed each element within a correlative semiotic discourse. The keys to the successful functioning of the templates, over time and space, were the cosmogonic twins: dynamism and flexibility.

Dynamism was that domain within which change became an element of constancy; in which we recognize the profound internalization of the axiom "The more things change, the more they remain the same." Within this paradigm, flexibility, or the ability and willingness to accept change at an integrative level, becomes the functional coefficient of dynamism. Only within a cosmogony configured as a circularity does dynamism operate as a key cultural element, with a high functional coefficient of flexibility. And this was, and is, the setting in which, and by means of which, the Seminoles have survived to the present as a coherent cultural group.

Their cosmogony has never failed them since its introduction by the Four Teachers: neither in the centuries of its florescence and complexification, nor in the relatively short period of its adulthood in the Southeast immediately prior to the coming of the Europeans, nor in the ensuing centuries of increasing cultural stressors. Nor has it remained static, forcing its adherents into tedious and untenable replications of rigid templates that would have placed them constantly at odds with the realities of outside stressors, particularly in the form of demands for negotiations from various European groups. The cultural matrix both engendered and replicated social systems that had been, and remained, sufficiently flexible to absorb shock, accept change, and endure. This was the consummate element of their survival: the flexibility and consequent endurance of the overall cultural matrix.

The central tool of cultural continuity among the social templates has been, and continues to be, the Clan system. The basic complementarity of its functioning is an institutionalization of the reciprocity that is a chief characteristic of the circular matrix. Within its elastic frontiers, the rhetoric of the Clan system also provided the continuity that permitted the tribe to weather transitional periods, such as the evolution of their Maskokálgî credo from its zenith of complexity, in about the fourteenth century, to the mature state in which the Spaniards first encountered it in the sixteenth century. This flexibility constituted the critical value of the Clan system to dynamism and, therefore, to the continuous vitality of the tribes. This same flexibility has ensured its continued functioning to the present.

Central to the functioning and survival of the Clan were the women who were its mothers. Within the mechanism of Clan membership and descent were juxtaposed two processes, at once static in a dedication to continuity and dynamic in a permeability that ensured its perpetuation. Women embodied the continuity of the Clan, passing membership to the children of their wombs and sustaining its bounds with their very lives. Males, as children, reinforced the Clan and, as husbands, broadened the Clans genetically and implemented their deferential orderings. As warriors, males augmented the Clans with women taken from affinity groups or from disparate cultures. In both of these cases, "outsider" women crossed the Clans' permeable boundaries to take up places already established for them socially. The mechanism by which the Clan was embedded in the larger social structure ensured the perpetuation of the template, even as the Clans' boundaries remained permeable. The seeming dichotomy was resolved repeatedly to the benefit of the people, as warfare recalibrated society and the mechanism of Clan affiliation operated to absorb the added nonlinear elements and to restore equilibrium.

This process of absorption and recalibration was a constant of the Maskokálgî, and it was a process developed over centuries prior to the arrival of Europeans and used time and time again over the ensuing five centuries to replicate Maskókî culture in the face of continuing external and internal stressors. Social requirements changed across the time and space of Maskókî-European negotiations, but major cultural templates continued to impart continuity. Ceremonies and rituals, whether perfectly or imperfectly transmitted, continued to function as the fonts of public utterances from which the people drew strength and reaffirmed themselves as people of the same fire.

In Chapter 3 we asked the question, How have the Maskokálgî survived almost five hundred years of contact with, and stress from, Euroamericans and still managed to remain a discrete and coherent cultural entity? We see now that the answer lies in the nature of their cosmogony, which is unique in its basis, and in the character of their own self-imaging as the Maskokálgî. They have survived through the replication of cultural templates that existed independently of social processes and have survived independently.

Further, they have survived because the processes of cultural replication were neither entirely dismantled nor destroyed just because so many Maskókî peoples' lives were lost during the continuing story of contact. Larger and smaller portions of the templates were held within each individual and were reassembled as affinity groups reassembled. If some of the social elements changed as a result of loss of memory keepers or replacement by extracultural absorption, the major templates nevertheless remained. It is neither new nor unique to the Maskókî peoples to conclude that individual cultural participants carry the seeds of culture within themselves. What was unique to the Maskókî peoples was the nature of the culture that they carried, its flexibility and dynamism, and the profound importance of its circular inclusionism.

In the history of the emergence of the Native American peoples known as Seminoles, the self-imaging of the Maskókî peoples as independent decision makers within a dynamic cultural system was critical. Propelled by the incessant demands of the Spaniards at the mission sites within the Spanish power corridor, from the sea islands below Santa Elena southward and westward to Abalachi, individual Natives began to withdraw from the negotiation process at least as early as the 1630s. Spanish reports of the second half of the seventeenth century frequently mention the wandering men or *cimarrones,* whose flagrant disregard of Spanish regulations seemed criminal to the Europeans. In the eyes of many of the Abalachi and the Guale and Timuguana peoples (at least those who had been willing to try life with the Spaniards), their experiments with white men's technology and clothing had been useful but their experiments with the white men's culture and god had proven to be too expensive. Obviously, in the final choice between Spanish demands for cultural suicide on the one hand and a life of independence on the other, independence was the more enticing choice for many.

Throughout the seventeenth century the numbers of *cimarrones* increased as the Spaniards tried unsuccessfully to stem the tide of defections. Across the traditional Abalachi and Timuguana territories, individual survivors found livelihoods as *mikî anópit* or *mikî suukî,* that is, as keepers of cattle and pigs: the same things that the British would find some of their descendants doing in the later eighteenth century. Others established marginal enterprises that allowed them to live freely without losing all access to European trade goods, their primary interest in contact with white persons.

Unfortunately for the Spaniards, their tenuous power corridor was destroyed in the early eighteenth century by the military raids of Carolina's Colonel James Moore, and still more *La Florida* Natives were sent spinning away from the white men's conflicts. The survivor villages that the Spaniards set up as interim sites after the Yamásî uprising of 1715 were excellent examples of the processes of rapid amalgamation of which the Maskókî peoples were capable. Further, contrary to the enduring Euroamerican myth of destruction, the Maskókî peoples who coalesced across the north-central peninsula early in the eighteenth century were legitimate derivatives of the commingling of a broad and culturally interrelated spectrum of Maskókî tribes, whose cultural frontiers had long ranged across the lower Southeast, including the area known today as geopolitical Florida, in a configuration totally unrelated to that unilaterally imposed by Europeans. Indeed, their own cultural reality recognized no European borders.

As we have seen, the realignment of cultural affinity groups and the genesis of villages were standard elements of the cultural dynamism that had marked the Maskókî peoples for centuries. However, the speed and proportion of change reached a profound degree during the period 1670 to 1763, and the impetus was the English interposition. For over a century and a half, from 1510 to 1670, the primary agents of European interposition in the Southeast had been Spaniards. The initial discourse of European power to which the Maskókî peoples responded in their ongoing negotiations was couched in Spanish cultural terms. Beginning in 1670, however, and increasingly during the period 1704 to 1763, the English and the French encroached more closely upon the Spanish core areas of *La Florida* than they had been able to in the preceding century and a half. New, demanding, and rapidly expanding elements, especially in the case of the English colonists, were added to the discourse of power.

With the establishment of Charles Towne in 1670, Oglethorpe's Georgia colony at Savannah in 1733, and French settlements at Mobile in 1711 and in Louisiana from 1714 forward, the level of cultural stress upon the Maskókî speakers of interior and peninsular *La Florida* increased exponentially. English traders, venturing into *La Florida*'s interior, encountered villages of potential trading customers living around the Oconee Creek, and the misnomer "Creeks" entered the English vocabulary as a generic for numerous Maskókî peoples whose true tribal affiliations would henceforth remain better known to themselves than to Euroamericans.

The raids effected by Colonel James Moore into the heart of the Spanish mission system, across the northern head of the peninsula, had the force of a shotgun blast fired into a crowded room, but their effects were far from random. Survivors, careening across the lower Southeast in search of peace, were set into motion yet again a mere six years later by the reactive Yamásî War, near the Atlantic coast southward from the Carolinas to San Agustín. The "fallout" from this war, as one historian has described it, was the demographic concentration of Maskókî peoples on *La Florida*'s north-central peninsula.[4]

However, despite the southward movement during this period of certain of their constituent groups into what Europeans saw as a geographic and military void along the region that would later become the northern border of Florida, these Natives were not, as previously held, all new settlers. Many were the same Hitchiti, Yamásî, Abalachi, Chisca, Abalachi-colo, and other groups who had moved northeastward away from the epicenter of Spanish-English warfare and now were returning to their traditional territorial ranges.

Nor was a strategic void synonymous with a cultural void. The period between 1704 and 1763 has been viewed as pivotal for the emergence of the "Seminoles" because it was during this period that several separate but critical demographic, social, and political processes began to coalesce within and across the head of the peninsula of *La Florida*. One was the reamalgamation of survivors from the destruction wreaked within Spain's power corridor, as has been outlined above. Another was the amalgamation of other Maskókî women and men from the interior of the Southeast who, propelled by the destruction of the Yamásî War and the trade demands of the English, pushed southward ahead of the advancing English settlements.

The final critical element that made this period pivotal was the external political intrigues among the European powers, especially the climactic Seven Years' War, which resulted in the replacement of Spanish settlers and soldiers in San Agustín with English settlers and soldiers in 1763. With the entrance of English speakers into the heart of *La Florida,* the base European language changed; the base documentary language of historians of *La Florida* changed as well. San Agustín became St. Augustine, and *La Florida,* that part that still existed south and west of the English Carolinas and Georgia and east of French Louisiana, became two administrative polities, East and West Florida.

The newly arrived English had no cultural memory of the creation and growth of the Spanish power corridor or of the numbers of Native peoples who had chosen to leave that corridor for the freedom of the Abalachi and southern peninsular La Chua wildernesses. When the English asked the Native people who had coalesced west of the St. John's River and across the "Alachua" savannah who they were, they responded that they were *istî siminolî* or *yat'siminolî*—free people, in the sense that they were unattached to villages and tribes, although they certainly knew who they were culturally. The linguistic reduction that the English speakers made has now become transparent: even though the Natives were "Siminolies" only after their own fashion, after the English fashion, "Siminolies" they have remained.

The fact that the process of disarticulation and amalgamation of affinity groups in *La Florida* had begun well over a century before the English arrived to witness it firsthand was irrelevant as well. The process was new to the English, who were new to *La Florida*. Therefore, in the English chronicles of United States formation, the Native peoples were new and the English unilaterally chose to rename them. Thus were "born" the Seminoles and, within two generations, the "Miccosukees."

The fact that the nexus of these processes occurred around and across what would become, although not until almost a century later, the northern geopolitical boundary of Euroamerican Florida was not wholly fortuitous. The settlement of the Natives there was a combination of geography and genetics, because the Native peoples who coalesced in the regions across the north-central head of the peninsula came neither immediately nor only from north of the area, but also from the area itself as we have seen. Moreover, they came from south of it also, a fact that was politically antithetical to the reportings of the Spaniards, as well as one that has been elided by the exigencies of Euroamerican cultural chauvinism from United States history. The location had geographic centrality, access to demographic centers, hardwood forests, lakes and rivers, plentiful game, and a moderate climate. From the point of view of the Native Americans who knew it well, it was a good place to be.

However, historical fortunes recontextualized the documentary imaging of those surviving Native peoples as an element of Florida's history only within the view of their cultural Other and thereby eclipsed their own continuous self-imaging with a discontinuity that has attempted to rob them of all but the last century and a half of their own past. The final element of these interrelated processes was the clothing of old Native

American groups in new guises through the powerful metadiscursive process of naming and the entrance into the social lexicon of United States citizens of three new, formalized discursive entities, wholly constructs of the Euroamerican Others: the Seminoles, Miccosukees, and Creeks.

For all of the sixteenth and seventeenth centuries and most of the eighteenth century, the Spaniards whose monarch sent them to *La Florida* attempted to use every conceivable element of the negotiating continuum to coerce, bribe, or otherwise intimidate the Maskókî peoples into a position of subservience. When it became obvious, early on, that the numbers of Spanish troops in *La Florida* would not be sufficient to effect change by force, Spanish administrators followed the mandate of the king and began to hand out gifts.

To a degree, this ploy worked. The problem with the system was that the Spaniards had no absolute way of gauging the degree to which it was working on any given person or group of persons at any place or time. Guale and Timuguana and Abalachi peoples who saw the power of Spanish guns and horses were sufficiently impressed with the possible power of the strangers that they sometimes agreed to stay and listen to their beliefs. Individuals who were satisfied with what they heard and, especially, with what they saw, remained and tried to live the Spanish way.

For a great many, however, the Spaniards were unable to provide the constant proofs of their powers that were required for Native acceptance. Among the Maskokálgî, the powers to mediate seen and unseen forces went hand in hand and practitioners of medicine regularly reconfirmed their abilities to interact with the forces of nature. Despite the occasional signs and wonders that could be used to Spanish advantage, in the long run the vast majority of Maskókî peoples in the Southeast were unimpressed by the ideology that the Spaniards offered, disbelieving of their powers, and unwilling to meet Spanish demands.

Cooperating governors and Franciscan friars caught the Native peoples up in a loaded negotiation that used both military force and religious cajoling to play upon human fears. The power of the Spanish monarch was great, so the ploy went, and if the Natives did not cooperate they would be crushed by his wrath. Their only refuge was the sanctity of the Roman Catholic Church and the sheltering care of the Franciscans. For many, the impetus was insufficient and the ploy was transparent. The peoples of Calus, for example, maintained their own prerogatives. They, and others, turned their backs on Spanish threats, countered Spanish aggressions with aggressions of their own, and took Spanish bribes of utilitarian trade goods with equanimity.

Even those peoples who accepted the Spaniards and succumbed to their ploys and blandishments did not all fully internalize Spanish culture and ideology. As it became apparent, over time, that protective friars could make as many demands as the belligerent military and that demands would regularly turn into threats and violence, and as it became all too obvious that there was no equilibrium in a Spanish world where Natives performed all the work and friars reaped all the profits, many "converts" chose to reassert their personal prerogatives and depart.

Spanish records do not follow these people, however, and Spanish reports do not dwell on them, so they seem to disappear from historical view. Our primary clues to the inefficacy of the Spaniards' negotiations are their frequent mentions of the need to protect Christianized Natives from the belligerence of "infidels" and "pagan indians" who increasingly harassed them and their regulations against wandering men who moved from village to village and refused to submit to Spanish authority. Moreover, there is the undeniable physical reality of the amount of land on *La Florida*'s peninsula that was available for occupation by the Natives juxtaposed against the very limited amount of contact with and reports about those lands that are evidenced in the Spaniards' documents.

In the final analysis, two realities prevailed. First, and foremost, the Spaniards radically underestimated the validity and functionality of the Maskókî cosmogony. Second, the commitment of the Spanish Crown to the settlement of *La Florida* never was sufficient to permit the Spaniards to exercise the ultimate negotiating gambit and force conversions based on the strength of overwhelming military odds. To put it more succinctly, the Spaniards told the Natives that, in order to obtain the goods and technology that they brought, it was necessary to accept the culture that they brought as well; but the Natives' own cultural system functioned too well for many to relinquish it and, as for the alternative of applying military or other types of force, the Spaniards in *La Florida* never reached critical mass.

Except for those few thousand Natives who found an intellectual state of accommodation and accepted the Spanish system in its totality—and paid for it with their lives in the Europeans' conflicts—the majority realized the low value of the offer and never accepted the deal. For most of the

Maskókî peoples, it was obvious that what the Spaniards were offering was not of equal value to what they were being asked to give up and, so, they chose to reject Hispanicization. So many, in fact, rejected the Spanish negotiations that their descendants still exist today, centuries later, as a discrete holding community: not decontextualized, not disarticulated, and not destroyed. Their self-imaging still places them firmly in the Maskókî universe. The Maskókî peoples continue to function as the Maskokálgî because their templates functioned. They had listened to the intruders and they had accepted many facets of the world that the intruders represented and introduced. But, ultimately, the Maskokálgî cosmogony did not fail them and they did not abandon it.

Today, almost 3,000 descendants of the process of Maskókî survival still reside in Florida. Including individuals whose blood quantum has fallen below that which would qualify them for membership in the Seminole Tribe of Florida, there are almost 10,000 descendants living in Oklahoma as well. In addition to this number, there are approximately one hundred "independents" in Florida today: Seminoles who are eligible for membership in the Seminole and Miccosukee Tribes, by virtue of their blood quantum. These individuals have had numerous opportunities to join the Tribes. The potential benefits, in terms of health care, housing, dividends, and access to social and financial resources, seem too obvious to be ignored. Yet, they steadfastly refuse to trade their autonomy for what they view as the white man's dole.

There is an interesting and obvious parallel between this tiny group and another such group, composed of independent remnants of a number of tribes that the white men conveniently called "Seminole," who made the same decision to maintain their autonomy, in the 1840s and 1850s, and who wound up taking refuge in the Everglades in their determination. In those days, the pressures to assimilate also were profound, because the United States government in its negotiations put forward the same three types of powerful inducements that had been employed by the Spaniards and the English: concern for the well-being of loved ones, financial inducements and technological benefits, and—the ultimate incentive—the preservation of their very lives.

Once again, as they had done in the seventeenth century, small bands of resistors gravitated together, drawn by the similarities in their languages and cultures and societies, only to have themselves derisively labeled "Siminolies"—renegades, holdouts, malcontents, untamed by civilization, in their denigrators' lexicon. However, this was a designation that the nineteenth-century Seminoles, once again, took proudly, for many of them had inherited this word as used in their own context for at least two centuries already. They internalized its message of determined freedom so well that a century and a half later, in the late twentieth century, their descendants still would be free people, "holding out" against the powerful and even more insidious inducements of non-Native culture.

They are, in fact, the survivors. All of Florida's Seminole, Miccosukee, and Creek people are, however, the survivors. If survival is the quintessential test of success, then they are the living, dynamic evidence of the success of numerous of the Maskókî traditions that the Euroamerican culture, with its far more numerous population, has chosen, for its own cultural reasons, to believe that it had eradicated, both advertently and inadvertently, by 1763. They still recall the last fights, one hundred fifty–plus years ago, to stay in their land. They still name their children with words from medicine songs that protected them from white soldiers and formalize memories of events from their fights. They still recall their strong affiliations with the *Spanalî*, the Spanish people. Their elders still pass down the knowledge, received from their own elders, that *ichî bomet* or "the nose of the deer," as they image Florida's long peninsula, was always destined to be their final refuge. They had been moving southward long before the arrival of the Europeans, they say. The white man, they say, likes to think that he pushed the people southward, but they know that they had already been moving there, following their own dictates.[5]

Ronnie Jimmie, a Seminole Tribe member who has lived along the Tamiami Trail, sums it all up eloquently. "Out the Trail, all my life I have heard the elders tell us about the memories of the people from long before the wars. And the old people spoke of *ichî bomet* as our final home, and they knew the area very well. The ancestors knew which areas were high and dry, where the hammocks were, where to find the food, and where to build the camps. The knowledge of *ichî bomet* had been with our people for a long, long time. And *ichî bomet* was more than just the nose of the deer. It was that thin, long land where the soft, fresh breezes would blow over us and set our spirits free. When we all lived in that land, our spirits would be able to blow gently over into the other world, to the West, without even having to cross over physically. They knew about Florida, and our people were here for a long, long time before the white people think we were."[6]

Appendixes

Appendix 1

Notes on Orthography and Pronunciation

In both Maskókî and Mikísuukî, the consonant *k* should be pronounced as a soft *g*. When the consonant *g* occurs, it indicates the hard *g* sound. Also, *b* and *p* sound much alike and are pronounced as a soft *b*. The notation *(t)* at the end of a word indicates that the *t* sound that closes the word is only partially vocalized. Among some of the younger generation today this subtlety is being ignored. The phonemes [ul] and [al] are very closely allied in many of their uses and are here transcribed as *al* unless the dichotomy is very clear in spoken use.

All syllables have been written out in this text, and I have chosen not to syllabicate them visually, for clarity of reading. The only exceptions to the extended syllables are two sounds that have no English equivalents. One is the Maskókî and Mikísuukî *s*. When placed within a word, this carries the sound of *sh* in English, spoken at the far back of the mouth (as most Maskókî and Mikísuukî words are). The other is an aspirated sound proximate to *-th* and represented as *ł* in the written form.

All vowels should be pronounced in their short forms, and when inserted into words as double letters they indicate lengthening of the sound. For example, the suffix *-alkî* should be pronounced *-al gî*, with a soft *g*. The final *i* is shorter than the *i* in *discourse* but is the sound constantly misspelled by English transcribers as *-ee*. So, for example, the word commonly mispronounced in English as "chikee" is actually "chikí(t)" in Mikísuukî and "chikó" in Maskókî.

Appendix 2

Seminole Sources

Judy Baker
Carl Baxley
Mike Bemo
Mike Berryhill
Ernie Bert
Charles Hiers Billie, Sr.
Edie Cypress Billie
Frank Billie
Frank J. Billie
Henry John Billie
James E. Billie
Joe Billie, Jr.
Joe Don Billie
Juanita Fewell Billie
Lonnie Billie
Marlin Billie
Martha Billie
Ronnie Billie
Sadie Billie
Sandy Billie, Sr.
Sonny Billie
Alice Billieboy
Dan Bowers
Mary Parker Bowers
Steven Bowers
Wanda Bowers
Mary A. Brown
Jonas Burgess
Andy Buster
Paul Buster
Jimmie Carbitcher, Jr.
Nancy Carbitcher
Lewis Carpitche

Louise Carpitche
Louis Chupco
Lottie Coody
Irene Cummings
Mickey Cummings
Agnes Cypress
Billy Cypress
Candy Cypress
Edna Cypress
Jeanette Cypress
Mitchell Cypress
Shane Cypress
Vivian Delgado
Agnes Denver
Claudia Doctor
Joe Doctor, Sr.
Lisa Dodd
Winifred Fife
Joe Frank
Joel Frank, Sr.
Larry Frank
Mabel Frank
Spencer Frank
Lesley Garcia
Carla Gopher
Lorene Gopher
Louise Gopher
Willie Gopher, Jr.
Sydney Gore
Dale Grasshopper
Jeremiah Hall
Mike Hall, Sr.
Bill Haney
Enoch Kelly Haney
George B. Harjo
Nan Harjo
Ronnie Harjo
Rick Harjochee
Mable Haught

Bobby Henry
John Wayne Huff
Mary Alice Huff
Mable Jim
Marie Jim
Noah Jim
Annie Jimmie
Ronnie Jimmie
Archie Johns, Sr.
Mary Frances Johns
Stanlo Johns
Wonder Johns
Lewis Johnson
Happy Jones
Martha Jones
Alan Jumper
Betty Mae Jumper
Daisy Jumper
Danny Jumper
David Jumper
Dolores Jumper
Elgin Jumper
Harley Jumper
James Jumper
Lucile Jumper
Moses "Big Shot" Jumper, Jr.
Pocahontas Jumper
Tommie Jumper
Teresa Jumper
Alice Kernell
Bob Kernell
Betty King
Leroy (Keeno) King
LaVonne Kippenberger
Mary Jene Koenes
Ryder Larney
Harry Long
Edna McDuffie
Virginia Mitchell

Jack Motlow
Jane Motlow
Nancy Motlow
Shirley Motlow
Christene Nelson
Juanita Noon
Erica North
Josephine North
Alice Nunez
Bill Osceola
Charlotte Osceola
Frances Osceola
Jacob Osceola, Sr.
Jacob Osceola, Jr.
Jimmie O'Toole Osceola
Joe Dan Osceola
Jo-Lin Osceola
Judybill Osceola
Laura Mae Osceola
Marcellus Osceola, Sr.
Marie Osceola
Max Osceola, Sr.
Max Osceola, Jr.
Pete Osceola
"Wild Bill" Osceola
Minnie Palmer
Tom Palmer
Corine Postoak
Ethel Santiago
Priscilla Sayen
Geneva Shore
Jim Shore
Jack Smith, Jr.
Lois Smith
Alice Snow
Elbert Snow
Peggy Stivers
Ed Tanyan
Frances Tanyan

Michelle Thomas
Buffalo Tiger
Lee Tiger
Marlin Tiger
Tema Tiger
Vernon Tiger
Winifred Tiger
Little Tigertail
Louise Tigertail
Daniel Tommie
Danny Tommie
Dorothy Tommie
Howard Tommie
Karen Tommie
Kevin Tommie
Samuel Tommie
Dorothy Tucker
Johnny Tucker, Jr.
Connie Whidden
Mary Jane Willie
Nancy Willie
Ben Yahola
Grace Youngblood
Cleo Yzaguirre

Notes

Preface

1.   Robert V. Remini, *Andrew Jackson and the Course of American Empire, 1767–1821*, 3 vols. (New York: Harper & Row, 1977), 1:231.

1. Introduction: A People Obscured by Their Past

1.   Bernard Bailyn, paper delivered to the Organization of American Historians, Dallas, Texas, 1981, cited in "General Introduction" to Peter H. Wood, Gregory A. Waselkov, and M. Thomas Hatley, *Powhatan's Mantle: Indians in the Colonial Southeast* (Lincoln: University of Nebraska Press, 1989), xvi n. 3.

2.   Some of the classic readings in Florida history that present and reaffirm this viewpoint are Frank Parker Stockbridge and John Holliday Perry, *Florida in the Making* (New York: de Bower Publishing, 1926); Frederick W. Dau, *Florida Old and New* (New York: G. P. Putnam's Sons, 1934); Rembert Patrick, *Florida Under Five Flags* (Gainesville: University of Florida Press, 1945); Michael V. Gannon, *The Cross in the Sand* (Gainesville: University of Florida Press, 1965); Charlton Tebeau, *The History of Florida* (Coral Gables: University of Miami Press, 1971); and Jerald T. Milanich and Samuel Proctor, eds., *Tacachale* (Gainesville: University Presses of Florida, 1978).

3.   *La Florida* first appears on the Cantino Map, 1502. See Carl Ortwin Sauer, *Sixteenth Century North America: The Land and the People as Seen by the Europeans* (Berkeley: University of California Press, 1971), 25. By 1521 Spanish slavers had already emptied the Bahama Islands of all its inhabitants in their searches. See Archivo General de Indias, Justicia 3, no. 3, fols. 40–41. For a short discussion of the primary sources supporting 1510 as the date of first Spanish discovery, see *Letter of Hernando de Soto and Memoir of Hernando de Escalante Fontaneda*, ca. 1575 (Washington, D.C.: privately printed for G. W. Riggs, 1854).

4.   Antonio de Herrera y Tordesillas, *Historia General de los Hechos de los Castellanos en las Islas y Tierra del Mar Oceano*, 9 vols. (Madrid, 1601–1615), decada 1, libro 9, p. 53.

5.   Amy Turner Bushnell, *Situado and Sabana: Spain's Support System for the Presidio and Mission Provinces of Florida*, American Museum of Natural History Anthropological Paper No. 74 (New York: American Museum of Natural History, 1994), 17.

6. Ibid., 17.

7. For discussion of the functionalist nature of discourse, see, for example, M. Halliday, *Language as a Social Semiotic* (London: Edward Arnold, 1978), and Deborah Schiffrin, *Approaches to Discourse* (Oxford: Blackwell Publishers, 1994).

8. Numerous attempts have been made over the past century to delineate these languages and their cultural frontiers. A useful current synthesis of data is Karen M. Booker, Charles M. Hudson, and Robert L. Rankin, "Place Name Identification and Multilingualism in the Sixteenth-Century Southeast," *Ethnohistory* 39:4 (Fall 1992), 399–451. Earlier interpretations have relied upon John R. Swanton's *Early History of the Creek Indians and Their Neighbors* (Washington, D.C.: Government Printing Office, 1922) and *The Indians of the Southeastern United States*, Bureau of American Ethnology Bulletin 137 (Washington, D.C.: Government Printing Office, 1946).

9. There is confusion over the origins and linguistic affiliations of what appear to be two separate Yuchî or Euchee tribes. One observer differentiated the two thus: "The Yuchi or Uchee tribe of Indians [differ] from the Creeks in race and language. But the Yutchitálgi or Euchitaws . . . are the Hitchiti tribe, not the Yuchi." See Albert Gatschet, *A Migration Legend of the Creek Indians with a Linguistic, Historical and Ethnographic Introduction*, vol. 2, Transactions of the St. Louis Academy of Science (Philadelphia: Daniel G. Brinton, 1888), 103.

10. The linguistic affiliation of this latter tribe, the Timuguana, is particularly problematic. Julian Granberry in his *A Grammar and Dictionary of the Timucuan Language*, 3d ed. (Tuscaloosa: University of Alabama Press, 1993), follows John R. Swanton but posits that Timuguana may actually have an Arawakan antecedent, while Swanton, in *Early History* and *Indians of the Southeastern United States*, makes it a Maskókî language.

11. See, for example, the statement of Lynda Norene Shaffer, *Native Americans Before 1492: The Moundbuilding Centers of the Eastern Woodlands* (Armonk, N.Y.: M. E. Sharpe, 1992), xxi. She concludes: "I was taken aback by the nature of some of the disputes in North American archaeology and by the ways in which they are pursued by some of the experts on the Eastern Woodlands. Long before I finished this study, it became clear to me that such controversies would make it exceedingly difficult to write a book about the moundbuilding region that would please all the archaeologists, especially since I did not want to write a book that would be more about their disagreements than about the peoples of this region."

12. John H. Hann, *A History of the Timucua Indians and Missions* (Gainesville: University Press of Florida, 1996), 2–17.

13. Ibid., 17, 326.

14. Ibid., 4–17, passim.

15. Ibid., 327–28.

16. Schiffrin, *Approaches to Discourse*, 8. Here Schiffrin builds upon the "ethnography of communication" approach advocated by Dell Hymes in two works, "Toward Ethnographies of Communication: The Analysis of Communicative Events," in P. Giglioli, ed., *Language and Social Context* (Harmonsworth, England: Penguin, 1972), and "Introduction: Toward Ethnographies of Communication," *American Anthropologist* 66:6 (1966), 12–25, and by A. Hallowell, "Ojibwa Ontology, Behavior and Worldview," in S. Diamond, ed., *Primitive Views of the World* (New York: Columbia University Press, 1964), 49–82.

17. Bushnell, *Situado and Sabana*, 35; Gannon, *Cross in the Sand;* Milanich and Proctor, *Tacachale;* and Jerald T. Milanich, *Archaeology of Precolumbian Florida* (Gainesville: University Presses of Florida, 1994), among others, also repeat this and recontextualize it as disappearance.

18. Milanich, *Archaeology of Precolumbian Florida*, xvi.

19. Tebeau, *History of Florida*, 38.

20. A clear statement of this mentality can be found in the introduction to Leslie Bethell, ed., *New Cambridge History of Latin America* (Cambridge: Cambridge University, 1984–), 1:4.

21. See, for example, Kathleen Deagan, *Spanish St. Augustine: The Archaeology of a Colonial Creole Community* (New York: Academic Press, 1983), and Deagan, "Accommodation and Resistance: The Process and Impact of Spanish Colonialization in the Southeast," in David Hurst Thomas, ed., *Columbian Consequences*, vol. 2, *Archaeological and Historical Perspectives on the Spanish Borderlands East* (Washington, D.C.: Smithsonian Institution Press, 1990), 297–314; John H. Hann, *Apalachee: The Land between the Rivers* (Gainesville: University Press of Florida, 1987), and Hann, ed. and trans., *Missions to the Calusa* (Gainesville: University Press of Florida, 1991); Paul Hoffman, *A New Andalucia and a Way to the Orient: The American Southeast during the Sixteenth Century* (Baton Rouge: Louisiana University Press, 1990); Marvin T. Smith, *Archaeology of Aboriginal Culture Change in the Interior Southeast: Depopulation during the Early Historic Period* (Gainesville: University Press of Florida, 1987); and Wood, Waselkov, and Hatley, *Powhatan's Mantle*.

22. Foremost among the developers of these approaches have been Steve J. Stern, *Peru's Indian Peoples and the Challenge of Spanish Conquest: Huamanga to 1640* (Madison: University of Wisconsin Press, 1982); Florencia E. Mallon, *The Defense of Community in Peru's Central Highland: Peasant Struggle and Capitalist Transition, 1860–1940* (Princeton: Princeton University Press, 1984); and Nancy M. Farriss, *Maya Society under Colonial Rule: The Collective Enterprise of Survival* (Princeton: Princeton University Press, 1984).

23. Anthony Pagden, *The Fall of Natural Man: The American Indian and the Origins of Comparative Ethnology,* 1982 (Cambridge: Cambridge University Press, 1989), 2.

24. Ibid., 6.

25. Gabriél Garciá Márquez, *Of Love and Other Demons* (New York: Random House, 1995).

26. Pagden, *Fall of Natural Man*, 4.

27. Ibid.

28. Kathleen Deagan, in "Sixteenth-Century Spanish-American Colonization in the Southeastern United States and the Caribbean," in Thomas, *Columbian Consequences*, 2:231, summarizes that all "Florida Indians [were] subdued in large measure by the end of the sixteenth century through the combined efforts of population loss, mission efforts, and the collaboration of the caciques with the Spaniards." Historian Amy Bushnell tempers this sweeping statement by pointing out that, in reality, "only a fraction of the tribal groups in the Southeast developed into full Spanish provinces." See Bushnell, *Situado and Sabana*, 60.

29. Charles Hudson, *The Southeastern Indians* (Knoxville: University of Tennessee Press, 1976), 3, cited in John H. Hann, "Summary Guide to Spanish Florida Missions and Visitas with Churches in the Sixteenth and Seventeenth Centuries," *The Americas* 46:4 (April 1990), 422.

30. See, for example, Mary Elizabeth Perry, *Gender and Disorder in Early Modern Seville* (Princeton: Princeton University Press, 1990), 177, 178; Bonnie S. Anderson and Judith P. Zinsser, *A History of Their Own: Women in Europe from Prehistory to the Present*, vol. 1 (New York: Harper & Row, 1989), 77, passim. Sarah B. Pomeroy, *Goddesses, Whores, Wives, and Slaves: Women in Classical Antiquity* (New York: Schocken Books, 1975), discusses the Aristotelian basis for the subordination of women; Marilyn French, *The War Against Women* (New York: Ballantine Books, 1992), provides an overview of the attitudes and teachings of various organized religions; Mary Daly, *The Church and the Second Sex* (Boston: Beacon Press, 1968), describes the continuing subjugation of women in orthodoxy. For background on all of the concerned issues, see James A. Brundage, *Law, Sex, and Christian Society in Medieval Europe* (Chicago: University of Chicago Press, 1987).

31. Bushnell, *Situado and Sabana*, 68.

32. Heinz-Otto Peitgen, Hartmüt Jurgens, and Dietmar Saupe, *Chaos and Fractals: New Frontiers of Science* (New York and Berlin: Springer-Verlag, 1992), vii–viii.

2. The Four-Cornered Circle

1. Marshall D. Sahlins, *Historical Metaphors and Mythical Realities: Structure in the Early History of the Sandwich Islands Kingdom*, ASAO Special Publication No. 1 (Ann Arbor: University of Michigan Press, 1981), 8.

2. Albert Gatschet, *A Migration Legend of the Creek Indians with a Linguistic,*

Historical and Ethnographic Introduction, vol. 2, Transactions of the St. Louis Academy of Science (Philadelphia: Daniel G. Brinton, 1888), 104.

3. This question has been addressed by modern archaeologists particularly in the peninsular regions of *La Florida,* where the earliest evidence of contact is discernible. See, for example, the discussion and references to other works in Jerald T. Milanich, *Archaeology of Precolumbian Florida* (Gainesville: University Presses of Florida, 1994), 360.

4. John F. Scarry, "The Late Prehistoric Southeast," in Charles Hudson and Carmen Chaves Tesser, eds., *The Forgotten Centuries: Indians and Europeans in the American South, 1521–1704* (Athens: University of Georgia Press, 1994), 29.

5. Vernon James Knight, Jr., "The Institutional Organization of Mississippian Religion," *American Antiquity* 51:4 (1986), 681.

6. Milanich, *Archaeology of Precolumbian Florida,* xvi, 263; Knight, "Institutional Organization," 681.

7. John H. Hann, *A History of the Timucua Indians and Missions* (Gainesville: University of Florida Press, 1996), 5.

8. Laura Kozuch, *Sharks and Shark Products in Prehistoric South Florida,* Institute of Archaeology and Paleoenvironmental Studies, Monograph No. 2 (Gainesville: University of Florida, 1993), 7, 31.

9. The exact dynamic of linguistic affinity among certain of the Maskókî speakers remains controversial. John R. Swanton in *Indian Tribes of the Lower Mississippi Valley and Adjacent Coast of the Gulf of Mexico,* Bureau of American Ethnology Bulletin 43 (Washington, D.C.: Government Printing Office, 1911), 7–8, excludes the Timucua of Florida from his Muskhogean speakers although in later works he would include them. More recent research classifies "Chickasaw" as a dialect of "Choctaw," both of which were western "Muskogean," along with the "Natchez," although the two former frequently penetrated the core areas of the Maskókî speakers. See Karen M. Booker, Charles M. Hudson, and Robert L. Rankin, "Place Name Identification and Multilingualism in the Sixteenth-Century Southeast," *Ethnohistory* 39:4 (Fall 1992), 414–16. "Timucuan," always problematic, is cited first as a "Muskogean language" and then as "a language of unclear genetic affiliation." Julian Granberry, *A Grammar and Dictionary of the Timucuan Language,* 3d ed. (Tuscaloosa: University of Alabama Press, 1993), 1, treats Timuguana as a Maskókî language. Booker, Hudson, and Rankin, however, do agree that "it seems probable, therefore [i.e., based on linguistic and archaeological evidence], that Muskogean-speaking peoples east of the Mississippi River originated and/or disseminated the package of social and economic changes that archaeologists call the Mississippian tradition" (p. 435).

10. Booker, Hudson, and Rankin, "Place Name Identification," 435.

11. Knight, "Institutional Organization," 675–79.

12.   Scarry, "Late Prehistoric Southeast," 34 n. 34.

13.   See, for example, J. Leitch Wright, Jr., *Creeks & Seminoles: The Destruction and Regeneration of the Muscogulge People* (Lincoln: University of Nebraska Press, 1986), 12, concerning the four founding towns of the Maskókî speakers; also Mary Frances Johns, Sonnie Billie, James Billie, and Suzie Jim, interviews with the author. An exception to the belief in the number four as a number of power occurred among the Timuguana, for whom there is some indication that six was the number of power. See Jerald T. Milanich, ed., *Francisco Pareja's Confessionario: A Documentary Source for Timucuan Ethnography* (Tallahassee: Division of Archives, History, and Records Management, Florida Department of State, 1972), 23–39.

14.   Anthony F. C. Wallace, *Religion: An Anthropological View* (New York: Random House, 1966), 75, cited in Knight, "Institutional Organization," 675.

15.   Knight, "Institutional Organization," 677.

16.   Ibid., 678.

17.   Some of the best-known descriptions are those of William Bartram, "Observations on the Creek and Cherokee Indians," *Transactions of the American Ethnological Society*, vol. 3, pt. 1 (1853), 54–56; James Adair, *History of the American Indians* (London: n.p., 1775), 17; Le Clerc Milfort, *Mémoire ou coup-d'œil rapide sur mes différens voyages et mon séjour dans la nation Crëck* (Paris: Giguet et Michaud, 1802), 255; and Caleb Swan, "Position and State of Manners and Arts in the Creek, or Muskogee Nation in 1791," in Henry R. Schoolcraft, *Historical and Statistical Information Respecting the History, Condition, and Prospects of the Indian Tribes of the United States,* vol. 5 (Philadelphia: Lippincott, 1855), 251–83. A classic discussion of these sources and others is in John R. Swanton, *Forty-Second Annual Report of the Bureau of American Ethnology to the Secretary of the Smithsonian Institution* (Washington, D.C.: Government Printing Office, 1928), 170–88.

18.   Mary Jene Koenes, Joe Frank, Sonny Billie, James Billie, Geneva Shore, Samuel Tommie, Henry John Billie, Lorene Gopher, Chitto Hadjo, among others, interviews with the author.

19.   Regarding ceremonial grounds or plazas as a standard feature of the lives of the Maskókî speakers, see Swanton, *Indian Tribes of the Lower Mississippi Valley;* Swanton, *The Indians of the Southeastern United States,* Bureau of American Ethnology Bulletin 137 (Washington, D.C.: Government Printing Office, 1946), 776, illus. pls. 99–104; and David J. Hally, "Archaeological Investigation of the Little Egypt Site (9MU102), Murray County, Georgia, 1969 Season," mimeograph (Athens: University of Georgia, Department of Anthropology, August 1976), 113.

20.   Interviews with Florida Seminoles Mary Frances Johns, Sonny Billie, James Billie, Samuel Tommie, and Ronnie Jimmie and with Oklahoma Seminoles Chitto Hadjo, Ryder Larney, and Harry Long. Mary Frances Johns also re-

calls being told by her Clan elders that there was a time when the number three was the number of power, but, she believes, that was before the coming of the Four Teachers.

21.   See, for example, the remarks of Jacques le Moyne de Morgues, French cartographer who accompanied the Huguenot expedition of René de Laudonnière to *La Florida* in 1564, in his *Brevis narratio eorum quae in Florida, Americae provincia, Gallis acciderunt, secunda in illa navegationae, duce renato de Laudonnière, closses praefecto, anno 1564 quae est secunda pars Americae. . . .* (Frankfort: Typis J. Wecheli, 1591), reprinted in Stefan Lorant, ed., *The New World: The First Pictures of America* (New York: Duell, Sloan & Pearce, 1946), pl. 12, p. 59; see also Swanton, *Indians of the Southeastern United States,* 774.

22.   William C. Sturtevant, "The Mikasuki Seminole: Medical Beliefs and Practices," 2 pts. (Ph.D. diss., Yale University, 1955), 2:321.

23.   Knight, "Institutional Organization," 678.

24.   Antonio J. Waring, Jr., and Preston Holder, "A Prehistoric Ceremonial Complex in the Southeastern United States," *American Anthropologist* 47 (1945), 1–34, and Antonio J. Waring, Jr., "The Southern Cult and Muskohogean Ceremonial: General Considerations," in Stephen Williams, ed., *The Waring Papers,* Papers of the Peabody Museum of Archaeology and Ethnology, 58 (1968), 30–69, both cited in Knight, "Institutional Organization," 678.

25.   See, for example, John R. Swanton, "The Interpretation of Aboriginal Mounds by Means of Creek Indian Customs," *Annual Report of the Smithsonian Institution* (Washington, D.C.: Government Printing Office, 1927), 495–507.

26.   Knight, "Institutional Organization," 682.

27.   Ibid., 681.

28.   Gatschet, *Migration Legend,* 219.

29.   Hudson and Tesser, *Forgotten Centuries,* 2.

30.   Swanton, *Indians of the Southeastern United States,* 218. There is no disagreement among non-Native scholars over this point.

31.   I have been reminded of this frequently, for example, by Mary Frances Johns, Jeanette Cypress, Agnes Cypress, Willie Johns, Mable Haught, Samuel Tommie, and others.

32.   Alexander McGillivray, "Minutes Taken from Genl. McGillivray Respecting the Creeks," General Henry Knox Papers, August 1790, XXVI-165, 2467a, microfilm, Massachusetts Historical Society Library, Boston.

33.   George Stiggins, *Creek Indian History: A Historical Narrative of the Genealogy, Traditions and Downfall of the Ispocoga or Creek Indian Tribe of Indians by One of the Tribe* (Birmingham: Birmingham Public Library Press, 1989), 24–25.

34. Marvin T. Smith, *Archaeology of Aboriginal Culture Change in the Interior Southeast: Depopulation during the Early Historic Period* (Gainesville: University Press of Florida, 1987), 72.

35. "The Letters of US Indian Agent Benjamin Hawkins," *Georgia Historical Society Collections* 9 (1916), 85, 86. See also the discussion in Albert Hazen Wright, *Our Georgia-Florida Frontier: The Okeefenokee Swamp, its History and Cartography* (Ithaca, New York: A. H. Wright, 1945), pt. 1, 3. Sixteenth-century documents referred to the swamp as "the great morass." The name Okefinocau, of which Okefinokee is a corruption, comes from the Chactá and Maskókî words *Okî finokau* for "water, quivering."

36. United States Indian Agent John Johnston to Caleb Atwater, 1819: quoted by Buckingham Smith in his translation of Hernando de Escalante Fontaneda, *Letter of Hernando de Soto and Memoir of Hernando de Escalante Fontaneda,* ca. 1575 (Washington, D.C.: privately printed for G. W. Riggs, 1854), 47.

37. Escalante Fontaneda, *Letter of Hernando de Soto and Memoir of Hernando de Escalante Fontaneda,* 47, cited in Wright, *Our Georgia-Florida Frontier,* pt. 3, 46; 46 n. 23.

38. "Letters of Benjamin Hawkins," 16, 17, 34, cited in Wright, *Our Georgia-Florida Frontier,* pt. 3, 46; 46 n. 23.

39. Wilbur R. Jacobs, ed., *Indians of the Southern Colonial Frontier: The Edmond Atkin Report and Plan of 1755* (Columbia: University of South Carolina Press, 1954), 64–66.

40. Dale Jumper Grasshopper, Lucille Jumper, and Alan Jumper, interviews with the author. Alan Jumper recalls being told this by Abraham Lincoln Clay (deceased).

41. Swanton, *Indians of the Southeastern United States,* 184.

42. "The Account by a Gentleman from Elvas," James Alexander Robertson, trans., in Lawrence A. Clayton, Vernon James Knight, Jr., and Edward C. Moore, eds., *The De Soto Chronicles: The Expedition of Hernando de Soto to North America in 1539–1543,* 2 vols. (Tuscaloosa: University of Alabama Press, 1993), 1:19–220.

43. Smith, *Archaeology of Aboriginal Culture Change,* 77, offers convincing archaeological proofs that the core villages of "Coosa" moved steadily southward during the period. Smith, however, narrows his period of migration to 1540–1740.

44. Wright, *Creeks & Seminoles,* 3. Variant spellings exist for each of these names. See also Swanton, *Indians of the Southeastern United States,* 126–28.

45. Swanton, *Indians of the Southeastern United States,* 127.

46. Ibid., 125.

47. Gatschet, *A Migration Legend,* 83. Gatschet explains them as "the four genii who brought fire from the four cardinal points to the ancestors of the Kasi'hta tribe, according to the legend related by Taskáya Miko. . . . The

term is connected with Cr. hayáyagi *light, radiance.* . . . These genii are what other Indian myths call the four pillars of the Sky." See also R. M. Loughbridge and David M. Hodge, *Dictionary in Two Parts: English and Muskogee, and Muskogee and English* (Philadelphia: Westminster Press, 1914), 44.

48. Interviews with Sonny Billie, currently considered the most powerful medicine man, or "Indian doctor" as he calls himself, among the Florida Seminoles. He learned this from Josie Billie and his father, Co-na-pa-hatchee Billie, two of the more powerful medicine practitioners of the early twentieth century. Also from interviews with Susie Jim, another protégée of Josie Billie, and with Mary Frances Johns, who has studied for many years with Susie Jim. Also from Mable Haught and from Celeste Billie Hall, who learned it from her grandfather, Jimmy Billie. All the accounts agree that the primary impetus came from the north and that the subsequent Illuminators appeared in clockwise sequence, rather than a counterclockwise sequence, even though the latter would be more consistent with Maskókî semiotics.

49. Gatschet, *A Migration Legend,* 95. Among the current Oklahoma Seminoles, the designator "Ofunga" is preferred by traditionalists, who view the other term as indicative of the Christian Christ. Jimmie and Nancy Carbitcher, Rev. Harry Long, Ryder Larney, and Louis Chupco, interviews with the author, September 1995.

50. Sonny Billie, interview with the author.

51. Mable Haught, Priscilla Sayen, and Leroy "Keno" King, interviews with the author.

3. The Tree That Bends

1. Greg Urban, *A Discourse-Centered Approach to Culture: Native South American Myths and Rituals* (Austin: University of Texas Press, 1991), 16–17.

2. Colin Gordon, ed., *Power/Knowledge: Selected Interviews & Other Writings, 1972–1977 by Michel Foucault,* 1972 (New York: Pantheon Books, 1980), 194, 195, 196, 197, 198–99, 208.

3. Nancy M. Farriss, *Maya Society under Colonial Rule: The Collective Enterprise of Survival* (Princeton: Princeton University Press, 1984), 300–5.

4. Ibid., 286.

5. Mary Frances Johns, interviews with the author.

6. Jerald T. Milanich, ed., *Francisco Pareja's Confessionario: A Documentary Source for Timucuan Ethnography* (Tallahassee: Division of Archives, History, and Records Management, Florida Department of State, 1972), fol. 124, p. 23.

7. Ibid., fol. 125, p. 24; fol. 130, p. 27.

8. J. Leitch Wright, Jr., *Creeks & Seminoles: The Destruction and Regeneration of the Muscogulge People* (Lincoln: University of Nebraska Press, 1986), 14–17.

9. Willie Johns, Sonnie Billie, Mary Frances Johns, Henry John Billie, Joe Billie, Jr., Danny Wilcox Tommie, Ronnie Billie, Frank J. Billie, and James Billie, interviews with the author.

10. John R. Swanton, *Forty-Second Annual Report of the Bureau of American Ethnology to the Secretary of the Smithsonian Institution* (Washington, D.C.: Government Printing Office, 1928), 164–66. Swanton discusses the red:white juxtapositions of towns and also asserts broader significances.

11. Dale Jumper Grasshopper referring to her great-uncle, Bert Fraser; also Alan Jumper and Danny Wilcox Tommie, interviews with the author.

12. Robert K. Merton, *Social Theory and Social Structure,* 1949 (New York: The Free Press, 1968), 178.

13. Heinz-Otto Peitgen, Hartmüt Jurgens, and Dietmar Saupe, *Chaos and Fractals: New Frontiers of Science* (New York and Berlin: Springer-Verlag, 1992), vii–viii.

14. Wright, *Creeks & Seminoles,* 17.

15. Vernon James Knight, Jr., "The Institutional Organization of Mississippian Religion," *American Antiquity* 51:4 (1986), 682.

16. Charles Hudson and Carmen Chaves Tesser, eds., *The Forgotten Centuries: Indians and Europeans in the American South, 1521–1704* (Athens: University of Georgia Press, 1994), 2.

17. Rochelle A. Marrinan, John F. Scarry, and Rhonda L. Majors, "Prelude to de Soto: The Expedition of Pánfilo de Naváez," in David Hurst Thomas, ed., *Columbian Consequences,* vol. 2, *Archaeological and Historical Perspectives on the Spanish Borderlands East* (Washington, D.C.: Smithsonian Institution Press, 1990), 2:78.

18. James Pierce, "Notices of the Agriculture, Scenery, Geology, and Animal, Vegetable and Mineral Production of the Floridas, and of the Indian Tribes, Made during a Recent Tour in These Countries," *American Journal of Science and Arts,* article 21, 9:1 (June 1825), 119–36.

19. Peggy V. Beck, Anna Lee Walters, and Nia Francisco, *The Sacred: Ways of Knowledge, Sources of Life,* 1977 (Tsaile, Arizona: Navajo Community College Press, 1992), 248.

20. See, for example, the extreme cultural chauvinism evidenced by Clifford M. Lewis in his "The Calusa," in Jerald T. Milanich and Samuel Proctor, eds., *Tacachale* (Gainesville: University Presses of Florida, 1978), 36. Lewis describes Calusa ritual, in terms reminiscent of those of sixteenth-century Roman Catholic missionaries, as "witchcraft"; doubts that there was any "real significance" to their ceremonies; and concludes, contrary to the documents, that the Calusa and Teguesta "were converted to Christianity without much resistance" because they had "no intelligible beliefs." See Chapter 9 of the present work for a review of the successful three hundred–year resistance of the Calusa and Teguesta to conversion.

21. Lawrence A. Clayton, Vernon James Knight, Jr., and Edward C. Moore, eds., *The De Soto Chronicles: The Expedition of Hernando de Soto to North America in 1539–1543,* 2 vols. (Tuscaloosa: University of Alabama Press, 1993).

22. Henry F. Dobyns, *Their Number Become Thinned: Native American Population Dynamics in Eastern North America* (Knoxville: University of Tennessee Press, 1983), passim; Peter Wood, "The Changing Population of the Colonial South: An Overview by Race and Region, 1685–1790," in Peter H. Wood, Gregory A. Waselkov, and M. Thomas Hatley, *Powhatan's Mantle: Indians in the Colonial Southeast* (Lincoln: University of Nebraska Press, 1989), 38–39, 51–61; Marvin T. Smith, *Archaeology of Aboriginal Culture Change in the Interior Southeast: Depopulation during the Early Historic Period* (Gainesville: University Press of Florida, 1987), 78; John R. Dunkle, "Population Change as an Element in the Historical Geography of St. Augustine," *Florida Historical Quarterly* 37 (July 1958), 3–22; Theodore G. Corbett, "Population Structure in Hispanic St. Augustine, 1629–1763," *Florida Historical Quarterly* 54 (January 1956), 263–84; and Kenneth W. Porter, "Negroes on the Southern Frontier, 1670–1763," *Journal of Negro History* 33 (1948), 53–78.

23. Dobyns, *Their Number Become Thinned,* 41.

24. John R. Swanton, *The Indians of the Southeastern United States,* Bureau of American Ethnology Bulletin 137 (Washington, D.C.: Government Printing Office, 1946), map 3.

25. Dobyns, *Their Number Become Thinned,* 43.

26. Wood, Waselkov, and Hatley, *Powhatan's Mantle.*

27. Lucy Wenhold, trans. and ed., *A Seventeenth-Century Letter of Gabriel Díaz Vara Calderón, Bishop of Cuba, Describing the Indians and Indian Missions of Florida,* Smithsonian Miscellaneous Collections, 95:16 (Washington, D.C.: Smithsonian Institution Press, 1936).

28. As passing examples of the Spaniards' imaging of their cultural Other, see the terms *barbarous and inhuman, heathen, idolaters,* and *lazy* in Garcilaso de la Vega's "La Florida del Ynca," in Clayton, Knight, and Moore, *De Soto Chronicles,* 2:67, 68, 87, 110, 126.

29. Helen Nader, *Liberty in Absolutist Spain: The Habsburg Sale of Towns, 1521–1700* (Baltimore: Johns Hopkins University Press, 1990), 8, 18, 27, 41–45.

30. Helen Hornbeck Tanner, "The Land and Water Communication Systems of the Southeastern Indians," in Wood, Waselkov, and Hatley, *Powhatan's Mantle,* 6–20. An earlier seminal work on this topic and area is William E. Myer, "Indian Trails of the Southeast," in *Forty-Second Annual Report of the Bureau of American Ethnology for 1924–1925* (Washington, D.C.: Government Printing Office, 1928), 727–857, especially 828, 846–48.

31. Andrés González de Barciá Carballido y Zúñiga, *Ensayo cronológico para la historia general de la Florida, 1512–1722,* 1723, Anthony Kerrigan, trans. (Gainesville: University Presses of Florida, 1951).

32. Julian H. Steward, "Theory and Application in a Social Science," *Ethnohistory* 2 (1955), 296–97.

33. Bill Osceola, Henry J. Billie, Little Tigertail, and Frank J. Billie, interviews with the author.

34. Dale Grasshopper, Daisy Jumper, and Charles Hiers Billie, interviews with the author.

35. Mark Williams and Gary Shapiro, eds., *Lamar Archaeology: Mississippian Chiefdoms in the Deep South* (Tuscaloosa: University of Alabama Press, 1990), 174.

36. Peter H. Wood, "Introduction to Part One," in Wood, Waselkov, and Hatley, *Powhatan's Mantle*, 3.

37. For a comprehensive view of the exotic materials and artifacts recovered from Florida's pre-Columbian occupational sites, see Jerald T. Milanich, *Archaeology of Precolumbian Florida* (Gainesville: University Presses of Florida, 1994), passim.

38. Ibid., 134.

39. Fray Juan Rogel, SJ, to Fray Didacus Avellaneda, November 1566–January 1567, in Felix Zubillaga, ed., *Monumenta Antiquae Floridae* (Rome: Monumenta Missionum Societatis Iesu, 1946), 101–40, translated in John H. Hann, ed. and trans., *Missions to the Calusa* (Gainesville: University Press of Florida, 1991), 279–82.

40. Vega, "La Florida del Ynca," 2:126.

41. René de Laudonnière, *Three Voyages,* 1586, Charles E. Bennett, trans. and ed. (Gainesville: University Presses of Florida, 1975), 86.

42. Stefan Lorant, ed., *The New World: The First Pictures of America* (New York: Duell, Sloan & Pearce, 1946), pl. 40, p. 115; Milanich, *Francisco Pareja's Confessionario,* fol. 124, p. 23; and John H. Hann, *Apalachee: The Land between the Rivers* (Gainesville: University Press of Florida, 1987), 79, 85, 336, 343.

43. Karen M. Booker, Charles M. Hudson, and Robert L. Rankin, "Place Name Identification and Multilingualism in the Sixteenth-Century Southeast," *Ethnohistory* 39:4 (Fall 1992), 432.

44. Swanton, *Indians of the Southeastern United States,* 137.

45. Ibid.; and Clayton, Knight, and Moore, *De Soto Chronicles,* 1:279. Booker, Hudson, and Rankin agree with this correlation: see Booker, Hudson, and Rankin, "Place Name Identification," 421.

46. Dobyns, *Their Number Become Thinned,* 4.

47. Ibid., 8. See also Peter H. Wood, "Introduction to Part One," in Wood, Waselkov, and Hatley, *Powhatan's Mantle,* 1. Wood reminds us that generations of Euroamericans have been educated to believe that the lands that the early colonists settled were void of previous settlers and wonders whether

the subliminal message of primacy was promulgated through ignorance, accident, or a conspiracy of silence.

48. See also the calculations by Wood, "Changing Population of the Colonial South," in Wood, Waselkov, and Hatley, *Powhatan's Mantle*, 54–55, 97 n. 39. The population figure varies among the sources. Eighty-three, eighty-six, or eighty-nine "Christianized Indians" chose to evacuate *La Florida* to avoid the incoming British. Cf. David J. Weber, *The Spanish Frontier in North America* (New Haven and London: Yale University Press, 1992), 199–200. Weber cites seven hundred evacuees from Pensacola.

49. I am grateful to Dr. Eugene Lyon for this information, which he gathered from personal research efforts in Cuban archives in 1989 and 1995.

50. Wood, "Changing Population of the Colonial South," in Wood, Waselkov, and Hatley, *Powhatan's Mantle*, 55, 97 n. 39.

51. See, for example, the pronouncement of Milanich, according to whom "no descendants of the Native Americans who had lived here since people first migrated into the land we now call Florida survived the European conquest." Milanich, *Archaeology of Precolumbian Florida*, xvi.

52. Marshall D. Sahlins, *Historical Metaphors and Mythical Realities: Structure in the Early History of the Sandwich Islands Kingdom*, ASAO Special Publication No. 1 (Ann Arbor: University of Michigan Press, 1981), 8.

53. Sonny Billie, Andy Buster, Ryder Larney, Ronnie Billie, Henry John Billie, and Mary Frances Johns, interviews with the author.

54. Alan Jumper. Variations of this same explanation have been offered by Sonny Billie, Celeste Billie Hall, Samuel Tommie, and David Jumper, among others, in interviews with the author. An interesting and useful exposition of elements of the social mechanics of bounding and replication in oral societies may be found in Walter J. Ong, *Orality and Literacy: The Technologizing of the Word*, 1982 (London: Routledge, 1988). See especially Ong's chapter 3, "Some Psychodynamics of Orality," 31–77, and pages 146, 166, 169, in which the author uses the results of researchers among oral societies from biblical times to the present and reaches conclusions quite similar to those presented here.

55. Luís Gerónimo de Oré, OFM, *The Martyrs of Florida (1513–1616)*, Maynard Geiger, OFM, trans. Franciscan Studies No. 18 (July 1936) (New York: Joseph F. Wagner, 1936).

56. George Stiggins, *Creek Indian History: A Historical Narrative of the Genealogy, Traditions and Downfall of the Ispocoga or Creek Indian Tribe of Indians by One of the Tribe* (Birmingham: Birmingham Public Library Press, 1989), 64–65.

57. There is, however, a transition that has been taking place among the members of the Seminole Nation of Oklahoma since the removal period from 1836 to 1858. United States military and government officials, in compiling prisoner and annuity lists, introduced the term *Band* to indicate members

of a single authority group. A Band comprised not only blood and fictive kin who had lived together in a Clan structure, but also pendant ex-slaves and freedmen as well. A male was always listed as the head of a Band, nuclear families were listed together, and slaves and freedmen were listed as a discrete segment of a Band list. The United States government has, by dint of its reporting and dispersing systems, required the Oklahoma Seminoles to preserve their Band affiliations for official purposes, even as they maintain their memories of their Clan affiliations. Within this continuing dual system of personal and corporate identifications, the weight of federal requirements is tipping the balance against the Clans. There are currently about six Clans still represented among the Oklahoma Seminoles and fourteen Bands (twelve of Native Americans and two Freedmen's Bands). Some of the people there no longer remember their Clans.

58. Some researchers continue to find ambiguity in the documentary comments and to posit that some of the Maskókî peoples functioned in patrilineal systems. Hann, for example, indicates that the Calusa were patrilineal, apparently because the leader traditionally took a sister as his first wife. However, the cacique Don Felipe indicated that only the cacique was permitted to do this, and, even so, marrying one's sister would support a matrilineal system rather than a patrilineal system, because then one's son and nephew would be the same child and would maintain the same Clan affiliation, as he would not if the cacique married outside his Clan.

59. Widowers are prime examples of this process. Mitchell Cypress and Charles Hiers Billie, among others, have experienced this: interviews with the author.

60. Thus, for example, the members of Toad Clan within the Seminole Tribe today retain their kinship but have rejected their Clan totem and changed their Clan name to Big Town because they have been derisively compared with toads so frequently. Conversations with Geneva Shore, Happy Jones, Willie Johns, James Billie, Samuel Tommie, and many others.

61. William Bartram, *Travels in Georgia and Florida, 1773–74: A Report to Dr. John Fothergill,* Transactions of the American Philosophical Society, new series, vol. 33, pt. 2 (Philadelphia: American Philosophical Society, 1943), 454. Also cited in Swanton, *Indians of the Southeastern United States,* 616.

62. Quoted in Steve Wall and Harvey Arden, *Wisdomkeepers: Meeting with Native American Spiritual Elders* (Hillsboro, Oregon: Beyond Words Publishing, 1990), 79.

63. Urban, *A Discourse-Centered Approach to Culture,* 9–10.

64. Deborah Schiffrin, *Approaches to Discourse* (Oxford: Blackwell Publishers, 1994), 57–59.

65. Fray Juan Rogel, SJ, to Fray Didacus Avellaneda, November 1566–January 1567, in Zubillaga, *Monumenta Antiquae Floridae,* 101–40, translated in Hann, *Missions to the Calusa,* 241.

66. Ibid., 246.

67. M. Le Page du Pratz, *The History of Louisiana or of the Western Parts of Virginia and Carolina: Containing A Description of the Countries that lye on both Sides of the River Missisipi: with An Account of the Settlements, Inhabitants, Soil, Climate, and Products. Translated from the French, (lately published,) by M. Le Page Du Pratz With Some Notes and Observations relating to our Colonies,* 2 vols. (London: T. Becket and P. A. De Hondt, 1763), 2:169.

4. Geography, Society, and Continuity

1. Marvin T. Smith, *Archaeology of Aboriginal Culture Change in the Interior Southeast: Depopulation during the Early Historic Period* (Gainesville: University Press of Florida, 1987), 7–8.

2. For the most cogent discussions of the Black Legend, which institutionalized the image of the Spaniards as rapacious plunderers of the Americas, see Charles Gibson, *The Black Legend: Anti-Spanish Attitudes in the Old World and the New* (New York: Knopf Publishers, 1971), and William S. Maltby, *The Black Legend in England: The Development of Anti-Spanish Sentiment, 1558–1660* (Durham, North Carolina: Duke University Press, 1971).

3. Smith, *Archaeology of Aboriginal Culture Change,* 6–7.

4. Frank J. Billie, Henry John Billie, James Billie, Mary Frances Johns, Alan Jumper, and Pete Osceola, interviews with the author.

5. Cited in Mark F. Boyd, "From a Remote Frontier: Letters and Documents Pertaining to San Marcos de Apalache, 1763–69, during the British Occupation of Florida," *Florida Historical Quarterly* 19:3, 4 (1941), 20:1, 2, 3, 4 (1941–42), and 21:1, 2 (1942).

6. John Stuart to Lieutenant Pampellone, July 16, 1764, Thomas Gage Collection, Clement Library, University of Michigan. Quoted in Charles H. Fairbanks, "Ethnohistorical Report of the Florida Indians. Before the United States Indian Claims Commission, The Seminole Indians of the State of Florida vs. The United States of America," Dockets No. 73 and 151 (1957), 4.

7. Fairbanks, "Ethnohistorical Report," 5.

8. Lawrence A. Clayton, Vernon James Knight, Jr., and Edward C. Moore, eds., *The De Soto Chronicles: The Expedition of Hernando de Soto to North America in 1539–1543,* 2 vols. (Tuscaloosa: University of Alabama Press, 1993), 2:124.

9. For an excellent review of the Spanish dynamic of individual pride of place and the competition of Spanish towns for advancement and royal preferment, see Helen Nader, *Liberty in Absolutist Spain: The Habsburg Sale of Towns, 1521–1700* (Baltimore: Johns Hopkins University Press, 1990), passim.

10. Ibid., 41; and John V. Lombardi, *People and Places in Colonial Venezuela* (Bloomington: University of Illinois Press, 1976), cited in Nader.

11.   Felix Zubillaga, SJ, remarks on this in his translations of Spanish *La Florida* documents regarding the Calusa: "Generally, in Spanish documents, the province and principal town, Calus, are referred to by the name of Carlos, their ruler." Felix Zubillaga, ed., *Monumenta Antiquae Floridae* (Rome: Monumenta Missionum Societatis Iesu, 1946), doc. 85, translated in Hann, *Missions to the Calusa* (Gainesville: University Press of Florida, 1991), 270 n. 3.

12.   "The Account by a Gentleman from Elvas," James Alexander Robertson, trans., in Clayton, Knight, and Moore, *De Soto Chronicles,* 1:76.

13.   Ibid., 1:58.

14.   Ibid., 1:65.

15.   Charles Hudson, Marvin Smith, David Hally, Richard Polhemus, and Chester DePratter, "Coosa: A Chiefdom in the Sixteenth-Century Southeastern United States," *American Antiquity* 50:4 (1985), 723–37.

16.   Albert Gatschet, *A Migration Legend of the Creek Indians with a Linguistic, Historical and Ethnographic Introduction,* vol. 2, Transactions of the St. Louis Academy of Science (Philadelphia: Daniel G. Brinton, 1888), 104.

17.   Variations in orthography include *Apica, Abihka, Apeka,* and *Abeka.* See, for example, Charles Hudson, Marvin T. Smith, Chester DePratter, and Emilia Kelley, "The Tristan de Luna Expedition, 1559–1561," in Jerald T. Milanich and Susan Milbrath, eds., *First Encounters: Spanish Explorations in the Caribbean and the United States, 1492–1570* (Gainesville: University of Florida Press, 1989), 119–34. See also Wilbur R. Jacobs, ed., *Indians of the Southern Colonial Frontier: The Edmond Atkin Report and Plan of 1755* (Columbia: University of South Carolina Press, 1954), 43, 64, 64 n. 93. The name appears as "Apéicah" on the Lamhatty Map of 1708. Lamhatty is thought to have been a Timuguana speaker from the Old Chatot area on the Gulf coast between what are now the Chipola and Ochlockonee rivers. See Gregory A. Waselkov, "Indian Maps of the Colonial Southeast," in Peter H. Wood, Gregory A. Waselkov, and M. Thomas Hatley, *Powhatan's Mantle: Indians in the Colonial Southeast* (Lincoln: University of Nebraska Press, 1989), 317, 318–19.

18.   Steven Bowers, Mary Frances Johns, Willie Johns, Stanlo Johns, and Geneva Shore, interviews with the author.

19.   Daniel G. Brinton, *Notes on the Floridian Peninsula, Its Literary History, Indian Tribes and Antiquities* (Philadelphia: J. Sabin, 1859), 8; Gatschet, *Migration Legend,* 2:248.

20.   "The Letters of US Indian Agent Benjamin Hawkins," *Georgia Historical Society Collections* 9 (1916), 82.

21.   John R. Swanton, *The Indians of the Southeastern United States,* Bureau of American Ethnology Bulletin 137 (Washington, D.C.: Government Printing Office, 1946), 216.

22.   George Stiggins, *Creek Indian History: A Historical Narrative of the Genealogy, Traditions and Downfall of the Ispocoga or Creek Indian Tribe of Indians*

by *One of the Tribe* (Birmingham: Birmingham Public Library Press, 1989), 34–35.

23. Ibid. Stiggins asserts that they used the affirmative particle *aw* rather than the *caw* used by other Maskókî speakers; a more comprehensive explanation is offered by the book's editor in 145–46 n. 19.

24. Swanton, *Indians of the Southeastern United States*, 216, avers that this definition is correct, but Karen M. Booker, Charles M. Hudson, and Robert L. Rankin, "Place Name Identification and Multilingualism in the Sixteenth-Century Southeast," *Ethnohistory* 39:4 (Fall 1992), did not collect this word in their "field guide lexica." They do, however, quote "Haas (ca. 1936)," whom they do not include in their bibliography, as being in substantial agreement. The word *tcilokit*, as understood to mean "people of a different language," is currently in common usage among the Mikísuukî Seminoles. Joe Billie, Jr., Dale Grasshopper, James E. Billie, Priscilla Sayen, Frank J. Billie, and others, interviews with the author.

25. This is the "Talimachusy" of Rodrigo Ranjel and the "Tallimuchase" of the Gentleman of Elvas. See Clayton, Knight, and Moore, *De Soto Chronicles*, vol. 1. See also Smith, *Archaeology of Aboriginal Culture Change*, 137.

26. Stiggins, *Creek Indian History*, 36.

27. John Stuart's opening speech to the tribal leaders assembled, the British-Indian Congress, Picolata, East Florida, November 15, 1765. In Rowland Dunbar, ed., *Mississippi Provincial Archives, English Dominion* I, 188–215. Cited in James W. Covington, *The British Meet the Seminoles*, Contributions of the Florida State Museum, Social Sciences No. 7 (Gainesville: University of Florida, 1961), 23.

28. James B. Dallam, in William D. Hoyt, "A Soldier's View of the Seminole War: Three Letters of James B. Dallam," *Florida Historical Quarterly* 25:4 (April 1947), 356–62. For the etymology of *tastanakî*, see R. M. Loughbridge and David M. Hodge, *Dictionary in Two Parts: English and Muskogee, and Muskogee and English* (Philadelphia: Westminster Press, 1914).

29. "Diary" of United States Army Assistant Surgeon Ellis Hughs, April 4, 1839, Collections of the Florida Historical Society, University of South Florida Library. See also John T. Sprague, *The Origin, Progress, and Conclusion of the Florida War*, 1848, reprint ed., John K. Mahon, ed. (Gainesville: University of Florida Press, 1964), 99; and John K. Mahon, *History of the Second Seminole War*, 1967 (Gainesville: University of Florida Press, 1991), 127–28, 204, 303–04, passim.

30. Juan López de Velasco, *Geográfia y descripción universal de las Indias, recopilado por el cosmógrafo-cronista . . . desde el año 1570 al de 1574. Publicada por primera vez en el Bolitín de la Sociedad Geográfica de Madrid. . . .* (Madrid: 1894), 164.

31. The documents relating the chain of events by which the Spaniards intervened in the internal affairs of the Escampaba or Calusa were published first

in Felix Zubillaga, ed., *Monumenta Antiquae Floridae* (Rome: Monumenta Missionum Societatis Iesu, 1946), as docs. 41 and 85, translated in John H. Hann, ed. and trans., *Missions to the Calusa* (Gainesville: University Press of Florida, 1991), 230–85.

32.   Zubillaga, *Monumenta Antiquae Floridae*, doc. 85, 337, translated in Hann, *Missions to the Calusa*, 223.

33.   John R. Swanton, *Early History of the Creek Indians and Their Neighbors* (Washington, D.C.: Government Printing Office, 1922), 343.

34.   Zubillaga, *Monumenta Antiquae Floridae*, doc. 85, 337.

35.   Greg Urban, *A Discourse-Centered Approach to Culture: Native South American Myths and Rituals* (Austin: University of Texas Press, 1991), 14.

36.   Ibid., 2. See also Walter J. Ong, *Orality and Literacy: The Technologizing of the Word,* 1982 (London: Routledge, 1988), 33.

5. Power and Gender

1.   Bartolomé Martínez to the Crown, Havana, February 17, 1577, Archivo General de Indias Santo Domingo, 125. Quoted in Eugene Lyon, "Settlement and Survival," in Michael V. Gannon, *The New History of Florida* (Gainesville: University Press of Florida, 1996), 58.

2.   Gerda Lerner, *The Creation of Patriarchy* (New York: Oxford University Press, 1986), 21. See also Gayle Rubin, "The Traffic in Women: Notes on the 'Political Economy' of Sex," in Reyna Rapp Reiter, ed., *Toward an Anthropology of Women* (New York: Monthly Review, 1978), 159.

3.   Amerigo Vespucci, "Mundus Novus Albericus Vespucius Laurencio Petri de Medicis salutem plurinam dicit. 1504/05," in *Vespucci Reprints, Texts, and Studies,* George T. Narthrup, trans. (Princeton: Princeton University Press, 1916), vol. 5.

4.   Lerner, *Creation of Patriarchy,* 31.

5.   Eleanor Leacock, "Women in Egalitarian Societies," in Renate Bridenthal and Claudia Koonz, eds., *Becoming Visible: Women in European History* (Boston: Houghton Mifflin, 1977), 27.

6.   See Martin and Vorhees, "Female of the Species," Judith K. Brown, "Iroquois Women: An Ethnohistoric Note," and Paula Webster, "Matriarchy: A Vision of Power," in Bridenthal and Koonz, *Becoming Visible,* 229, 127–56, 235–51.

7.   John R. Swanton, *Forty-Second Annual Report of the Bureau of American Ethnology to the Secretary of the Smithsonian Institution* (Washington, D.C.: Government Printing Office, 1928), 388.

8.   Bonnie S. Anderson and Judith P. Zinsser, *A History of Their Own: Women in Europe from Prehistory to the Present,* vol. 1 (New York: Harper & Row, 1989), 2:5.

9.   See, for example, John Pope, *A tour through the southern and western territories of the United States of North America: the Spanish dominions on the river Mississippi, and the Floridas; the countries of the Creek nations; and many uninhabited parts* (Richmond: J. Dixon for the author, 1792), 60; Bernard Romans, *A Concise Natural History of East and West Florida,* facsimile ed. (Gainesville: University Presses of Florida, 1962), 93; and "The Letters of US Indian Agent Benjamin Hawkins," *Georgia Historical Society Collections* 9 (1916), 83.

10. William Bartram, *Travels in Georgia and Florida, 1773–74: A Report to Dr. John Fothergill,* Transactions of the American Philosophical Society, new series, vol. 33, pt. 2 (Philadelphia: American Philosophical Society, 1943), 3:31–32. For examples of the formality of relations in public, see Caleb Swan, "Position and State of Manners and Arts in the Creek, or Muskogee Nation in 1791," in Henry R. Schoolcraft, *Historical and Statistical Information Respecting the History, Condition, and Prospects of the Indian Tribes of the United States,* vol. 5 (Philadelphia: Lippincott, 1855), 272.

11. Vernon James Knight, Jr., "The Institutional Organization of Mississippian Religion," *American Antiquity* 51:4 (1986), 679.

12. Stanley J. Folmsbee and Madeline Kneberg Lewis, eds., "Journals of the Juan Pardo Expeditions, 1566–1567," *East Tennessee Historical Society's Publications* 37 (1965), 114 (fol. 469) and 119 (fol. 483).

13. "The Account by a Gentleman from Elvas," James Alexander Robertson, trans., in Lawrence A. Clayton, Vernon James Knight, Jr., and Edward C. Moore, eds., *The De Soto Chronicles: The Expedition of Hernando de Soto to North America in 1539–1543,* 2 vols. (Tuscaloosa: University of Alabama Press, 1993), 1:85–86.

14. Ibid., 1:86.

15. Garcilaso de la Vega, "La Florida del Ynca," in Clayton, Knight, and Moore, *De Soto Chronicles,* 2:102–8.

16. Richard Hakluyt, *The Principal Navigations, Voyages, Traffiques and Discoveries of the English Nation* (Glasgow: The Hakluyt Society, 1904), 9:51–52.

17. Jerald T. Milanich and Charles Hudson, *Hernando de Soto and the Indians of Florida* (Gainesville: University Presses of Florida, 1995), 119.

18. Karen M. Booker, Charles M. Hudson, and Robert L. Rankin, "Place Name Identification and Multilingualism in the Sixteenth-Century Southeast," *Ethnohistory* 39:4 (Fall 1992), 419.

19. Anthony Pagden, *The Fall of Natural Man: The American Indian and the Origins of Comparative Ethnology,* 1982 (Cambridge: Cambridge University Press, 1989), 105.

20. Anderson and Zinsser, *A History of Their Own,* 8.

21. Morton H. Fried, *The Evolution of Political Society: An Essay on Political Anthropology* (New York: Random House, 1967); Elman Service, *Primitive So-*

cial Organization: An Evolutionary Perspective (New York: Random House, 1962); Henry T. Wright, "Prestate Political Formation," in T. K. Earle, ed., *On the Evolution of Complex Societies: Essays in Honor of Harry Hoijer, 1982* (Malibu, California: Undena Publications, 1984), cited in Mark Williams and Gary Shapiro, eds., *Lamar Archaeology: Mississippian Chiefdoms in the Deep South* (Tuscaloosa: University of Alabama Press, 1990), 177; John F. Scarry, "The Rise, Transformation, and Fall of Apalachee: A Case Study of Political Change in a Chiefly Society," in Williams and Shapiro, *Lamar Archaeology,* 175–86.

22.   Scarry, "Rise, Transformation, and Fall of Apalachee," 175–76.

23.   Ibid., 77.

24.   David G. Anderson, *The Savannah River Chiefdoms: Political Change in the Late Prehistoric Southeast* (Tuscaloosa: University of Alabama Press, 1994), 120.

25.   Fray Juan Rogel, SJ, to Fray Jéronimo Ruiz del Portillo, April 25, 1568, Codex Peru 19, fols. 7–20, translated in John H. Hann, ed. and trans., *Missions to the Calusa* (Gainesville: University Press of Florida, 1991), 245.

26.   Jacques le Moyne de Morgues, *Brevis narratio eorum quae in Florida, Americae provincia, Gallis acciderunt, secunda in illa navegationae, duce renato de Laudonnière, closses praefecto, anno 1564 quae est secunda pars Americae. . . .* (Frankfort: Typis J. Wecheli, 1591), pl. 29.

27.   Clayton, Knight, and Moore, *De Soto Chronicles;* and Antonio de Arguelles, "Record of the visitation of the Province of Guale and Mocama," Archivo General de Indias Escribanía de Camera, leg. 156B, Stetson Collection, fols. 527v–528, translated in John H. Hann, "Twilight of the Mocamo and Guale Aborigines as Portrayed in the 1695 Spanish Visitation," *Florida Historical Quarterly* 66:1 (1987), 12.

28.   M. Le Page du Pratz, *The History of Louisiana or of the Western Parts of Virginia and Carolina: Containing A Description of the Countries that lye on both Sides of the River Missisipi: with An Account of the Settlements, Inhabitants, Soil, Climate, and Products. Translated from the French, (lately published,) by M. Le Page Du Pratz With Some Notes and Observations relating to our Colonies,* 2 vols. (London: T. Becket and P. A. De Hondt, 1763), 212.

29.   Jerald T. Milanich, ed., *Francisco Pareja's Confessionario: A Documentary Source for Timucuan Ethnography* (Tallahassee: Division of Archives, History, and Records Management, Florida Department of State, 1972), fols. 128, 129.

30.   Scarry, "Rise, Transformation, and Fall of Apalachee," 175–86.

31.   Chester B. DePratter, "Late Prehistoric and Early Historic Chiefdoms in the Southeastern United States" (Ph.D. diss., University of Georgia, 1983); Booker, Hudson, and Rankin, "Place Name Identification," 401.

32.   Swanton, *Forty-Second Annual Report,* 406.

33. Booker, Hudson, and Rankin, "Place Name Identification," 419.

34. Swanton, *Forty-Second Annual Report,* 405.

35. Robert K. Merton, *Social Theory and Social Structure,* 1949 (New York: The Free Press, 1968), 178.

36. Read, for example, the comments of an English volunteer in the United States Army, John Bemrose, during the Second Seminole War (1835–1842), who noted how Osceola, the Tallassee warrior, watched the United States troops drill and realized how much he was learning from his enemies' tactics. See John K. Mahon, ed., *Reminiscences of the Second Seminole War* (Gainesville: University Presses of Florida, 1966).

37. James Adair, *History of the American Indians* (London: n.p., 1775), 159–64.

38. Louis Capron, *The Medicine Bundles of the Florida Seminoles and the Green Corn Dance,* Bureau of American Ethnology Bulletin 51 (Washington, D.C.: Smithsonian Institution, 1953), 155–210; William C. Sturtevant, "The Medicine Bundles and Busks of the Florida Seminoles," *Florida Anthropologist* 7 (May 1954), 31–70; John R. Swanton, "Social Organization and Social Usages of the Indians of the Creek Confederacy," in *Forty-Second Annual Report.* Joe Billie, Jr., Dan Bowers, Henry John Billie, Wild Bill Osceola, James E. Billie, Samuel Tommie, Sonny Billie, and numerous others, interviews with the author.

39. James W. Covington, *Pirates, Indians and Spaniards: Father Escobedo's "La Florida,"* A. F. Falcones, trans. (St. Petersburg: Great Outdoors Publishing, 1963), 151–52.

40. Clayton, Knight, and Moore, *De Soto Chronicles,* 1:101.

41. Charles Hudson, Marvin Smith, David Hally, Richard Polhemus, and Chester DePratter, "Coosa: A Chiefdom in the Sixteenth-Century Southeastern United States," *American Antiquity* 50:4 (1985), 729.

42. Ibid.

43. Adair, *History of the American Indians,* 388–91; Romans, *A Concise Natural History,* 9.

44. Le Page du Pratz, *History of Louisiana,* 252.

45. Le Moyne de Morgues, *Brevis narratio,* 63, pl. 14.

6. The Entrada Model in the Southeast

1. From Gonzalo Fernández de Oviedo y Valdés, *Historia general y natural de las Indias* (Madrid: Imprenta de la Real Academia de la Historia, 1851), in Lawrence A. Clayton, Vernon James Knight, Jr., and Edward C. Moore, eds., *The De Soto Chronicles: The Expedition of Hernando de Soto to North America in 1539–1543,* 2 vols. (Tuscaloosa: University of Alabama Press, 1993), 1:273.

2. William C. Sturtevant, "Spanish-Indian Relations in Southeastern North America," *Ethnohistory* 9 (Winter 1962), 42.

3. *La Florida* first appears on the Cantino Map, 1502. See Carl Ortwin Sauer, *Sixteenth Century North America: The Land and the People as Seen by the Europeans* (Berkeley: University of California Press, 1971), 25; and Archivo General de Indias Justicia 3, no. 3, fols. 40–41. For a short discussion of the primary sources supporting 1510 as the date of first Spanish discovery, see Buckingham Smith's "Notes by the Translator," in Hernando de Escalante Fontaneda, *Letter of Hernando de Soto and Memoir of Hernando de Escalante Fontaneda,* ca. 1575 (Washington, D.C.: privately printed for G. W. Riggs, 1854), note NN.

4. The *Patronato Real* was actually a series of concessions made to the Spanish Crown by the papacy between 1486 and 1523. By papal bulls, the Roman Catholic Church conceded to the Spanish monarchs the rights of patronage and presentation to major ecclesiastical benefices in Granada, in Castilla, and, finally, in all of Spain and in all of the newly claimed territories of the Indies. For a concise discussion of the values of these concessions to Spanish royal power, see J. H. Elliott, *Imperial Spain 1469–1716,* 1963 (London: Penguin Books, 1990), 99–110.

5. James Billie, Juanita Billie, Joe Frank, Henry John Billie, Mable Haught, Sadie Billie, Wild Bill Osceola, and others, interviews with the author.

6. Anthony Pagden, *The Fall of Natural Man: The American Indian and the Origins of Comparative Ethnology,* 1982 (Cambridge: Cambridge University Press, 1989), 105.

7. Helen Nader, *Liberty in Absolutist Spain: The Habsburg Sale of Towns, 1521–1700* (Baltimore: Johns Hopkins University Press, 1990), 45. On the same topic, see also Richard L. Kagan, *Lawsuits and Litigants in Castile, 1500–1700* (Chapel Hill: University of North Carolina Press, 1981).

8. Reverend La A. Vigneras, *The Journal of Christopher Columbus,* Cecil Jane, trans. (London: The Hakluyt Society, 1960), 194–200.

9. Carl Ortwin Sauer, *The Early Spanish Main* (Berkeley: University of California Press, 1966), 291.

10. Ibid., 148–49.

11. John E. Kicza, "Patterns in Early Spanish Overseas Expansion," *William and Mary Quarterly* 49:2 (April 1992), 239.

12. Bartolomé de las Casas, *The Devastation of the Indies: A Brief Account,* 1552, Herma Briffault, trans. (Baltimore: Johns Hopkins Press, 1974), 41.

13. Sauer, *Early Spanish Main,* 149.

14. Pietro Martire d'Anghiera [Peter Martyr], *Decadas del Nuevo Mundo,* 2 vols., edited by Edmundo O'Gorman (Mexico City: n.p., 1964–1965), 2:595.

15. Paul Hoffman, *A New Andalucia and a Way to the Orient: The American*

Southeast during the Sixteenth Century (Baton Rouge: Louisiana University Press, 1990), xi, 125, 210–11, 219, 308.

16.   Ibid., 7–13.

17.   Archivo General de Indias Justicia 3, no. 3, fols. 8, 35, 49–51, 62v–63, 66, 69; Anghiera, *Decadas* 2:595, cited in Hoffman, *A New Andalucia,* 16–17.

18.   Archivo General de Indias Justicia 3, no. 3, fols. 21v–23, cited in Hoffman, *A New Andalucia,* 53.

19.   Fernández de Oviedo y Valdés, *Historia general,* 3:626.

20.   John H. Hann, *Apalachee: The Land between the Rivers* (Gainesville: University Press of Florida, 1987), 9.

21.   Hoffman, *A New Andalucia,* 87.

22.   Rolena Adorno, "The Discursive Encounter of Spain and America: The Authority of Eyewitness Testimony in the Writing of History," *William and Mary Quarterly* 49:2 (April 1992), 220.

23.   Paul E. Hoffman, "Introduction: The De Soto Expedition, a Cultural Crossroads," in Clayton, Knight, and Moore, *De Soto Chronicles,* 1:7.

24.   John R. Swanton, *The Indians of the Southeastern United States,* Bureau of American Ethnology Bulletin 137 (Washington, D.C.: Government Printing Office, 1946), 150–51.

25.   "Relación de la Florida para el Ilamo. Señor Visorrei de la Nueva Españala qual trajo Fr. Gregorio Beteta," in Buckingham Smith, ed. and trans., *Colección de varios Documentos para la historia de la Florida y tierras adycentes* (London: Trubner and Company, 1857); and Victor Francis O'Daniel, OP, *Dominicans in Early Florida* (New York: The United States Catholic Historical Society, 1930), cited in Michael V. Gannon, *The Cross in the Sand* (Gainesville: University of Florida Press, 1965), 10–14.

26.   Hoffman, *A New Andalucia,* 144.

27.   Clayton, Knight, and Moore, *De Soto Chronicles,* 2:321.

28.   Ibid., 1:239.

29.   Alvar Núñez Cabeça de Vaca, *Relation of Alvar Núñez Cabeça de Vaca,* 1542, Buckingham Smith, trans., 1871 (New York: Readex Microprint, 1966), 69.

30.   See, for example, ibid., 53, 70, 90, 130.

31.   Ibid., 136.

32.   Clayton, Knight, and Moore, *De Soto Chronicles,* 1:154.

33.   Stefan Lorant, ed., *The New World: The First Pictures of America* (New York: Duell, Sloan & Pearce, 1946), 61.

34.   Cabeça de Vaca, *Relation,* 59.

35.   Clayton, Knight, and Moore, *De Soto Chronicles,* 1:278.

36.   Ibid., 1:288.

37. See, for example, ibid., 1:145–47 and 213 n. 267; and Cabeça de Vaca, *Relation*, 41.

38. See, for example, Cabeça de Vaca, *Relation*, 38–39, 40, 53–54; and Clayton, Knight, and Moore, *De Soto Chronicles*, 1:145–46.

39. Cabeça de Vaca, *Relation*, 135.

40. Ibid., 39; and Clayton, Knight, and Moore, *De Soto Chronicles*, 1:234.

41. In Clayton, Knight, and Moore, *De Soto Chronicles*, 1:234, the authors express specifically the kind of Conquest rhetoric that has long disempowered the Maskókî peoples. They explain: "Fighting under soldiers equipped in this manner [i.e., with European arms and armor] was demoralizing for native peoples who, *however*, showed great courage and ingenuity when facing them" [emphasis added]. This demeaning characterization of the people as having diminished capacities and prerogatives is belied by the statements of the Spaniards themselves.

42. Cabeça de Vaca, *Relation*, 136. See also David J. Weber, *The Spanish Frontier in North America* (New Haven and London: Yale University Press, 1992), 27 and the quotation from one of Coronado's soldiers cited in chapter 1, note 49: "The most essential thing in this new land is horses. They instill the greatest fear in the enemy and make the Indians respect the leaders of the army."

43. See, for example, Cabeça de Vaca, *Relation*, 81, 116, 117, 120, 151.

44. Clayton, Knight, and Moore, *De Soto Chronicles*, 1:120.

45. Jacques le Moyne de Morgues, *Brevis narratio eorum quae in Florida, Americae provincia, Gallis acciderunt, secunda in illa navegatione, duce renato de Laudonnière, classes praefecto, anno 1564 quae est secunda pars Americae. . . .* (Frankfort: Typis J. Wecheli, 1591), 55 pl. 10.

46. Cabeça de Vaca, *Relation*, 80.

47. See, for example, Clifford M. Lewis, "The Calusa," in Jerald T. Milanich and Samuel Proctor, eds., *Tacachale* (Gainesville: University Presses of Florida, 1978), 19–49.

48. A classic statement of this Conquest viewpoint is made in Rochelle A. Marrinan, John F. Scarry, and Rhonda L. Majors, "Prelude to de Soto: The Expedition of Pánfilo de Narváez," in David Hurst Thomas, ed., *Columbian Consequences*, vol. 2, *Archaeological and Historical Perspectives on the Spanish Borderlands East* (Washington, D.C.: Smithsonian Institution Press, 1990), 78.

49. For a short but important discussion of the interrelationships of epidemics, demographic decline, and culture change, see Paul E. Hoffman, "Introduction: The De Soto Expedition, a Cultural Crossroads," in Clayton, Knight, and Moore, *De Soto Chronicles*, 1:12–13. Profound culture loss is still assumed but the author is, at least, open to the reality that a single-factor cause is no longer acceptable. See also the conclusions of John E. Worth, *The*

Struggle for the Georgia Coast: An Eighteenth-Century Retrospective on Guale and Mocama, American Museum of Natural History Anthropological Papers No. 75 (New York: American Museum of Natural History, 1995).

7. El Sombrero de Tres Picos

1. Eugene Lyon, *The Enterprise of Florida: Pedro Menéndez de Avilés and the Spanish Conquest of 1565–1568* (Gainesville: University Presses of Florida, 1976), 49.

2. Jean Ribault, *The Whole & True Discouerye of Terra Florida,* 1563, facsimile ed. (Gainesville: University of Florida Press, 1964), 66–67.

3. Paul Hoffman, *A New Andalucia and a Way to the Orient: The American Southeast during the Sixteenth Century* (Baton Rouge: Louisiana University Press, 1990), 165.

4. Ibid., 167.

5. Ibid., 129; Paul E. Hoffman, *The Spanish Crown and the Defense of the Caribbean, 1535–1585: Precedent, Patrimonialism, and Royal Parsimony* (Baton Rouge: Louisiana State University Press, 1980), 79–88.

6. Dr. Pedro de Santander to King Felipe II, Sevilla, July 15, 1557, in Fernández de Navarrete, *Colección de documentos inéditos relativos al descubrimiento* (Madrid: Sucesores de Rivadeneyra, 1885–1932), 26:353–65.

7. Cited in Hoffman, *A New Andalucia,* 149–50.

8. "Auto of the adelantado, Pedro Menéndez de Avilés, reporting on the damages and murders caused by the coast Indians of La Florida," January 15, 1573–July 28, 1574, Archivo General de Indias [hereinafter AGI] Patronato 2-5-4/12 (Patronato 257), in Jeannette Thurber Connor, *Colonial Records of Spanish Florida* (Deland: Florida Historical Society, 1925), 30–81. Also see Amy Turner Bushnell, *Situado and Sabana: Spain's Support System for the Presidio and Mission Provinces of Florida,* American Museum of Natural History Anthropological Paper No. 74 (New York: American Museum of Natural History, 1994), 42; and Lyon, "The Enterprise of Florida," in David Hurst Thomas, ed., *Columbian Consequences,* vol. 2, *Archaeological and Historical Perspectives on the Spanish Borderlands East* (Washington, D.C.: Smithsonian Institution Press, 1990), 2:291.

9. Ribault, *Whole & True Discouerye of Terra Florida,* xx; and René de Laudonnière, *Three Voyages,* 1586, Charles E. Bennett, trans. and ed. (Gainesville: University Presses of Florida, 1975), xx.

10. Laudonnière, *Three Voyages,* 4–5.

11. Ibid., 5.

12. Amy Turner Bushnell, "Research Design: The Menéndez Family of Spanish Florida, 1565–1743: Nepotists and Entrepreneurs in a Border Province,"

typescript, November 18, 1975, p. 6, in the collections of the St. Augustine Foundation, St. Augustine, Florida.

13. The primary contemporary account is that of Gonzalo Solís de Merás, *Pedro Menéndez Avilés,* Jeannette Thurber Connor, trans. (Deland: Florida State Historical Society, 1923). See also Lyon, *Enterprise of Florida;* Verne E. Chatelain, *The Early Defenses of Spanish Florida, 1565–1763* (Washington, D.C.: Carnegie Institution, 1941); and Connor, *Colonial Records of Spanish Florida.*

14. Bushnell, *Situado and Sabana,* 18; William C. Sturtevant, "Spanish-Indian Relations in Southeastern North America," *Ethnohistory* 9 (Winter 1962), 42–94.

15. Bushnell, *Situado and Sabana,* 207.

16. Ibid., 18.

17. Ibid., 36; and Max L. Moorehead, *The Presidio: Bastion of the Spanish Borderlands* (Norman: University of Oklahoma Press, 1975), cited in ibid.

18. Eugene Lyon, "Richer Than We Thought: The Material Culture of Sixteenth-Century St. Augustine," *El Escribano: The St. Augustine Journal of History* (1992), 16.

19. Ibid.; and James Cusick, "Across the Border: Commodity Flow and Merchants in Spanish St. Augustine," cited in Lyon, 111 n. 49.

20. Bushnell, *Situado and Sabana,* 64.

21. For a clear understanding of the seeming ironies in the Spanish Crown's positions on centralization and decentralization, see Helen Nader, *Liberty in Absolutist Spain: The Habsburg Sale of Towns, 1521–1700* (Baltimore: Johns Hopkins University Press, 1990), especially 41–45.

22. See Lyon, *Enterprise of Florida,* appendix 2, 220–23, for the salient characteristics of Pedro Menéndez's *asiento* and a comparison of these with the characteristics of other, contemporary, *asiento* grantees.

23. Bushnell, *Situado and Sabana,* 41; and Engle Sluiter, *The Florida Situado: Quantifying the First Eighty Years, 1571–1651,* Research Publications of the P. K. Yonge Library of Florida History, University of Florida No. 1 (Gainesville: University of Florida Libraries, 1985).

24. See Hoffman, *The Spanish Crown and the Defense of the Caribbean;* Bushnell, *Situado and Sabana;* and Sluiter, *Florida Situado,* 3–9, concerning the early expenditures of the Crown on defense in *La Florida* and how they constituted a major portion of Spain's Caribbean defense budget.

25. Charles W. Arnade, *Florida on Trial, 1593–1602* (Coral Gables: University of Miami Press, 1959), 89.

26. Lyon, "Richer Than We Thought," 17; see also the reinterpretations of Hoffman, *A New Andalucia;* Sluiter, *Florida Situado;* and John H. Hann, *Apalachee: The Land between the Rivers* (Gainesville: University Press of Florida, 1987).

27. Bushnell, "Menéndez Family of Spanish Florida." See also Helen Hornbeck Tanner, *Zéspedes in East Florida 1784–1790* (Coral Gables: University of Miami Press, 1963), 115, concerning British and French garrisons of the same period.

28. Amy Bushnell, *The King's Coffers: Proprietors of the Spanish Florida Treasury, 1565–1702* (Gainesville: University Presses of Florida, 1981); Bushnell, *Situado and Sabana;* and Sluiter, *Florida Situado.*

29. Juan Fernández de Olivera to the Crown, December 15, 1611, in AGI Santo Domingo [hereinafter SD] 229/67; Juan Treviño Guillamas to the Crown, 1615?, summary in AGI SD 225; and Maynard Geiger, *The Franciscan Conquest of Florida* (Washington, D.C.: The Catholic University of America, 1937), 52, cited in Bushnell, *Situado and Sabana,* 55.

30. Bushnell, *Situado and Sabana,* 53.

31. Sluiter, *Florida Situado,* 6; Spanish Crown, Cedula to the Royal Officials of Florida with a copy to the Royal Officials of Mexico City, August 21, 1646; and Spanish Crown, Cedula to the Governor and Royal Officials of Florida, July 26, 1658, in Bushnell, *Situado and Sabana,* 54.

32. John H. Hann, "Summary Guide to Spanish Florida Missions and Visitas with Churches in the Sixteenth and Seventeenth Centuries," *The Americas* 46:4 (April 1990), 417–514.

33. Troy Floyd, *The Columbus Dynasty in the Caribbean, 1492–1526* (Albuquerque: University of New Mexico Press, 1973), 183, cited in Hoffman, *A New Andalucia,* 37.

34. Joaquin F. Pacheco, Francisco de Cardenas, and Luís Torres de Mendoza, eds., *Colección de documentos inéditos relativos al descubrimiento, conquista y organización de las antiguas posesiones españoles de América y Oceania, sacados de los archivos del reino, y muy especialmente del de Indias,* 42 vols. (Madrid: Real Academia de la Historia, 1864–1884), vol. 8, no. 58, p. 505. Cited in Lyon, *The Enterprise of Florida,* 25 n. 14.

35. Lyon, *The Enterprise of Florida,* appendix; and Hoffman, *A New Andalucia,* 227, 228.

36. Bushnell, *Situado and Sabana,* 208.

37. Testimony of Agustín and Juan, Natives from San Juan del Puerto, in Havana, Cuba, July 2, 1636, AGI SD 27/28, in Connor, *Colonial Records of Spanish Florida,* 2; Francisco Menéndez Márquez and Pedro Benedit Horruytiner, July 27, 1647, AGI SD 235, in Connor, *Colonial Records of Spanish Florida,* 4, cited in Bushnell, *King's Coffers,* 13.

38. Joseph de Prado, Treasurer, report with comments appended by the fiscal of the San Agustín council, December 30, 1654, AGI SD 229/115, in Connor, *Colonial Records of Spanish Florida,* 3, cited in Bushnell, *King's Coffers,* 28.

39. Eugene Lyon, "Settlement and Survival," in Michael V. Gannon, ed., *The New History of Florida* (Gainesville: University Press of Florida, 1996), 48.

40. Laureano de Torres y Ayala and Tomás Menéndez Márquez to the Crown, April 20, 1697, cited in Bushnell, *Situado and Sabana,* 55.

41. Bushnell, *King's Coffers,* 13.

42. Bushnell, "Republic of Spaniards, Republic of Indians," in Michael V. Gannon, ed., *New History of Florida,* 63.

43. Bushnell, "Republic of Spaniards," 63.

8. Fear as the Forerunner of Faith

1. Andrés González de Barciá Carballido y Zúñiga, *Ensayo cronológico para la historia general de la Florida, 1512–1722,* 1723, Anthony Kerrigan, trans. (Gainesville: University Presses of Florida, 1951), 170–71, cited in Maynard Geiger, *The Franciscan Conquest of Florida* (Washington, D.C.: The Catholic University of America, 1937), 90; John Tate Lanning, *The Spanish Missions of Georgia* (Chapel Hill: University of North Carolina Press, 1935), 82–85.

2. Eugene Lyon, *The Enterprise of Florida: Pedro Menéndez de Avilés and the Spanish Conquest of 1565–1568* (Gainesville: University Presses of Florida, 1976), 137.

3. Gary B. Nash, "Notes on the History of Seventeenth-Century Missionization in Colonial America," *American Indian Culture and Research Journal* 2:2 (1978), 7; see also Marshall W. Murphee, *Christianity and the Shona* (London, 1969), 2, cited in Nash, 8 n. 30.

4. Henry F. Dobyns, *Their Number Become Thinned: Native American Population Dynamics in Eastern North America* (Knoxville: University of Tennessee Press, 1983), 8–26.

5. Ibid.

6. Marvin T. Smith, *Archaeology of Aboriginal Culture Change in the Interior Southeast: Depopulation during the Early Historic Period* (Gainesville: University Press of Florida, 1987), 6–7.

7. Dobyns, *Their Number Become Thinned,* 25.

8. Ibid.

9. Ibid., 26.

10. Smith, *Archaeology of Aboriginal Culture Change,* 89–103.

11. Dobyns, *Their Number Become Thinned,* 51, 291–95.

12. This practice has been substantiated by many of the Seminole sources.

13. There is no consensus among Mikísuukî or Maskókî speakers about the translation of *tahkóshat.* All agree that it is a very old word and that it is either an ant or a mole, depending upon whether it came originally from the core Maskókî or from Hitchiti.

14. Jacques le Moyne de Morgues, *Brevis narratio eorum quae in Florida, Ameri-*

cae provincia, Gallis acciderunt, secunda in illa navegationae, duce renato de Laudonnière, closses praefecto, anno 1564 quae est secunda pars Americae. . . . (Frankfort: Typis J. Wecheli, 1591), 115, pl. 40.

15. Smith, *Archaeology of Aboriginal Culture Change,* 75–85.

16. Dobyns, *Their Number Become Thinned,* 311.

17. Ibid., 181.

18. John E. Worth, *The Struggle for the Georgia Coast: An Eighteenth-Century Retrospective on Guale and Mocama,* American Museum of Natural History Anthropological Papers No. 75 (New York: American Museum of Natural History, 1995), 13.

19. Nash, "Notes on the History of Seventeenth-Century Missionization," 7; and J. Frederick Fausz, "The Powhatan Uprising of 1622: A Historical Study of Ethnocentrism and Cultural Conflict" (Ph.D. dissertation, College of William and Mary, 1977), 339, cited in Nash, 8 n. 12 and n. 24.

20. John H. Hann, "Summary Guide to Spanish Florida Missions and Visitas with Churches in the Sixteenth and Seventeenth Centuries," *The Americas* 46:4 (April 1990), 424.

21. Amy Turner Bushnell, *Situado and Sabana: Spain's Support System for the Presidio and Mission Provinces of Florida,* American Museum of Natural History Anthropological Paper No. 74 (New York: American Museum of Natural History, 1994).

22. Paul Hoffman, *A New Andalucia and a Way to the Orient: The American Southeast during the Sixteenth Century* (Baton Rouge: Louisiana University Press, 1990), 61, 77, 79, 81, 90; Michael V. Gannon, *The Cross in the Sand* (Gainesville: University of Florida Press, 1965), 9.

23. See Luís Gerónimo de Oré, OFM, *The Martyrs of Florida (1513–1616),* Maynard Geiger, OFM, trans. Franciscan Studies No. 18 (July 1936) (New York: Joseph F. Wagner, 1936), 101–2; Zubillaga, *La Florida: La Misión Jesuitica (1566–1572) y la colonización española* (Rome: Instituto Historicum S. I., 1941), passim; and Gannon, *Cross in the Sand,* 9.

24. David Hurst Thomas, "The Spanish Missions of La Florida: An Overview," in Thomas, ed., *Columbian Consequences,* vol. 2, *Archaeological and Historical Perspectives on the Spanish Borderlands East* (Washington, D.C.: Smithsonian Institution Press, 1990), 2:388–89.

25. David J. Weber, "Blood of Martyrs, Blood of Indians: Toward a More Balanced View of Spanish Missions in Seventeenth-Century North America," in Thomas, *Columbian Consequences,* 2:439.

26. Fray Juan Rojel to Fray Jerónimo Ruiz del Portillo, April 25, 1568, in Felix Zubillaga, ed., *Monumenta Antiquae Floridae* (Rome: Monumenta Missionum Societatis Iesu, 1946), 272–311, translated in John H. Hann, ed. and trans., *Missions to the Calusa* (Gainesville: University Press of Florida, 1991), 239.

27.   Lyon, *Enterprise of Florida*, 202.

28.   Archivo General de Indias [hereinafter AGI] Patronato 19, fol. 477.

29.   AGI Santo Domingo [hereinafter SD] 125, 150-D.

30.   James W. Covington, *Pirates, Indians and Spaniards: Father Escobedo's "La Florida,"* A. F. Falcones, trans. (St. Petersburg: Great Outdoors Publishing, 1963), 22.

31.   Fray Juan Rojel to Fray Jerónimo Ruiz del Portillo, April 25, 1568, in Zubillaga, *Monumenta Antiquae Floridae*, 272–311, translated in Hann, *Missions to the Calusa*, 239.

32.   Fray Francisco Pareja to the Crown, San Juan del Puerto mission, September 14, 1602, AGI 54-5-20, Stetson Collection [hereinafter SC] [SD 235].

33.   Covington, *Father Escobedo's "La Florida,"* 11.

34.   Governor Méndez de Canzo to the Crown, April 24, 1601, AGI 54-5-9, SC [AGI SD 224].

35.   Fray Francisco Pareja to the Crown, San Juan del Puerto mission, September 14, 1602, AGI 54-5-20, SC [SD 235].

36.   Fray Baltasar López to the Crown, San Pedro mission, September 16, 1602, AGI 54-5-20, SC micro. 62-A, Woodbury Lowrey Collection, 4.

37.   "Auto para hacer Vicita General en la provincia de Apalache," January 17–February 13, 1657, AGI Escribanía de Camera, leg. 155, pp. 1, 7–10, SC.

38.   "Auto para hacer Vicita General en la provincia de Apalache," January 17–February 13, 1657, AGI Escribanía de Camera, leg. 155, p. 1, SC.

39.   "Auto para hacer Vicita General en la provincia de Apalache," January 17–February 13, 1657, AGI Escribanía de Camera, leg. 155, p. 17, SC.

40.   Amy Bushnell, "'That Demonic Game': The Campaign to Stop Indian Pelota Playing in Spanish Florida, 1675–1684," *The Americas* 35:1 (July 1978), 2, 2 n. 5. See also Robert Allen Matter, "The Spanish Missions of Florida: The Friars Versus the Governors in the 'Golden Age,' 1606–1690" (Ph.D. diss., University of Washington, 1972).

41.   Smith, *Archaeology of Aboriginal Culture Change*, 1.

42.   Hann, *Missions to the Calusa*, 4.

43.   Bushnell, *Situado and Sabana*, 96.

44.   Nash, "Notes on the History of Seventeenth-Century Missionization," 4.

45.   Ibid.

46.   John Smith, *The Generall Historie of Virginia, New England, and the Summer Isles* (London, 1624), cited in Nash, "Notes on the History of Seventeenth-Century Missionization," 7 n. 7.

47.   Nash, "Notes on the History of Seventeenth-Century Missionization," 4; and Patrick Copland, *A Sermon of Thanksgiving for the Happie successe of the Affayres in Virginia* (London, 1622), cited in Nash, 8 n. 11.

48. Neal E. Salisbury, "Red Puritans: The 'Praying Indians' of Massachusetts Bay and John Eliot," *William and Mary Quarterly,* 3d. ser., 31 (1974), 50, cited in Nash, "Notes on the History of Seventeenth-Century Missionization," 6, 8 n. 24.

49. Ibid., 51, cited in Nash, 6–7, 8 n. 25.

50. Bushnell, "'That Demonic Game,'" 2, 2 n. 3.

51. Amy Bushnell, "Republic of Spaniards, Republic of Indians," in Michael V. Gannon, ed., *New History of Florida* (Gainesville: University Press of Florida, 1995), 63.

52. Bushnell, "'That Demonic Game,'" 3.

53. Bushnell, *Situado and Sabana,* 104–8.

54. Francisco Menéndez Márquez I, Juan de Cueva, and Francisco Ramírez to the Crown, January 30, 1627, AGI SD 229, fol. 87, cited in Bushnell, *Situado and Sabana,* 108.

55. Bushnell, "'That Demonic Game,'" 2; Charles H. Fairbanks, "Ethnohistorical Report of the Florida Indians. Before the United States Indian Claims Commission, The Seminole Indians of the State of Florida vs. The United States of America," Dockets No. 73 and 151 (1957), 4; Mark F. Boyd, Hale G. Smith, and John W. Griffin, *Here They Once Stood: The Tragic End of the Apalachee Missions* (Gainesville: University of Florida Press, 1951), passim.; Dobyns, *Their Number Become Thinned;* Matter, "The Spanish Missions of Florida."

56. Bushnell, "'That Demonic Game,'" 2–3.

57. See the examples in ibid., 2, 2 n. 5; Bushnell, *Situado and Sabana;* and John H. Hann, *Apalachee: The Land between the Rivers* (Gainesville: University Press of Florida, 1987).

58. See "Ordenanzas," in Fernández de Navarrete, *Colección de documentos inéditos relativos al descubrimiento* (Madrid: Sucesores de Rivadeneyra, 1885–1932), 8:26, 353–65, encomienda, no. 58, 505; and repartimiento, no. 61, 506, and no. 145, 535; and tributo, no. 146, 535–36.

59. Amy Bushnell, "Patricio de Hinachuba: Defender of the Word of God, the Crown of the King, and the Little Children of Ivitachuco," *American Indian Culture and Research Journal* 3:3 (1979), 5.

60. "Consejo de las Indias to Fray Juan Luengo, comisario general de Indias de la orden de S. Francisco," November 5, 1976, AGI 58-1-2, fol. 166 [SD 834], North Carolina 4-33, SC micro., 62-A.

9. Children of Self-Interest

1. Mark F. Boyd, trans., "Documents Describing the Second and Third Expeditions of Lieutenant Diego Peña to Apalachee and Apalachicolo in 1717 and 1718," *Florida Historical Quarterly* 31:2 (1952), 128.

2.   Archivo General de Indias [hereinafter AGI] 58-1-20 [Santo Domingo (SD) 833], leg. 82. Quoted in Boyd, "Documents Describing the Second and Third Expeditions," 109–39.

3.   Wilbur R. Jacobs, ed., *Indians of the Southern Colonial Frontier: The Edmond Atkin Report and Plan of 1755* (Columbia: University of South Carolina Press, 1954), 39.

4.   Patent of Sir Robert Heath, 5 Charles I, October 30, 1629, in *Collections of the South Carolina Historical Society,* vol. 5 (Richmond: Wm. Jones, 1897), 3.

5.   Charles H. Fairbanks, "Ethnohistorical Report of the Florida Indians. Before the United States Indian Claims Commission, The Seminole Indians of the State of Florida vs. The United States of America," Dockets No. 73 and 151 (1957), 18.

6.   For an overview of sixteenth-century Spanish *asiento* stipulations, see Eugene Lyon, *The Enterprise of Florida: Pedro Menéndez de Avilés and the Spanish Conquest of 1565–1568* (Gainesville: University Presses of Florida, 1976), table 2, "A Comparison of Provisions of Various Sixteenth-Century Asientos," 220–23. The classic requirements were to conquer, pacify, populate, and Christianize.

7.   These are taken from the Virginia Charter of April 10, 1606, in Alexander Brown, *The Genesis of the United States,* 1890 (New York: 1964), 54; and from Samuel Lucal, *Charters of the Old English Colonies in America* (London, 1850), 32, 89, 48, 106, cited in Patricia Seed, "Taking Possession and Reading Texts: Establishing the Authority of Overseas Empires," *William and Mary Quarterly* 49:2 (April 1992), 186, 186 n. 10. Seed's article is comprehensive and an excellent short treatment of the divergent mindsets of the English, which had such profoundly negative impacts upon the lives of Native Americans.

8.   Mark F. Boyd, Hale G. Smith, and John W. Griffin, *Here They Once Stood: The Tragic End of the Apalachee Missions* (Gainesville: University of Florida Press, 1951), 19.

9.   W. L. McDowell, ed., *Journals of the Commissioners of Indian Trade, 1710–1718,* The Colonial Records of South Carolina, vol. 1 (1955), cited in Fairbanks, "Ethnohistorical Report," 19. See also Governor Zúñiga to the Crown, "Upon the raid into Santa Fé and the expedition upon which Captain Romo was sent," San Agustín, September 30, 1702, AGI 58-2-8 [SD 858], leg. B3, pp. 7–10, in Boyd, Smith, and Griffin, *Here They Once Stood,* 36–38.

10.   See, for example, Don Laureano e Torres y Ayala to the Crown, San Agustín, April 15, 1696, AGI 54-5-13 [SD 228], leg. 72.

11.   Gerda Lerner, *The Creation of Patriarchy* (New York: Oxford University Press, 1986), 181.

12.   Alexander McGillivray, "Sketch of the Creek Indians," written for General

Henry Knox, 1790. Manuscript in the Collections of the Massachusetts Historical Society, Boston.

13. John R. Swanton, *The Indians of the Southeastern United States,* Bureau of American Ethnology Bulletin 137 (Washington, D.C.: Government Printing Office, 1946), 127.

14. For locations of these towns as ascertained by archaeologists, see Marvin T. Smith, *Archaeology of Aboriginal Culture Change in the Interior Southeast: Depopulation during the Early Historic Period* (Gainesville: University Press of Florida, 1987), 16–18 and passim.

15. Swanton, *Indians of the Southeastern United States,* 127, 128, 153; see also discussions under the headings of various tribes.

16. George Stiggins, *Creek Indian History: A Historical Narrative of the Genealogy, Traditions and Downfall of the Ispocoga or Creek Indian Tribe of Indians by One of the Tribe* (Birmingham: Birmingham Public Library Press, 1989), 25.

17. John Walton Caughey, *McGillivray of the Creeks* (Norman: University of Oklahoma Press, 1938), passim.

18. Smith, *Archaeology of Aboriginal Culture Change,* 22; and Vernon J. Knight and Sheree Adams, "A Voyage to the Mobile and Tomen in 1700 with Notes on the Interior of Alabama," *Journal of Alabama Archaeology* 27 (1981), 48.

19. Fray Alonso de Moral to the Crown, November 5, 1676, AGI 54-5-20 [SD 235], fol. 105, Stetson Collection [hereinafter SC].

20. Henry Woodward, "A faithfull relation of my westoe voiage," 1674, in Alexander S. Salley, Jr., ed., *Narratives of Early Carolina, 1650–1708* (New York: Charles Scribner's Sons, 1911), 130–34, cited in Fred Lamar Pearson, Jr., *Spanish-Indian Relations in Florida: A Study of Two Visitas, 1657–1678* (New York: Garland Publishing, 1990), 183–85.

21. John E. Worth, *The Struggle for the Georgia Coast: An Eighteenth-Century Retrospective on Guale and Mocama,* American Museum of Natural History Anthropological Papers No. 75 (New York: American Museum of Natural History, 1995), 26.

22. Ibid.

23. Amy Turner Bushnell, *Situado and Sabana: Spain's Support System for the Presidio and Mission Provinces of Florida,* American Museum of Natural History Anthropological Paper No. 74 (New York: American Museum of Natural History, 1994), 96.

24. Don Patricio, Cacique of Ivitachuco, and Don Andrés, Cacique of San Luis, to the King, February 12, 1699, AGI 54-5-19 [SD 234], leg. 439, translated in Boyd, Smith, and Griffin, *Here They Once Stood,* 24–26.

25. Sebastián de Covarrubias Horozco, compiler, *Tesoro de la Lengua Castellana o Española* (Madrid: Luís Sánchez, 1611); Gonzalo Fernández de Oviedo y Valdés, *Historia general y natural de las Indias,* 1535 (Madrid: Imprenta de la

Real Academia de la Historia, 1851), 1:256, cited in Joan Corominas, *Diccionario Crítico Etimológico Castellano e Hispánico,* vol. 2 (Madrid: Editorial Gredos, 1954), 76–77.

26.   Georg Friederici, *Hilfswörterbuch für den Amerikanisten: Lehnwörter aus Indianer-Sprachen und Erklärungen Altertümlicher Ausdrücke, Deutsch-Spanisch-Englisch* (Halle: Max Niemeyer, 1926), 30–31.

27.   Real Academia Española, *Diccionario de la Lengua Española* (Madrid: Real Academia, 1992).

28.   See the comments of Domingo Sarmiento quoted in Corominas, *Diccionario Crítico,* 2:76–77.

29.   Kathleen Deagan and Darcie MacMahon, *Fort Mose: Colonial America's Black Fortress of Freedom* (Gainesville: University Presses of Florida, 1995), 13; and Paul Hoffman, *A New Andalucia and a Way to the Orient: The American Southeast during the Sixteenth Century* (Baton Rouge: Louisiana University Press, 1990), 73–79.

30.   Pedro de San Martín, Petition, 1635, AGI SD 233. My sincere thanks to Dr. John H. Hann, historian, San Luís Archaeological and Historic Site, Division of Historical Resources, Florida Department of State, Tallahassee, for assisting me in locating these references.

31.   Diego de Rebolledo, Orden to Antonio de Arguelles, March 10, 1655, AGI SD 23.

32.   Amy Bushnell, "'That Demonic Game': The Campaign to Stop Indian Pelota Playing in Spanish Florida, 1675–1684," *The Americas* 35:1 (July 1978), 4.

33.   Pearson, *Spanish-Indian Relations in Florida,* 134–35.

34.   Auto of the Visita General of Capitán Antonio de Arguelles, January 5, 1678, AGI Escribanía de Camera, leg. 156, p. 529, SC, cited in Pearson, *Spanish-Indian Relations in Florida,* 210.

35.   Bushnell, *Situado and Sabana,* 15.

36.   John H. Hann, personal communication, December 4, 1995; and John H. Hann, ed. and trans., *Missions to the Calusa* (Gainesville: University Press of Florida, 1991), 45–46. Hann also outlines the events surrounding this expedition in "Twilight of the Mocamo and Guale Aborigines as Portrayed in the 1695 Spanish Visitation," *Florida Historical Quarterly* 66:1 (1987), 1–24.

37.   Hann, *Missions to the Calusa,* 45.

38.   Stuart to Gage, December 14, 1771, Thomas Gage Collection, Clements Library, University of Michigan, quoted in Fairbanks, "Ethnohistorical Report," 4.

39.   Geneva Shore from her mother, Lottie Bowers Shore, interview with the author. The now-deceased father and husband of these women, Frank Shore, was a powerful medicine man among the Maskókî and Mikísuukî

peoples of the Seminole Tribe and, consequently, a holder of esoteric information.

40. Albert Manucy, *The Houses of St. Augustine* (St. Augustine: St. Augustine Historical Society, 1978), 15.

41. Colonel James Moore to the Lords Proprietors, April 16, 1704, "Spanish Papers," MSS, Library of Congress, 6:888, cited in Boyd, Smith, and Griffin, *Here They Once Stood,* 92–93.

42. Bushnell, *Situado and Sabana,* 211.

43. See, for example, Governor Zúñiga to the Crown, San Agustín, March 30, 1704, AGI 58-1-20 [SD 833], leg. 92, in Boyd, Smith, and Griffin, *Here They Once Stood,* 48–50.

44. See Colonel James Moore to Sir Nathaniel Johnson, April 16(?), 1704, "Spanish Papers," MSS, Library of Congress, 6:892–96; and Colonel James Moore to the Lords Proprietors, April 1, 1704, "Spanish Papers," 6:888, reproduced in Boyd, Smith, and Griffin, *Here They Once Stood.*

45. AGI Papeles de Cuba, leg. 206, fols. 105–6. The descendants still reside in Rapide Parish and in Pineville, near Alexandria, Louisiana. Their current "chief" is Gilmer Bennett.

46. Commandant at Pensacola [Joseph de Guzmán] to Viceroy, Santa Maria de Galve, August 22, 1704, AGI 58-2-7 [SD 857], leg. 2, pp. 15–17; Governor Zúñiga to the Crown, San Agustín, September 3, 1704, AGI 58-2-2 [SD 852], leg. 83 1/2; Governor Zúñiga to the Crown, San Agustín, September 10, 1704, AGI 58-2-7 [SD 857], leg. 2, pp. 44–45; and "Summary of Martyrdoms Experienced in Florida by the Franciscans," Franciscans to the Crown, San Agustín, May 7, 1707, AGI 58-2-14 [SD 863], leg. 61, in Boyd, Smith, and Griffin, *Here They Once Stood,* 62–64, 65–68, 85–89, 102 n. 84.

47. John H. Hann, "St. Augustine's Fallout from the Yamasee War," *Florida Historical Quarterly* 48:2 (October 1989), 193–94.

48. Bushnell, *Situado and Sabana,* 202–4; see also Boyd, Smith, and Griffin, *Here They Once Stood;* and Verne E. Chatelain, *The Early Defenses of Spanish Florida, 1565–1763* (Washington, D.C.: Carnegie Institution, 1941); Landers and MacMahon, *Fort Mose;* and James Moore, *The St. Augustine Expedition of 1740, A Report to the South Carolina General Assembly,* reprinted from the Colonial Records of South Carolina (Columbia: South Carolina Archives Department, 1954).

49. Hann, "St. Augustine's Fallout from the Yamasee War," 180.

50. Verner W. Crane, *The Southern Frontier, 1670–1732* (Durham: Duke University Press, 1928), 162.

51. Jacques le Moyne de Morgues, *Brevis narratio eorum quae in Florida, Americae provincia, Gallis acciderunt, secunda in illa navegationae, duce renato de Laudonnière, closses praefecto, anno 1564 quae est secunda pars Americae. . . .* (Frankfort: Typis J. Wecheli, 1591), 115, pl. 40; see also the "Journal of John

Lee Williams," *Florida Historical Quarterly* 1:1 (1908), 18–29 and 1:2 (1908), 37–44; and Captain Daniel E. Burch, *Pensacola Gazette,* October 9, 1824, quoted in Boyd, Smith, and Griffin, *Here They Once Stood,* 2–4.

52. Burch, *Pensacola Gazette,* quotes a "Creek" man who lived near Tallahassee and who said that he personally recalled the war that drove the Spaniards out of the missions. It seems unlikely that he could have witnessed Moore's raids personally, but one or both of his parents may have done so. Quoted in Boyd, Smith, and Griffin, *Here They Once Stood,* 2–4.

53. Hann, "St. Augustine's Fallout from the Yamasee War," 193–94.

54. Spanish governor of Pensacola to the Spanish governor of Florida, at San Agustín, on July 24, 1717, in Mark F. Boyd, "Documents Describing the Second and Third Expeditions," 128.

55. See, for example, Bushnell's discussion of the 1702 killing of three Abalachi traders who failed to provide horses in exchange for muskets, in Amy Bushnell, "Patricio de Hinachuba: Defender of the Word of God, the Crown of the King, and the Little Children of Ivitachuco," *American Indian Culture and Research Journal* 3:3 (1979), 6.

56. Pablo Rodriguez, Deposition, Palica, October 16, 1736, in Auto, Depositions on Governor Moral Sánchez, 1736, AGI SD 861. Cited in Bushnell, *Situado and Sabana,* 201.

57. Francisco de San Buenaventura Martínez Tejada, letter to the Crown, April 29, 1736, AGI SD 863/119. Cited in Bushnell, *Situado and Sabana,* 201.

58. Francisco de Buenaventura, Bishop of Tricale, April 29, 1736, AGI SD 863/119, in Jeannette Thurber Connor, *Colonial Records of Spanish Florida* (Deland: Florida Historical Society, 1925), 6, cited in Bushnell, "Patricio de Hinachuba," 18 n. 26.

59. John H. Hann, *Apalachee: The Land between the Rivers* (Gainesville: University Press of Florida, 1987), 47.

60. Bishop Geronimo Valdés to the King, December 9, 1711, AGI SD 860 SC. Quoted in Hann, *Apalachee,* 47.

61. Joseph María Monaco and Joseph Javier Alaña, OFMs, to Governor Juan Francisco de Güemes y Horcasitas, 1760, "Report on the Indians of Southern Florida and its Keys," AGI SD 1210, translated by John Hann and compared with its original version, written July 1743, in AGI SD 1210, in Hann, *Apalachee,* 419–22.

62. John Jay TePaske, *The Governorship of Spanish Florida, 1700–1763* (Durham: University of North Carolina Press, 1964), 215; Michael V. Gannon, *The Cross in the Sand* (Gainesville: University of Florida Press, 1965), 82; Robert L. Gold, "The Departure of Spanish Catholicism from Florida, 1763–1765," *The Americas* 22:4 (1966), 386; Hann, "St. Augustine's Fallout from the Yamasee War," 192–93; Kathleen A. Deagan, "Accommodation and Resistance: The Process and Impact of Spanish Colonialization in the Southeast," in David Hurst Thomas, ed., *Columbian Consequences,* vol. 2, *Archaeological*

and Historical Perspectives on the Spanish Borderlands East (Washington, D.C.: Smithsonian Institution Press, 1990), 297–314; and Robert Allen Matter, *Pre-Seminole Florida: Spanish Soldiers, Friars, and Indian Missions, 1513–1763* (New York: Garland Press, 1990), 166.

63. Bushnell, *Situado and Sabana*, 206.

10. Conclusions: The Past as Prelude

1. Cited in James Glick, *Chaos: Making a New Science* (New York: Penguin Books, 1987), 38.

2. Robert V. Remini, *Andrew Jackson and the Course of American Empire, 1767–1821* (New York: Harper & Row, 1977), 231.

3. John R. Swanton, *The Indians of the Southeastern United States,* Bureau of American Ethnology Bulletin 137 (Washington, D.C.: Government Printing Office, 1946), 153.

4. John H. Hann, "St. Augustine's Fallout from the Yamasee War," *Florida Historical Quarterly* 48:2 (October 1989), 193–94.

5. Frank J. Billie, Henry John Billie, James Billie, Mary Jene Koenes, Ronnie Jimmie, and Edie Cypress Billie, interviews with the author.

6. Ronnie Jimmie, interview with the author, 1996.

Bibliography

Primary Sources

Archivo General de Indias [hereinafter AGI] 58-1-20, leg. 82, 124 pp.

AGI Justicia 3, no. 3, fols. 8, 21v–23, 35, 40–41, 49–51, 62v–63, 66, 69.

AGI Patrimonio 1-1, leg. 1-19, fol. 477.

Santander, Pedro de, Dr., to the Crown. Sevilla. July 15, 1557. In *Colección de documentos inéditos relativos al descubrimiento,* by Fernández de Navarrete, 26:353–65. Madrid: Sucesores de Rivadeneyra, 1885–1932.

Rogel, Fray Juan, SJ, to Fray Didacus Avellaneda. November 1566–January 1567. In *Monumenta Antiquae Floridae,* Felix Zubillaga, ed., 101–40. Rome: Monumenta Missionum Societatis Iesu, 1946.

Rogel, Fray Juan, SJ, to Fray Jerónimo Ruiz del Portillo. April 25, 1568. In *Monumenta Antiquae Floridae,* Felix Zubillaga, ed., 272–311. Rome: Monumenta Missionum Societatis Iesu, 1946.

Menéndez de Avilés, Pedro. "Auto of the adelantado, Pedro Menéndez de Avilés, reporting on the damages and murders caused by the coast Indians of la Florida." January 15, 1573–July 28, 1574. AGI Patrimonio 257.

Moyne de Morgues, Jacques Le. *Brevis narratio eorum quae in Florida, Americae provincia, Gallis acciderunt, secunda in illa navegationae, duce renato de Laudonnière, closses praefecto, anno 1564 quae est secunda pars Americae. . . .* Frankfort: Typis J. Wecheli, 1591.

Méndez Canzo, Gonzalo, Governor, to the Crown. April 24, 1601. AGI Santo Domingo [hereinafter SD] 224.

Pareja, Francisco, Fray, to the Crown. San Juan del Puerto mission. September 14, 1602. AGI SD 235, Stetson Collection [hereinafter SC].

López, Baltasar, Fray, to the Crown. San Pedro mission. September 16, 1602. AGI 54-5-20, SC micro. 62-A, Woodbury Lowrey Collection, 4.

Fernández de Olivera, Juan, to the Crown. December 15, 1611. AGI SD 229/67.

Treviño Guillamas, Juan, to the Crown. 1615? Summary in AGI SD 225.

Menéndez Márquez, Francisco, I, Juan de Cueva, and Francisco Ramírez to the Crown. January 30, 1627. AGI SD 229/87.

Patent of Sir Robert Heath. 5 Charles I. October 30, 1629. In *Collections of the South Carolina Historical Society.* Vol. 5. Richmond: Wm. E. Jones, 1897.

Alonso de Jesús, Francisco, Fray, to the Crown. November 14, 1630. AGI Mexico leg. 302.

San Martín, Pedro de. Petition, 1635. AGI SD 233.

Testimony of Agustín and Juan, Natives from San Juan del Puerto. Havana, Cuba. July 2, 1636. AGI SD 27/28. In *Colonial Records of Spanish Florida,* by Jeanette Thurber Connor, 2. Deland: Florida Historical Society, 1925.

Spanish Crown, to the Governor and Royal Officials of Florida. "Cedula." July 26, 1648. AGI SD 834/4.

Prado, Joseph de. Report with comments appended by the fiscal of the San Agustín council. December 30, 1654. AGI SD 229/115. In Connor's *Colonial Records of Spanish Florida*, 3.

Rebolledo, Diego de, to Antonio de Arguelles. "Orden." March 10, 1655, AGI SD 23.

Arguelles, Antonio de. "Record of the visitation of the Province of Guale and Mocama." AGI Escribania de Camera, leg. 156B, fols. 527v–528, SC.

"Auto para hacer Vicita General en la provincia de Apalache." January 17–February 13, 1657. AGI Escribania de Camera, leg. 155, SC.

Woodward, Henry. "A faithful relation of my westoe voiage." 1674. In *Narratives of Early Carolina, 1650–1708*, Alexander S. Salley, Jr., ed., 130–34. New York: Charles Scribner's Sons, 1911.

Moral, Alonso de, Fray, to the Crown. November 5, 1676. AGI 54-20/105, SC.

"Consejo de las Indias to Fray Juan Luengo, comisario general de Indias de la orden de S. Francisco." November 5, 1676. AGI 58-1-21/166. North Carolina 4-33, SC micro. 62-A.

Arguelles, Antonio de. Auto of the Vista General of Captitán Antonio de Arguelles. January 5, 1678. AGI Escribania de Camera, leg. 156, SC.

Torres y Ayala, Laureano de, to the Crown. San Agustín. April 15, 1696. AGI 54-5-13, leg. 72.

Torres y Ayala, Laureano de, and Tomás Menéndez Márquez to the Crown. April 20, 1697. AGI SD 230/120.

Patricio, Don, Cacique of Ivitachuco and Don Andrés, Cacique of San Luis, to the Crown. February 12, 1699. AGI 54-5-19, leg. 439.

Zúñiga y Cerda, Joseph de, Governor, to the Crown. "Upon the raid into Santa Fé and the expedition upon which Captain Romo was sent." San Agustín. September 30, 1702. AGI 58-2-8, leg. B3.

Zúñiga y Cerda, Joseph de, Governor, to the Crown. San Agustín. March 30, 1704. AGI 58-1-20, leg. 92.

Moore, James, Colonel, to Sir Nathaniel Johnson. April 16(?), 1704. "Spanish Papers," MSS, Library of Congress, 6:892–96.

Moore, James, Colonel, to the Lords Proprietors. April 16, 1704. "Spanish Papers," MSS, Library of Congress, 6:888.

[Guzmán, Joseph de]. Commandant at Pensacola to Viceroy. Santa María de Galve. August 22, 1704. AGI 58-2-7/2.

Zúñiga y Cerda, Joseph de, Governor, to the Crown. San Agustín. September 3, 1704. AGI 58-2-2, leg. 83 1/2.

Zúñiga y Cerda, Joseph de, Governor, to the Crown. San Agustín. September 10, 1704. AGI 58-2-7/2.

Franciscans to the Crown. "Summary of Martyrdoms experienced in Florida by the Franciscans." San Agustín. May 7, 1707. AGI 58-2-14, leg. 61.

[Nairn, Thomas]. *A Letter from South Carolina: Giving an Account of the Soil, Air, Product, Trade, Government, Laws, Religion, People, Military Strength, &c. of that Province; Together with the Manner and necessary Charges of Settling a Plantation there, and the Annual Profit it will produce. Written by a Swiss*

Gentleman, to his Friend at Bern. 1710. Facsimile ed. Ann Arbor: University Microfilms, 1996.

Valdés, Bishop Geronimo, to the King. December 9, 1711. AGI SD 860 SC.

Spanish governor of Pensacola to the Spanish governor at San Agustín. July 24, 1717. In "Documents Describing the Second and Third Expeditions of Lieutenant Diego Peña to Apalachee and Apalachicolo in 1717 and 1718," by Mark F. Boyd. *Florida Historical Quarterly* 31, no. 2 (1952): 128.

Buenaventura, Francisco de, Bishop of Tricale. April 29, 1736. AGI SD 863/119. In Connor's *Colonial Records of Spanish Florida*, 6.

Martínez Tejada, Francisco de San Buenaventura, to the Crown. April 29, 1736. AGI SD 863/119.

Rodríguez, Pablo. Auto. Depositions on Governor Moral Sánchez. October 16, 1736. AGI SD 861.

Monaco, Joseph María, OFM, and Joseph Javier Alaña, OFM, to Governor Juan Francisco de Güemes y Horcasitas. "Report on the Indians of Southern Florida and its Keys." 1760. AGI SD 1210.

Page du Pratz, M. Le. *The History of Louisiana or of the Western Parts of Virginia and Carolina: Containing A Description of the Countries that lye on both Sides of the River Missisipi: with An Account of the Settlements, Inhabitants, Soil, Climate, and Products. Translated from the French, (lately published), by M. Le Page Du Pratz With Some Notes and Observations Relating to our Colonies*. 2 vols. London: T. Becket and P. A. De Hondt, 1763.

Stuart, John, Agent, to Lt. Pampellone. July 16, 1764. Thomas Gage Collection, Clements Library, University of Michigan.

Stuart, John, Agent, to Gen. Thomas Gage. December 14, 1771. Thomas Gage Collection, Clements Library, University of Michigan.

McGillivray, Alexander. "Minutes taken from Genl. McGillivray respecting the Creeks." Genl. Henry Knox Papers, August 1790, XXVI-165, 2467a. micro. Massachusetts Historical Society Library, Boston.

Hughes, Ellis, United States Army Asst. Surgeon. "Diary." April 4, 1839. Collections of the Florida Historical Society, University of South Florida Library, Tampa.

Secondary Sources

Unpublished Works

Boniface, Brian. "A Historical Geography of Spanish Florida circa 1700." Master's thesis, University of Georgia, 1971.

Bushnell, Amy. "Research Design: The Menéndez Family of Spanish Florida 1565–1743: Nepotists and Entrepreneurs in a Border Province." Typescript prepared for the Historic St. Augustine Preservation Board, St. Augustine, November 18, 1975.

Deagan, Kathleen A. "Sex, Status and Role in the Mestizaje of Spanish Colonial Florida." Ph.D. dissertation, University of Florida, 1974.

DePratter, Chester B. "Late Prehistoric and Early Historic Chiefdoms in the Southeastern United States." Ph.D. dissertation, University of Georgia, 1983.

Fairbanks, Charles H. "Ethnohistorical Report of the Florida Indians. Before the United States Indian Claims Commission, The Seminole Indians of the State of Florida vs. The United States of America," Dockets No. 73 and 151, 1957.

Fausz, J. Frederick. "The Powhatan Uprising of 1622: A Historical Study of Ethnocentrism and Cultural Conflict." Ph.D. dissertation, College of William and Mary, 1977.

Gannon, Michael V. "The Conflict between Church and State in Spanish Florida: The Administration of Juan Márquez Cabrera, 1680–1687." Paper delivered at the Congreso de la Rábida, "Impacto de España en la Florida, el Caribe y la Luisiana, 1500–1800." La Rábida, Spain, September 13–17, 1981.

Hally, David J. "Archaeological Investigation of the Little Egypt Site (9MU102) Murray County, Georgia 1969 Season." Mimeographed. Athens: University of Georgia, Department of Anthropology, August 1976.

Hann, John H. "Political Organization among Southeastern Indians in the Early Historic Period." Typescript prepared for San Luís Archaeological and Historical Site, Florida Department of State, Tallahassee, n.d.

Marchena Fernández, Juan. "Las Floridas y la Luisiana." Typescript prepared for the Facultad de Geografia e Historia, Universidad de Sevilla, n.d.

Matter, Robert Allen. "The Spanish Missions of Florida: The Friars Versus the Governors in the 'Golden Age,' 1606–1690." Ph.D. dissertation, University of Washington, 1972.

Schwaller, John. "Nobility, Family, and Service: Menéndez and His Men." Typescript. N.d.

Smith, Marvin. "The Rise and Fall of Coosa, AD 1350–1700." Paper presented to the annual meeting of the Southern Anthropological Association symposium, "Societies in Eclipse: Eastern North America at the Dawn of Colonization," Pittsburgh, Pennsylvania, April 1992.

Sturtevant, William C. "The Mikasuki Seminole: Medical Beliefs and Practices." Ph.D. dissertation, Yale University, 1955.

Articles

Adorno, Rolena. "The Discourse Encounter of Spain and America: The Authority of Eyewitness Testimony in the Writing of History." *William and Mary Quarterly* 49, no. 2 (April 1992): 210–28.

Anderson, David G. "Stability and Change in Chiefdom-Level Societies: An Examination of Mississippian Political Evolution on the South Atlantic Slope." In *Lamar Archaeology: Mississippian Chiefdoms in the Deep South*, M. Williams and G. Shapiro, eds., 187–213. Tuscaloosa: University of Alabama Press, 1990.

Anderson, David G., David J. Hally, and James L. Rudolph. "The Mississippian Occupation of the Savannah River Valley." *Southeastern Archaeology* 5, no. 1 (1986): 32–51.

Baber, Adin. "Food Plants of the de Soto Expedition." *Tequesta* 1, no. 2 (1942): 34–40.

Bartram, William. "Observations on the Creek and Cherokee Indians." 1789. *Transactions of the American Ethnological Society* 3, pt. 1 (1853): 1–8.

Blakely, Robert L., and David Mathews. "Bioarchaeological Evidence for a Spanish–Native American Conflict in the Sixteenth-Century Southeast." *American Antiquity* 55 (1990): 718–44.

Bonvillian, Nancy. "Gender Relations in Native North America." *American Indian Culture and Research Journal* 13, no. 2 (1989): 1–28.

———. "The Iroquois and the Jesuits: Strategies of Influence and Resistance." *American Indian Culture and Research Journal* 10, no. 1 (1986): 29–32.

Booker, Karen M., Charles M. Hudson, and Robert L. Rankin. "Place Name Identification and Multilingualism in the Sixteenth-Century Southeast." *Ethnohistory* 39, no. 4 (Fall 1992): 399–451.

Boyd, Mark F. "From a Remote Frontier: Letters and Documents Pertaining to San Marcos de Apalache, 1763–69, during the British Occupation of Florida." *Florida Historical Quarterly* 19:3, 4 (1941); 20:1, 2, 3, 4 (1941–42); 21:1, 2 (1942).

Boyd, Mark F., trans. "Diego Peña's Expedition to Apalachee and Apalachicolo in 1716." *Florida Historical Quarterly* 28, no. 1 (1949): 1–27.

———. "Documents Describing the Second and Third Expeditions of Lieutenant Diego Peña to Apalachee and Apalachicolo in 1717 and 1718." *Florida Historical Quarterly* 31, no. 2 (1952): 109–39.

Boyd, Mark F., and José Navarro LaTorre. "Spanish Interest in British Florida, and in the Progress of the American Revolution: Part 1, Relations with the Spanish Faction of the Creek Indians." *Florida Historical Quarterly* 31, no. 1 (1953): 93–103.

Brown, Judith K. "Iroquois Women: An Ethnohistoric Note." In *Becoming Visible: Women in European History,* Renate Bridenthal and Claudia Koonz, eds., 127–56. Boston: Houghton Mifflin, 1977.

Bushnell, Amy. "The Ménendez Cattle Barony at La Chua and the Determinants of Economic Expansion in 17th Century Florida." *Florida Historical Quarterly* 56, no. 4 (1978): 407–31.

———. "Patricio de Hinachuba: Defender of the Word of God, the Crown of the King and the Little Children of Ivitachuco." *American Indian Culture and Research Journal* 3, no. 3 (1979): 1–21.

———. "Republic of Spaniards, Republic of Indians." In *The New History of Florida,* Michael V. Gannon, ed., 62–77. Gainesville: University Press of Florida, 1995.

———. " 'That Demonic Game': The Campaign to Stop Indian Pelota Playing in Spanish Florida, 1675–1684." *The Americas* 35, no. 1 (July 1978): 1–19.

Capron, Louis. *The Medicine Bundles of the Florida Seminoles and the Green Corn Dance.* Bureau of American Ethnology Bulletin 51, Anthropological Paper 35. Washington, D.C.: Smithsonian Institution, 1953, 159–210.

Corbett, Theodore G. "Migration to a Spanish Imperial Frontier in the Seventeenth and Eighteenth Centuries: St. Augustine." *Hispanic American Historical Review* 54, no. 3 (August 1974): 414–30.

———. "Population Structure in Hispanic St. Augustine, 1629–1763." *Florida Historical Quarterly* 54 (January 1956): 263–84.

Crouch, Dora F. "Roman Models for Spanish Colonization." In *Columbian Consequences*. Vol. 3, *The Spanish Borderlands in Pan-American Perspective,* David Hurst Thomas, ed., 21–35. Washington, D.C.: Smithsonian Institution Press, 1990.

Curren, Caleb B., Keith J. Little, and Harry O. Holstein. "Aboriginal Societies Encountered by the Tristan de Luna Expedition." *Florida Anthropologist* 42 (1989): 381–95.

Cusick, James. "Across the Border: Commodity Flow and Merchants in Spanish St. Augustine." *Florida Historical Quarterly* 69 (1991): 277–99.

Deagan, Kathleen A. "Accommodation and Resistance: The Process and Impact of Spanish Colonialization in the Southeast." In *Columbian Consequences.* Vol. 2, *Archaeological and Historical Perspectives on the Spanish Borderlands East,* David Hurst Thomas, ed., 297–314. Washington, D.C.: Smithsonian Institution Press, 1990.

———. "The Material Assemblage of Sixteenth Century Spanish Florida." *Historical Archaeology* 12:25–50.

———. "Sixteenth-Century Spanish-American Colonization in the Southeastern United States and the Caribbean." In *Columbian Consequences.* Vol. 2, *Archaeological and Historical Perspectives on the Spanish Borderlands East,* David Hurst Thomas, ed., 225–50. Washington, D.C.: Smithsonian Institution Press, 1990.

DePratter, Chester. "The Route of Juan Pardo's Explorations in the Interior Southeast, 1566–1568." *Florida Historical Quarterly* 62, no. 2 (1983): 125–58.

Dunkle, John R. "Population Change as an Element in the Historical Geography of St. Augustine." *Florida Historical Quarterly* 37 (1958): 3–22.

Folmsbee, Stanley J., and Madeline Kneberg Lewis, eds. "Journals of the Juan Pardo Expeditions, 1566–1567." *East Tennessee Historical Society's Publications* 37 (1965): 106–21.

Galloway, Patricia. "The Archaeology of Historical Narrative." In *Columbian Consequences*. Vol. 3, *The Spanish Borderlands in Pan-American Perspective,* David Hurst Thomas, ed., 453–69. Washington, D.C.: Smithsonian Institution Press, 1990.

Galloway, Patrick. "Basic Patterns in Annual Variations in Fertility, Nuptuality, Mortality, and Prices in Pre-Industrial England." *Population Studies* 42 (1988): 275–303.

García-Gallo, Alfonso. "Las Bulas de Alejandro VI y el ordenamiento jurídico de la expansión portuguesa y castellana en Africa e Indias." *Anuario de Historia del Derecho Español* 27–28 (1957–58): 461–829.

———. "La ciencia jurídica en la formación del Derecho Hispanoamericano en los siglos XVI al XVIII." *Anuario de Historia del Derecho Español* 44 (1974): 157–200.

———. "La ley como fuente del Derecho en Indias en el siglo XVI." *Anuario de Historia del Derecho Español* 21 (1951): 607–730.

Gold, Robert L. "The Departure of Spanish Catholicism from Florida, 1763–1765." In *Primitive Views of the World: Essays from Culture in History,* Stanley Diamond, ed., 49–82. New York: Columbia University Press, 1964.

Hann, John H. "Demographic Patterns and Changes in Mid-Seventeenth Century Timucua and Apalachee." *Florida Historical Quarterly* 64, no. 4 (April 1896): 371–92.

———. "Florida's Terra Incognita: West Florida's Natives in the Sixteenth and Seventeenth Centuries." *Florida Anthropologist* 41 (1988): 61–107.

———. "St. Augustine's Fallout from the Yamasee War." *Florida Historical Quarterly* 48, no. 2 (October 1989): 193–94.

———. "Summary Guide to Spanish Florida Missions and Visitas with Churches in the Sixteenth and Seventeenth Centuries." *The Americas* 46, no. 4 (April 1990): 417–513.

———. "Twilight of the Mocamo and Guale Aborigines as Portrayed in the 1695 Spanish Visitation." *Florida Historical Quarterly* 66, no. 1 (1987): 1–24.

Haring, Clarence Henry. "El origen del gobierno real en las Indias." *Boletín del Instituto e Investigaciones Históricos* [Buenos Aires] 3, no. 24 (1925): 297–327.

Hawkins, Benjamin. *Letters of Benjamin Hawkins, 1796–1806.* Collections of the Georgia Historical Society 9. Savannah: n.p., 1916.

———. *A Sketch of the Creek Country in 1798 and 1799.* Collections of the Georgia Historical Society 3:1 (1848).

Henige, David. "The Content, Context, and Credibility of La Florida del Ynca." *The Americas* 43 (1986): 1–23.

Hoffman, Paul E. "Introduction: The De Soto Expedition, a Cultural Crossroads." In *Columbian Consequences.* Vol. 2, *Archaeological and Historical Perspectives in the Spanish Borderlands East,* David Hurst Thomas, ed., 12–13. Washington, D.C.: Smithsonian Institution Press, 1990.

Hoyt, William D. "A Soldier's View of the Seminole War: Three Letters of James B. Dallam." *Florida Historical Quarterly* 25, no. 4 (April 1947): 356–62.

Hudson, Charles. "Conversations with the High Priest of Coosa." In *Lamar Archaeology: Mississippian Chiefdoms in the Deep South,* M. Williams and G. Shapiro, eds., 214–30. Tuscaloosa: University of Alabama Press, 1990.

Hudson, Charles, Marvin T. Smith, Chester DePratter, and Emilia Kelley. "The Tristan de Luna Expedition, 1551–1561." In *First Encounters: Spanish Explorations in the Caribbean and the United States, 1492–1570,* Jerald T. Milanich and Susan Milbrath, eds., 119–34. Gainesville: University of Florida Press, 1989.

Hudson, Charles, Marvin T. Smith, David Hally, Richard Polhemus, and Chester DePratter. "Coosa: A Chiefdom in the Sixteenth-Century Southeastern United States." *American Antiquity* 50 (1985): 723–37.

———. "A Spanish-Coosa Alliance in Sixteenth-Century North Georgia." *Georgia Historical Quarterly* 72 (1988): 599–626.

Hussey, Roland D. "Text of the Laws of Burgos, 1512–1513, Concerning the Treatment of the Indian." *Hispanic-American Historical Review* 12 (1932): 301–26.

Hymes, Dell. "Toward Ethnographies of Communication: The Analysis of Communicative Events." In *Language and Social Context,* P. Giglioli, ed. Harmonsworth: Penguin, 1972.

Jackson, Robert H. "Patterns of Demographic Change in the Missions of Central

Alta California." *Journal of California and Great Basin Anthropology* 9, no. 2 (1987): 251–72.

Jennings, Francis. "A Growing Partnership: Historians, Anthropologists, and American Indian History." *Ethnohistory* 29, no. 1 (1982): 21–34.

Jennings, Jesse D. "Nutt's Trip to the Chickasaw Country." *Journal of Mississippi History* 9 (1947): 34–61.

Johnson, Sherry. "The Spanish St. Augustine Community, 1784–1795: A Reevaluation." *Florida Historical Quarterly* 68, no. 1 (July 1989): 27–54.

Jones, Calvin B. "Southern Cult Manifestations at the Lake Jackson Site, Leon County, Florida: Salvage Excavation of Mound 3." *Midcontinental Journal of Archaeology* 7, no. 1 (1982): 3–44.

Kicza, John E. "Patterns in Early Spanish Overseas Expansion." *William and Mary Quarterly* 49, no. 2 (April 1992): 229–53.

———. "The Social and Ethnic Historiography of Colonial Latin America: The Last Twenty Years." *William and Mary Quarterly* 45, no. 3 (July 1988): 453–88.

Knight, Vernon James, Jr. "The Institutional Organization of Mississippian Religion." *American Antiquity* 51, no. 4 (1986): 675–87.

Knight, Vernon J., and Sheree Adams. "A Voyage to the Mobile and Tomen in 1700 with Notes on the Interior of Alabama." *Journal of Alabama Archaeology* 27 (1981): 48.

Knight, Vernon J., and Marvin T. Smith. "Big Tallassee: A Contribution to Upper Creek Site Archaeology." *Early Georgia* 8 (1980): 59–74.

Konetzle, Richard. "La imigracíon de mujeres españolas a América durante la época colonial." *Rivista Internacional de Sociología* [Madrid] 9 (1945): 123–50.

———. "El mestizaje y su importancia en el desarrollo de la población hispanoamericano durante la época colonial." *Revista de Indias* 23 (1946): 7–44, and 24 (1946): 215–37.

Landers, Jane. "Black-Indian Interaction in Spanish Florida." *Colonial Latin America Historical Review* 2, no. 2 (Spring 1993): 141–62.

Lankford, George E., III. "Legends of the Adelantado." In *The Expedition of Hernando de Soto West of the Mississippi, 1541–1543,* Gloria Young and Michael P. Hoffman, eds., 173–91. Fayetteville: University of Arkansas Press, 1993.

Leacock, Eleanor. "Women in Egalitarian Societies." In *Becoming Visible: Women in European History,* Renate Bridenthal and Claudia Koonz, eds. Boston: Houghton Mifflin, 1977.

Lewis, Clifford M. "The Calusa." In *Tacachale: Essays on the Indians of Florida and Southeastern Georgia during the Historic Period,* Jerald Milanich and Samuel Proctor, eds., 19–49. Gainesville: University of Florida Press, 1978.

Lynch, John. "The Institutional Framework of Colonial Spanish America." *Journal of Latin American Studies* 24 (Quincentenary Supplement 1992): 69–81.

Lyon, Eugene. "Aspects of Pedro Menéndez the Man." *El Escribano* 24 (1987): 39–52.

———. "The Enterprise of Florida." In *Columbian Consequences.* Vol. 2, *Archaeological and Historical Perspectives on the Spanish Borderlands East,* David Hurst Thomas, ed., 281–96. Washington, D.C.: Smithsonian Institution Press, 1990.

———. "Pedro Menéndez' Strategic Plan for the Florida Peninsula." *Florida Historical Quarterly* 67 (1988): 1–14.

———. "Richer Than We Thought: The Material Culture of Sixteenth-Century St. Augustine." *El Escribano: The St. Augustine Journal of History* 29 (1992).

———. "Settlement and Survival." In *The New History of Florida*, Michael V. Gannon, ed., 40–61. Gainesville: University of Florida Press, 1996.

———. "Spain's 16th Century North American Settlement Attempts: A Neglected Aspect." *Florida Historical Quarterly* 59 (1981): 275–91.

McDowell, W. L., ed. *Journals of the Commissioners of Indian Trade, 1710–1718.* The Colonial Records of South Carolina, vol. 1. 1955.

Marquardt, William H. "Politics and Production among the Calusa of South Florida." In *Hunters and Gatherers 1: History, Evolution, and Social Change,* Tim Ingold, David Riches, and James Woodburn, eds., 161–83. Oxford: St. Martin's Press, 1988.

Marrinan, Rochelle A., John F. Scarry, and Rhonda L. Majors. "Prelude to De Soto: The Expedition of Pánfilo de Narváez." In *Columbian Consequences.* Vol. 2, *Archaeological and Historical Perspectives in the Spanish Borderlands East,* David Hurst Thomas, ed. Washington, D.C.: Smithsonian Institution Press, 1990.

Matter, Robert Allen. "Economic Basis of the Seventeenth Century Florida Missions." *Florida Historical Quarterly* 52, no. 1 (1973): 18–38.

Milanich, Jerald T. "Corn and Calusa: De Soto and Demography." In *Coasts, Plains and Deserts: Essays in Honor of Reynold J. Ruppe,* Sylvia W. Gaines, ed., 173–84. Tempe: Arizona University Press, 1987.

Milner, George R. "Epidemic Disease in the Postcontact Southeast: An Appraisal." *Midcontinental Journal of Anthropology* 5 (1980): 39–56.

Moreno, Frank Jay. "The Spanish Colonial System: A Functional Approach." *Western Political Quarterly* 20, no. 2 (June 1967): 308–20.

Myer, William E. "Indian Trails of the Southeast." In *Forty-Second Annual Report of the Bureau of American Ethnology for 1924–1925,* 727–857. Washington, D.C.: Government Printing Office, 1928.

Narthrup, George T., trans. "Mundus Novus Albericus Vespucius Laurencio Petri de Medicis salutem plurinam dicit. 1504/05." In *Vespucci Reprints, Texts, and Studies.* Vol. 5. Princeton: Princeton University Press, 1916.

Nash, Gary B. "Notes on the History of Seventeenth-Century Missionization in Colonial America." *American Indian Culture and Research Journal* 2, no. 2 (1978): 3–8.

Pérez de Tudela Bueso, Juan. "La Gran Reforma Carolina de las Indias en 1542." *Revista de Indias* 18, nos. 73/74 (1958): 463–509.

Pierce, James. "Notice of the Agriculture, scenery, geology and animal, vegetable and mineral production of the Floridas, and of the Indian Tribes, made during a recent tour in these countries." *American Journal of Science and Arts* 9, no. 1 (June 1825): 119–36 (article 21).

Poitrineau, Able. "Demography and the Political Destiny of Florida during the Second Spanish Period." *Florida Historical Quarterly* 64, no. 4 (April 1988): 420–43.

Porter, Kenneth W. "Negroes on the Southern Frontier, 1670–1763." *Journal of Negro History* 33 (1948): 53–78.

Rubin, Gayle. "The Traffic in Women: Notes on the 'Political Economy' of Sex." In *Toward an Anthropology of Women,* Reyna Rapp Reiter, ed. New York: Monthly Review, 1978.

Salisbury, Neal E. "Red Puritans: The 'Praying Indians' of Massachusetts Bay and John Eliot." *William and Mary Quarterly* 3d. ser., 31 (1974): 27–54.

Scarry, John F. "The Late Prehistoric Southeast." In *The Forgotten Centuries: Indians and Europeans in the American South, 1521–1704,* Charles Hudson and Carmen Chaves Tesser, eds., 17–35. Athens: University of Georgia Press, 1994.

———. "The Rise, Transformation, and Fall of Apalachee: A Case Study of Political Change in a Chiefly Society." In *Lamar Archaeology: Mississippian Chiefdoms in the Deep South,* M. Williams and G. Shapiro, eds., 175–86. Tuscaloosa: University of Alabama Press, 1990.

Seed, Patricia. "Taking Possession and Reading Texts: Establishing the Authority of Overseas Empires." *William and Mary Quarterly* 49, no. 2 (April 1992): 183–209.

Sempat Assadourian, Carlos. "The Colonial Economy: The Transfer of the European System of Production to New Spain and Peru." *Journal of Latin American Studies* 24 (Quincentenary Supplement 1992): 55–68.

Sivaramakrishnan, K. "Colonialism and Forestry in India: Imagining the Past in Present Politics." *Comparative Studies in Society and History* 37, no. 1 (1995): 3–40.

Smith, Buckingham, ed. and trans. "Relación de la Florida para el Ilmo. Señor Visorrei de la Nueva España la qual trajo Fr. Gregorio Beteta." In *Colección de varios Documentos para la historia de la Florida y tierras adyacentes.* London: Trubner and Company, 1857.

Stannard, David E. "The Consequences of Contact: Toward an Interdisciplinary Theory of Native Responses to Biological and Cultural Invasion." In *Columbian Consequences.* Vol. 3, *The Spanish Borderlands in Pan-American Perspective,* David Hurst Thomas, ed., 519–39. Washington, D.C.: Smithsonian Institution Press, 1990.

Steckley, John. "The Warrior and the Lineage: Jesuit Use of Iroquoian Images to Communicate Christianity." *Ethnohistory* 39, no. 4 (Fall 1992): 478–509.

Stern, Steve J. "Paradigms of Conquest: History, Historiography, and Politics." *Journal of Latin American Studies* 24 (Quincentenary Supplement 1992): 1–34.

Steward, Julian H. "Theory and Application in a Social Science." *Ethnohistory* 2 (1955): 296–97.

Sturtevant, William C. "The Medicine Bundles and Busks of the Florida Seminoles." *Florida Anthropologist* 7, no. 2 (May 1954): 31–70.

———. "Spanish-Indian Relations in Southeastern North America." *Ethnohistory* 9 (Winter 1962): 41–94.

Swaggerty, W. R. "Spanish-Indian Relations, 1513–1821." In *Scholars and the Indian Experience,* W. R. Swaggerty, ed., 36–78. D'Arcy McNickle Center for the History of the American Indian, Newberry Library. Bloomington: University of Indiana Press, [1982].

Swan, Caleb. "Position and State of Manners and Art in the Creek, or Muskogee Nation in 1791." In *Historical and Statistical Information Respecting the History, Condition and Prospects of the Indian Tribes of the United States*, 6 vols., Henry R. Schoolcraft, 251–83. Philadelphia: Lippincott, 1855.

Swanton, John R. "The Interpretation of Aboriginal Mounds by Means of Creek Indian Customs." In *Annual Report of the Smithsonian Institution*, 495–507. Washington: Government Printing Office, 1927.

Tanner, Helen Hornbeck. "The Land and Water Communication Systems of the Southeastern Indians." In *Powhatan's Mantle: Indians in the Colonial Southeast*, Peter H. Wood, Gregory A. Waselkov, and M. Thomas Hatley, 6–20. Lincoln: University of Nebraska Press, 1989.

———. *Zéspedes in East Florida, 1784–1790*. Coral Gables: University of Miami Press, 1963.

Thomas, David Hurst. "The Spanish Missions of La Florida: An Overview." In *Columbian Consequences*. Vol. 2, *Archaeological and Historical Perspectives on the Spanish Borderlands East*, David Hurst Thomas, ed., 388–89. Washington, D.C.: Smithsonian Institution Press, 1989.

Vega, Garcilaso de la. "La Florida, By the Inca." Charmion Shelby, trans. In *The De Soto Chronicles: The Expedition of Hernando de Soto to North America in 1539–1543*, vol. 2, Lawrence A. Clayton, Vernon James Knight, Jr., and Edward C. Moore, eds., 126. Tuscaloosa: University of Alabama Press, 1993.

Vidal, Hernán. "The Concept of Colonial and Postcolonial Discourse: A Perspective from Literary Criticism." *Latin American Research Review* 20, no. 10 (1993): 113–52.

Waring, Antonio J., Jr. "The Southern Cult and Muskohegean Ceremonial: General Considerations." In *The Waring Papers*, Stephen Williams, ed., 30–69. Papers of the Peabody Museum of Archaeology and Ethnology, 58 (1968).

Waring, Antonio J., Jr., and Preston Holder. "A Prehistoric Ceremonial Complex in the Southeastern United States." *American Anthropologist* 47 (1945): 1–34.

Waselkov, Gregory A. "Indian Maps of the Colonial Southeast." In *Powhatan's Mantle: Indians in the Colonial Southeast*, Peter H. Wood, Gregory A. Waselkov, and M. Thomas Hatley, 292–343. Lincoln: University of Nebraska Press, 1989.

Weber, David J. "Blood of Martyrs, Blood of Indians: Toward a More Balanced View of Spanish Missions in Seventeenth-Century North America." In *Columbian Consequences*. Vol. 3, *The Spanish Borderlands in Pan-American Perspective*, David Hurst Thomas, ed. Washington, D.C.: Smithsonian Institution Press, 1990.

Webster, Paula. "Matriarchy: A Vision of Power." In *Becoming Visible: Women in European History*, Renate Bridenthal and Claudia Koonz, eds., 235–51. Boston: Houghton Mifflin, 1977.

Williams, John Lee. "Journal of John Lee Williams." *Florida Historical Quarterly* 1, no. 1 (1908): 18–29 and 1, no. 2 (1908): 37–44.

Wood, Peter H. "The Changing Population of the Colonial South: An Overview by Race and Region, 1685–1790." In *Powhatan's Mantle: Indians in the Colonial Southeast*, Peter H. Wood, Gregory A. Waselkov, and M. Thomas Hatley, 35–103. Lincoln: University of Nebraska Press, 1989.

———. "Introduction to Part One." In *Powhatan's Mantle: Indians in the Colonial Southeast*, Peter H. Wood, Gregory A. Waselkov, and M. Thomas Hatley, 1–5. Lincoln: University of Nebraska Press, 1989.

Periodicals

Bahama Advertiser, October 2, 1819.
Pensacola Gazette, October 9, 1824.

Published Works

Acosta Rodríguez, Antonio. *La Población de Luisiana Española*. Madrid: Ministerio de Asuntos Esteriores, 1979.

Adair, James. *History of the American Indians*. 1775. Reprint ed., Samuel Cole Williams, ed. Johnson City, Tennessee: National Society of Colonial Dames of America, 1930.

Agnew, Brad. *Fort Gibson: Terminal of the Trail of Tears*. Norman: University of Oklahoma Press, 1980.

Alegre, Francisco Javier. *Historia de la Provincia de la Compañia de Jesús de Nueva España. Tomo I.* New ed., Ernest Burrus and Félix Zubillaga, eds. Rome: Institutum Historicum, Bibliotheca Instituti Historici S.J., vol. 9, 1956.

Anderson, Bonnie S., and Judith P. Zinsser, *A History of Their Own: Women in Europe from Prehistory to the Present*. 2 vols. New York: Harper & Row, 1989.

Anderson, David G. *The Savannah River Chiefdoms: Political Change in the Late Prehistoric Southeast*. Tuscaloosa: University of Alabama Press, 1994.

Andrews, Kenneth R. *The Spanish Caribbean: Trade and Plunder, 1530–1630*. New Haven: Yale University Press, 1978.

Anghiera, Pietro Martire 'd [Peter Martyr]. *Decadas del Nuevo Mundo*. 2 vols. Edited by Edmundo O'Gorman. Mexico City: n.p., 1964–1965.

Annual Report of the Smithsonian Institution. Washington: Government Printing Office, 1927.

Arac, Jonathan, ed. *After Foucault: Humanistic Knowledge, Postmodern Challenges*. New Brunswick, New Jersey: Rutgers University Press, 1988.

Arnade, Charles. *Florida on Trial*. Coral Gables: University of Miami Press, 1959.

Atlman, Ida, and James Lockhart, eds. *Provinces of Early Mexico: Variants of Spanish American Regional Evolution*. Los Angeles: University of California at Los Angeles, 1976.

Bailyn, Bernard. *The Peopling of British North America, An Introduction*. New York: Vintage Books, 1986.

———. *Voyagers to the West: A Passage in the Peopling of America on the Eve of the American Revolution*. New York: 1986. New York: Vintage Press, 1988.

Barcía Carballido y Zúñiga, Andrés González de [pseudo., Gabriel de Cardensa z Cano]. *Ensayo cronológico para la historia general de la Florida, 1512–1722*.

1723. Anthony Kerrigan, trans. Gainesville: University Presses of Florida, 1951.

Bartram, William. *Travels through North and South Carolina, Georgia, East and West Florida.* 1791. Reprint ed. New Haven: Yale University Press, 1958.

Beck, Peggy V., Anna Lee Walters, and Nia Francisco. *The Sacred: Ways of Knowledge, Sources of Life.* 1977. Tsaile, Arizona: Navajo Community College Press, 1992.

Bemrose, John. *Reminiscences of the Second Seminole War.* John K. Mahon, ed. Gainesville: University Presses of Florida, 1966.

Benítez, Fernando. *The Century After Cortez.* Chicago: University of Chicago Press, 1965.

Bennassar, Bartolomé. *The Spanish Character: Attitudes and Mentalities from the Sixteenth through the Nineteenth Century.* Benjamin Keen, trans. Berkeley: University of California Press, 1979.

Bennett, Charles E. *Laudonnière and Fort Caroline: History and Documents.* Gainesville: University of Florida Press, 1964.

Bethell, Leslie, ed. *Cambridge History of Latin America.* 8 vols. Cambridge: Cambridge University Press, 1984.

Blakely, Robert L., ed. *The King Site: Continuity and Contact in Sixteenth-Century Georgia.* Athens: University of Georgia Press, 1988.

Bloch, Marc. *Feudal Society.* Chicago: University of Chicago Press, 1961.

Boas, Franz. *Race, Language, and Culture.* 1940. Reprint ed. New York: McMillan Company, 1955.

Bolton, Herbert E., and Thomas M. Marshall. *The Colonization of North America, 1492–1783.* New York: n.p., 1932.

Boorstin, Daniel J. *The Americans: The Colonial Experience.* New York: Vintage Books, 1958.

———. *The Discoverers.* New York: Vintage Books, 1985.

Bossu, Jean-Bernard. *Nouveaux voyages dans l'Amerique Septentrionale.* 1777. Seymour Feiler, trans. and ed. Norman: University of Oklahoma Press, 1962.

Boyd, Mark F., Hale G. Smith, and John W. Griffin. *Here They Once Stood: The Tragic End of the Apalachee Missions.* Gainesville: University of Florida Press, 1951.

Braudel, Fernand. *The Mediterranean and the Mediterranean in the Age of Philip II.* 2 vols. New York, Hagerstown, San Francisco, London: Harper & Row, 1972.

———. *The Structure of Everyday Life: The Limits of the Possible.* New York: Harper & Row, ca. 1981.

Bridenthal, Renate, and Claudia Koonz, eds. *Becoming Visible: Women in European History.* Boston: Houghton Mifflin, 1977.

Brinton, Daniel G. *Notes on the Floridian Peninsula, Its Literary History, Indian Tribes and Antiquities.* Philadelphia: Joseph Sabin, 1859.

Brown, Alexander. *The Genesis of the United States.* 1890. New York: 1964.

Brundage, James A. *Law, Sex, and Christian Society in Medieval Spain.* Chicago: University of Chicago Press, 1987.

Burkhart, Louise M. *The Slippery Earth: Nahua-Christian Dialogue in Sixteenth-Century Mexico.* Tucson: University of Arizona Press, 1989.

Burkholder, Mark A., and D. S. Chandler. *From Impotence to Authority: The Spanish*

Crown and the American Audiencias, 1687–1808. Columbia: University of Missouri Press, 1977.

Burns, Robert Ignatius. *Muslims, Christians, and Jews in the Crusader Kingdom of Valencia: Societies in Symbiosis.* Cambridge: Cambridge University Press, 1984.

Bushnell, Amy. *The King's Coffer: Proprietors of the Spanish Florida Treasury, 1565–1702.* Gainesville: University Presses of Florida, 1981.

Bushnell, Amy Turner. *Situado and Sabana: Spain's Support System for the Presidio and Mission Provinces of Florida.* American Museum of Natural History Anthropological Paper No. 74. New York: American Museum of Natural History, 1994.

Cabeça de Vaca, Alvar Núñez. *Relation of Alvar Núñez Cabeça de Vaca.* 1542. Buckingham Smith, trans., 1871. New York: Readex Microprint, 1966.

Campbell, Richard L. *Historical Sketches of Colonial Florida.* Cleveland: n.p., 1892.

Casas, Bartolomé de las. *The Devastation of the Indies: A Brief Account.* 1552. Herma Briffault, trans. Baltimore: John Hopkins Press, 1974.

Caughey, John Walton. *McGillivray of the Creeks.* Norman: University of Oklahoma Press, 1938.

Chatelain, Verne E. *The Early Defenses of Spanish Florida, 1565 to 1753.* Carnegie Institute of Washington Publication No. 511. Washington, D.C.: Carnegie Institute, 1941.

Chaunu, Pierre, and Huguette Chaunu. *Séville et l'Atlantique: 1504–1650.* 10 vols. Paris: S.E.V.P.E.N., 1955–1959.

Cipolla, Carlo M. *Guns, Sails and Empire: Technological Innovation and the Early Phases of European Expansion, 1400–1700.* N.p.: Minerva Press, 1965.

Clayton, Lawrence A., Vernon James Knight, Jr., and Edward C. Moore, eds. *The De Soto Chronicles: The Expedition of Hernando de Soto to North America in 1539–1543.* 2 vols. Tuscaloosa: University of Alabama Press, 1993.

Clendinnen, Inga. *Ambivalent Conquests.* Cambridge: Cambridge University Press, 1987.

Connor, Jeannette Thurber. *Colonial Records of Spanish Florida.* Deland: Florida Historical Society, 1925.

Corominas, Joan. *Diccionario Crítico Etimológico Castellano e Hispánico.* 2 vols. Madrid: Editorial Gredos, 1954.

Covington, James W. *The British Meet the Seminoles.* Contributions of the Florida State Museum, Social Sciences No. 7. Gainesville: Florida State Museum, 1961.

———. *Pirates, Indians and Spaniards: Father Escobedo's "La Florida."* A. F. Falcones, trans. St. Petersburg: Great Outdoors Publishing, 1963.

Crane, Verner W. *The Southern Frontier, 1670–1732.* Durham: Duke University Press, 1928.

Crosby, Alfred W. *The Columbian Exchange: Biological and Cultural Consequences of 1492.* Westport, Connecticut: Greenwood Press, 1972.

Daly, Mary. *The Church and the Second Sex.* Boston: Beacon Press, 1968.

Dau, Frederick W. *Florida Old and New.* New York: G. P. Putnam's Sons, 1934.

Deagan, Kathleen A. *Artifacts of the Spanish Colonies of Florida and the Caribbean,*

1500–1800. Vol. 1, *Ceramics, Glassware, and Beads*. Washington, D.C.: Smithsonian Institution Press, 1987.

——. *Spanish St. Augustine: The Archaeology of a Colonial Creole Community*. New York: Academic Press, 1983.

Deagan, Kathleen A., and Darcie MacMahon. *Fort Mose: Colonial America's Black Fortress of Freedom*. Gainesville: University of Florida, 1995.

Defourneaux, Marcelin. *Daily Life in Spain in the Golden Age*. Newton Branch, trans., 1970. Stanford: Stanford University Press, 1979.

Delbrück, Hans. *History of the Art of War [Geschichte der Kriegskunst im Rahmen der politischen Geschichte]*. 1920. 4 vols. Walter J. Renfroe, Jr., trans. 1st English ed., 1975. Lincoln: University of Nebraska Press, 1990.

Dillard, Heath. *Daughters of the Reconquest: Women in Castillian Town Society, 1100–1300*. Cambridge: Cambridge University Press, 1963.

Dobyns, Henry F. *Their Number Become Thinned: Native American Population Dynamics in Eastern North America*. Knoxville: University of Tennessee Press, 1983.

Duby, Georges. *The Three Orders: Feudal Society Imagined*. Chicago: University of Chicago Press, 1980.

Elliott, J[ohn] H[uxtable]. *The Count-Duke of Olivares*. Boston: Yale University Press, 1986.

——. *Imperial Spain, 1469–1716*. 1963. New York: Mentor Books, 1966.

——. *The Revolt of the Catalans: A Study in the Decline of Spain (1598–1640)*. Cambridge: Cambridge University Press, 1963.

Elvas, Gentleman of. "The Account by a Gentleman from Elvas." James Alexander Robertson, trans. In volume 1 of *The De Soto Chronicles: The Expedition of Hernando de Soto to North America in 1539–1543*, Lawrence A. Clayton, Vernon James Knight, Jr., and Edward C. Moore, eds., 19–219. Tuscaloosa: University of Alabama Press, 1993.

Escalante Fontaneda, [Hernando] de. *Letter of Hernando de Soto and Memoir of Hernando de Escalante Fontaneda, ca. 1575*. Buckingham Smith, trans. and ed. Washington, D.C.: privately printed for G. W. Riggs, 1854.

Farriss, Nancy M. *Maya Society under Colonial Rule: The Collective Enterprise of Survival*. Princeton: University Press, 1984.

Fernández de Navarrete. *Colección de documentos inéditos relativos al descubrimiento*. Vol. 8. Madrid: Sucesores de Rivadeneyra, 1885–1932.

Fernández y Oviedo, Gonzalo. *Historia general y natural de las Indias*. 4 vols. Madrid: Real Academia de la Historia, 1851–1855.

Fichtenau, Heinrich. *Living in the Tenth Century: Mentalities and Social Orders*. Chicago: Chicago University Press, 1984.

Flinn, Michael W. *The European Demographic System, 1500–1820*. Baltimore: Johns Hopkins University Press, 1981.

Floyd, Troy. *The Columbus Dynasty in the Caribbean, 1492–1526*. Albuquerque: University of New Mexico Press, 1973.

Fori Aragonum vom Codex von Huesca (1247) bis zur Reform Philipps II (1547) nach der Ausgabe Zaragoza 1476/1477, mit den Handschriftlichen Glossen des

Martín de Pertusa und mit Ergängzungen nach den Ausgaben Zaragoza 1542, 1548, und 1576. Vaduz/Liechtenstein: Topos Verlag, 1979.

French, Marilyn. *The War Against Women*. New York: Ballantine Books, 1992.

Fried, Morton H. *The Evolution of Political Society: An Essay on Political Anthropology*. New York: Random House, 1967.

Friederici, Georg. *Hilfswörterbuch für den Amerikanisten: Lehnwörter aus Indianer-Sprachen und Erklärungen Altertümlicher Ausdrücke, Deutsch-Spanisch-Englisch*. Halle: Max Niemeyer, 1926.

Gannon, Michael V. *The Cross in the Sand*. Gainesville: University of Florida Press, 1965.

Garciá Márquez, Gabriél. *Of Love and Other Demons*. New York: Random House, 1995.

Garner, Richard L., and William B. Taylor. *Iberian Colonies, New World Societies: Essays in Memory of Charles Gibson*. Privately printed in the United States, 1985/1986.

Gatschet, Albert A. *Migration Legend of the Creek Indians with a Linguistic, Historical and Ethnographic Introduction*. Brinton's Library of Aboriginal Literature No. 4. Philadelphia: Daniel G. Brinton, 1884–1888.

Geiger, Maynard J. *The Spiritual Conquest of Florida (1573–1818)*. Washington, D.C.: Catholic University of America, 1937.

George, Anita. *Annals of the Queens of Spain, from the period of the conquest of the Goths . . . to . . . Isabel II*. New York: Baker & Scribner, 1850.

Gibson, Charles. *The Aztecs under Spanish Rule: A History of the Indians of the Valley of Mexico, 1519–1810*. Stanford: Stanford University Press, 1964.

——. *The Black Legend: Anti-Spanish Attitudes in the Old World and the New*. New York: Knopf, ca. 1971.

Gordon, Colin, ed. *Power/Knowledge: Selected Interviews & Other Writings, 1972–1977 by Michel Foucault*. 1972. New York: Pantheon Books, 1980.

Granberry, Julian. *A Grammar and Dictionary of the Timucua Language*. 3d. ed. Tuscaloosa: University of Alabama Press, 1993.

Green, Michael D. *The Politics of Indian Removal: Creek Government and Society in Crisis*. Lincoln: University of Nebraska Press, ca. 1982.

Gutmann, Myron P. *War and Rural Life in the Early Modern Low Countries*. Princeton: Princeton University Press, 1980.

Hakluyt, Richard. *The Principal Navigations, Voyages, Traffiques and Discoveries of the English Nation*. Glasgow: The Hakluyt Society, 1904.

Halliday, M. *Language as Social Semiotic*. London: Edward Arnold, 1978.

Hann, John H. *Apalachee: The Land between the Rivers*. Gainesville: University Presses of Florida, 1988.

Hann, John H., ed. and trans. *Missions to the Calusa*. Gainesville: University of Florida Press, 1991.

Haring, Clarence Henry. *The Spanish Empire in America*. New York: Oxford University Press, 1947.

Harris, Marvin. *Patterns of Race in the Americas*. 1964. Westport, Connecticut: Greenwood Press, 1980.

Hawkins, Benjamin. *A Sketch of the Creek Country*. 1848. Reprint ed. Americus, Georgia: Americus Book Co., 1938.

Herrera y Tordesillas, Antonio de. *Historia general de los hechos de los castellanos en las islas i tierra firme del mar oceano*. 4 vols. Madrid, 1601–1615.

Hillgarth, J. N. *The Spanish Kingdoms, 1250–1516*. 2 vols. Oxford: Clarendon Press, 1978.

Hobsbawm, Eric, and Terence Ranger, eds. *The Invention of Tradition*. New York: Cambridge University Press, 1983.

Hoffman, Paul E. *A New Andalucia and a Way to the Orient: The American Southeast during the Sixteenth Century*. Baton Rouge and London: Louisiana State University Press, 1990.

———. *Spain and the Roanoke Voyages*. North Carolina: Department of Cultural Resources, 1987.

———. *The Spanish Crown and the Defense of the Caribbean, 1535–1585: Precedent, Patrimonialism, and Royal Parsimony*. Baton Rouge: Louisiana State University Press, 1980.

Holland Braund, Kathryn E. *Deerskins and Duffels: Creek Indian Trade with Anglo-America, 1685–1815*. Lincoln: University of Nebraska Press, 1993.

Hudson, Charles. *The Southeastern Indians*. Knoxville: University of Tennessee Press, 1976.

Hudson, Charles, ed. *Red, White, and Black: Symposium on Indians in the Old South*. Southern Anthropological Society Proceedings No. 5. Athens: University of Georgia Press, 1971.

Hudson, Charles, and Carmen Chaves Tesser, eds. *The Forgotten Centuries: Indians and Europeans in the American South, 1521–1704*. Athens: University of Georgia Press, 1994.

Israel, J. I. *Race, Class, and Politics in Colonial Mexico, 1610–1670*. London: Oxford Press, 1975.

Jacobs, Wilbur R., ed. *Indians of the Southern Colonial Frontier: The Edmond Atkin Report and Plan of 1775*. Columbia: University of South Carolina Press, 1954.

Jordan del Asso y del Rio, Ignatius, and Miguel de Manuel y Rodríguez. *Institutes of the Civil Law of Spain*, 6th ed., materially corrected. Madrid, 1805. Lewis F. C. Johnston, trans. London: Joseph Butterworth and Son, 1825.

Jornadas Americanistas. *El Consejo de las Indias en el siglo XVI*. D. Ramos, et al., ed. Valladolid: Universidad de Valladolid, 1970.

Kagan, Richard L. *Lawsuits and Litigants in Castile, 1500–1700*. Chapel Hill: University of North Carolina Press, 1981.

Knight, Vernon James, Jr. "Tuckabatchee: Archaeological Investigations at an Historic Creek Town, Elmore County, Alabama, 1984." Report of Investigations 45. Office of Archaeological Research, Alabama State Museum of Natural History, The University of Alabama, 1985.

Kozuch, Laura. *Sharks and Shark Products in Prehistoric South Florida*. Institute of Archaeology and Paleoenvironmental Studies Monograph No. 2. Gainesville: University of Florida, 1993.

Krupat, Arnold. *Ethnocriticism: Ethnography, History, Literature.* Berkeley: University of California Press, 1992.

Lanning, John Tate. *The Spanish Missions of Georgia.* Chapel Hill: University of North Carolina Press, 1935.

Laudonnière, René Goulaine de. *Three Voyages, 1586.* Charles E. Bennett, trans. and ed. Gainesville: University Presses of Florida, 1975.

Lerner, Gerda. *The Creation of Patriarchy.* New York: Oxford University Press, 1986.

Liss, Peggy K. *Isabel the Queen.* New York and Oxford: Oxford University Press, 1992.

——. *Mexico Under Spain, 1521–'56: Society and the Origins of Nationality.* Chicago: University of Chicago Press, 1976.

Lockhart, James, and Enrique Otte, eds. *Letters and People of the Spanish Indies.* Cambridge: Cambridge University Press, 1976.

López de Velasco, Juan. *Geografia y descripción universal de las Indias, recopilado por el cosmógrafo-cronista . . . desde el año 1570 al de 1574.* Publicada por primera vez en el Bolitín de la Sociedad Geográfica de Madrid. . . . Madrid: 1894.

Lorant, Stefan, ed. *The New World: The First Pictures of America.* New York: Duell, Sloan & Pearce, 1946.

Loughbridge, R. M., and David M. Hodge. *Dictionary in Two Parts: English and Muskokee, and Muskokee and English.* Philadelphia: Westminster Press, 1914.

Lowrey, Woodbury. *The Spanish Settlements within the Present Limits of the United States.* New York: G. P. Putnam's Sons, 1901.

Lucal, Samuel. *Charters of the Old English Colonies in America.* London: 1850.

Lunenfeld, Marvin. *1492: Discovery, Invasion, Encounter: Sources and Interpretations.* Lexington, Massachusetts: D. C. Heath, 1991.

Lynch, John. *Spain Under the Hapsburgs.* 2 vols. Oxford: A. Blackwell, 1964–1969.

Lyon, Eugene. *The Enterprise of Florida: Pedro Menéndez de Avilés and the Spanish Conquest of 1565–1568.* Gainesville: University Presses of Florida, 1976.

McAlister, Lyle N. *Spain and Portugal in the New World, 1492–1700, Europe and the New World in the Age of Exploration.* Vol. 3. Minneapolis: University of Minnesota, 1984.

Macias Domínguez, Isabela. *Cuba en la primera mitad del siglo XVII.* Sevilla: Escuela de Estudios Hispanoamericanos, 1978.

MacLachlan, Colin M. *Spain's Empire in the New World: The Role of Ideas in Institutions and Social Change.* Berkeley: University of California Press, ca. 1988.

Mahon, John K. *History of the Second Seminole War.* 1967. Gainesville: University of Florida Press, 1991.

Mallon, Florencia E. *The Defense of Community in Peru's Central Highland: Peasant Struggle and Capitalist Transition, 1860–1940.* Princeton: Princeton University Press, 1984.

Maltby, William S. *Alba: A Biography of Fernando Alvarez de Toledo, Third Duke of Alba, 1507–1582.* Berkeley, Los Angeles, and London: University of California Press, 1983.

——. *The Black Legend in England: The Development of Anti-Spanish Sentiment in England, 1558–1660.* Durham, North Carolina: Duke University Press, 1971.

Manucy, Albert. *The Houses of St. Augustine.* St. Augustine Historical Society, 1978.

Martin, M. Kay, and Babara Vorhees. *Female of the Species.* New York: Columbia University Press, 1975.

Matter, Robert Allen. *Pre-Seminole Florida: Spanish Soldiers, Friars, and Indian Missions, 1513–1763.* New York: Garland Publishing, 1990.

Merriman, Roger Bigelow. *The Rise of the Spanish Empire on the Old World and the New.* 3 vols. New York: McMillan Company, 1925.

Merton, Robert K. *Social Theory and Social Structure.* 1949. New York: Free Press, 1968.

Milanich, Jerald T. *Archaeology of Precolumbian Florida.* Gainesville: University Presses of Florida, 1994.

———. *Florida Indians and the Invasion from Europe.* Gainesville: University Press of Florida, 1995.

Milanich, Jerald T., and Charles Hudson. *Hernando de Soto and the Indians of Florida.* Gainesville: University Presses of Florida, 1993.

Milanich, Jerald T., and Susan Milbrath, eds. *First Encounters: Spanish Explorations in the Caribbean and the United States, 1492–1570.* Gainesville: University Presses of Florida, 1989.

Milanich, Jerald T., and Samuel Proctor, eds. *Tacachale.* Gainesville: University Presses of Florida, 1978.

Milanich, Jerald T., and William C. Sturtevant, eds. *Francisco Pareja's Confessionario: A Documentary Source for Timucuan Ethnography.* Tallahassee: Division of Archives, History, and Records Management, Florida Department of State, 1972.

Milfort, Le Clerc. *Mémoire ou coup-d'œil rapide sur mes différens voyages et mon séjour dans la nation Crëck.* Paris: Giguet et Michaud, 1802.

Mitchell, Timothy. *Colonizing Egypt.* Berkeley: University of California Press, 1988.

Moore, James. *The St. Augustine Expedition of 1740: A Report to the South Carolina General Assembly.* Reprinted from the Colonial Records of South Carolina. Columbia: South Carolina Archives Department, 1954.

Moorehead, Max L. *The Presidio: Bastion of the Spanish Borderlands.* Norman: University of Oklahoma Press, 1975.

Morales Padron, Francisco. *Historia de hispanoamerica.* Sevilla: Escuela de Estudios Hispanoamericanos, 1972.

———. *Historia del descubrimiento y conquista de America.* Madrid: Editoria Nacional, 1963.

———. *Teoria y Leyes de la Conquista.* Madrid: Ediciones Cultura Hispánica del Centro Iberoamericano de Cooperacion, 1979.

Nader, Helen. *Liberty in Absolutist Spain: The Habsburg Sale of Towns, 1516–1700.* Baltimore: Johns Hopkins University Press, 1990.

O'Daniel, Victor Francis, OP. *Dominicans in Early Florida.* United States Catholic Historical Society Monograph Series 12. New York: United States Catholic Historical Society, 1930.

Oman, Charles, Sir. *A History of the Art of War in the Sixteenth Century.* New York: E. P. Dutton and Company, [1937].

Ong, Walter J. *Orality and Literacy: The Technologizing of the Word.* 1982. London: Routledge, 1988.

Oré, Luís Geronimo de, OFM. *The Martyrs of Florida (1513–1616).* Maynard Geiger, OFM, trans. Franciscan Studies 18. New York: Joseph F. Wagner, July 1936.

Otero, Gustavo Adolfo. *La Vida Social del Coloniaje: Esquema de la Historia del Alto Perú, hoy Bolivia/Life in the Spanish Colonies: With Particular Reference to Upper Peru, Now Bolivia.* New York: Bertrand Publishers, 1955.

Ots y Capdequi, José Maria. *El Estado Español en las Indias.* Mexico, D.F.: Fondo de Cultura Economica, 1957.

Pacheco, Joaquin F., Francisco de Cardenas, and Luís Torres de Mendoza, eds. *Colección de documentos inéditos relativos al descubrimiento, conquista y organización de las antiguas posesiones españoles de América y Oceania, sacados de los archivos del reino, y muy especialmente del de Indias.* 42 vols. Madrid: Real Academia de la Historia, 1864–1884.

Pagden, Anthony. *The Fall of Natural Man: The American Indian and the Origins of Comparative Ethnology.* Cambridge: Cambridge University Press, 1982, 1989.

Parker, Geoffrey. *The Army of Flanders and the Spanish Road, 1567–1659: The Logistics of Victory and Defeat in the Low Countries' Wars.* Cambridge: Cambridge University Press, 1972.

———. *Europe in Crisis, 1598–1648.* Brighton: Harvester Press [Fontana Paperbacks], 1980.

———. *Philip II.* Boston, Toronto: Little, Brown and Company, 1978.

Parker, Geoffrey, and Angela Parker. *European Soldiers, 1550–1650.* Cambridge: Cambridge University Press, 1977.

Parker, Geoffrey, and Lesley M. Smith, eds. *The General Crisis of the Seventeenth Century.* London: Rutledge & Kegan Paul, 1978.

Parry, J. H. *The Spanish Seaborne Empire.* New York: Alfred A. Knopf, 1966.

———. *The Spanish Theory of Empire in the Sixteenth Century.* Folcroft, Pennsylvania: Folcroft Library Editions, 1973.

Patrick, Rembert. *Florida Under Five Flags.* Gainesville: University of Florida Press, 1945.

Pazzis Pi Corrales, Magdalena de. *Felipe II y la Lucha por el Dominio del Mar.* Madrid: Editorial San Martín, [ca. 1988].

Pearson, Fred Lamar, Jr. *Spanish-Indian Relations in Florida: A Study of Two Visitas, 1657–1678.* New York: Garland Publishing, 1990.

Peitgen, Heintz-Otto, Helmüt Jurgens, and Dietmar Saupe. *Chaos and Fractals: New Frontiers of Science.* New York and Berlin: Springer-Verlag, 1992.

Penicaut Narrative. R. G. McWilliams, trans. 1953. Tuscaloosa: University of Alabama Press, 1988.

Pérez de Tudela Bueso, Juan. *Las Armadas de Indias y los Origines de la Política de Colonización, 1492–1505.* Madrid: 1956.

Perry, Mary Elizabeth. *Gender and Disorder in Early Modern Seville.* Princeton: Princeton University Press, 1990.

Pettrich, Ferdinand [artist]. *Portraits of Distinguished Indians From Several Tribes, Who Visited Washington in 1837; Also A Faithful Representation of the Indian*

War Dance, Which Took Place During Their Visit. Drawn on the Spot by Ferdinand Pettrich. The above portraits were originally drawn from life, full size, on the four walls of Pettrich's Studio and now for the first time reduced and presented to the public by Ferd. Pettrich. Lithographed by Edward Weber & Co. Baltimore. 1842.

Pomeroy, Sarah B. *Goddesses, Whores, Wives, and Slaves: Women in Classical Antiquity.* New York: Schocken Books, 1975.

Pope, John. *A tour through southern and western territories of the United States of North America; the Spanish dominions on the river Mississippi, and the Floridas; the countries of the Creek nations; and many uninhabited parts.* Richmond: J. Dixon for the author, 1792.

Priestley, Herbert Ingram, ed. and trans. *The Luna Papers: Documents Relating to the Expedition of Don Tristán de Luna y Arellano for the Conquest of La Florida in 1559–1561.* 2 vols. Deland: Florida State Historical Society, 1928.

Rabinow, Paul, ed. *The Foucault Reader.* New York: Pantheon Books, 1984.

Ramírez, Susan E. *Provincial Patriarchs: Land Tenure and the Economics of Power in Colonial Peru.* Albuquerque: University of New Mexico Press, 1986.

Real Academia Española. *Diccionario de la Lengua Española.* Madrid: Real Academia, 1992.

Reiter, Renya Rapp, ed. *Toward an Anthropology of Women.* New York: Monthly Review, 1978.

Remini, Robert V. *Andrew Jackson and the Course of American Empire, 1767–1821.* Vol 1. New York: Harper & Row, 1977.

Ribault, Jean. *The Whole & True Discouerye of Terra Florida.* London: 1563. Facsimile ed. Gainesville: University of Florida Press, 1962.

Rojas, María Teresa de. *Indice y Estractos del Archivo de Protocolos de la Habana.* 3 vols. Habana: n.p., 1950–1957.

Romans, Bernard. *A Concise Natural History of East and West Florida.* 1775. Facsimile ed. Gainesville: University of Florida Press, 1962.

Rouse, Irving. *The Tainos: Rise and Decline of the People Who Greeted Columbus.* New Haven: Yale University Press, 1992.

Sahlins, Marshall. *Islands of History.* Chicago: University of Chicago Press, 1985.

Sánchez-Albornoz, Nicolas. *The Population of Latin America, A History.* W. A. R. Richardson, trans. Berkeley: University of California Press, 1974.

Sarfatti [Larson], Magali. *Spanish Bureaucratic-Patrimonialism in America.* Berkeley: University of California Press, 1966.

Sauer, Carl Ortwin. *The Early Spanish Main.* Berkeley: University of California Press, 1966.

———. *Seventeenth Century North America.* Berkeley: University of California Press, 1980.

———. *Sixteenth Century North America: The Land and the People as Seen by the Europeans.* Berkeley: University of California Press, 1971.

Schiffrin, Deborah. *Approaches to Discourse.* Cambridge, Massachusetts: Blackwell, 1994.

[Schoolcraft] Colcraft, Henry Rowe. *Historical and statistical information respecting* the history, condition and prospects of the Indian tribes of the United States. 6 vols. Philadelphia: Lippincott, 1851–1857.

Service, Elman. *Primitive Social Organization: An Evolutionary Perspective.* New York: Random House, 1962.

Shaffer, Lynda Norene. *Native Americans Before 1492: The Moundbuilding Centers of the Eastern Woodlands.* Armonk, New York: M. E. Sharpe, 1992.

Simpson, Lesley Byrd. *The Encomienda in New Spain: The Beginnings of Spanish Mexico.* Berkeley: University of California Press, 1966.

Sluiter, Engel. *The Florida Situado: Quantifying the First Eighty Years, 1571–1651.* Research Publications of the P. K. Yonge Library of Florida History, University of Florida No. 1. Gainesville: University of Florida Libraries, 1985.

Smith, Buckingham, ed. and trans. *Colección de varios documentos para la historia de la Florida y tierras adyacentes.* London: Trubner and Company, 1857.

Solano, Francisco de, and Pilar Ponce. *Cuestionarios para la formacion de las relaciones geograficas de Indias: siglos XVI–XIX.* Madrid: Consejo Superior de Investigaciones Cientificas, Centro de Estudios Historicos, Departamento de Historia de America, 1988.

Solís de Merás, Gonzalo. *Memorial of Pedro Menéndez de Avilés.* 1567. Jeannette Thurber Connor, trans., 1923. Facsimile ed. Gainesville: University of Florida Press, 1964.

Spalding, Karen. *Haurochirí: An Andean Society under Inca and Spanish Rule.* Stanford: Stanford University Press, 1984.

Sprague, John T. *The Origin, Progress, and Conclusion of the Florida War.* 1848. Reprint ed. John K. Mahon, ed. Gainesville: University of Florida Press, 1964.

Stern, Steve J. *Peru's Indian Peoples and the Challenge of Spanish Conquest: Huamanga to 1640.* Madison: University of Wisconsin Press, 1982.

Stiggins, George. *Creek Indian History: A Historical Narrative of the Traditions and Downfall of the Ispocoga or Creek Indian Tribe of Indians, by One of the Tribe.* Virginia Pounds Brown, ed. Birmingham, Alabama: Birmingham Public Library Press, 1989.

Swanton, John R. *Early History of the Creek Indians and Their Neighbors.* Bureau of American Ethnology Bulletin 73. Washington, D.C.: Government Printing Office, 1922.

——. *Forty-Second Annual Report of the Bureau of American Ethnology to the Secretary of the Smithsonian Institution.* Washington, D.C.: Government Printing Office, 1928.

——. *Indian Tribes of the Lower Mississippi Valley and Adjacent Coast of the Gulf of Mexico.* Bureau of American Ethnology Bulletin 137. Washington, D.C.: Government Printing Office, 1928.

——. *The Indians of the Southeastern United States.* Smithsonian Institution, Bureau of American Ethnology Bulletin 137. Washington, D.C.: Government Printing Office, 1946.

Tannen, Deborah, ed. *Framing in Discourse.* New York and Oxford: Oxford University Press, 1993.

Tebeau, Charlton. *The History of Florida.* Coral Gables: University of Miami Press, 1971.

TePaske, John Jay. *The Governorship of Spanish Florida, 1700–1763.* Durham: University of North Carolina Press, 1964.

Thomas, David Hurst, ed. *Columbian Consequences.* Vol. 1, *Archaeological and Historical Perspectives on the Spanish Borderlands West;* vol. 2, *Archaeological and Historical Perspectives on the Spanish Borderlands East;* vol. 3, *The Spanish Borderlands in Pan-American Perspective.* Washington, D.C.: Smithsonian Institution Press, 1990.

Thompson, I. A. A. *War and Government in Hapsburg Spain, 1560–1620.* London: 1976.

Urban, Greg. *A Discourse-Centered Approach to Culture: Native South American Myths and Rituals.* Austin: University of Texas Press, 1991.

Vega, Garcilaso de la. *The Florida of the Inca.* John G. and Jeannette J. Varner, trans. Austin: University of Texas Press, 1951.

Viaud, Pierre. *Shipwreck and Adventures of Monsieur Pierre Viaud.* 1768. Robin F. A. Fabel, trans. and ed. Pensacola: University of West Florida Press, 1990.

Wall, Steve, and Harvey Arden. *Wisdomkeepers: Meetings with Native American Spiritual Elders.* Hillsboro, Oregon: Beyond Words Publishing, 1990.

Wallace, Anthony F. C. *Religion: An Anthropological View.* New York: Random House, 1966.

Ward Hunt, Lynn, ed. *The New Cultural History.* Berkeley: University of California Press, ca. 1989.

Weber, David J. *The Spanish Frontier in North America.* New Haven: Yale University Press, 1992.

Weddle, Robert S. *The Spanish Sea: The Gulf of Mexico in North American Discovery, 1500–1685.* College Station: Texas A & M Press, 1985.

Wenhold, Lucy, trans. and ed. *A Seventeenth-Century Letter of Gabriel Díaz Vara Calderón, Bishop of Cuba, Describing the Indian Missions of Florida.* Smithsonian Miscellaneous Collections Vol. 95, No. 16. Washington, D.C.: Smithsonian Institution Press, 1936.

Willey, Gordon R. *Archeology of the Florida Gulf Coast.* Smithsonian Institution Miscellaneous Collections No. 113. Washington, D.C.: Smithsonian Institution, 1949.

Williams, Mark, and Gary Shapiro, eds. *Lamar Archaeology: Mississippian Chiefdoms in the Deep South.* Tuscaloosa: University of Alabama Press, 1990.

Wood, Peter H., Gregory Waselkov, and M. T. Hatley. *Powhatan's Mantle: Indians in the Colonial Southeast.* Lincoln and London: University of Nebraska Press, 1989.

Worth, John E. *The Struggle for the Georgia Coast: An Eighteenth-Century Retrospective on Guale and Mocama.* American Museum of Natural History Anthropological Papers No. 75. New York: American Museum of Natural History, 1995.

Wright, Albert Hazen. *Our Georgia-Florida Frontier: The Okeefenokee Swamp, Its History and Cartography.* Ithaca, New York: A. H. Wright, 1945.

Wright, J. Leitch, Jr. *Creeks & Seminoles: The Destruction and Regeneration of the Muscogulge People.* Lincoln: University of Nebraska Press, 1986.

Zavala, Silvio Arturo. *Las instituciones jurídicas en la conquista de America.* Madrid:

Junta para Ampliación de Estudios e Investigaciones Cientificas, Centro de
Estudios Historicos, Sección Hispanoamericana, 1935; 2d ed., rev. & exp.
Mexico, D.F.: Editorial Porrua, 1971.

Zubillaga, Felix. *Monumenta Antiquae Floridae*. Rome: Monumenta Historica Societatis Iesu, 1946.

Index

About the Author

Patricia Riles Wickman is Director, Department of Anthropology and Genealogy, Seminole Tribe of Florida. She is also author of *Osceola's Legacy*, published by The University of Alabama Press.